T0313856

# A NEW DEAL

### FOR

# CHINA'S WORKERS?

*Cynthia Estlund*

Harvard University Press

*Cambridge, Massachusetts*
*London, England*

2017

First printing

*Library of Congress Cataloging-in-Publication Data*
Names: Estlund, Cynthia, author.
Title: A New Deal for China's workers? / Cynthia Estlund.
Description: Cambridge, Massachusetts: Harvard University Press, 2017. |
Includes bibliographical references and index.
Identifiers: LCCN 2016017881 | ISBN 9780674971394
Subjects: LCSH: Industrial relations--China. | Labor policy—China. | Labor
unions—China. | Comparative industrial relations.
Classification: LCC HD8736.5 .E87 2017 | DDC 331.0951—dc23
LC record available at https://lccn.loc.gov/2016017881

*To Jerry Cohen,*
*whose brilliance and vitality are rivaled only*
*by his unfailing kindness*

# Contents

# Preface

CHINA BECKONED to me at a time when my old stomping ground in American labor and employment law was looking far too familiar. For my whole professional life as a labor lawyer and scholar, China had loomed as the bottom of the notorious "race to the bottom" in global labor standards—a one-party state that proclaimed itself socialist, but that had invited global capital to exploit its multitudes of poor workers, its low wages, and its seemingly lawless factories. By 2007, thanks to excellent coverage in the *New York Times*, I knew that things were changing—that new laws, enacted over employer opposition, sought to raise labor standards and improve enforcement; that the official union was actively organizing in those factories; and that workers, emboldened by labor shortages (labor shortages in China!) were making noise. That sounded intriguing but still distant and hazy.

Beginning with my first visit to China in the summer of 2009, I began to see a larger landscape that was full of contradictions and surprises. The Beijing airport, the Shanghai skyline, and the ubiquitous construction cranes hinted that the twenty-first century might belong to China. Freewheeling political discussions with Chinese scholars over great food (and weak beer) clashed with my preconceptions about political discourse in China. And accounts of a government scrambling to cope with mass protest incidents across multiple domains—labor, environment, appropriation of land—gave a tantalizing glimpse of the dilemmas of maintaining stability in a rapidly developing one-party state. Along the way I saw that labor issues had a salience and urgency in China that they had lost in the United States, and that workers there might be on the cusp of real progress that would reverberate throughout the world.

When I returned to NYU after that visit, energized and captivated, I met for the first time with my colleague Jerry Cohen, the dean of American China law scholars and one of the most extraordinary individuals I have ever met. He insisted that I—as a newcomer to China with decades of teaching and writing on U.S. labor law and its evolution under my belt— would bring a distinct and important perspective to China's labor scene, and that I should seize the opportunity to do so. China was far too important, he said, to leave to China scholars alone. This book is dedicated to Jerry, whose encouragement and inspiration allowed me to embark on this unexpected scholarly journey.

Jerry did more than encourage and inspire me, however. He was thrilled to have a new recruit to the remarkable China law program at NYU School of Law, mainly through its U.S.–Asia Law Institute. He and his colleagues at USALI provided an ideal launching pad and a wealth of connections, beginning in that first meeting in his office in June 2009. In particular, in explaining why I was just the person he and his colleagues had been waiting for, Jerry mentioned three people who were urging him to start a labor project. It so happened that I already knew all of them independently. A remarkable element of serendipity in that first conversation with Jerry— what Benjamin Van Rooij and I took to calling "Jerrendipity"—helped persuade me to jump into China headfirst.

Seth Gurgel, a 2009 NYU law graduate, had just moved to Shanghai to work for USALI, and hoped to expand its work in the labor field. I already knew Seth as a brilliant former student (and fellow Wisconsinite); I came to learn that he was also extraordinarily resourceful, engaging, and insightful about China. Beginning with my first research visit in 2010, and in several subsequent visits, he arranged and joined in scores of meetings with leading labor scholars, lawyers, officials, and NGO activists in Beijing, Shanghai, Shenzhen, and a half-dozen other mainland cities, as well as in Hong Kong. In those meetings Seth bridged the language gap as well as other gaps in understanding, and in between meetings he helped me to digest and make sense of the torrent of information and impressions. Early on, we set out to write a joint paper, parts of which evolved into a co-authored book chapter on union elections, and into parts of this book.[1] But Seth was drawn to a more active role in China, where he has been working with young public interest lawyers, many in the labor arena, since 2013.

The two other people whom Jerry mentioned in that first meeting in 2009 were Aaron Halegua and Arnold Zack. Aaron was then a recent graduate of Harvard Law School and a young scholar of Chinese labor law. He had been my student during a visiting stint at Harvard in 2008, and had helped me set up the very first informal meetings with labor experts that had sparked my interest in China and brought me to Jerry's office. Aaron has continued to be an invaluable source of insight, information, and connections in the field of Chinese labor law, especially in the world of labor rights advocates—lawyers, lay advocates, and labor NGOs. Arnold Zack was Jerry's law school classmate and a prominent longtime labor arbitrator whom I had already known for several years. Arnold had become an energetic proselytizer for the role that arbitrators could play in improving labor standards in the developing world, especially in Asia. We later shared a study trip to China, along with Seth, Jerry, and my colleague Sam Estreicher, to explore the expansion of mediation of labor disputes.

And so I took the leap. Since 2009, over the course of more than a dozen trips to China and many conferences, I have had hundreds of conversations with Chinese scholars, lawyers, officials, and activists. (Food and drink often paved the way to more candid discussions.) Initially with Jerry's good offices and excellent assistance from Seth and Aaron, I developed a network of close and thoughtful observers of and participants in China's labor scene. Through other avenues, I was also able to meet with a number of Party-friendly intellectuals and Party policy officials who challenged my thinking about China (and the United States). Those many discussions helped to deepen the understanding of China's labor troubles and of its culture and political system that I was gathering from piles of books and articles—journalism as well as scholarship from many disciplines. For sources available only in Chinese, I had outstanding help from colleagues and research assistants at NYU. (My own study of Chinese, starting in 2010, got me to a basic level that was helpful in signaling respect, embellishing introductions, and getting around China, but wholly inadequate for research or real conversation.)

Nearly thirty-five years of studying, practicing, teaching, and writing in the field of labor and employment law, almost entirely its rather distinctive American variant, has obviously shaped my understanding of China's labor landscape, as it will shape that of many readers. But the converse is also true. My exposure to China has provoked reflections on America's labor and employment law as well as its political institutions. I have sought to make those critical reflections in both directions explicit in this book, for they may help to orient and enlighten readers whose starting point is similar to my own seven years ago.

A few housekeeping details: First, an earlier version of Chapter 8 of this book appeared in the *Comparative Labor Law and Policy Journal*.[2] Second, regarding Chinese names: In the text, per Chinese convention, surnames appear first except in the acknowledgments below; in source information in endnotes, for the sake of consistency, surnames appear last (with some notable exeptions such as Mao Zedong).

Many people helped to make this book possible. I feel constrained from identifying many of my Chinese interlocutors, given the increasingly chilly atmosphere there for engagement with foreigners on sensitive topics. (As a general matter, interviews were conducted in confidentiality, and names are withheld here by mutual agreement.) And those who have shared their insights on China are too numerous to mention. I am grateful to all of them. (All errors, errant opinions, and misunderstandings are my own.) With those provisos, I would especially like to thank Joel Andreas, Earl Brown, William Brown, Kai Chang, Sean Cooney, Wenwen Ding, Baohua Dong, Sam Estreicher, Eli Friedman, Mary Gallagher, Dan Guttman, Xin He, Virginia Harper Ho, Sam Issacharoff, Junlu Jiang, Dimitri Kessler, Margaret Lewis, Ben Liebman, Cheng Liu, Mingwei Liu, Xiaonan Liu, Martin Ma, Carl Minzner, Pasquale Pasquino, Eva Pils, Jian Qiao, Benjamin Van Rooij, Bo Rothstein, Teemu Ruskola, Xiuyin Shi, Karla Simon, Frank Upham, Isabelle Wan, Kan Wang, Tianyu Wang, Zengyi Xie, Tian Yan, Arnold Zack, Wei Zhang, Weiwei Zhang, Wei Zhao, and Earnest Changzheng Zhou. In addition, I am grateful to two anonymous reviewers for Harvard University Press (HUP) for their deeply thoughtful comments on an earlier draft of the whole manuscript, and to two editors at HUP, Michael Aronson and especially Thomas LeBien, for their support and guidance.

NYU has proven to be an extraordinary platform for this scholarly foray into China. Two successive deans at NYU, Richard Revesz and Trevor Morrison, provided support in many forms. My past and present colleagues at USALI warmly encouraged my efforts at every step. In addition to Jerry, Seth, and Aaron, I am indebted to Ira Belkin, Yu-jie Chen, Chaoyi Jiang, Ling Li, Chao Liu, and Han Yu. In addition, I had outstanding research assistance at NYU from Gabriel Ascher, Alvin Cheung, Iris Hsiao, Regina Hsu, Jesse Klinger, Bing Le, Rousang Li, Weili Li, Hannah McDermott, Yingying Wu, Jo Yizhou Xu, Wentao Yuan, Luping Zhang, Tianpu Zhang, and Han Zhu, and especially from Ellen Campbell, whose work was above and beyond. I also had invaluable help from research librarians Gretchen Feltes and Meredith Rossi. I have enjoyed generous financial support from the NYU School of Law, in part through the Filomen D'Agostino and Max E. Greenberg Research Fund.

Finally, I am endlessly grateful for the love and support of my children, Jessica and Lucas, who are kind, generous, funny, and accomplished young adults, and my husband, Sam Issacharoff, who has been a treasured colleague, critic, and fan, as well as a wonderful life partner for thirty-five years and counting.

A NEW DEAL FOR CHINA'S WORKERS?

# CHAPTER ONE

# Introduction

IF THE WORKERS of the world are united in anything, it may be in the degree to which their working lives and their futures are being shaped by China. This is no surprise to American workers and the politicians who court them. China's deep pool of "cheap labor" has been a recurring motif in modern American politics, most recently in the 2016 presidential campaign. But China's workers are increasingly speaking up for themselves, and we should all be listening.

In the first decade or two after China opened its doors to the world and began to churn out much of the clothing, shoes, toys, and other mass consumer goods sold in Western stores, the prevailing Western image of Chinese workers—if there was one—was of an endless, faceless, voiceless mass. The millions of poor rural migrants flowing into the grim factories in China's coastal areas seemed to tolerate the intolerable—working for pennies an hour at a brutal pace for unimaginably long days and weeks. Behind them, and ready to replace those who were chewed up and spit out, were the hundreds of millions who remained in the impoverished rural villages of the interior. That seemingly bottomless supply of cheap labor gave a geographic location if not a human face to the "race to the bottom" that for many Western observers was shaping the bleak future of workers, their unions, and their families in the developed economies of the world.

One does not have to be a close China watcher to know that things have changed. To begin with, China has become an economic powerhouse—the world's second-largest national economy, home to a sizable share of global manufacturing and to a large and growing fraction of the world's middle-income consumers. Since 1981, as many as six hundred million people in China have climbed out of poverty, partly through the wrenching process of migration out of destitute rural areas and into China's vast and countless factories.[1] That process has transformed product markets, labor markets, and workers' lives both within and beyond its borders.

The rise from destitution has brought rising expectations. China's workers may still be a faceless mass to many Westerners, but they are no longer voiceless, and they are increasingly unwilling to tolerate the intolerable. That is most vividly true in the factories of the newly-industrialized coastal areas, with their mostly migrant workforces, which churn out much of the world's consumer goods. After years of widespread submission to miserable wages and working conditions, punctuated by occasional outbursts of wrath, Chinese workers are increasingly resorting to both "exit" and "voice" in response to their discontentment.[2] They are exercising their market freedom to quit and seek better conditions elsewhere, and they are protesting, loudly and in larger numbers, against abuse and low wages.

An important spur to both "exit" and "voice" lies in the surprising appearance of labor shortages starting in the mid-2000s.[3] The supply of new migrant workers, and especially of the skilled workers needed in the more advanced product sectors now growing up in China, began to slow as the smaller "one-child generation," born starting in 1980, entered the industrial workforce.[4] In the meantime, enough capital had trickled into the interior to create factory jobs closer to home, so that a teenager's decision to leave home for a brutally demanding, poorly paid, and faraway factory job became more of a choice and less of a dire necessity.[5] A tighter labor market changed the labor market calculus in the more developed coastal regions, and it emboldened many of China's workers to join together to protest against injustice, to demand a bigger share of the growing economic pie and a greater voice in their working lives. More recently, an economic slump has brought layoffs and factory closings in some areas; but those events, too, have triggered strikes, for China's migrant workers have become increasingly willing and able to mount a collective response to their grievances.

The rise of labor unrest, and especially the rise of strikes, has unsettled Chinese officialdom. For two decades after the opening of its economy, China's Communist Party leaders pursued rapid economic growth above all else, paying little heed to the social and environmental costs of growth or to the increasingly unequal distribution of its benefits. But China's restive workers have helped to push those problems up to the top of the policy agenda, and to underscore the need for reform and redistribution (and not only repression) in order to build a "harmonious society."

An American observer might imagine (as I did upon first learning of these developments) that China's workers had arrived at the cusp of their own "New Deal moment"—a moment when workers' political and economic power and mobilization converge to produce major industrial relations reforms and redistributive policies. Even without the ability to vote for candidates promising labor reform, labor protest and the threat of serious unrest undoubtedly put political pressure on an authoritarian regime, and China's leaders had already responded with some pro-worker reforms. Indeed, those leaders might well take note that it is not only workers who might have something to gain from a "New Deal with Chinese characteristics," for the American New Deal was both transformative and conservative. It dramatically enhanced some workers' ability to shape their own working lives and livelihoods through unionization and collective bargaining, and at the same time it helped to deflect and defuse demands for more radical political and economic change and to bolster the political legitimacy of the established order among the working classes.

In short, China is both changing the world, and is itself changing, in ways that we cannot afford to ignore. It is worth watching closely as the most populous nation in the history of the world grapples before our twenty-first-century eyes (albeit often behind closed doors) with the question of how to redefine the rights and entitlements of workers and the governance of labor relations in an increasingly advanced industrial economy. That big question may seem remote from a bigger question that has gripped many Western observers since the 1970s: is economic liberalization and growth leading, inevitably or otherwise, to political liberalization and democratization? But the two questions are linked. China's workers are demanding not only higher wages but a greater voice in their working lives. China's response to those demands will both reflect and potentially reshape the structure of governance and the prospects for broader political reform in China.

## China's Rise and the "Race to the Rising Bottom"?

China's economic past and future—its unprecedented growth in recent decades and its hotly disputed capacity to sustain future growth—are inextricably intertwined with its unfolding labor relations story and with the welfare of workers elsewhere. For one thing, the sheer magnitude of future labor unrest in China may both affect and be affected by its ability to keep its now-troubled economy afloat and growing, and to avoid massive factory closings and layoffs.[6] The stability of China's economy preoccupies policy makers and others in China and across the world, and it is a matter of vigorous debate among economists; but it is not my topic here. Suffice it to say that the economic turmoil of the past few years does not encourage those who might have hoped that a steadily and vigorously growing economy would by itself solve the problem of labor unrest and avert the need for reform by meeting the rising material expectations of China's workers.

China's economic performance in recent decades does, however, raise another question that warrants brief attention here. Scholars and activists have debated for many decades whether the globalization of the economy has generated more of a "race to the bottom" or a "rising tide that lifts all boats."[7] But the rise of China, along with the wages and labor standards of its workers, suggests a better metaphor: a "race to the rising bottom." And China's increasingly restive workers are helping to raise that bottom.

Some industries and firms do chase cheap, unorganized labor and weakly regulated labor markets. The migration of much of the American textile and apparel industry to China in the 1990s, for example, was largely a quest for cheap labor, facilitated by falling trade barriers and transportation costs.[8] The rise of labor shortages and of wages in China, in turn, has sent shudders through the ranks of foreign corporations that have profited so handsomely from China's "cheap labor" model of development. Some industries and firms, especially in footwear, apparel, and other light mass manufacturing industries, have gravitated to even cheaper labor markets in Bangladesh, Vietnam, and elsewhere. That dynamic may encourage some poor countries' leaders to make suppression of unions and lack of regulation part of a national development strategy. That is, of course, the "race to the bottom" story, and there is clearly something to it.

But China (among other developing economies) has complicated the story line. The "race to the bottom" was once seemingly embodied by China, with its apparently bottomless supply of poor farmers who could be drawn into its burgeoning factories. But the flow of capital to China has also helped to bring about the most dramatic reduction in poverty the world has ever seen: The percentage of China's population living in "extreme poverty" fell from 84 percent in 1981 to 12 percent in 2010.[9] Moreover, it is because labor is not so cheap in China anymore (not just because cheaper labor can be found elsewhere) that some firms are moving manufacturing jobs to lower-wage countries.[10] Real wage levels have increased during the whole post-opening period by an average of nearly ten percent per year, as shown in Figure 1.1; and real minimum-wage levels have increased by an average of 8 percent per year from 2010 to 2014, and by as much as 20 percent in some provinces.[11] That is partly because China's workers have loudly demanded wage hikes; their struggle is at the heart of this book. But it underscores the fact that, at least in recent years, China's rulers have not sought to suppress wages to keep bottom-tier manufacturing jobs in China. On the contrary, up to a point the loss of those jobs is in keeping with China's development strategy, which is to move up the value chain and into more lucrative sectors and phases of production. Whether China can do so, and thus avoid the so-called "middle-income trap," is a subject of anxious speculation in China and elsewhere.[12] But these developments obviously do not reflect a simple "race to the bottom."

The "race to the bottom" story gives short shrift to the fact that many industries and firms—especially those that drive a prosperous economy, and that China now aims to cultivate—depend on a more productive and stable workforce than may be found in a "cheap labor" locale. China's continued growth thus requires developing the skills of its labor force, its gargantuan domestic consumer market, and its relatively sophisticated infrastructure and supplier networks; those are advantages that lower-wage jurisdictions cannot offer.[13] Moreover, the flow of capital to "cheap labor" countries, even when it is attracted by their less demanding, less

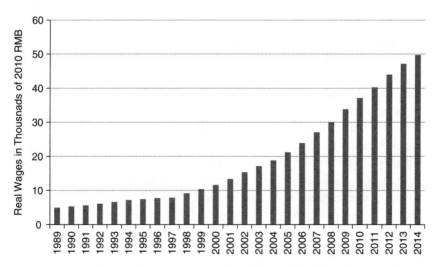

FIGURE 1.1 Real annual average wages of on-duty staff and workers in urban units, China, in 2010 RMB, 1989–2014. *Sources:* China Ministry of Human Resources and Social Security (MOHRSS); China National Bureau of Statistics (NBS); IMF World Economic Outlook Database 2015.

organized workers and weak or compliant regulators, tends to both enable and stimulate worker organizing, regulatory development, and rising wage levels.[14] That is what has happened in China. Those dynamics might evoke the "rising tide" story.

Yet the rising tide is not quite lifting all boats. In particular, many blue-collar workers of the world's richest industrial countries have seen their jobs disappear, and their hard-won wage gains and generous benefit packages erode, under competitive pressure from lower-cost workers in China and elsewhere.[15] That is the kernel of truth that underlies recurring populist appeals in the United States, most recently in the 2016 presidential campaign, to reconstruct trade barriers and punish China for "stealing our jobs." Many former steelworkers and autoworkers, and especially their children and grandchildren, have drifted into service-sector jobs that are much worse paid and less secure.[16] And their fate might foreshadow that of many others. Much of the work that is currently done in the developed world—including skilled service work in technical, medical, legal, and financial fields—will be exportable to lower-wage countries as technology enhances firms' ability to divide up work and transport its inputs and outputs across borders. Predictions vary as to how much of that work will be exported (or simply replaced by software and smart machines).[17]

The amalgam of the two stories that I mean to capture in the phrase "race to the rising bottom" offers little solace to workers at the top of the global economic ladder, for it is a long way down to even a rising bottom. But a rising bottom would be good news for many of the world's poorest workers, who may reap economic gains from globalization even if they work under conditions that are appalling to us (and even if global business and financial elites take an outsized share of the gains). A simplistic anti-globalization line is hard to square with the rising fortunes of China's hundreds of millions of formerly impoverished rural citizens, not to mention the aspirations of hundreds of millions of still-destitute citizens in South and Southeast Asia and Africa who need capital investment (among other things) to climb up the economic ladder in China's footsteps. (Of course, China's own development casts a shadow—or rather a noxious layer of smog—over the question of whether and how continued economic development can be made compatible with the habitability of the planet.[18] That is another enormous question that will be set aside here.)

One piece of good news is that the "bottom" may now be in sight, as both manufacturers and anti-sweatshop activists are recognizing. Auret van Heerden, a veteran of the campaign to compel corporations to take responsibility for ensuring decent labor standards in their supply chains, described the lay of the land in 2011 from the vantage point of manufacturers:

They're wondering if they could push more stuff to Bangladesh or Vietnam or Indonesia and so on, but the options are limited . . . [T]here are only one or two places left. People are looking at Africa again to see if there isn't something that they've overlooked there. Finding another cheap platform, another cheap country, was the default until now, but frankly that's no longer an option. There's nowhere else to go.[19]

Indeed, some production that had left the United States has even returned there—albeit with fewer jobs and more robotics—as the advantages of proximity and productivity have begun to rival or outrun the diminishing advantages of cheap labor.[20]

So let us give a half-hearted cheer for the "race to the rising bottom" and for the Chinese workers who are among its beneficiaries. And let us recognize that Chinese workers are not only the beneficiaries but also among the agents of the "rising bottom" part of the story. The bottom of the global labor market rises in part because workers' rising expectations and demands push it up; and they do that in part, as they have in China, by agitating collectively for a larger share of growing returns from a developing economy. That brings us back to the main story line here: the rise of labor unrest in China and the evolving official response.

## The Rise of Labor Unrest: Snapshots of China's Workers in Motion

The 1990s and 2000s saw rising numbers of so-called "mass incidents"—variously defined, but usually involving at least one hundred people—protesting a perceived injustice at the hands of government officials, wealthy developers, or bosses. The proliferation of these mostly spontaneous protests, many of them labor related, was a growing source of concern to the regime, one that contributed to the mid-2000s shift away from economic growth at all costs toward greater attention to mitigating the costs and spreading the benefits of growth. But the more recent rise of larger, often longer lasting, and more organized strikes, or collective work stoppages, was more deeply alarming and put collective labor relations on the front burner of policy makers.

### A Rising Tide of "Mass Incidents"

The central government reported 10,000 mass incidents in 1994, rising to 74,000 in 2004, and 87,000 in 2005.[21] The government has not reported the total figures since 2005, but there is no doubt they are keeping track.

In 2008, a senior Party source put the total number of mass incidents at 127,467,[22] and a Chinese scholar estimated that there were 180,000 such incidents in 2010.[23] Informed observers have estimated that anywhere from 30 to 45 percent of these incidents arise out of labor disputes.[24]

When mass incidents are depicted from afar in such large numbers, they tend to blur into an abstraction, much as "Chinese workers" numbering in the hundreds of millions can blur into an undifferentiated mass. So it is worth trying to picture one of these labor-related mass incidents. Here is a report of one such incident from the official People's Daily on October 12, 2010:

> Lei Yong and Liao Xinglong were two of eight construction workers who went to their employer . . . at around 5 p.m. Monday to claim unpaid wages. A fight ensued. Lei and Liao were severely beaten by the company staff. Lei died in the hospital on Monday evening . . . Shortly after Lei's death, hundreds of his co-workers blocked Erhuan Road in Dujiangyan City. The furious workers clashed with police and toppled a police vehicle. They dispersed at around 3:30 a.m. Tuesday, [but] they protested again, with more people, a few hours later at the highway exit. The crowd dispersed and traffic resumed at around 11:30 a.m. after [the local police chief] promised the protesters that the criminals would be punished according to law and that unpaid wages would be paid.[25]

This incident was larger and more violent than most, as was the provocation—a worker's death at the hands of the employer's agents. But in other respects the incident was fairly typical of the labor protests that mounted in China's rapidly developing regions during the 2000s: The underlying grievance of unpaid wages was the single most common trigger for labor protest in the non-state economy. (China's labor laws are more comprehensive and demanding than most Westerners assume, but the large gap between the law on the books and conditions on the ground has triggered much protest.) The police response to the protest, and their use of both force and appeasement to end the incident, was characteristic of the mixed repertoire of "stability maintenance" techniques that local officials bring to the scene. Also typical was the spontaneity of the protest action, and in particular the utter absence from the scene of China's official trade union, the All-China Federation of Trade Unions (ACFTU), or its provincial and local branches.

Coincidentally, this particular incident was reported in the official press just two days after jailed political dissident Liu Xiaobo was awarded the Nobel Peace Prize, an event that was aggressively purged from public discourse in China. The contrasting treatment of the two events in the official press hints at the comparatively tolerant official attitude toward most labor unrest as compared to more overtly political (even peaceful) forms of dissent in China.

Yet collective labor protest risks turning political, and its rise has provoked deep anxiety among China's leaders. That anxiety stems in part from the historic role of workers' rebellions both in the birth of Communist regimes and in their demise, and it rose to a fever pitch in 1989. In April of that year, Poland's Solidarity Union, an independent worker movement that had grown up outside of Poland's own Leninist-style official union and in opposition to Communist rule, forced the regime to agree to hold democratic elections.[26] That same month in China, an unofficial, independent worker organization—the Beijing Workers' Autonomous Federation—formed to support the student-led protest movement that was building momentum and swirling around Tiananmen Square.[27] Both branches of that movement were brutally shut down, and many of their leaders were killed, jailed, or pushed into exile, in the crackdown on June 4. That happens to be the very day that Solidarity—the Polish trade union turned political party—won the first round of semi-free elections that eventually ended Communist Party rule there.

Before Tiananmen, some officials in the top layers of the Communist Party of China (CPC) had pressed from within for greater tolerance of political dissent and association, and also for greater autonomy for the ACFTU and its branches. But Tiananmen came to be seen as the moment when all could have been lost—when the Party might have lost control, casting China again into chaos. As one astute observer put it, "If the Chinese Communist Party has learned anything from the 1989 democracy movement and the Soviet experience, it is the lesson that 'a single spark can start a prairie fire,' as the Chinese saying goes."[28] Since 1989, China's leaders, from Deng Xiaoping to Xi Jinping and the top levels of the CPC under them, have been united in their commitment to consolidate Party control, to suppress political dissent, and to prevent the rise of any independent organization or movement that could become a vehicle for political opposition.[29] China's now vast and costly "stability maintenance" apparatus "is designed to nip any sign of opposition, real or imagined, in the bud," less by repressing it than by preventing it, for "violent suppression of protests is seen as a sign of failure. China's strong state is reflected not so much in its sharp teeth as in its nimble fingers."[30] The heavy investment in "stability maintenance" and suppression of dissent in turn reflects an often-expressed conviction that, without stable and united Communist Party leadership, China would be "ungovernable."[31]

The rising number of labor-related "mass incidents"—mostly spontaneous outbursts against broken laws and broken promises—was thus a source of concern in Beijing, and a spur to reforms, as we will see. But even more unsettling was the advent of larger labor actions that required a greater measure of planning, organizing, and leadership. In particular, the strikes that began at a Honda parts factory and gripped the auto industry for several weeks in 2010 seemed to mark a turning point in China's industrial relations development.

### A Wake-Up Call from Honda

In May of 2010, over 1,800 workers at the Nanhai Honda transmission factory in Foshan, China, went on strike. The Nanhai Honda strike was the biggest and longest-running strike ever in a foreign-invested Chinese factory. It stalled work in three downstream Honda assembly plants for nearly two weeks and cost Honda up to 2.4 billion RMB (about $350 million) a day.[32] The Nanhai strike was followed by strikes at another Honda component factory and several other foreign and domestic automakers.[33] Within Honda alone, the strike wave idled over 4,000 workers at four factories and stalled work at other downstream factories. In all, some twenty-five factories were affected by the strike wave.[34]

Casual observers of China's labor scene might have assumed that the workers were striking over the sort of Dickensian working conditions for which China—a nominally socialist workers' state—had become notorious. Egregiously exploitative working conditions have indeed triggered many mass incidents, but the Honda strike was different in several ways.

First, this was a strike about economic interests, not legal rights: the workers were seeking higher wages and better working conditions than the law required. Ironically, one government official suggested that it was partly *because* "Nanhai Honda follows the laws so strictly," especially in limiting overtime to the statutory ceiling of thirty-six hours a month, that it had "affected the workers' incomes."[35] That irony aside, these workers were demanding something that state enforcement of minimum labor standards could not deliver: a bigger share of the revenues that flowed from a leading company in an advanced sector of the economy. Workers were able to make Honda's own economic strength and profitability, together with its "just-in-time" production strategy, into a source of power for workers.

Second, both the ambition of their demands and their seriousness and skill in pursuing those demands showed that the Honda strikers were unusually "[w]ell organized, strategic and assertive," and had built up collective "solidarity and a determination to win."[36] They demanded not only sizable wage hikes but also "a pay scale and a career ladder." And they demanded something else that set them apart from most protesting workers in China—not only material improvements but also a measure of democracy and an institutional voice in determining future wages and working conditions. Strikers elected their own representatives from each of the factory's five sections of production to participate in multiple negotiating sessions with Nanhai Honda management. By the end of their week-long high-profile strike, the company had offered a 24 percent raise (32 percent for interns) and had promised future democratic elections for union representatives.[37]

Third, a strike in the automotive industry was especially threatening to China's leaders. In the global history of industrial relations, auto workers had often featured as a sort of militant vanguard whose uprising was a catalyst for significant change.[38] (And China's leaders are assiduous students of history.[39]) Auto workers in China and elsewhere have often managed to form connections and communication networks across their industry that greatly magnified the risk of contagion and of generalized unrest.[40] This was particularly unsettling because the automotive industry in China straddles the state sector and the private and foreign-invested sector, and is considered a "strategic" industry.[41] So this was a loud wake-up call indeed.

Nothing of this magnitude happens in China without the involvement of the party-state. Its key representative in the Honda strike was Zeng Qinghong, a provincial representative of the National People's Congress. An official newspaper report glowingly described Zeng as a mediator who "earnestly and patiently won acceptance from the workers," who almost single-handedly forced wrongdoers to apologize and saw to it that the workers' major demands were met, and who got the workers back to work.[42] Zeng had a strong incentive to settle the strike and was in a strong position to exact concessions from management, as he was in fact the general manager of the Guangzhou Auto Group, Honda's Chinese partner in this joint enterprise, which was losing hundreds of millions of dollars in the strike.[43] Wearing his Party hat, however, he assumed the role of mediator in its resolution.

So both management and the Party were on the scene, at least in the singular person of the two-hatted Zeng. But the ACFTU and the factory trade union branch that officially represented the workers were at first silent.[44] The union said nothing during prestrike negotiations with worker representatives when management offered a 55 RMB per month raise (about $9, or 5 percent of the workers' demands); that paltry offer was the immediate trigger for the work stoppage. Even after the strike began, the union did nothing. When a local ACFTU official was asked what the union was doing to help the workers in their negotiations for higher wages, he replied, "This is a matter between labor and employers. It is inappropriate for the trade union to intervene."[45] (The statement hints at features of the ACFTU that confound Western observers, to be explored in Chapter 3.)

When the union finally did begin to intervene, it only inflamed the situation. For example, on May 31, more than a hundred union members, sent to the factory by the local government, tried to block workers who were trying to talk to reporters. " 'They're mafia,' fumed one employee, as another showed a long cut on his face that he blamed on the union men."[46] Reports that two workers had their faces "beaten bloody" by twelve men wearing union badges prompted hundreds of workers who had returned to the lines to leave again.[47] According to one report, "at the Honda plant, employees fume more about the factory's trade union than about Japanese managers."[48]

These events—the workers' election of their own leaders, their successful negotiations with management, and the ACFTU's utterly marginal and unhelpful role—highlighted both the possibility and the necessity of reform within the ACFTU. They showed that both real collective bargaining and real elected leadership were possible, and that, absent serious reform, both might take place entirely outside the officially designated trade union structure. Some observers even saw signs of a long-awaited independent workers' movement and a challenge to the ACFTU's monopoly on representation of workers. But the stated goal of the strike leaders was not to form their own union; that would have sharply politicized their strike and brought them into a direct conflict with the state that they would have surely lost. They sought instead the right to elect leaders within the official trade union framework who would better represent their interests vis-à-vis management.[49]

The Honda strike was a spur to official and academic discussion of reforms within the ACFTU and in the sensitive domain of collective labor relations. But while those policy discussions have dragged on, events on the ground have followed their own course as workers have grown increasingly willing and able to press their own demands through collective action. Especially in Guangdong Province, workers have learned a lot in recent decades about how to organize collective action and how to walk the line between too little and too much agitation—enough to draw official attention and intervention, but not so much as to pose a political threat and provoke a harshly repressive official response. And so strike levels have continued to rise.

## A Follow-Up Call at Yue Yuen

The biggest strike in China's recent history took place in 2014 at Yue Yuen, a major Taiwanese-invested supplier for Nike, Adidas, Puma, and New Balance. The strike grew from a single worker's claim for workplace injury compensation to a strike involving some forty thousand workers. Although different in many ways from the Honda strike, the 2014 Yue Yuen strike sent its own alarming signals to both employers and officials, in part because of its utterly mundane origins.

In early April 2014, when a worker at Yue Yuen's large shoe factory in Dongguan City, in Guangdong Province, sought compensation for a workplace injury, he learned that Yue Yuen had not been making the legally mandated social insurance contributions for workers. He and his coworkers concluded that not only the company but "the local government, labor bureau, social security bureau and the company were all tricking [them] together" by skimping on social insurance contributions. On April 5, six hundred workers took to the streets around the factory, blocked roads, and demanded that the company pay full social insurance contributions, including past due amounts (estimated at $30 million).[50] By April 14, the action had escalated into a strike involving one thousand workers, and by April 17, the strike had spread to all seven Yue Yuen factories in Dongguan and involved as many as forty thousand employees.[51] Along the way, the workers' demands expanded to include wage increases of 30 percent. (Before the strike, the average monthly wage at Yue Yuen was about 2,500 yuan, or $400.) According to one fifteen-year veteran of Yue Yuen who was involved in the strike, the social security issues "were the trigger but there [were] many other reasons . . . [W]orkers just took this opportunity to vent their anger," mostly over low wages.[52]

The Yue Yuen strike met a more violent response than the Honda strike. Police used dogs and batons to break up marches and detained dozens of workers. They also arrested two worker advocates associated with Chunfeng (Spring Wind), a non-governmental organization (NGO) that supports workers in Dongguan. Chunfeng's leader, Zhang Zhiru, was detained for several days, and his colleague Lin Dong was jailed for thirty days on criminal charges of "picking quarrels and creating trouble." Lin's offense was apparently to post "rumors" about another strike involving thirty thousand electronics workers that might have been inspired by the Yue Yuen strike.[53] The second strike was real: two strikes, each involving tens of thousands of workers, in one municipality in one week.

The strike finally came to an end, and most of the workers returned to the factories, by April 28. The strike had cost Yue Yuen about $27 million in lost production, and the settlement would cost another $31 million in 2014 alone, according to the company. For its part, the Ministry of Human Resources and Social Security said that Yue Yuen had failed to "truthfully report" social security payments it was making for employees at its Dongguan factories and that the agency would step up auditing and enforcement of social security insurance payments.

One Yue Yuen worker summed up profoundly mixed feelings upon the conclusion of the strike in an online posting:

> Yes, we failed. Under the violence of batons and police dogs we had to resume work. Yet deep in our hearts we feel proud as we participated in this great *wei quan* [rights-protection] struggle. This action is going to be seen as a milestone in the history of Chinese workers' *wei quan*. It symbolizes that the Chinese labour movement has now advanced from merely demanding wage raises to demanding more social security (although this is what the laws stipulate in the first place). This is a great advancement! In the future when one looks back at the history of Chinese labour movement one will see a great monument, with the words, "Yue Yuen" inscribed on it . . . After the baptism of this struggle, in the future the Yue Yuen workers will only be more organized, more courageous in fighting for their interests!"[54]

The invocation of the "Chinese labour movement," the sense of collective identity and historic destiny, and the determination to continue the struggle were among the signs that China's workers had reached a new stage of self-organization and that China's labor pains were likely to continue for some time.

Several features of the Yue Yuen strike are noteworthy. First, many of the strikers were middle-aged, and their initial focus on social security contributions—even if other grievances were brewing as well—was a sign of the maturation of China's migrant labor force. Long-term economic security was far from the minds of young migrant workers in the first decades of China's "opening." The social security system in particular was virtually irrelevant to migrant workers, given the impact of China's *hukou,* or "household registration," system: local officials in the place of work had little interest in collecting contributions on behalf of workers from outside the locality, and the funds were not transferable to workers' home localities.[55] But today's migrant workers are older, more focused on future economic security, and less likely to envision returning to the countryside and living off their small farm plots there. They are also more demanding of employers and the state to provide what the law purports to ensure them but in fact has largely denied. This hints at both the changing nature of China's *hukou* system and the changing nature of the industrial labor force.

The Yue Yuen strike also put the fragmented nature of the Chinese party-state on vivid display. To begin with, the underlying dispute over social security contributions arose out of collusion between local officials and the employer to evade legal mandates emanating from Beijing. Local governments in Guangdong Province and elsewhere routinely indulge the local businesses from which economic growth (and graft) flow, and tacitly condone companies' skipping their social security contributions. The massive Yue Yuen uprising over this very common practice thus sent ripples of anxiety through the managerial ranks in Dongguan's thousands of factories and beyond.

The local government's involvement in the underlying dispute also put a potentially political cast on the Yue Yuen strike from the beginning. That potential was magnified by the aggressive response of police and security officials. The veteran worker quoted above described the workers' sentiment as the strike was coming to a close: "We all feel aggrieved today. Outwardly, the strike has been resolved but the underlying problems are still there. All in all, we are frustrated. We feel especially dissatisfied because of the government's suppression of workers." He continued: "In the end, all three sides suffered losses in this strike—workers were suppressed, the employer had to pay billions in compensation and fines, and the legitimacy of the government was eroded."[56]

The role of the trade union was more equivocal at Yue Yuen than it had been at Honda. Some reports had the official trade union intervening constructively on strikers' behalf. The Guangdong Federation of Trade Unions, the provincial branch of the ACFTU, announced that it was "taking a clear-cut stand" that the workers' rights must be protected, and had instructed its municipal branch in Dongguan to mediate the labor dispute.[57] (The idea of a trade union "mediating" a dispute between workers and their employer may be puzzling to Western observers, but that turns out to be a signature feature of one form of "collective bargaining" that is emerging in China, described in Chapter 6.) That might have represented a step forward for local unions that had long been dismissed as "useless" and submissive to local businesses. But the veteran worker cited above found that the Guangdong FTU's "mediation" made things worse for the workers: "After seeking workers' opinions, they issued a Proposal of Resumption of Work, calling on everyone to return to work. Then, the cops sealed the factory gates. The workers couldn't punch in, and those inside were not allowed to go out . . . I think they are on the same side— the Federation, the cops and the employer."[58] If the union had learned a lesson from the Honda strikes, it seemed to have had more impact on its public pronouncements than on its actions.

The grassroots activists from Chunfeng, by contrast, were more helpful, according to the worker activist: they offered some ideas that were "basically pertinent and reasonable," especially "the establishment of a workers' committee to lead the strike."[59] But Chunfeng did not and could not purport to replace the union; instead, its activists encouraged strikers to seek a more democratic trade union election as part of their demands.

## Why Labor Protest Is Different

What is happening in the labor field is in some ways typical of other arenas of simmering social discontent in China, and in some ways distinct. Collective protest is on the rise in disputes over demolition of housing, appropriation of rural lands, and environmental abuse, as well as in labor disputes. In all those arenas, the proliferation of protest incidents raises anxiety at both local and national levels of officialdom; that stems partly from the fear that localized social mobilization outside the state might coalesce into something larger and more threatening to political stability. Local officials have responded with a mixture of reform and repression— efforts to address underlying social concerns, in part through better laws and better enforcement, alongside ad hoc efforts to silence the most disruptive, ambitious, or visible protest leaders. NGOs are often found around the edges, or sometimes at the center, of protest, and they meet an official response that reflects China's increasing chilliness toward civil society. China's unelected regime faces a range of dilemmas in dealing with popular discontent. By closely examining one of those arenas of social discontent—labor unrest—and the mixture of official responses to it, this book aims to cast some light on a wider landscape of challenges and changes in China.

But labor is also a distinct field of social conflict. First, workers have a potential source of collective power—beyond the power to create a ruckus— that other citizens lack: they can shut down or disrupt production of goods and services by refusing to work. That gets the attention both of the proprietors of an enterprise, who profit directly from continued production, and of the political actors whose ability to govern successfully and to stay in power may depend on steady economic output and growth.

Second, labor protest generally takes place in urbanized areas, where news travels faster and further and arrives more quickly at centers of power than in rural areas. Industrial workers are connected to each other and to larger and denser social networks by way of modern channels of communication and transportation. Rural uprisings may be easier to bottle up within a single village or town.

Third, workers also have some diffuse structural advantages that tend to make labor unrest both more organizable and potentially more contagious than other forms of social protest. For centuries and across the globe, the experience of shared work—within the same workplace, the same occupation, or the same labor market—has often provided a fertile medium for organizing. Common work fosters both solidarity—a sense of common fate and interdependence—and an awareness of collective power that comes from manning the productive engines of the economy, and can make it easier to organize collective action across various boundaries, both geographic and social.

These are some of the factors behind the remarkable rise in the number of strikes and of striking workers in China, especially in the past decade, and some of the factors that make that development so unsettling to the regime. There are no official, publicly available statistics on strikes in China, but the best data available shows strike levels increasing dramatically every year for the past five years—from 185 strikes in 2011 to 2,774 in 2015.[60]

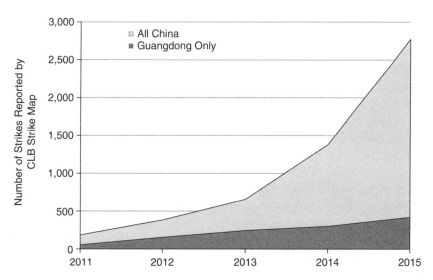

FIGURE 1.2 Strikes in China as a whole and in Guangdong Province, 2011–2015. *Note:* While this is the best data known to be available, we are aware that this data is likely not exhaustive of strikes in China, given restrictions on reporting. *Source:* China Strike Map, China Labour Bulletin, available online at http://strikemap.clb .org.hk/strikes/en.

## Is China Headed Toward a "New Deal" for Labor?

These distinctive features of labor unrest and labor organizing are not unique to China. They begin to suggest the value of looking at China's labor pains against the backdrop of labor unrest and organizing elsewhere. This book examines China's current labor troubles and the reforms that are taking shape in their wake in part through the comparative lens of American experience with industrial conflict. The point of such a comparison is neither to predict China's path nor to show how China falls short of some universal ideal—U.S. labor law and institutions are neither universal nor ideal. The point is to use both the parallels and the contrasts between Chinese and U.S. experiences with industrial conflict to illuminate China's labor relations and its political system and policy choices, especially for the American reader. Indeed, one point of deploying this comparative lens is to show how it might distort as well as clarify the Chinese labor scene. Things are quite different from how they may appear when seen through the lens through which many U.S. observers view China. The friction between China's contemporary reality and U.S.-inflected preconceptions and patterns can generate sparks of insight into China's struggle to regulate work and industrial relations in a developing market economy.

Some recent developments in China—rising strike levels, rising worker demands, rising economic inequality, and rising resentment over inequality—seem to echo the American experience with industrial unrest in the 1930s. China's leaders worry, as some U.S. leaders did in the 1930s, that if workers' just grievances are not addressed constructively, they might turn political, and might undermine the legitimacy of the political system among workers and their allies. China's leaders aspire to peaceful and productive industrial relations, continuing growth and widely shared prosperity, and renewal of the government's legitimacy among the working classes. Those were among the key economic and political achievements of the New Deal in the United States. When viewed through that historical lens, China might seem to be headed either toward a "New Deal" of sorts—a major recalibration of the rewards of industry, including some system of collective bargaining through independent trade unions—or toward the kind of wrenching and destabilizing industrial conflict that the New Deal helped bring to a close in the United States.

Yet a closer look at China takes one "through the looking glass," where nothing is as it first appears. One big reason is obvious and inescapable: China has a one-party authoritarian system whose leaders do not stand for popular election and do not intend to do so in the foreseeable future. Even as China's leaders might hope to replicate some of the major achievements of the American New Deal, they are bound and determined to avoid the sort of bottom-up, tumultuous, politicized mobilization that helped to bring about the New Deal, and to continue to deny the political liberties and democratic institutions that made the New Deal possible. In particular, they are deeply committed to preventing the rise of independent trade unions of the sort that played a central, defining role in the American New Deal and in industrial relations in the advanced industrial economies of the West. In China it is the *specter* of independent trade unions—more than the Party-controlled trade union itself—that plays that central, defining role. For China's rulers, an independent labor movement is seen as an existential political threat to one-party rule.

Hence, the overarching thesis of this book: The regime's unwavering determination to avoid the rise of an independent labor movement is a driving force behind China's multifaceted approach to labor unrest. That determination has spurred both reforms and repression, while at the same time shaping and constraining both.

The commitment to preventing the rise of an independent labor movement is reflected in the continuing threat and use of repression against individuals and groups that threaten to grow into union-like organizations; but it is also reflected in efforts to economize on the use of overt repression that might provoke a popular backlash and an escalation of oppositional activity. So alongside the continuing but restrained use of repression against potentially political forms of collective worker activity, the regime has undertaken a range of reforms and initiatives that aim to address some of the grievances—economic and otherwise—that fuel workers' protests. Yet those reforms and initiatives have also been constrained, even stunted, by the determination to prevent labor unrest from veering into political opposition. Underlying every part of this oscillating mix of repression and restraint, reform and retrenchment, is the fear that localized protests against particular employers, mixed with discontentment over the government's role in labor relations, will coalesce into a larger labor movement that could challenge the prevailing political order.[61]

China's multifaceted struggle to contain labor conflict and head off independent labor organizing thus displays a mix of repression and reform, rigidity and pragmatism, corruption and meritocracy, and even a dash of freedom and democracy, that will surprise many readers. The biggest surprise might be the apparent durability and functionality of a system that is both deeply flawed and deeply different from our own. China's response to labor unrest reveals both entrenched barriers to democratizing reforms, including the toleration and recognition of independent unions, and a range of alternative strategies for managing labor conflict. By adroitly opening and closing various pressure valves on organized discontent, China's leaders might be able to keep labor unrest within manageable bounds, and keep the political status quo intact, for a long time.

## Chinese Labor Reform in Four Dimensions

The basic thesis, again, is that the regime's determination to avoid the rise of an independent labor movement has spurred both reforms and repression while at the same time constraining both. That dynamic is reflected in four dimensions of China's labor reform strategy that will occupy much of this book.

*The regulatory strategy:* China's first choice of reform strategies consisted of upgrading minimum labor standards and official institutions for the redress of individual complaints about rights violations. Drawing workers off the streets and into the courts and arbitration tribunals, where the state could deliver better labor standards, seemed a fine strategy for pre-empting collective action. That was much of the impetus for China's enactment of three major labor statutes in 2007, including the Labor Contract Law (LCL).

But if the goal was stemming the tide of labor protest, the regulatory reform strategy fell short. Indeed, the new statutes probably widened the gap between the law on the books and the law in action by raising standards while enforcement was already poor. The disparity between law and practice—a frequent focus of protest and a source of vulnerability for the regime—reflects in part regulatory flaws that are characteristic of China's still-early stage of economic and legal development. But it stems partly from China's unwillingness to unleash the civil society actors that might help workers enforce their rights under the new laws. The constricted and shrinking space for workers' lawyers and advocacy groups stems in turn from the fear of organized social activism, and particularly labor activism that is independent of the state.

But that is not the whole story, for if China had hoped to solve the problem of labor unrest by legislating and enforcing minimum standards, it was destined to fail. Across the industrial world, legislated minimum standards inevitably fall short for many workers in the most advanced and profitable sectors of the economy, like the autoworkers at Honda. Once "interest disputes"—disputes over the distribution of revenues above and beyond compliance with legal minima—rise to the fore, as they have in China, better enforcement of uniform minimum standards is not enough.

*Collective bargaining and the response to strikes:* The tried-and-true institutional response to workers' collective interest disputes in industrial economies has been collective bargaining through representative trade unions,
either at the enterprise level or at the sectoral or regional levels. Especially
in the wake of the Honda strikes, the spotlight soon turned to industrial
relations policy and practices. But even basic terminology suggests differences between Chinese and Western conceptions of industrial relations.
The Chinese term for "collective bargaining" (*jiti tanpan*) is not the pre-
ferred official term for what is supposed to take place in China between
workers and managers in determining wages and other matters. Officially,
that process is usually called "collective consultation" (*jiti xieshang*). "Collective bargaining" has more combative connotations than "collective consultation," which suggests a more consensus-based process in keeping with
the official aspiration to "harmonious labor-management relations." The
term "collective bargaining" seems to be gaining currency, especially in
Guangdong Province, as the daily reality of strikes suggests the inevita-
bility of conflict between labor and capital over basic distributional issues.

Collective agreements are a central feature of China's system of labor
regulation. But both the content of those agreements and the standard
process for securing them in the private sector is a far cry from collective
bargaining as it takes place in the West. Local union officials are charged
by their bosses with concluding large numbers of collective agreements,
which are filled with boilerplate provisions that replicate legal standards.
These collective agreements are generally devoid of real concessions and
take little or no account of the specific demands of workers.[62]

Then there is the atypical bargaining that takes place in the midst of an
actual strike. A strike of any size requires some kind of organization,
informal though it may be, and that is cause for alarm in Chinese officialdom. The alarm that is set off by a sizable strike brings out the local
"firefighters"—a coterie of union officials and police and security forces,
all charged with restoring stability. One part of the "firefighting" arsenal
often consists of local union officials negotiating with employers and
exacting concessions—usually wage hikes. But the negotiating process that
takes place during a strike is better seen as part of local officials' "stability
maintenance" toolbox than as an industrial relations process.

So there are strikes and there are collective negotiations between
employers and union officials, sometimes in the midst of a strike. But there
is no prescribed or practical process for collective negotiations under the
shadow of a strike threat—before and perhaps instead of a strike. For one
thing, strikes exist in a legal no-man's land in China: they are not explicitly
recognized or protected by Chinese labor law, nor are they unlawful

(though employers are free to promulgate rules against work stoppages and to enforce them by dismissing strikers). One thing is clear: strikes are not part of the official process for securing collective agreements with employers, nor are they part of the repertoire of the official trade union.

*Trade union democratization:* That brings us to the ACFTU, and proposals for its reform. With its legal monopoly on worker representation, the ACFTU is a major actor in the regime's effort to stave off independent organizing. But the official union's perceived uselessness to China's restive workers has also made it largely useless to the regime in that effort. So the ACFTU has come under pressure from above, below, and within to become a better representative, and thus a better regulator, of China's workers.

By 2010, some striking workers, at least in Guangdong, were demanding, and sometimes getting, more democratic elections for "grassroots" union leaders.[63] A closer look at this trend, what is behind it, what it amounts to, and what it is up against, reveals much about the meaning of "democracy" in China as well as China's response to labor unrest. It appears that electoral democracy may be another tool in the "stability maintenance" toolkit—one to be dealt out cautiously and sparingly when circumstances (and workers) demand it, but to be kept within narrow bounds. In particular, China's characteristic insistence on "selection" before election—on official screening of candidates—has proven to be a point of contention in grassroots union elections, much as it has been in village elections (and indeed in elections in Hong Kong).

The regime's continuing commitment to party-state control of organized labor activity stands in ironic contrast to its more liberal treatment of "organized capital." In China's planned economy, productive activity was an integral dimension of the party-state. Enterprises—both their capital and their labor—were administered through managers and union officers, all party cadres. "Reform and opening"—the corporatization of the state-owned sector and the expansion of the private sector—brought a shift toward a more familiar (to us) conception of firms as relatively autonomous market actors. They were to be *regulated* but no longer directly administered by the state. In short, China moved strongly in the direction of Western-style "regulatory capitalism" in the governance of "organized capital."[64] But it did not make the parallel shift in its posture toward organized labor. Unions in the West are regulated to varying degrees but not administered by the state. By contrast, the ACFTU remains an integral component of the Party-directed system of governance. Organized labor, unlike most organized capital, is still subject to administrative control through the CPC's hierarchy.

Ironically, the aggregation of capital and capitalists has come to be seen as less of a challenge to China's nominally socialist regime than collective labor activity. At the level of ideology, it seems that China has managed to square the circle and to reconcile private ownership of much of the means of production, and substantial entrepreneurial autonomy for capital, with its socialist commitments.[65] Yet it has held fast to the idea that the CPC, through its labor arm the ACFTU, is the one true representative of the workers. That is partly because, at the level of practical politics, "organized labor" outside the party-state is seen as a greater threat to the regime than "organized capital." China has proven remarkably adept at cultivating the loyalty of the domestic capital-owning class and defusing the political threat it might otherwise pose.[66] At the same time, officials have acquired a large private stake in the prosperity of China's business enterprises. The intertwined membership and interests of business and Party elites have enriched both, and have helped to entrench one-party rule against challenges from capital. But workers have not been sharing in the feast. The powers-that-be in China fear that, if workers were permitted to organize themselves autonomously, they would pose a significant threat to the stability of the political-economic status quo. That fear puts sharp limits on the liberalization of collective labor activity and the democratization of the official union.

*"Democratic management"*: The first three dimensions of reform taken up here concern China's continuing commitment to manage "organized labor"—to contain autonomous worker organizations and to make the official union more responsive without its becoming independent. "Organized capital" in China is comparatively autonomous. But we should not overstate that autonomy. China may be imposing some procedural restraints on managerial autonomy in an effort to give workers a formal voice of some kind in workplace governance.

Let us step back briefly: The modernization and expansion of China's economy over a few short decades is one of the most impressive economic accomplishments of any society in history. For some Western observers, and especially for the "market fundamentalists" among them, that accomplishment is a testament to the virtues of markets and private enterprise. What China did right, in their view, was to abandon its ideological commitment to a planned economy, and the suffocating fetters it placed on private initiative, and to let markets and self-interested entrepreneurs do what they have been doing in the West for a few centuries. On that view, China's continued development would presumably follow a course of further privatization and economic liberalization—albeit tamed by a more competent regulatory state. Moreover, economic liberalization would inevitably impel China down a path of political liberalization. In other words, private property rights and market freedoms were indispensable to successful development, and would in turn beget demands for other rights and freedoms and eventually to democracy. That was to be "the end of history" for some, and in any event the future of China.[67]

China watchers have begun to question that account, and to discern a different model of development that might compete with, or even surpass in some respects and some settings, the traditional Western prescription of markets, rule of law, and electoral democracy. Whether it is called "state capitalism" or the "socialist market economy," all indications are that the state in China will retain a large stake in the productive economy and in the financial sector. And it may maintain levers of control over the private economy beyond what is entailed by "regulatory capitalism," or at least by its American version. That might be seen in one widely neglected aspect of recent labor reforms: the apparent revival, at least on paper, of institutions of "democratic management," including what might have seemed a doomed relic of the planned economy, the Staff and Worker Representative Congress (SWRC) system.

The SWRCs are analogous in some ways to German works councils. If they were genuinely representative and able to exercise their rather substantial statutory functions, they might serve as real vehicles of worker voice inside the enterprise and real constraints on enterprise management. As such, they might better enable workers to enforce their rights and resolve their interest disputes inside the enterprise and keep problems from spilling onto the streets in the form of labor unrest. But the SWRCs probably cannot do any of those things, and they are destined to remain a rubber stamp for management, unless they are able to work in tandem with trade unions that are themselves accountable to workers. The tentative and partial revival of the SWRCs may be another reform effort that is simultaneously driven, shaped, and constrained by the determination to quell labor unrest while avoiding the rise of independent labor activism.

THE NEXT THREE chapters will lay some necessary foundations for the rest of this book. Chapter 2 will briefly survey the evolution of contemporary labor protest in China and its political, economic, and institutional context, particularly in the non-state sector of the economy that has grown up since the "opening" to foreign capital. Chapter 3 will explore the official and unofficial organizations that represent workers, and provide a window on civil society and its governance in China. It will begin with the official ACFTU, along with the many branches and the millions of enterprise trade unions that it supervises, and will then introduce some of the unofficial and informal non-governmental organizations that serve and advocate for workers. Chapter 4 will put some comparative cards on the table. Western readers may be predisposed to see China's current labor pains through the lens of historical experience with industrial conflict and labor law reforms in the advanced industrial world, much as I did when I first began studying China's labor scene in 2009. That lens clarifies some features of the latter while blurring or distorting others. So it will be useful to put that lens itself into clearer focus before turning back to China.

Chapters 5 through 8 will examine key components of the official response to labor unrest: the effort to upgrade minimum labor standards and their enforcement (Chapter 5); the evolving approaches to strikes and collective bargaining (Chapter 6); efforts to democratize the grassroots unions at the base of the ACFTU pyramid (Chapter 7); and the tentative revival of "democratic management," with the SWRC as its main vehicle (Chapter 8). Chapter 9 will conclude.

As workers in China have grown both more willing and more able to join together and assert their shared rights and interests, China's leaders have responded with a mix of repression, concessions, and reform. At the local level, officials respond to labor protesters with everything from police dogs, batons, and detentions to concessions and even cash. At the top, policy makers have invested billions in internal "stability maintenance," but they have also put forward a variety of reform measures that aim to satisfy some of workers' demands and to better live up to the regime's proclaimed pro-worker ideology. They have raised the legal floor on wages and labor standards, expanded access to judicial and arbitral enforcement of workers' rights, experimented with collective bargaining, and sought to rejuvenate the official trade unions and other avenues of worker voice. And they have done all those things, and much more in other policy arenas, while maintaining the political stability of a one-party regime that Western elites had once consigned to its deathbed.

China's defiance of Western prescriptions and predictions is exquisitely self-conscious. Its leaders, and many of its citizens, insist that China's unique history, culture, values, and even geography require it to develop its own way of governing and its own way of fulfilling even the aspirations that they share with Western liberal democracies. China thus claims to be developing its own forms of civil society, rule of law, human rights, and democracy, all with distinctive "Chinese characteristics." This book seeks to illuminate some of those Chinese characteristics through a comparative look at the struggle with labor unrest. If China's workers do get their own New Deal, it will be a New Deal with Chinese characteristics, and it will look very different from what workers in the United States or elsewhere in the West achieved in the mid-twentieth century.

Perhaps that should not be surprising of a country that in thirty years transformed itself from a deeply impoverished and economically backward totalitarian state, closed to the world and torn by periodic political upheaval, into one of the world's largest and most dynamic economies. Rising labor unrest is a serious challenge for China and a major spur to reform, but China's leaders draw on an increasingly sophisticated toolkit in their determined effort to keep unrest from boiling over while staving off major political change. China's vertiginous economic rise has taught us one thing: just because something has never been done before does not mean that China cannot do it.

# CHAPTER TWO

# The Rise of China, and of Labor Protest, in the Reform Era

THE CONTEXT FOR China's current labor scene and the regime's many-faceted response to it lies in China's political and regulatory institutions. Those institutions have their roots, of course, in China's history. And China has a very long history. But we will begin this story not in the dynastic era, nor in the short-lived republic launched in 1911, nor in the chaotic period of civil war and foreign occupation that followed it, nor even with the Communist Revolution in 1949. We will begin instead in the late 1970s, after Mao's death and the end of the Cultural Revolution, when Deng Xiaoping and other pragmatists within the Communist Party elite took charge and began to build modern China. The Cultural Revolution had decimated many of China's institutions, including some of the prescribed structures for governance of the planned economy and the state enterprises that populated it.[1] Deng found it necessary to reestablish many of those institutions before transforming them. So we begin this brief account of the emergence of a modern system of workplace governance, and of the parallel emergence of labor activism and unrest, on the cusp of Deng's "reform and opening."

## "Reform and Opening" and the Attendant Labor Pains

"Reform and opening," though often uttered in the same breath, were two different dimensions of a vision of development through the gradual and partial unleashing of market forces. "Reform" was the process of restructuring the state-owned enterprises (SOEs) of the planned economy, concentrated in the urban northeast of China, and subjecting them to competition and market pressure. "Opening" stands for the welcoming of private entrepreneurship and capital, foreign and domestic, into largely rural areas of the coastal south, and the incorporation of millions of poor farmers into the industrial workforce. Reforming the planned economy was a more complex and drawn-out process than opening the door to private entrepreneurship and capital; and so reform lagged behind opening. The following account of both processes is ruthlessly condensed into a background narrative for the more recent reforms that occupy the bulk of this book.[2] Let us begin with the nature of the planned economy that was to be reformed and opened up.

### From Mao to Markets, and from the Danwei to the Labor Contract

In the planned economy that had taken shape under Mao, and that was reestablished for a time under Deng, enterprises were owned and administered by the party-state. State-appointed enterprise managers were accountable to administrators for fulfillment of their production quotas; but they were also responsible for the livelihood of the staff and workers who were assigned, more or less permanently, to the *danwei*, or enterprise work unit.[3] Andrew Walder describes the role of the factory director in the twilight years of the *danwei* system:

> [He is] more than a manager of an economic enterprise. He is also the leader of a socio-political community. This community often contains thousands of people, and in some cases tens of thousands. He is responsible not only for their income, but for their welfare and that of their dependents. Housing has to be built for the many families that need larger quarters and the many young employees who want to marry and start a family. The factory must strive to establish and maintain a health-care system, schools, meal services, entertainment facilities, a guest house, and car pool. It must find employment for the offspring of employees. It has to fund the pensions of retired workers. It organizes sports teams and cultural events. The manager is responsible for all these things, and he will be judged both by his superiors and his subordinates on his effectiveness in these areas, not just on meeting production and financial plans.[4]

This was the "iron rice bowl" model of the urban industrial economy, and it was not based on labor markets or employment contracts. Labor was not "commodified," and workers could rarely either quit or be fired.[5] Workers were only nominally the masters of the factory, given the pervasive control of the Party and its appointee, the factory director; but they were indeed members of the *danwei* rather than mere employees.

Workers were kept within the *danwei* system, and poor rural citizens were kept out of it, in part through a household registration *(hukou)* system that tied nearly all social welfare benefits to one's work unit or place of registration.[6] Chinese workers described the "iron rice bowl" system as *"jin bu qu, chu bu lai"* (you can't get in, and you can't come out). The "labor contract system" existed around the edges of the *danwei* system, but it was reserved for small numbers of migrant workers who were drawn into the bottom floors of China's economy, and it was disparaged as unfit for the urban "masters of the workers' state."[7]

During the Cultural Revolution, the overall disorder roiled industry, causing shortages of raw materials, disruptions in transport, and work stoppages.[8] Red Guard students targeted *danwei* directors and trade union leaders, among other authority figures, for abuse. Urban youth and cadres were sent to the countryside to learn to "eat bitterness," removing them from their *danwei* (and interrupting their education). Moreover, urban planning was considered "tainted by bourgeois ideology," and government investment in urban factories shrank.[9] All of this weakened the urban *danwei* system.

Although reform of the system was in the offing, at the beginning of the Deng era the *danwei* system was initially shored up and its official governing institutions restored. Those governing institutions, apart from the factory director and supervisory corps, were the trade union (an enterprise or "grassroots" chapter of the All-China Federation of Trade Unions (ACFTU)), the Staff and Worker Representative Congress (SWRC), and the enterprise chapter of the Communist Party of China (CPC), which stood above both of those. Those "old three bodies" *(lao san hui)* were later supplemented, and many of their powers were absorbed by the "new three bodies" *(xin san hui)* established by the Company Law in 1994: the corporate board of directors, the supervisory board, and the shareholders.[10] But we are getting ahead of the story, for before reform got seriously under way, a dramatically different economy started to emerge in the wake of the opening to private and foreign capital.

Beginning with "special economic zones" in the largely rural Pearl River Delta in the south and elsewhere along the coast, foreign investors were invited in, often into joint ventures. Collectively owned "town and village enterprises" (TVEs) began to operate more like private companies, and domestic private entrepreneurs were allowed to form and expand businesses.[11] Labor was bought and sold through labor markets that were largely unconstrained by legal labor standards. Foreign firms began to beat a path to China's factories and its burgeoning low-wage labor market. And China's impoverished rural peasants, spurred on by poverty and family necessity, dreams of prosperity, and even patriotism, began to beat their own tortured paths to those factories. The long hours, low wages, and dangerous and degrading conditions that they found there—appalling as they were to many observers from the advanced economies of the West—were apparently still preferable for most migrants to a rural life devoid of prospects.[12]

For the first decade or so after the opening, China's "socialist market economy" looked like two glaringly divergent economies: a socialist economy and a market economy. The socialist economy was still planned and administered by the party-state, and its workers were still members, not mere employees, of the enterprise. The market economy, though its domain was confined to particular regions and industry sectors, was virtually unfettered by the state, at least in its treatment of labor.

The opening to private capital and market competition helped pave the way for market-based reforms even in the state sector. As Professor Mary Gallagher has shown, the rapid growth of private and foreign-invested enterprises and the introduction of product markets, labor markets, and the profit motive helped to spur the rationalization, partial privatization, and "corporatization" of the state-owned enterprises (SOEs).[13] The corporatization of the state economy was further advanced as state-owned enterprises became integrated into global supply chains and were compelled to follow many of the rules of the global economy that had been established by Western multinational corporations.[14] Labor became commodified as the labor contract system and market-based employment relations came to dominate China's labor market, even in the large remaining SOE sector.[15] Egalitarian (but low) salary structures gave way to much more disparate (though eventually higher) salaries.[16] Gradually but deliberately, the "iron rice bowl," and the privileges and security of the urban industrial workforce, were smashed, and millions of urban workers were laid off from their once-permanent positions in the all-encompassing *danwei* system.[17]

The SOEs continued to dominate major capital-intensive sectors concentrated in the northeast, and to employ almost exclusively urban-registered workers, albeit in shrinking numbers and with less fulsome benefits and job security, though eventually higher wages. By contrast, the growing private and foreign-invested sector was initially concentrated in labor-intensive mass manufacturing of garments, toys, and other consumer goods, primarily in the coastal areas of China's southeast. This workforce was composed largely of rural migrants with no prior industrial experience. As

Professor Ching Kwan Lee has elaborated, the two groups of workers—the urban workers of the declining "rustbelt" of the northeast and the rural migrants of the booming but brutally exploitative factories of the "sunbelt"—developed their own characteristic but distinct sets of grievances.[18]

### Blue-Collar Blues in China's Rustbelt

From the "rustbelt" came the grievances of the urban working class, whose relatively high wages, benefits, and lifetime job security in the SOEs, and their proclaimed standing as "masters of the factory," were all upended in the more competitive and profit-oriented environment that followed liberalization. Many enterprises closed, others were wholly or partly privatized, and efficiencies and profits were wrung out of those that remained. The dismantling of the *danwei* system and the iron rice bowl was carried out gradually, even haltingly; for China's leaders were justifiably anxious about labor unrest at the heart of the workers' state, especially in the wake of the Tiananmen protests.[19] But for the previously privileged urban workers, some of whom had bypassed higher education in favor of a "permanent" SOE job, their eventual plunge into the market economy meant a precipitous decline in living standards, security, and status.[20]

The distress of workers in China's SOE sector would not be wholly unfamiliar to the unionized auto workers and steel workers of America's rustbelt around the same time. Those blue-collar industrial workers had been the proud and prosperous core of the New Deal coalition and of the American middle class, with wages, benefits, and expectations of economic security built up through decades of U.S. industrial dominance. But they suffered a steep decline in status and political clout, in material security, and in sheer numbers from the late 1970s through the 1990s, as global competition, falling trade barriers, and new technologies of production and transportation converged to produce devastating waves of layoffs.[21] Whole regions suffered economic decline as hundreds of thousands of well-paid, previously secure jobs with generous enterprise-based pension, health, and welfare benefits disappeared.

Obviously the "rust belt" experiences in China and the United States were very different. To begin with, Chinese SOE workers were much poorer in absolute terms than U.S. steel- and autoworkers and faced far bleaker conditions than the latter when their industries contracted. After decades of relying on the "iron rice bowl" model of enterprise-based welfare, China struggled (and has thus far still failed) to construct a decent social safety net of public welfare benefits and social insurance to replace it. Though much better off than their rural compatriots, laid-off urban workers in China's "rust belt" landed harder than their American blue-collar counterparts. On the other hand, they landed in an economy that was on its way up and expanding rapidly. Within a decade or so after their disruptive loss of status and security, some former SOE workers—especially younger, skilled male workers—had surpassed their previous income levels, while others suffered long-term economic losses.[22] (Whether even the former are better off depends on one's view—or rather their view—of the value of absolute wealth versus relative economic well-being, status, and security). For laid-off U.S. steel and autoworkers, their fall from economic grace, starting in the 1970s, proved to be the harbinger of a painful and continuing slide in real wages for the average American worker. Many of those workers suffered lasting losses on all fronts—income, status, and security. And many of them blame China and its workers, at least in part, for their losses.

The domestic politics of "rust belt" decline were also very different in the two countries. For one thing, privatization and restructuring in China's SOEs were directly engineered by the state from above, and enormous gains flowed visibly to a favored few—typically local party elites, often the workers' former bosses. The continuing flow of wealth to a politically wired upper crust has become one of China's most divisive social issues.[23] But the first wave of elite enrichment in the 1980s and 1990s had a nasty twist: workers' own bosses and party leaders—previously all part of a rel-atively egalitarian *danwei* system—were pulling the economic rug out from under the workers, appropriating the productive assets that were supposed to provide them and their families with the permanent livelihood they had been promised. That alone made the restructuring of China's "rust belt," and the economic pain it caused, far more politically charged than the corresponding process in the United States.

The impact of China's urban transformation was not just political; it was deeply ideological. That points to another important difference between the two "rust belt" experiences: in the United States, the New Deal commitment to decent work and industrial democracy, and the decades of collectively bargained prosperity enjoyed by some blue-collar workers until the 1970s, had long coexisted, albeit more or less in tension, with an underlying acceptance of markets, competition, and capitalism. To be sure, a more unfettered commitment to "free markets" came to the fore in the 1980s, and spurred waves of deregulation and trade liberalization.[24] But in the United States, markets and commodification of labor had never been demonized, and workers had never been lionized as the "masters of the factory" and of the "worker state," as they had been for decades in

Mao's China. The turnabout from Maoism to markets brought a sense of shock and betrayal for many urban Chinese workers that American blue-collar workers might find hard to imagine.

In the wake of the dismantling of the planned economy and the ideological shift that it entailed, Chinese workers angrily protested both the enrichment of the elite few and the crumbling of their own former entitlements.[25] The ACFTU—the workers' official and only lawful trade union—was a relatively minor player in this drama. Answerable to Party officials rather than workers, and charged not only with representing workers but also with maintaining production and upholding Party rule, the union struggled, mostly ineffectually, to contain workers' anger and cushion their fall.[26] (The ACFTU, given its importance in the labor landscape and its distinctive organization and mission, requires its own Chapter 3, below.)

The wave of unrest triggered by the "reform" of the state sector, which crested around 2002, was deeply threatening to the regime.[27] Its potential impact on political legitimacy and stability was magnified by both geography and ideology, for these protests emanated from the industrial heartland of the northeast, near Beijing, and from the urban workers who were the CPC's core constituency and still nominally the "masters" of the "workers' state."[28] In those SOE protests, some observers saw the emergence of a new working-class consciousness.[29] Others saw instead the response of jilted "masters of the factory."[30] Either way, these protests by laid-off workers decried the passing of a political economic order that was clearly not coming back. Workers' ability to disrupt production, much less to change the course of China's future development, was limited.[31] That is among the ways in which the "rust belt" protests differed sharply from the unrest that has arisen in the wake of the opening of China's once-rural "sun belt" regions to foreign and domestic capitalist development, and is the chief focus of this book.

## Migrant Workers' Woes in China's Sunbelt

China's "sun belt" development, starting in the late 1970s, was largely driven by private capital, domestic and foreign. Unlike the state sector with its capital-intensive heavy industries, the private companies of the coastal south were concentrated for the first two decades in labor-intensive manufacturing of apparel, footwear, and toys for export. This new profit-driven non-state sector has generated much of China's economic growth in the decades since its opening to private investment.

The workers of the "sun belt" differed from their northern compatriots in important ways. Unlike the state sector's urban workers, whose former privileges made their initial fall especially crushing and politically perilous, the migrant workers of the "sun belt" had long languished in rural poverty before moving to the coastal manufacturing regions. Their social marginalization, the recent memories of starvation and upheaval in the 1960s and 1970s, and their voluntary flight to the factories initially fostered a certain stoicism—even pride in their willingness to "eat bitterness"—and then made their mounting grievances easier for the state to ignore. While the ACFTU was not a very effective representative for its core urban constituency, rural migrant workers were not on its radar; they were not even allowed to join the ACFTU until 2003.[32] And while urban workers were suffering from the dismantling of the "iron rice bowl," the rural migrants of the south were still scarred by its remnants: the *hukou* system, which had insulated the privileged urban economy by excluding rural migrants, remained a major barrier to fair pay and equal treatment for the latter, especially in linking social benefits to one's official place of residence.[33] As mass migration became not just a social fact but a central tenet of China's economic development strategy, the *hukou* system came under greater pressure for reform.[34] Yet even now it continues to supply legal scaffolding for the second-class citizenship of China's migrant workers.

The state also played dramatically different roles in the "sun belt" and the "rust belt." Unlike the pervasive and highly visible role of the party-state in the state sector and its "reform," the state seemed to recede in the new non-state sector for the first decade and a half, at least from the standpoint of its workers. In fact, the state both orchestrated the post-Mao rise of capitalist development and retained enormous leverage over these enterprises, both the foreign-invested "joint enterprises" that dominated the first decade of development and the purely domestic.[35] The state established the "special economic zones" in which foreign-invested, export-oriented factories first flourished, and it even enacted some early labor laws for the regulation of those foreign-invested enterprises.[36] But the "law on the books" did not translate into serious regulation of wages and working conditions, partly because China had not yet constructed public regulatory structures to govern the companies that were not directly managed and controlled by the party-state. What evolved in this regulatory near-vacuum was a bare-knuckled laissez faire version of capitalism that made the regime's continuing invocation of socialist ideology seem farcical.[37]

Workplace disasters punctuated this period in China. The 1993 Shenzhen Zhili toy factory fire, in which more than eighty workers died and more than forty others suffered severe injuries, was a turning point.[38] Like the Triangle Shirtwaist fire in 1911 in New York City, the Zhili tragedy stemmed partly from the absence or blockage of emergency exits. And like the Triangle Shirtwaist fire, the Zhili fire provoked public outrage and helped spur governing authorities to usher in some much-needed reforms, to which we will return in Chapter 5. Unfortunately, in neither the United States nor in China were these tragedies or the succeeding reforms enough to avert eerily similar disasters in more recent years: in Hamlet, North Carolina, in 1991, and in northeast China in June 2013, poultry plant fires killed dozens of workers—in China over one hundred—many of whom were once again trapped by locked or blocked exits.[39]

The Triangle Shirtwaist fire and the Hamlet fire are reminders that the United States has its own experiences, both historical and contemporary, with dangerous and underregulated low-wage work. China's brutal factories and their population of poor migrant workers in the early decades of its burgeoning private-sector economy are reminiscent of the pre–New Deal era of laissez faire capitalism in the United States. Although U.S. workers and their allies were able to press for labor standards laws through democratically elected legislatures, those laws were swatted down by an unelected judiciary armed with the constitutional doctrine of "liberty of contract."[40] The resulting regulatory vacuum and sweatshop conditions of that period of U.S. history are not wholly unlike what China's migrant workers experienced in its first decades of post-Mao profit-driven growth.

Unfortunately, that past is not quite past, for America is still home to a large low-wage labor market in which labor standards are chronically underenforced, work is often dirty and dangerous, and "wage theft," or denial of wages or benefits that are lawfully due an employee,[41] is common. As in China, the brunt of these conditions is borne by poor migrant workers with tenuous legal status—that is, undocumented immigrants.[42] As one would hope, given the advantages of economic and legal development and democratic institutions, underregulated low-wage work in the United States is less dismal and less widespread than in China, though more widespread than in other advanced industrial economies.[43] The American struggle for decent labor standards thus has a long history and a vivid present, both of which may cast light on the challenges facing China's factory workers today.

Yet there is an obvious irony in the analogy between low-wage labor markets in China and in brashly capitalist America, in both its pre–New Deal and modern-day versions: how could a self-proclaimed socialist workers' state permit such rank exploitation of workers at the hands of their profit-seeking capitalist bosses? Chapter 5 will return to the puzzle of low labor standards. For now it is enough to know that although labor laws have now been on the books in China for many decades—a fact that surprises many newcomers to China's labor scene—enforcement has lagged and evasion has been endemic in the non-state sector. Both in modern China's "sun belt" and in pre–New Deal America's laissez faire labor markets, a flood of migrant labor from poorer countries or regions kept wages low and enabled profit-driven bosses, unconstrained by effective regulation, to exploit and mistreat workers.

If that is how we see the recent period of rapid industrial development in China, the rise of collective labor unrest should come as no surprise, either to us or to China's leaders. Indeed, for some in China, a "scientific" understanding of the stages of socialist development may have foretold, or even prescribed, a period of labor exploitation.[44] Exploitation breeds unrest. Chronically long hours, low wages, and hazardous conditions created tinderbox conditions in which a spark—an industrial accident, a worker's collapse from exhaustion, the discharge of a pregnant worker, or the failure to pay even the promised subminimum wages—could produce an explosion of angry protest. There have been many sparks and, especially in the past two decades, many explosions.[45]

## A Rising Tide of Workers' Rights Disputes: Causes and Changes

We have already noted the rising numbers of "mass incidents"; estimates rose from 87,000 in 2005 to 180,000 in 2010.[46] Experts estimated that about one-third were labor related; many others stemmed from appropriation of rural lands and forced demolition of housing for private development, or from environmental problems. A government report on mass incidents in 2012 conspicuously omitted the total number of mass incidents—that was apparently too sensitive—but it did report some interesting percentages: nearly 25 percent of the incidents lasted for more than a day, and some for up to three months; 71 percent led to physical injuries (including 9 percent with fatalities). In 62 percent of these cases, public authorities responded with "negative measures," including "dispersal using force" and arrests and detentions.[47] So these are not trivial incidents.

Lest one conclude that China is a boiling cauldron of unrest, however, let us recall that China is a very big country. Even 180,000 protest incidents in a year—many of them small, in isolated rural villages, and scattered across China's very large territory and its 1.4 billion people—may pose little threat to overall social stability. Nonetheless, the trend line is steep, and the rising number of mass incidents in the labor context and beyond had become a major preoccupation of the regime by the mid-2000s.

Before turning to the official responses to unrest, let us briefly take up a question that has occupied many in China: what underlies the rising tide of labor unrest, especially among China's long-suffering migrant workers? Obviously workers have had plenty of cause for discord given the grueling hours, dangerous conditions, and low pay in the factories of the non-state economy. But why have China's migrant workers been increasingly inclined to take their grievances to the streets? A serious answer to that question would occupy a book all by itself, but let us here take note of a few factors that might not be evident to outside observers.

## The Roles of Demographics and Economics in the Surge of Labor Protest

Clearly one factor in rising unrest is generational: many in the first wave of migrant workers, having experienced the dire poverty of the 1960s and 1970s and the paroxysms of the Cultural Revolution, were willing to tolerate miserable factory conditions, to "eat bitterness," and even to "let a few get rich first," as Deng Xiaoping famously urged.[48] Today's migrant workers, most of them born after 1980 in the "one-child" era, are far less acquiescent. They face choices and burdens that their parents did not. More educated than their parents, they know nothing of farming and do not plan to return to the countryside. Nor do they see themselves as participants in a patriotic Party-led national movement. The new generation is said to be more disposed to seek gratification of their own desires and to see their interests as diverging from those of the rich (even if they want to be rich themselves). Only-children in particular are the sole vessels for the hopes and affections, and the sole source of future support, not only for their parents but possibly for all four grandparents, without siblings or cousins to share the burden or familial limelight. This so-called "4–2–1 problem" is exacerbated by a low mandatory retirement age (currently sixty for men and fifty for women in labor-intensive fields) and a much longer life expectancy (seventy-five years in 2012 versus forty-nine years in 1964).[49] The rising aspirations and expectations of China's workers are tinged with strains of individualism that may curb workers' collective impulses, at least if material conditions continue to improve. For now those rising aspirations may be contributing to the rise of collective labor protest.

At the same time, discontented workers are taking to the streets not only in protest but also in search of better jobs and higher wages. They are, in short, resorting to "exit," the quintessential market response to dissatisfaction, as well as that peculiar hybrid of "exit" and "voice" that is the strike.[50] The focus here is on the latter, but the former is more pervasive and at least as unsettling to China's employers. Workers' willingness to migrate from the interior provinces to the factories of the more developed coastal provinces has faltered as development in the interior has begun to create factory jobs closer to home. Rural citizens are not as desperate as they were just a decade ago. Add to that the demographic cliff created by the entry of the "one-child" generation (born after 1980) into the labor market.[51] The net result has been recurring labor shortages since at least 2004—to the surprise of many in the West who had envisioned China as a bottomless source of cheap labor.[52] Even with minimum-wage levels rising quite substantially—largely in response to labor unrest—some employers have been paying a wage premium to keep experienced workers from jumping ship.[53]

The tight labor market might have done as much for China's workers as either government intervention or collective protest, and it has also helped to underwrite both regulation and protest. For example, China's quick recovery and the reappearance of labor shortages after the global financial crisis largely quieted employers' alarmist claims about the "job-killing" Labor Contract Law (LCL). And while tight labor markets and high turnover pose real challenges to organizing collective action, they also emboldened workers to exercise that noisier and more vocal exit option, the strike. For even though strikers might lose their jobs, most would readily find another one. (It is unclear whether that continues to be true in the economic doldrums that have set in since 2014.)

### Law as a Catalyst for Protest

One surprise for Western observers is that the proliferation of labor-related "mass incidents" since the "reform and opening" may have had more to do with the *presence* of labor laws and formal legal rights than with their absence. As noted, substantive labor standards have been on the books for decades; they were not well enforced, but they were widely publicized. As part of its effort in the 1980s and 1990s to establish a "rule of law," the regime conducted legal education campaigns to inform officials and citizens of the laws' requirements.[54] Chinese workers were exhorted to "use the law as a weapon" and to take their claims to state agencies of adjudication and enforcement.[55] Many workers took up the challenge.

Unfortunately, official paths of recourse were strewn with obstacles.[56] Many of those obstacles would be familiar to low-wage workers in the United States: burdens of proof, lack of legal representation, and fly-by-night or insolvent employers from whom one might recover nothing even after winning a case.[57] In addition, Chinese workers were often unable to prove the existence of an employment relationship or were pressured by officials to accept a paltry settlement, or rebuffed altogether because of the "sensitivity" of their complaints.[58] After one or more fruitless visits to the local labor bureau or labor arbitration body, some workers took to the streets to demand their rights.[59] Wage arrears were the single most frequent trigger for these outbursts: it was common for employers to withhold months of wages and then simply refuse to pay them, with or without some pretext.[60] Workers demanded simply what they were legally entitled to, but their protests—at least once rebuffed by the courts—were often addressed to the government, not just employers. In short, law often shaped both the substance and the expression of most labor protests, especially in the years before China enacted the LCL in 2007.[61]

The role of law in shaping and mobilizing popular protest in China is not confined to the labor arena. Protests over land appropriation, pollution, excessive taxation, and corruption also typically take the form of what Kevin O'Brien and Lianjiang Li call "rightful resistance."[62] Protesters appeal to higher authority, sometimes traveling to provincial capitals or beyond, for redress against localized wrongdoing; rather than challenging the established order, they seek to uphold it against errant business owners or unresponsive local officials.[63] "Rightful resistance" seeks to use law both as a weapon against wrongdoers and as a shield against repression. Organized collective action outside of Party-sanctioned channels is always risky, but the invocation of legal rights proclaimed by the regime itself was sure to meet a less repressive response than more political protests.

The contrast to workers' protests in the United States is revealing. Workers, and especially low-wage workers, have plenty of complaints against employers, some of them surprisingly similar to those of Chinese workers. In particular, journalists, advocates, and scholars have found rampant "wage theft" by employers—for example, demands for "off-the-clock" work, covert cuts in recorded hours, or failure to pay legally required overtime premiums or minimum wage rates (though only rarely the sheer refusal to pay past wages, common in China).[64] And while the American legal system is more developed than China's, it is still cumbersome, and does not always afford speedy resolution of those "rights disputes." So workers sometimes stage protest rallies and boycotts, both to pressure employers to resolve disputes and to organize workers.[65] In China those events would count as "mass incidents." But in the United States those protests rarely target the government, are rarely disorderly much less violent, and never pose a threat to social stability. In part that is because peaceful protest activity—and, crucially, the *organizing* of protest activity—is constitutionally protected. So even large and noisy protests are both organized and peaceful—peaceful in part because they are organized and in part because legal protections keep the police at bay.

Ironically, China's hostility to organized protest and to its leaders means that protests are more likely to be spontaneous, leaderless, and chaotic; and when chaotic protests meet a show of force from the police, violent clashes often result. On the other hand, disorganized protests are also likely to remain localized rather than merging into a larger protest movement. Disorganization has its virtues for a regime preoccupied with political stability, and China's regime and its supporters may be willing to pay the price in localized unrest. We will return to this theme when we turn to the official response to strikes in Chapter 6.

### The Changing Official Response: From Repression toward Appeasement (and Back?)

Given the regime's firm commitment to unelected one-party rule, it is not surprising that labor-related mass incidents have sometimes triggered police violence and detentions. That is the dark side of the regime's commitment to social stability, or what the Hu administration called a "harmonious society." Officials fear that organized protests, and especially protest-oriented organizations, might spread or turn political. Most threatening, and most likely to trigger serious repression, are labor protests or labor groups that straddle multiple factories; such organizing remains rare. But for ordinary localized incidents, repression risks provoking an escalation of conflict, and drawing unwelcome attention from outside and above, especially in the increasingly wired and interconnected society that China has become. (Chinese workers were quick to acquire cell phones, useful for spreading word of protests both among co-workers and to the wider world.) So for local officials who fear the consequences of "mass incidents" for their careers, appeasement became a large part of their repertoire for dealing with protest.

Appeasement often takes a very simple form: labor officials and judges have resorted to offering cash to protesting workers in the streets to induce them to end their protest![66] Until about 2007, that kind of remunerative response was said to be limited to protests that appeared spontaneous, unorganized, and leaderless; repression was likely whenever there were identifiable protest leaders or glimmers of organization.[67] Workers thus learned how to organize a "spontaneous" ruckus, usually by text messages to co-workers. In the past decade or so, however, official hostility to leadership has sometimes given way to a pragmatic effort to identify someone with whom to negotiate an end to the incident.[68] And cash on the street has become less effective as workers' demands have become more ambitious, as we will see in Chapter 6.

Local officials take their cues in part from changing signals from above. Since the early 2000s, top leaders have been expressing more solicitude for workers and their grievances; that is the other side of the call for a "harmonious society." Most labor unrest, although troubling, is not overtly political, especially when workers are asking only for fulfillment of employer promises or legal obligations. It has been deemed a "minor contradiction," not a direct challenge to the regime.[69] Moreover, Party leaders have become increasingly concerned about the growing and corrosive gap between rich and poor. By conventional measures of economic inequality, China's is among the highest in the world.[70] In a nominally socialist country, this is more than an embarrassment. There is growing recognition that workers have legitimate grievances that, if left unaddressed, are likely to fester and to undermine the regime's legitimacy in more dangerous ways. Whether these concerns stem solely from an interest in political stability or also from genuine sympathy with the workers, the regime has been moved to address workers' grievances on several fronts.

### From Rights Disputes to Interest Disputes, and from "Mass Incidents" to Strikes

The rise of organized labor activism in the wake of industrial development—particularly capitalist-led industrial development—is hardly unique to China.[71] And however unusual China's recent economic rise has been, the rise of organized labor activism is one of its less surprising features. It became evident to China's leaders several years ago that the growing problem of labor unrest called for a more systemic response. So policy makers have reexamined and to varying degrees reformed official channels of redress for workers' grievances.

The initial focus, and the regime's favored response, was on improving minimum labor standards, including wages, and the judicial, arbitral, and administrative systems for their enforcement. This generated a flurry of national legislation in 2007, including the LCL. But the ambitious regulatory response to labor unrest (the subject of Chapter 5)—better laws, stronger enforcement, and higher minimum-wage levels—can do only so much to meet workers' demands for a larger share of growing revenues, especially in the most productive sectors of the economy. So even as China continues to raises labor standards and improve enforcement, China's workers have created a new sort of problem that calls for a different solution.

In 2010, the convergence of two dramatic episodes put China's labor pains into headlines worldwide. The first was the Honda strike, previewed in Chapter 1, which stalled three downstream Honda assembly plants for nearly two weeks and cost Honda up to 2.4 billion RMB (about $350 million) a day. Around the same time, Taiwan-based mega-manufacturer Foxconn, one of the world's largest corporations and a supplier for Apple and other major technology brands, became infamous for a string of worker suicides and for the highly regimented working conditions that might have fostered such despair.[72] Eighteen Foxconn workers were found to have attempted suicide during a ten-month period in 2010.[73]

To the average Western consumer, and perhaps even to the average Chinese middle-class urbanite, the plight of Chinese workers and their growing discontent had long been rather abstract. But the Foxconn suicides and the Honda strikes put a more human face on Chinese labor. Due to their duration, the coincidence of their timing, their direct ties to major global brands, or the unusually open coverage in the Chinese media (for a while), Foxconn and Honda grabbed national and international headlines for weeks.[74] While Foxconn epitomized the desperation of Chinese workers, Honda seemed to confirm their agency and to suggest a way forward.[75]

One common feature of the two cases is noteworthy: neither Foxconn nor Honda was regarded within China as among its worst employers. Unlike the Dickensian apparel, footwear, and toy factories of the early phase of export-led industrialization, Honda and Foxconn both employed relatively skilled workers in more advanced sectors of the economy, and on most accounts those companies were more compliant with most domestic labor standards than the average employer in China. (Recall the complaint of some Honda workers that the factory's compliance with maximum hours laws was adversely affecting their pay!) So the combination of despair and militancy that boiled over in those companies was a dramatic announcement of a new stage in the development of China's industrial relations.

Another common feature of the two incidents was the virtual absence of the trade union from the scene. Although both Honda and Foxconn, as large foreign companies, had official trade union chapters at the affected plants, workers at both factories were either oblivious or dismissive of the trade union. In the West, we associate strikes with trade unions. And indeed the frequency of strike activity in the United States has fallen with the decline of private-sector union density. But since the 1949 revolution in China, the ACFTU has had little to do with strikes—except for trying to stop them.[76] Indeed, preventing work stoppages has been a core official mission of the ACFTU and its chapters in the post-revolutionary era. Judging by the rising numbers of strikes in China in recent years, the

ACFTU has not been succeeding in that core mission. There are no official statistics available on the incidence of strikes, and so scholars almost universally turn to the best independent source of information on strikes, the *China Labour Bulletin* and its online Strike Map.[77] CLB finds almost seven thousand strikes from 2011 through 2015; and the number nearly double from each year to the next—from 185 in 2011, to 382 in 2012, to 656 in 2013, to 1379 in 2014, to 2774 in 2015 (as shown in Figure 1.2 in Chapter 1).[78] These figures come with two big caveats, each pointing in the opposite direction: First, CLB data include only verifiable reports of labor activity; per CLB estimates, that could be as little as ten to fifteen percent of actual incidents.[79] Second, CLB "strike" numbers include not only actual strikes, or collective work stoppages, but other collective protest incidents involving labor issues. In short, they appear to include anything that the government reports as a "mass incident" if it involves workplace grievances.

We will return in Chapter 6 to the rise of strikes and the official response. But first it is important to fill in the outlines of a very large but thus far blurry presence in the Chinese labor landscape: the official trade union. The ACFTU is not really a trade union as the term is generally understood in the West. But as the official representative of all of China's workers, it will be central to any official strategy for dealing with the problem of labor unrest. In fact, as we will see, the national ACFTU was quick to respond to the Honda strikes with its own reform proposals. In order to understand those reform proposals, however, one must understand what is being reformed. We will also take a preliminary look at the unofficial organizations that have grown up in the chasm that separates China's workers from their official collective representative. So let us populate the labor landscape sketched in this chapter with the very different kinds of organizations that purport to speak for China's workers.

# CHAPTER THREE

# Who Speaks for China's Workers?

## *The ACFTU and Labor NGOs*

O FFICIALLY, CHINESE WORKERS' SOLE legitimate representative is the All-China Federation of Trade Unions (ACFTU) and its many branches and affiliates. Unofficially, workers have been speaking out, individually and collectively, through a variety of channels, more or less formal, more or less visible, and more or less tolerated by the party-state. This tension between the official and unofficial outlets of worker voice captures the dilemma that China's leaders face in attempting to keep worker unrest from boiling over.

The ACFTU, for its part, is a nationwide trade union federation, headquartered in Beijing, with branches in ten industry sectors as well as branches at the provincial, municipal, county, rural township, and district levels. As of 2012, it reported having 2.7 million "grassroots" branches at the enterprise level and 280 million members, and a union density rate of 80 percent.[1] Yet this gargantuan union is often described as "useless" by workers seeking to improve their wages and working conditions.[2] One reason is quite simple: the ACFTU, although it is the only lawful labor union in China, is not a genuine representative chosen by the workers but a creature of the ruling Communist Party and a vehicle for consolidating Party power and regime stability. But important contradictions and changes within the ACFTU complicate that simple account. This chapter will sketch the ACFTU's history, structure, and function within the Chinese political and economic system and will introduce a few crucial complications, contradictions, and changes within the ACFTU.[3]

This chapter will also introduce some alternative organs of worker representation that have arisen to address some of the grievances that the ACFTU has neglected, especially among migrant workers. China's leaders look warily upon the rise of non-governmental organizations (NGOs) devoted to improving the lot of labor, or "labor NGOs," for they are seen as potential seedbeds of independent organized labor activism. Yet the labor NGOs also address real needs—real needs of workers and, by extension, of the regime. The regime's suspicious posture toward labor NGOs reflects in part a broader skepticism toward civil society; yet the rise of workers' collective disputes, and the involvement of some labor NGOs in those disputes, also triggers the particular anxieties that surround independent labor activism. This chapter will survey the major candidates for the role of representing China's workers. It will begin, inevitably, with the ACFTU.

## ACFTU: Arm of the Party, Tool of Management, or Voice of the Workers?

The ACFTU, first established in 1925 as an ordinary trade union federation, soon became a crucial element of the revolutionary coalition of the Communist Party of China (CPC).[4] With the Communist revolution in 1949 and the establishment of one-party rule, its function became a subject of fierce ideological dispute: what need did workers have for a trade union in the "workers' state"?[5] Indeed, once industry was brought firmly under the ownership and control of the party-state in the 1950s, to be administered on behalf of the whole people, the vestiges of traditional trade unionism in the ACFTU—of representation of workers as against owners—became highly suspect in some quarters. The dominant Leninist view was that the ACFTU was to be firmly subordinate to the Party, and was to serve as one of the primary "transmission belts" between the masses and Party leaders—conveying the masses' concerns up to the leaders, and the decisions and dictates of party leaders down to the masses.[6] Occasionally, a recessive strain of support for a more independent role on behalf of workers surfaced, as it did during a strike wave in Shanghai in 1957: some ACFTU leaders saw the unrest as an opportunity to move closer to workers and argued that the strikers were justly aggrieved. For such sins, the then-leader of the ACFTU was deposed in the Anti-Rightist campaigns that soon followed.[7]

The ACFTU, like other institutions in China, was decimated in the Cultural Revolution, and was then revived on the cusp of economic reform and liberalization in 1978.[8] The 1980s saw renewed flashes of independent activism within the ACFTU, and for a time the trade unions were officially described as "independent social entities, which should not, in terms of organizational affiliation, be equivalent to working departments of the Party."[9] But after 1989—and Tiananmen and the union-led challenge to communist rule in Poland—the ACFTU was brought under tighter Party control, and the union branches were directed to "dedicate themselves to helping consolidate the Party's basis of rule, to realise its ruling mission and uphold the cause of the Party."[10] The commitment to Party control of the ACFTU has not wavered since 1989, and has sharply circumscribed, though not wholly precluded, experimentation and change within the ACFTU and its provincial and local branches.

Experimentation and change within the ACFTU, and their limits, are central to this book's thesis. But even the quick sketch of the ACFTU's post-1949 history offered so far reveals one recurring theme: in the history of labor policy in China, and especially in the arena of collective labor activity and the ACFTU, reformist strains—rhetoric, proposals, experiments, pilot projects—tend to rise and fall and rise again rather than move steadily forward. That cyclical or oscillating pattern must temper any temptation to extrapolate from reform proposals to real progress.

In the case of the ACFTU, both the cyclical pattern of reformist talk and action and the relatively narrow spectrum within which they take place stem in part from two deep sources of tension built into the current mission of the ACFTU, which is to protect the interests of workers while advancing the interests of the Party and "the overall interests of the entire Chinese people."[11] Most obviously, this multi-faceted mission glosses over any potential conflict between the workers' interests and those of Party leaders. As long as real power resides in the Party, the latter is bound to trump the former when those interests do conflict. In the simpler terms often heard in China, the ACFTU is supposed to both protect worker rights *(weiquan)* and protect stability *(weiwen)*; but when those two aims conflict, *weiwen* has generally won out.

The ACFTU's mission also glosses over the inevitable conflicts between the interests of workers and of their employers. The union's commitment to "the overall interests of the entire Chinese people" traditionally entailed a role in maintaining production and discipline and promoting economic growth.[12] In the planned economy, in which factory management was charged with sustaining the *danwei* and its members, there was a certain logic in the trade union's functioning as a branch of management, more oriented toward maintaining production than toward representing workers' distinct interests. But the ACFTU retained that basic character and structure even as the state-owned enterprises (SOEs) began to mimic their market-driven private counterparts in many respects, and even as private capital and rural migrant workers began to flow into China's "sunbelt." Since the 1990s, the ACFTU has been "organizing" chapters in foreign enterprises (albeit in an unusual way described below), and since 2003 it has included migrant workers among its constituents.[13] But the dramatic transformation of the planned economy into a mixed economy populated largely by for-profit enterprises, capitalist and state-owned alike, brought no fundamental alteration of the ACFTU's structure or of its official mission. Management still commands the loyalty of trade union officials at the enterprise level.[14]

The combination of managerial domination at the bottom level of the ACFTU hierarchy and Party domination above has weighed especially heavily against workers' competing interests because the interests of managers and the Party have been strongly aligned along the axes of both social stability and economic growth. Party-state officials and managers, with their varied levers of power over workers and within the trade union structures, have generally been able to count on each other to reinforce efforts to suppress any signs of militancy among the workers. That is not to say that they always do or must succeed, but they generally present a powerful united front against rebellious workers or independent-minded worker leaders. And although the ACFTU's ability to represent workers' interests is clearly compromised, the regime tolerates no alternative institutions of collective worker representation. The ACFTU's official monopoly is aggressively enforced on the ground. Independent union-like groups that organize workers across factories are illegal and virtually non-existent. As we will see below, even labor NGOs that represent individual workers in ordinary legal disputes find only a tenuous and shifting toehold.

At the same time, the relatively simple account of the ACFTU presented so far obscures both crucial distinctions and interesting recent developments within the ACFTU, only a few of which are highlighted here. Let us begin with the ACFTU hierarchy outside the enterprises before turning to the enterprise chapters.

### The ACFTU outside the Enterprise: Arm of the Party

The ACFTU hierarchy mirrors the organization of the Party, from national to provincial and local levels of administration, and its officials are appointed by and answerable to the parallel party branch. So at every level, the ACFTU is subject to Party control; but Party control operates horizontally—from the national party to the national ACFTU, from provincial party organizations to provincial ACFTU chapters, and so on down to the local level—rather than vertically from higher to lower levels of the ACFTU (Figure 3.1).[15] In that very concrete sense, the ACFTU is an arm of the Party, not a voice of the workers. But the Party itself purports to speak and act for the workers, and it often does so through the ACFTU. So let us take a closer look.

At the national level, the ACFTU functions as a potential and sometimes actual voice for the interests of workers in policy discussions. But the ACFTU plays this role as an integral part of the party-state. The head of the ACFTU (as of January 2016, Li Jianguo) sits on the Politburo, the twenty-five-member body that oversees the CPC, and is vice-chairman and secretary general of the National People's Congress. The ACFTU's central role in national policy making has allowed it to push forward some controversial labor legislation, including the Labor Contract Law (LCL) in 2007, and the 2012 LCL amendments, which tightened up on the use of "labor dispatch" workers.[16] Both laws (discussed in more detail in Chapter 5) were strongly opposed by foreign employers and by many domestic employers; their enactment is some evidence of the clout that the ACFTU can wield within the Party, and of its deployment in support of laws that employers oppose and that at least aim to improve labor standards and protection of workers. In that sense, the ACFTU can fairly be characterized as a voice *for* China's workers if not a voice *of* the workers.

Below the national level, positions in the provincial and local ACFTU branches are staffed by Party cadres whose tenure has often been a stepping stone in a career within the Party apparatus.[17] The provincial and local governments have no formal sovereignty or autonomy from the central party-state in Beijing; yet the sheer size and complexity of China confers a kind of de facto local autonomy.[18] The deep roots of this local autonomy are captured in the Chinese aphorism "the mountains are high, and the emperor is far away." De facto local autonomy has created some space for local innovation. For example, officials in Guangdong province (in the Pearl River Delta) and their counterparts in Zhejiang province (near Shanghai) have experimented off and on with both direct election of union officials and sectoral collective bargaining.[19] Those experiments, explored in more detail in Chapters 6 and 7, laid a possible foundation for national reforms (or perhaps just for new rounds of "experiments"). Usually, however, local autonomy has worked in favor of local businesses and against workers. In particular, during the first decades of "reform and opening," the central government's pursuit of economic growth above all, and its

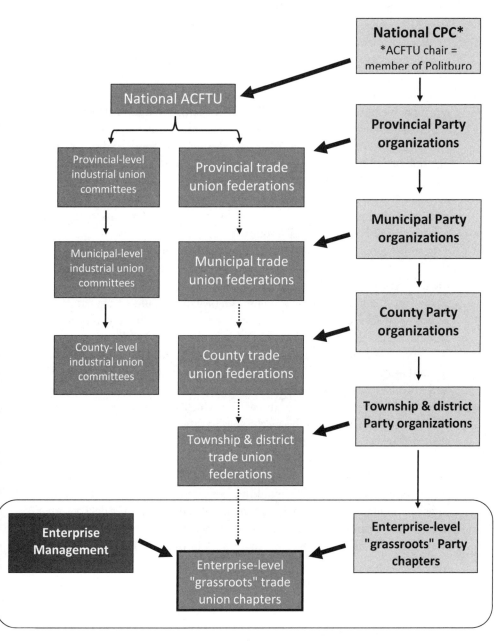

FIGURE 3.1 ACFTU Structure and Relationship to CPC

evaluation and promotion of local cadres on the basis of local economic growth, went hand in hand with local officials' indulgence of the local businesses that were often the source of personal enrichment as well as growth. The combination of party-state domination *and* the local influence of business interests have made the ACFTU a very poor vehicle of worker representation at the local level.

As central government priorities shifted in the Hu-Wen era (after 2002) toward addressing the causes of social unrest and "rebalancing" the economy, local autonomy and local officials' ties to local businesses became more problematic to the regime. This is a key to what Eli Friedman calls the "insurgency trap": entrenched and "endemic collusion between capital and local governments" has frustrated the central state's ability to carry out policies that require constraints on capital, including those aimed at addressing workers' grievances, and that fuels workers' frustration and activism.[20] The political constraints on central state control of local officials, though largely of the center's own making, threaten its own overriding imperative of political stability.

In the wake of the 2010 Honda strikes, the issue of labor unrest moved to the front burner of Chinese politics. Powerful voices within the ACFTU questioned the two-way "transmission belt" conception of its function, as well as its role in reconciling the interests of workers and employers.[21] The reformist voices contended that employers were adequately represented through other channels and sought to shift the ACFTU's function toward the representation of workers' interests vis-à-vis employers. That did not mean that they saw the union's role in the adversarial terms familiar to U.S. and other Western labor relations systems, nor that they sought to arm the union with the "economic weapons" by which this adversarial contest is traditionally carried out in the West. Nor did those views translate into a call for making the ACFTU as a whole directly accountable to the workers through bottom-up electoral mechanisms. Moreover, even if a more worker-centered conception of the union's role were to be fully embraced at higher levels, as Friedman shows, it would take a gargantuan long-term effort to alter the habits of local officials and managers, cultivated over decades, that anchor the status quo. Still, a changing conception of the union's mission may both explain and trigger other changes in the ACFTU's structure and conduct.

### *The ACFTU inside the Enterprise: Arm of Management?*

The enterprise trade union chapters, or "grassroots unions," have a rather different character. As a formal matter, the ambiguous mission of the national ACFTU is mirrored at the enterprise level: the enterprise unions are officially charged with both representing workers within the enterprise and promoting discipline and production. And as a formal matter, Party control of the ACFTU is also mirrored at the enterprise level, for the trade union chapter is officially supervised by the enterprise chapter of the Party. (Yes, even foreign-invested and private enterprises in China, unless they are very small, must generally have a CPC chapter, which is usually led by a manager who is a Party member.[22]) One important formal difference, and a major focus here, is that the enterprise trade union officers, unlike trade union officials outside the enterprise, are supposed to be elected by the worker-members. But in fact the enterprise trade union chapters have been almost uniformly dominated by enterprise management.[23] Despite the longstanding formal mandate of elections, management has usually been able to appoint (or to arrange for the election of) one from its own ranks, usually a high-level manager who is also a Party member, to lead the enterprise union.[24]

It is worth pausing for a moment to note the irony (at least from an American perspective) of the ACFTU encompassing *both* a massive nation-wide wing of the Communist Party of China *and* over a million enterprise-level unions that are dominated by profit-seeking managers of private corporations. Americans generally imagine Communists and capitalists to be in opposing camps. Their cooperative coexistence within the ACFTU (and beyond) captures something essential about China's political economy since the unleashing of capitalism, and we will return to it. For now, let us focus on the character of those enterprise-level unions themselves.

The subordination of enterprise unions to management is partly a hold-over from the SOE era in which the ACFTU's present structure and functions were forged. In the SOEs of the planned economy, managers were appointed by the Party; their responsibilities ran not to shareholders but to the workers of the enterprise and the "worker state"; and their pay, per-quisites, and status were quite similar to those of ordinary workers in the enterprise.[25] That legacy helps to explain a number of puzzles regarding the ACFTU—especially the reluctance to recognize a conflict of interest between labor and capital and its managers. But that explanation again begs the question as to why the union structure has not been overhauled to suit the needs of workers within privately owned profit-making enter-prises. One answer is that until the last decade the ACFTU had almost no presence in the non-state sector (where rural migrant workers predomi-nated), and found itself mostly struggling to quell the anger and cushion the fall of urban SOE workers whose security, benefits, and status were crumbling in the wake of privatization and restructuring.

More recently, and especially in the era of the "harmonious society," it has become clear to the regime that social and political stability requires addressing the concerns of the millions of mostly migrant workers in the enormous and growing non-state sector.[26] With these marching orders, the ACFTU set out with much fanfare to organize the operations of Fortune 500 firms in China, most famously including Wal-Mart, with the stated goal "to establish union organizations in all foreign-invested enterprises in China."[27] And it has had some well-publicized successes. By the beginning of 2009, the ACFTU claimed to have organized more than 83 percent of the headquarters of the Fortune 500 companies that do business within China.[28] Especially against the background of declining union fortunes in the United States and across much of the Western world, this sounds impressive. But what does it mean for workers on the ground?

At least until recently, most of the ACFTU's "organizing" of foreign-owned enterprises was a strictly top-down affair. (One question on the table is whether the pattern described here is changing; it does not appear to have changed much yet, but I will use the past tense to describe it.) Typically, management got a call from the local ACFTU office, which announced that the enterprise had been targeted for formation of a union chapter. When management in turn called its lawyers in a panic, the lawyers delivered the "bad news" and the "good news"—both of which sharply distinguish union organizing in China from such efforts in the United States.

The "bad news" was that management had little choice but to accede to the demand to "organize" a trade union—much as it was compelled to maintain a Party chapter—and thereafter to channel two percent of the firm's payroll to the union to fund its activities. But if the "bad news" was that management could not actively resist the formation of a union chapter, the "good news" was that they had relatively little reason to do so, for the union's presence would make little difference to the firm's operations beyond the two percent payroll tax. First, management ordinarily could select the union chair (with or without the trappings of an election), and could select someone who was not only friendly to management but part of management (albeit perhaps wearing his or her other hat as a CPC cadre). Second, if a union sought to secure a "collective agreement," it would be unlikely to demand anything more than the law's minimum wage and other mandatory labor standards (along with some innocuous worker welfare provisions, like better food and occasional breaks for women workers).[29] Nor would these union chapters foment labor unrest or work stoppages. On the contrary, the official unions took seriously their responsibility to avoid work stoppages, and touted their ability to prevent strikes in their negotiations with foreign-owned corporations.[30]

The pattern of top-down organizing, and of appealing to management's interests rather than organizing workers to assert their own interests, contrasts sharply with the nature of union organizing in the United States, which necessarily consists of a bottom-up campaign for majority support among employees. Under the law that governs most private sector labor relations, for example, workers in a particular enterprise (and in an "appropriate bargaining unit" within the enterprise) must choose, by majority vote, whether to form a union. The campaign often culminates in a formal election under the supervision of a labor board, which is officially neutral in the workers' decision whether to form a union. The union may alternatively present other evidence of majority support, such as signed authorization cards, and attempt to induce the employer to voluntarily recognize and bargain with the union. Either way, majority support from the employees is crucial. Employers are not permitted to bargain collectively with a union that lacks majority support from the employees, and unions are not permitted to put economic pressure on employers to recognize and bargain with the union unless they have demonstrable majority support. Those "top-down organizing" techniques were once quite prevalent but are now illegal under U.S. labor law.

Unfortunately, U.S. law has done too little to prevent employers from resisting the bottom-up organizing efforts of employees and unions. The law prohibits employer reprisals or threats, but employers often overstep that line, and remedial action is usually too little and too late to either remedy or deter misconduct.[31] And the law's inflated commitment to freedom of expression allows managers to mount aggressive antiunion campaigns—including "captive audience" meetings with employees on working time—while excluding union organizers from the workplace.[32] Those are large and crucial qualifications to the express commitment of U.S. labor law to employee "freedom of choice," and part of the reason why over 93 percent of private sector employees in the United States have no union representation.

In China, by contrast, the trade union is a branch of the party-state, which has many tentacles and levers by which it can influence employer conduct. Managers of foreign and privately owned enterprises in China do sometimes resist union organizing.[33] But employer resistance is tempered by the interest in good relations with the party-state, and it is not directed toward workers, who have little choice in the matter. To be sure, even though employees are not the agents of union organizing, they might still benefit from top-down organizing of union chapters. But that depends on how and by whom unions are directed once they are organized. Therein lies another set of problems to which we will turn below.

There have been exceptions to the pattern of top-down, management-focused organizing. For example, there was a flurry of excitement among labor advocates when grassroots union activists organized the first Walmart store, striking an unprecedented blow against Walmart's global anti-unionism by winning recognition over management opposition. But excitement soon subsided when Walmart's union chapters fell back into old habits of compliance and coziness with management. After the local ACFTU chapter negotiated a framework agreement with senior Walmart management, Gao Haitao, the union chairman at Walmart's Nanchang store who had led the grassroots organizing drive, sought to add specific clauses that would benefit his members. But he was simply bypassed by management, who got a union representative from another store to sign the boilerplate agreement. Gao resigned in frustration in September 2008.[34] For a time, Walmart touted its excellent labor relations in China as evidence of its new commitment to social responsibility, while workers still had no organization of their own to assert their interests.

More recently, Wal-Mart workers began to fight back, putting a dent in the company's rebranding efforts. Workers began to complain about low pay. "Wal-Mart only pays minimum wage, and it doesn't have overtime," labor scholar Anita Chan explained. "When the wage is minimum wage and there is no overtime, it's not possible to live on what you're making. So a lot of workers just leave for something better."[35] As Chan indicated, most discontented Wal-Mart workers, like most discontented Chinese workers elsewhere, chose "exit" over "voice." But some workers in Shenzhen began to consider a more vocal collective response. In 2012, they began attending training sessions on collective bargaining held not by the official trade union but by an activist labor lawyer, Duan Yi. Forty workers at a Wal-Mart distribution center eventually went on strike over pay issues, and Wal-Mart fired several workers involved in organizing efforts.[36] But we are again getting ahead of the story, which will continue in Chapter 6 on strikes and collective bargaining.

For a U.S. observer, management domination of China's enterprise trade unions may evoke the "company unions" that were popular with some U.S. companies in the 1920s and early 1930s, largely as a device to fend off independent union organizing. Company unions were outlawed by the National Labor Relations Act (NLRA) in 1935 and have since been largely extinct (or invisible).[37] In recent decades, labor law scholars and reformers have debated whether the NLRA's broad ban on employer domination of and assistance to "labor organizations," and the broad definition of the latter, should be narrowed to permit some structures of employee representation that are initiated and supported by management in workplaces where employees are not represented by an independent union. But the contestants in that debate take for granted (or seek to fortify) employees' right to form independent unions, controlled by worker-members, free from management interference. By contrast, given the ACFTU's monopoly on lawful union organizations, workers who are fed up with their union's submissiveness to management have no outside option.

Management domination of enterprise unions in China has several dimensions. For one, China's enterprise unions—and indeed the whole ACFTU structure—are largely funded by the two percent payroll tax that goes to the union upon the formation of a union chapter. (Members pay only a token amount in union dues.) By sharp contrast, it is unlawful in the United States for employers to "assist" a union through financial contributions or otherwise. A Chinese labor law scholar alluded to the comparison in the official China Daily:

> Unlike their Western counterparts, which are independent of management, China's labor unions get most of the funds from their companies, Li Xiaoping said. "That undermines the independence of labor unions, whose leaders find themselves in an awkward position. While they are supposed to defend workers' rights, they do not dare offend company management that pays their salaries."[38]

But the funding issue is only the beginning. The bigger problem is management control of union leadership. The law on the books has long called for elections, but elections have typically been easily manipulated by management when they occur at all.[39] Indeed, until recently, it was typical for a firm's head of human resources to also serve as chair of the union. As recently as 2006, for example, the ACFTU reported that nearly all union chairmen at private domestic and foreign-invested companies in Guangzhou were serving concurrently as corporate officers.[40]

That pattern has begun to change. The Chinese labor academy has rallied around the notion that workers need their own representatives free from management control.[41] Official ACFTU policy now prohibits executives, deputy executives, human resources managers, and partners of an enterprise, as well as their close relatives, from serving as chair of the enterprise union.[42] The role of managerial employees in the enterprise unions is partly a product of the comprehensive definition of the "workers and staff members" of an enterprise that are represented by the union: supervisors and most managers are not only entitled to ACFTU representation; they are part of a single all-inclusive "bargaining unit" (a term they do not use) along with the lowest-paid rank-and-file workers.

To most Western observers, it seems obvious that managers and production workers have fundamentally different interests on many issues of concern to the latter; managerial employees seem likely to side with "the employer" on such issues, and in any case simply do not share the same conditions of employment.[43] The conflicting interests of different groups of employees are reflected in U.S. labor law both in the exclusion of managers (and supervisors) from the definition of covered "employees," and in the concept of a "bargaining unit," the members of which are supposed to share a "community of interest." To be sure, U.S. labor law is a bit of an outlier within the West—and on some accounts an outlaw within international labor law—in its exclusion of ordinary supervisors and low-level managers from unions and from the protections of the labor laws.[44] Still, China is unusual in including top managers and factory workers in an enterprise—wall to wall and top to bottom—within the same union's constituency.[45]

The comprehensive scope of the ACFTU's constituency has its origins, again, in the planned economy. In the heyday of the "iron rice bowl," enterprises were run for the benefit of all of the workers, both as citizens of the enterprise and as citizens of the Chinese state, which owned the enterprise and received any surplus proceeds.[46] Workers' social status and economic security rivaled that of managers (though poverty and repression were endemic). In the relatively egalitarian planned economy, there was some sense to the notion that the participants of an enterprise were all in it together and required no separate representation. The question is how that notion managed to survive in the decades since, with the advent of the "labor contract system," the commodification of labor, the growth of private profit-making enterprises, and the spectacular economic inequalities that have followed.

Why hasn't China overhauled its conception of the unions' role in the enterprise to meet the challenges that workers face within a private for-profit enterprise? It is true that, in response to rising labor conflict, the ACFTU has been gradually refocusing its mission on the representation of workers and not employers. But there is still resistance to the notion of explicitly recognizing and institutionalizing conflict among workers or between workers and managers. This is one of the signal "Chinese characteristics" of its labor relations system: among and within the legitimate social relationships and actors in the society, "contradictions" can and should be mediated within comprehensive institutions, not fought out between contesting ones.[47]

One might have thought (as I did upon first coming to China) that official adherence to Marxist-Leninist thought would render all the more transparent the conflict of interest between labor and private capital. Paradoxically, however, ideology does more to obscure that conflict than to clarify it, and more to discourage than to encourage its forthright recognition. For China's leaders insist, even after decades of capitalist-led development, that China is not a capitalist society, but is in the "beginning stages of socialism." To explicitly acknowledge the conflict of interest between labor and capital, and the need for workers to have their own representatives in this conflict, might appear to retreat from that ideology and to embrace capitalism and the labor-management conflict that is emblematic of capitalism. Ironically, this effort to preserve Communist ideology and rhetoric contributes to workers' lack of meaningful collective representation and protection against their capitalist employers.

Once again, however, it is important not to compare the real, flawed Chinese system to an idealized American system. Recall that the great majority of American workers also lack meaningful collective representation vis-à-vis their capitalist employers. The basic assumption of U.S. labor law is that there are conflicting interests between workers and employers, peaceable resolution of which requires arm's-length bargaining by agents that are strictly loyal and accountable to those whom they represent. That has produced fairly vigorous and effective representation, and significant gains through collective bargaining, for the shrinking minority of U.S. workers who are represented by independent unions. It has also helped to spur aggressive managerial resistance to union organizing and bargaining. And that has curbed the appeal of unions to many American workers, who express little appetite for open conflict with their employers. Indeed, most say they would prefer more cooperative structures of worker representation even if that would mean less powerful representation.[48] It seems that many American workers would prefer more "harmonious" labor relations, provided that they had an effective opportunity to speak and to be heard. In principle, workers in the United States have the right to form or join an independent union—to go into opposition, as it were, against their employers—if they see fit. In practice, the hurdles along that path are notorious.

The problem in China is different. Management domination at the enterprise level and Party domination above that has rendered the ACFTU largely "useless" in pressing ordinary workers' concerns at that level.[49] Not just coincidentally, the ACFTU's organizing efforts have met relatively little managerial resistance, allowing for rapid membership growth in the last decade. In short, the ACFTU's organizing successes in the early 2000s stemmed as much from the union's weakness—its failure to challenge management or to increase labor's share of revenues—as from its strength, which lies in its party backing, not in workers' support and solidarity. By the same token, if the ACFTU were to shift toward a more adversarial and worker-centered conception of its mission, it would surely trigger greater managerial resistance to its organizing efforts. For now, the power of the CPC on which the ACFTU can draw may be enough to overcome that managerial resistance. But employers, too, have their fingers on levers of power in the party, especially at the local level.

### The ACFTU and "Freedom of Association": Some Preliminary Comparative Reflections

The Party-controlled ACFTU, with its official monopoly on worker representation, is the defining feature of China's labor landscape. Workers who are dissatisfied with its representation—as many workers apparently are—are not free to form their own union independent of the state or the ACFTU. Neither the ACFTU's monopoly over organized labor activity nor its active control by the party-state is under serious reconsideration by China's leadership; nor is either openly challenged by Chinese labor law scholars. The ACFTU's monopoly and Party control in turn make management domination of the enterprise-level unions an especially serious problem for workers. Both features set China's unions apart from the conception and, for the most part, the reality of unions in Western democracies.

Let us pause briefly, however, to adjust our comparative lens, lest this account of Party and management domination of China's official trade unions imply that their American counterparts are pristine exemplars of independence and democratic control—unimpeachably loyal, strictly accountable to their worker-members, and unscathed by state control.

The American labor movement has had its own bitter struggles with management-dominated "sweetheart unions," entrenched incumbents, corruption, and bureaucratic sclerosis, all of which have compromised unions' responsiveness to their worker members. American trade unions have also been subject to government interference in various forms, some of which has sought to combat the aforementioned evils and reinforce unions' democratic accountability, but some of which has annulled workers' autonomy, sometimes in the interest of political stability (as in the Cold War purges of left-wing unions and union activists).[50] Chapter 4 will turn directly to the American history of industrial relations, but for now it is worth noting two points about that history: both U.S. employers and the government have sometimes sought to control trade unions in order to temper their independence and militancy, and they have sometimes succeeded. But the norm of union independence from both employers and the state that has held sway since the New Deal has limited the extent and the nature of both employer and government interference in union self-governance. No such norm is recognized in China.

In other advanced industrial democracies of the West, the same basic norm of union independence coexists with elements that superficially recall aspects of China's system of worker representation. For example, many Western unions are affiliated with political parties, including parties that sometimes hold the reins of government. But those political parties do not control the trade unions, whose officers are elected by worker-members, and in a multiparty system those parties must themselves compete for citizens' allegiance and political power through competitive elections. A party-controlled monopoly union in a one-party state is quite another thing.

It is also true that constraints on individual workers' freedom of choice are endemic to systems of collective representation and bargaining. In the United States, for example, the choice of union representation is exercised by majorities, whose choice is binding on both those who do want union representation and can't get it and those who don't want representation but are saddled with it. (The former greatly outnumber the latter, partly because of the inordinate de facto power that management exerts over employees' freedom to choose union representation.) In some European countries, workers are effectively represented in economic bargaining by the dominant trade union in an industry, whether they choose to join that union, another union, or none at all.[51] The classic corporatist institution of "peak bargaining" between a single dominant union and an employer federation at the sectoral level, with extension of the results throughout the sector, obviously constrains individual workers' choice regarding union representation. Still, multiple unions compete for workers' allegiance, often on political grounds, and workers can join whatever union they wish.

In all of these Western systems, workers have a wide measure of collective freedom of choice at some level of aggregation, and they have collective control of their own unions through some electoral system or another. And in all of these systems, workers who are fed up with their union, or with the dominant union, are free to join or form a different union and to attempt to gain the allegiance of fellow workers. That generates some systemic pressure on unions to respond to workers' concerns. China is different, and it is at sharp odds with Western patterns and principles in its prohibition of any trade union organization other than the one designated and maintained by the one-party state.

China's continuing commitment to hierarchical and monopolistic party-state control of organized labor activity stands in ironic contrast to its more liberal posture toward "organized capital." In the planned economy, productive enterprises were effectively branches of the party-state; both capital and labor were administered by the state through managers and union officers, all party cadres. But since the "reform and opening," firms, or aggregations of capital, became relatively autonomous, self-organized, and self-directed market actors. China has thus shifted away from direct control or *administration* of productive capital, and toward its *regulation*.[52] But China still aspires to direct *administration* of organized labor through the ACFTU, an integral component of the Party-directed system of governance.

For China's leaders, autonomous collective labor activity appears to pose a greater challenge to China's nominally socialist regime than the autonomous aggregation of capital and of investors in the corporate form. As an ideological matter, China has sought to reconcile substantial entrepreneurial autonomy for capital, and private ownership of much of the means of production, with its socialist commitments through the ambiguous and still-evolving concept of the "socialist market economy." As a pragmatic matter, China's regime has managed to cultivate the loyalty of the domestic capital-owning class, while many of its officials have joined that class.[53] The overlapping membership and interests of business and Party elites, from the local level on up, largely defuse the threat that organized capital might pose to one-party rule. But workers, who are excluded from that cozy coalition, might pose a greater threat to political stability if they were permitted to organize themselves autonomously. "Organized labor" outside the party-state is thus seen as a much greater political threat to the regime than "organized capital." And so the CPC, through its labor arm the ACFTU, remains the one legitimate representative of the workers.

There is no sign that China will give up on this central tenet of its political system in the foreseeable future, either by allowing independent unions or by giving up party-state control over the ACFTU and its branches. That represents an unusually frontal rejection of workers' "freedom of association," a central organizing principle of the International Labor Organization (ILO), of which China is a member.[54] During the era of Mao and through the early years of "reform and opening," that put China on one side of a Cold War divide, for the Soviet Union and its satellite states in Eastern Europe also maintained a single official trade union and prohibited independent union organizing.[55] Indeed, so did other authoritarian anti-communist countries of East Asia, such as South Korea and Taiwan.[56] But with the collapse of the Soviet Union and the democratization of several East Asian societies, China became more of an outlier on this score. For many years, the ACFTU was a pariah among mainstream Western, and especially U.S., labor organizations. But attitudes began to change as China's continuing economic growth, its integration into the world economy, and its impact on global labor standards made some form of engagement look increasingly vital, and as the regime's successful resistance to political change discouraged hopes for the development of an independent labor movement.[57] The ACFTU, however flawed a vehicle of worker representation, has come to be seen as "the only game in town" in a town that could not be ignored.[58] Many foreign trade union federations have thus looked for ways to engage, critically but constructively, with the ACFTU.

Yet workers' rising assertiveness has been making a mark in China, and provoking a measure of official responsiveness along with repression. The possibility that workers in China might defect from the system and defy the ACFTU's monopoly by forming their own labor organizations does supply a systemic motivation for the party-state to respond to workers' concerns in some manner (even as it triggers surveillance and reprisals). That political pressure operates less on the ACFTU itself than on the regime as a whole, and its consequences are seen across multiple fronts, some of which are the topics of later chapters.

### Is the ACFTU a "Trade Union"?

The complex and contradictory nature of the ACFTU has produced sharply divergent assessments among knowledgeable observers. On one view, the ACFTU remains simply an instrument of party control, and its recent "organizing" campaign simply a vehicle for extending the party-state's reach into the relatively dynamic and free-wheeling private business sector. Some liberal minded friends of workers thus find the ACFTU's organizing drive counterproductive because it postpones the advent of workers' freedom of association and of independent democratic unions. Others, especially U.S. corporations doing business in China, object because it injects more Party meddling (or at least its potential) into managers' ability to govern their Chinese operations as they see fit.

By contrast, many scholars and worker advocates see the ACFTU as more than an instrument of Party control (if not a genuine union). They believe that, given the regime's steadfast commitment to avoiding the rise of independent unions, the ACFTU is likely to remain the only game in town, and workers' best hope for a real voice at work, for a long time. Indeed, they argue, workers might benefit from greater vertical control of the ACFTU from outside the enterprise and above the local level. Although that would hardly seem likely to enhance accountability and responsiveness to workers, it might do just that indirectly by countering employer domination. For those observers, a more centrally directed ACFTU that is committed to representing workers, raising wages, and reversing trends toward growing inequality could be a powerful ally for workers in their disputes with private and foreign businesses.

That is the view taken by Bill Taylor and Qi Li, who argue that, while the ACFTU is not a union as Westerners understand the term, it may nonetheless be Chinese workers' best source of support in their struggles for a better life. Chinese workers "are not oppressed by anyone else but their employers,"[59] and are in desperate need of powerful allies. As a relatively worker-friendly arm of the CPC, the ACFTU is "the only organ with the capacity or interest to do anything for labour on a nationwide systematic basis."[60] The ACFTU can be a crucial inside advocate in closed-door policy discussions in which worker interests are considered (as they were in the enactment of the LCL in 2007 and the recent amendments regulating the labor dispatch system). Taylor and Li argue that it might even be counterproductive for workers to weaken the ACFTU's party ties, though all the more important to combat its domination by employers at the enterprise (and local) level.

Along similar lines, Anita Chan, a leading scholarly critic of China's labor policies,[61] has proposed two structural reforms, both of which combat management domination, and neither of which presents a frontal challenge to party control of the ACFTU: First, like others, she argues that union leaders at the enterprise level should be directly elected by the workers they represent. (The move toward direct elections is elaborated in Chapter 7.) Second, she argues that the enterprise trade unions should be put under the direction of higher levels of the ACFTU—provincial union officials—rather than either enterprise-level Party officials or local party and union officials, who are notoriously intertwined with local business elites.[62] Chan argues that these two reforms could help transform the ACFTU into a more genuine representative of the workers and a real force for the promotion of a "harmonious society," in keeping with its designated role within the party-state.

It may be hard for democratic-minded Westerners to wrap their minds around this second cluster of views, which not only assumes the inability of Chinese workers to form their own unions, but find some advantages in the ACFTU's status as an arm of the Party for China's workers in their struggle for decent wages and working conditions. One may be convinced—as I am—that strong and independent unions that workers themselves control would be better for workers. But is that what Chinese workers would have if they were allowed to form their own unions (even apart from the extremely remote chance of that happening)? That is certainly not what most low-wage workers in the United States have. Most have no union representation at all and little realistic prospect of getting it.

Moreover, one wonders what low-wage workers in the United States would prefer if they were given a choice: a powerful worker-friendly arm of the state to bargain with economically powerful employers on their behalf or an independent union that pools workers' own meager bargaining power and is vigorously opposed by employers?[63] It is not obvious to me that they would choose the latter, nor that they should.

As for Chinese workers, they have had neither a powerful arm of the state nor an independent union to back them up in dealings with employers. The harsh suppression of independent trade unionism constantly prunes and thins the tenuous organizational threads that connect worker activists to each other. Even so, many Chinese workers have managed to mobilize themselves in recent years to carry out industrial actions, large and small, and rising in both number and size. A central question that this book asks is whether China is on the cusp of a major breakthrough in industrial relations, one that enables workers to speak for themselves through accountable and responsive, or even independent, labor organizations. To begin to address that question, let us look at the unofficial outlets of worker representation in China—comparatively independent *and* comparatively weak, but nonetheless important in China's labor landscape.

## Labor NGOs and a Glimpse of "Civil Society with Chinese Characteristics"

Workers in China, and especially migrant workers—marginalized or excluded from official support systems in the places where they live and work—have sought out and sometimes formed organizations to serve their interests. Labor NGOs, almost by definition, pose a challenge to the ACFTU's official monopoly on collective worker representation and attract official scrutiny and skepticism. But they are also part of a growing "civil society" that gradually achieved a modicum of legitimacy after the end of the Cultural Revolution, and is now under pressure. So let us expand the frame to take in a glimpse of the changing nature of Chinese civil society before zooming in on the uneasy status of labor NGOs.

### *The Blooming (and Pruning) of Chinese Civil Society since the Maoist Era*

Apart from the Party itself, the ACFTU is one of the stronger surviving components of what once was a more comprehensive system of Party control of collective social activity. China's version of "state corporatism" provided for representation of group interests—women, youth, workers, and other groups—through a single hierarchically organized, officially approved channel under the control of the CPC.[64] The ACFTU is thus one of several national "mass organizations," each standing atop a pyramid of provincial and local branches, and each charged with the mission of conveying the interests of the masses up to Party leaders and conveying the "party line" down to the masses. That Leninist "transmission belt" system, once the backbone of China's official system of social organization, has been challenged and eroded by social and economic change, but it continues to shape and constrain the legal and political space for independent social organizations.

One challenge to the official mass organizations is that, in the wake of economic growth and urbanization, the "masses" are increasingly differentiated, even individualistic, in their life experiences, interests, and views. In the planned economy, an individual's entire life and support system was administered through the permanently assigned *danwei*, or work unit. The *danwei* system facilitated social control, and it did so partly by generating relatively homogeneous experiences, interests, and views. That social reality lent a certain logic to the assignment of each recognized group (women, for example, or workers) to a single official channel of representation. It was a totalitarian logic, to be sure, and it was the antithesis of Western pluralist conceptions of civil society; but it was a logic nonetheless. The mass organizations' monopoly on associational life was doomed, however, with the demise of the *danwei* system, the rise of markets, the loosening of ties between individuals and the party-state, and the diversification of experiences, aspirations, and opinions that followed.

China's 1982 constitution established the basic principles that still govern the regulation of most nongovernmental civic organizations.[65] At its heart is a system of registration: Organizations must register with the local Civil Affairs office; and in order to register, they have to "attach themselves" *(guakao)* to some branch of the party-state that is willing and able to serve as their sponsor *(zhuguan danwei)*.[66] A labor NGO might seek to affiliate with the local ACFTU chapter; an NGO serving female workers might opt to approach the local branch of the All-China Women's Federation; a legal aid group might try to register with the Department of Justice. The two-part registration system symbolically preserves partystate leadership of collective social activity. But it is more than symbolic, for the sponsoring entity effectively vouches to higher-ups for the political trustworthiness of the NGO, and has both a motive and a means of keeping the NGO's activities within permissible (and non-political) bounds. Politically "sensitive" organizations with no official sponsor violate the registration requirement by their very existence. Behind this registration system lies a suspicion—one not strictly limited to Chinese officialdom—that "nongovernmental organizations" *(feizhengfuzuzhi)* are a small step removed from "antigovernment organizations" *(fanzhengfuzuzhi)*. That suspicion is one reflection of the strong antipluralist currents that have inhibited the development of civil society in China.

Early in the post-Mao era, the registration system tended to perpetuate the single-channel model of social organization even as associational life began to come alive. As Jonathan Unger and Anita Chan relate:

> when two national associations of calligraphy connoisseurs emerged in the 1980s, Beijing decreed that one and only one could be legally registered, and ordered that they therefore needed to merge into one national association. [And] when fans of a popular soccer team in the city of Shenyang in the late 1980s spontaneously organized themselves into two fan clubs encompassing two different social constituencies, the city authorities demanded that even fan clubs had to be legally recognized and that the two clubs would accordingly need to merge, since only one could be recognized and registered.[67]

These stories are almost funny to Western ears, but they attest to the totalistic control that party-state officials once sought to exercise over associational life.

Chinese civil society has come a long way since the 1980s.[68] The Fourth World Conference on Women in Beijing in 1995, which brought together over twenty-five thousand representatives, mostly from NGOs, was eye-opening to Chinese observers and inspired some to start their own NGOs.[69] More recently, the devastating Sichuan earthquake of 2008 evoked an outpouring of help from self-organized groups across China and underscored the value of volunteer associations for a regime that is easily unnerved by autonomous collective activity.[70] As NGOs and voluntary associations have bubbled up across China, foreign NGOs have been seeking out Chinese partners to support financially and otherwise. So the capabilities and public profile of Chinese NGOs have risen dramatically along with their numbers.

The official treatment of civil society has become somewhat bifurcated in recent years, with growing acceptance and legitimacy for some kinds of organizations and greater scrutiny and suspicion toward others. In 2013, China moved toward liberalizing the registration system for some NGOs (or allowing localities to do so).[71] In Beijing, for example, industry and commercial associations, community-based welfare groups and charities, and groups promoting scientific research were allowed to register directly with the Ministry of Civil Affairs without the need for a party-state sponsor. But this liberalized regime appeared to exclude most organizations engaged in advocacy on contentious social issues, as well as religious organizations, which still require a sponsor to register.[72] The more "sensitive" the group's mission and activities—with "sensitivity" being subject to a shifting barometer—the harder it remains to secure a sponsor, and thus to function lawfully. Many Chinese NGOs have been unable to register with the Ministry of Civil Affairs and have registered as businesses or not at all.[73]

In 2016 the Xi administration enacted a new law imposing draconian restrictions on the activities of foreign NGOs in China, many of which are seen as sowing the seeds of Western-inspired dissent.[74] The draft law led some to ask, as Ira Belkin and Jerome Cohen did in their op-ed: "Will China Close Its Doors?"[75] The draft law provoked a torrent of critical comments from the West, including many submitted through official channels in hopes of softening the final version.[76] But the final version adopted in April 2016 softened very little. The vast majority of foreign NGOs operating in China now have their own dual registration system: they must find an official party-state sponsor and they must register not with the Ministry of Civil Affairs but with the Ministry of Public Security—that is, the police. Informed observers believe that these new restrictions were intended chiefly to constrain the Chinese NGOs that had benefited from alliances with Western organizations.[77]

Other forms of oversight have also been tightened under the Xi administration. In 2015, the Political Bureau of the CPC began to require each domestic NGO to form a Party Members' Group to be the NGO's "core leadership," and to "see to it that the Party's line, principles and policies are implemented, to discuss and decide on matters of major importance . . . , to rally the non-Party cadres and the masses in fulfilling the tasks assigned by the Party and the state and to guide the work of the Party organization of the unit and those directly under it."[78] Increasingly the message seems to be that the only legitimate NGOs are those that submit to party-state authority and support the Party line.

The hostility to autonomous social organizations is strongest as to overtly political associations. While many Chinese citizens freely speak their minds as individuals, even on political matters, they cannot freely join with like-minded others to pursue political aims, however peacefully.[79] Liu Xiaobo, the imprisoned Nobel laureate, spoke his mind in China for many years, but when he circulated a petition in support of freedom and democracy, he crossed the line from speaking to organizing and became a "criminal." The court that upheld Liu's conviction asserted: "[Liu] incite[d] subversion of our country's state power and the socialist system . . . [by] publishing slanderous essays and extensively collecting signatures online";

his actions "conspicuously overstepped the bounds of free speech and constitute a crime."[80]

Xu Zhiyong crossed a similar line. As part of a loosely affiliated group of journalists, scholars, and lawyers who advocated a transition from authoritarianism to constitutionalism and a more just and transparent civil order, Xu was subject to official harassment for several years. But when Xu wrote an online essay in 2012 calling for a New Citizens Movement with those same goals,[81] and when the group began to sponsor peaceful rallies as well as informal indoor meetings, official harassment escalated into multiple detentions, arrests, and prosecutions. Xu himself was sentenced to four years in prison in 2014 for allegedly "assembling crowds with the intent to disrupt public spaces."[82]

Even individual legal representation may be regarded as out-of-bounds political advocacy if it invokes human rights or constitutional rights against the state, especially in the newly chilly environment under President Xi. In 2015, in the space of a few weeks, over two hundred "rights defense" lawyers and activists were detained, arrested, or jailed across China; the charges of "picking quarrels" and exploiting controversial cases for self-aggrandizement and enrichment were a transparent pretext for suppressing the tiny but vigorous rights defense movement.[83] Another prominent rights lawyer, Pu Zhiqiang, in jail since 2014, was convicted in December 2015 of "inciting ethnic hatred" and "picking quarrels and provoking trouble" based on comments he had made on the Internet; he was given a suspended sentence, but was disbarred.[84]

The 2015 crackdown is a reminder that lawyers are potentially "sensitive" members of civil society, given their professional advocacy role. The legal profession as a whole has regained legitimacy since the end of the Cultural Revolution and has played an invaluable and recognized role in China's entry into the global economy and community.[85] But lawyers remain subject to political as well as professional regulation, in part through the official All-China Lawyers Association and its provincial and local branches. Lawyers who overstep the boundaries of acceptable legal advocacy risk losing their license; that is rare, though it happened in 2009 to more than a dozen leading "rights lawyers" in Beijing.[86] China's contemporary bar associations conduct political oversight as a branch of the party-state—part of the single-channel system of social representation—with at best a fragile and provisional claim to professional autonomy. (U.S. bar associations operate a system of professional self-regulation. In the Cold War they sometimes functioned as political overseers, wielding disbarment as a sanction.[87] But that has rarely happened in the past half century.)

Religious groups are also deemed "sensitive," and they are subject to a strict version of the single-channel model of representation, owing to their faith in and allegiance to higher authority above the CPC. For example, China's only officially sanctioned Catholic organization, the Chinese Patriotic Catholic Association (CPCA), operates under Party supervision and denies papal authority. Chinese Catholics are not allowed to organize themselves outside of the CPCA's umbrella, nor to openly assert the higher authority of the Vatican, which is beyond Party control and beyond China's borders. As in the labor context, China's response has been measured as to the average Catholic, but harsh as to leaders of any organized challenge to the CPCA's monopoly; several have been sentenced to long prison terms.[88] In Zhejiang, where CPC officials have been demolishing churches and destroying crosses since 2013, pastors who publicly opposed the policy or organized protests have been harassed or even jailed.[89] (The United States has its own history of anti-Catholic sentiment and discrimination, based partly on the "foreign" allegiance ascribed to believers.[90] But it did not take the harsh official forms that it does today in China.)

Labor groups occupy a distinct yet ambiguous zone in this civil society landscape, owing to ideology and history: official Communist ideology endorses efforts to advance workers' interests, but it condemns collective representation of workers outside of official Party-led channels. And the history of independent labor movements across the world makes such organizing politically threatening even if it avoids any overt challenge to Party rule or the ACFTU's monopoly. Groups that approach that line by organizing across enterprise boundaries still court prosecution. In October 2010, for example, a worker activist in Xi'an was sentenced to three years in prison for "organizing more than 380 workers from about 20 [SOEs] to form a labour rights group tasked with overseeing and monitoring SOE restructuring, and reporting corruption and abuses of power."[91] But even worker organizations that steer clear of such "political" organizing, and confine themselves to representation of workers' rights claims, occupy a closely watched space that has narrowed since 2014.

Almost all labor NGOs engage in forms of advocacy that appear to disqualify them from the new streamlined registration process. That means they must secure a party-state sponsor in order to register as a civic organization. NGOs that cannot find a party-state sponsor—and most labor NGOs cannot—may attempt to register as business entities. That is simpler and requires no official sponsor, but it risks being seen as an evasion of the social management system.[92] (It also means that any revenues are taxable, which can lead to both financial and legal difficulties.) The level of monitoring and enforcement of the registration requirement for labor

NGOs varies over time and across regions, but it has intensified in recent years as the number of labor NGOs has grown and as they have become more active in strike situations.[93]

Once again, ironies abound in modern China's treatment of labor versus capital: Capital and capitalists are comparatively free to associate. Individuals may aggregate their capital by incorporating, and corporations may form trade associations and the like, using the liberalized single registration process. In short, associations of capitalists enjoy greater autonomy, even formally, than associations of workers. The former (and especially corporations themselves) are regulated to be sure, as they are in the West; but the latter remain subject to more comprehensive and illiberal forms of control that harken back to the totalitarian era. Underlying this irony, as already noted in Chapter 1, is an uncomfortable reality in a nominally socialist country: Relatively autonomous associations of capital and capitalists are essential for China's growth and lucrative for officialdom, but autonomous associations of workers, who have a long list of grievances against both employers and officialdom, are regarded as a dangerous rivals to the CPC and potentially existential political threats. So labor NGOs of all kinds are closely monitored lest they overstep the boundaries of permissible advocacy and venture into "political" terrain.

Groups that represent workers in their pursuit of legal claims may fall at various points along the spectrum of political acceptability depending partly on their relation to the official systems of supervision (for lawyers and for NGOs) and partly on the scope of their activities: Do they involve themselves with workers who engage in or even lead disruptive protest actions? Do they press rights claims that are "sensitive," or not officially sanctioned, or even officially off-limits? (Some of these relate to the special problems faced by lawyers who work with or for these groups, or even independently, as we will see below.) In short, some labor NGOs in China accept the constraints and the benefits that go with official legitimacy, and others do not, and try to operate independently.

In the first group, a handful of labor NGOs find or create space for worker and community engagement while maintaining positive relations with local labor departments or ACFTU officials. The draw of governmental approval is a potent force in Chinese society, and it is actively sought by many labor NGOs as a source of legitimacy as well as safety. Moreover, local party-state officials control access to much of what workers need—particularly when what they need requires policy changes. The willingness of some labor NGOs to take the officially approved path, and to accept the constraints that come with it, has led some scholarly critics to label those organizations as "anti-solidarity machines," and to question their autonomy.[94] But some of these organizations manage to do a lot of good for workers within the system. For example, the Beijing Legal Aid Office for Migrant Workers (known informally in China as *Zhicheng*) has secured grants of over one million yuan from the China Legal Aid Foundation and the All-China Lawyers Foundation, along with permission from the Beijing Justice Bureau to legally represent migrant workers. Those official ties have helped this NGO to operate safely and to win some high-profile cases.[95] But those ties may also come with fetters on its ability to offer aid, especially to unregistered migrant workers and groups of workers seeking to proceed collectively.[96]

By contrast, the labor NGOs that seek to remain independent, and to engage in activities that foreclose registration with the local ACFTU or Labor Department or Justice Department, face a more tense and tenuous existence. They may attempt to register as businesses; but even if they manage to retain a business license, they face hostility from local officials, including police, and pressure in the form of detentions, surveillance, and canceled leases, all in the name of "stability maintenance." Labor NGOs uniformly report that pressure has increased since 2006, even before the Xi administration. Many worker advocates were unsettled by the 2009 "Investigative Report on the Question of 'Professional Citizen Legal Agents" issued by the Guangdong Provincial Communist Party's Committee on Politics and Law, which oversees police, prosecutors, and judges. (Yes, the Party supervises courts; we will return to this striking fact in Chapter 5.) Worker allies read the report as "a deliberate attempt to discredit" unregistered labor NGOs and advocates (several of which were named in the report), and to push for tighter control or suppression.[97]

Before the recent turn toward greater repression, labor NGOs were caught in some interesting cross-currents, for China's party-state is not monolithic. The director of one Guangdong labor NGO related in 2011 that, even as five different local departments were trying to pressure the landlord to evict his organization, local and provincial ACFTU leaders had approached him about studying his worker training and outreach methods. Especially lately, however, the officials who might speak up in support of labor NGOs have been outnumbered and overmatched by those who seek tighter government control of civil society and labor advocacy. At the same time, the shift in workers' own sense of entitlement and their collective impulses—from enforcement of recognized legal rights toward assertion of broader interests—has sharpened both the tension with the ACFTU's monopoly and the regime's fear of independent labor activism.

The environment for labor NGOs has clearly grown more hostile since 2012. Some of these organizations have been shut down—seven in

Guangdong in 2012 alone—and some activists have faced arbitrary detention.[98] In April 2014, Lin Dong, who advised workers at Yue Yuen, was
charged and held for thirty days in the first use of an amended law prohibiting use of the Internet to disturb "social order."[99] In March 2015, Beijing
Yirenping, a major anti-discrimination organization that had rallied support for the "Feminist Five" (who were detained for a month without
charges after a public campaign against sexual harassment in China[100]),
was raided, its computers confiscated, and an employee detained.[101] Then
in December 2015, almost two dozen labor activists in Guangdong were
detained and their belongings confiscated. Three were charged with "inciting
crowds to disrupt public order" and one with "embezzlement," and two
simply disappeared.[102] As strikes have skyrocketed in Guangdong, run-ins
with police have risen concurrently. Labor activists said that the levels of
official intimidation in 2015 were "unprecedented."[103] In short, some
NGOs that represent workers have become politically sensitive and are
beginning to face the same risk of arbitrary detention, imprisonment, psy-
chiatric commitment, house arrest, and physical abuse that other human
rights advocates do.[104]

CHINA'S LABOR NGOS and the two overlapping spheres in which
they operate—rights enforcement and interest disputes—will reappear in
Chapters 5 and 6 as we take up China's first-choice regulatory response to
labor unrest and its more hesitant and hemmed-in industrial relations
response. Before turning to China's many-faceted response to labor unrest,
however, it is time for a comparative interlude. This book addresses some
large questions about China's future: How far and in what direction will
workers' initiatives and government reforms go in China? Will China
manage to construct reasonably effective regulatory institutions that can
enforce decent labor standards and reasonably functional industrial relations institutions for the resolution of labor conflict? Will China's workers
gain the fundamental rights of association and collective bargaining that
are embodied in international labor law and that were established in
some form or another many decades ago across the Western world? My
aim is not to answer those questions (though I will venture some provisional guesses along the way), but to illuminate what is at stake and what
dilemmas China faces as it attempts to answer those questions for itself.

In my own effort to understand those issues, however, I inevitably
brought American eyes and a very Western-tinged lens to China's labor
scene. What I saw—the similarities and historical analogies as well as
the many differences—was surprising in many ways, and disrupted my

expectations. Over the past several years of travels and studies in China, I have tried to look beyond that lens, and to scrutinize it for the imperfections and distortions that it might impart to my understanding. Especially for those readers who are starting from the same vantage point as I did, it may be useful to put that lens itself into clearer focus.

# CHAPTER FOUR

# How Did the New Deal Resolve the American "Labor Question"?

*Bringing a Comparative Lens into Focus*

WHEN SEEN THROUGH Western-tinted glasses, both China's workers, in their increasingly well-organized forms of collective action, and China's government, in its response to that collective action, appear in some ways to be following in the footsteps of the United States and other major industrial economies of the world during the twentieth century. As mass industrialization brought conflict between labor and capital, the resulting "labor question"—what to do about the disorder and violence surrounding labor conflict—became a leading domestic concern, and the predicate for major pro-worker labor reforms.[1] Those reforms have been of roughly two types: regulation of terms and conditions of employment, chiefly through minimum labor standards and mechanisms for their enforcement; and legal frameworks for peaceful collective self-help and collective bargaining through trade unions. Government regulation of wages and working conditions alone has never been sufficient to meet the challenges of industrial unrest, especially in the more productive sectors of the economy. And so institutions of collective self-help and national frameworks for collective bargaining are at the core of the industrial relations systems of "regulatory capitalism," varying forms of which emerged across the developed world in the twentieth century.[2] Much of the initial construction of these institutions in the United States was compressed into the dramatic New Deal period of reform in the 1930s.

The history of labor conflict and its resolution among the early industrializers of the world, and the United States in particular, might illuminate the dilemmas China faces as it seeks to manage labor unrest in its increasingly advanced industrial market economy. The point here is neither to predict nor to prescribe China's path in the years ahead. For their part, China's leaders view the twentieth-century history of industrial conflict and reform in the West as more of a cautionary tale than a model. They hope to replicate some of the results of those reforms—reasonably peaceful and productive industrial relations and greater economic equality and prosperity—without repeating either the history of independent labor activism or the democratic politics and mass movements that brought them about. Yet that history may contain clues as to whether and how China's leaders can pull off that feat. In particular, a closer look at the central role of independent unions in resolving America's twentieth-century labor troubles may cast light on the question of whether or how China can resolve its twenty-first-century labor troubles without allowing independent unions.

The history and shape of labor unrest and reform in the West, or in our own particular corner of the West, is also worth examining because it is likely to color, consciously or otherwise, the lens through which outsiders observe China's development from afar. That experience inevitably colored my own early impressions of China's labor landscape, and it surely continues to do so in some measure. That is all the more reason to bring into better focus the comparative lens that I bring to this project before proceeding to examine China's response to recent labor conflict. My chief point of comparative reference is the U.S. history of industrial relations and reform—or a highly compressed version of it. At times, however, I widen the lens to offer generalizations about "Western" experience in this domain. Varied though it is, that experience has some common features that are worth casting into sharper relief.

## A Brief History of Labor Conflict and Reform in the United States

Conflict between labor and capital, and between workers and employers, has been a persistent feature of social and political life in the industrialized market economies of the world. As owners and managers seek greater control, higher productivity, and a bigger share of revenues, workers seek to protect their rights and advance their interests. They may do so as individuals through labor markets with whatever bargaining power they can muster under varying market conditions. They may do so through politics when they can, pressing for the enactment of legal rights and minimum standards, and for state support in enforcing them.[3] And when neither labor markets nor legal mandates alone enable them to get what they think they deserve, workers have sought to aggregate their economic power and amplify their individual voices through collective self-help.

Workers' political-regulatory strategy as well as their collective self-help strategy correspond to societal strategies for dealing with labor conflict. In other words, policy makers may well conclude that stronger and better-enforced legal rights and labor standards and fair frameworks for peaceful collective bargaining may reduce conflict by addressing workers' grievances. The regulatory strategy is not incompatible in principle with China's current political system and has been under construction for over a quarter century. That strategy for dealing with labor conflict has its own complications, and it invites its own comparative perspective, undertaken in Chapter 5. This chapter will focus chiefly on workers' collective self-help strategies and the industrial relations structures that the United States and other modern developed economies have devised for channeling and accommodating those self-help strategies. That dimension of labor reform meets resistance in China because of the threat that collective labor activism poses to China's one-party system. But collective labor activism once loomed as a threat to basic social, economic, and political order in the United States, too. Let us turn to that history, sketched here in broad strokes.

## The Rise of the "Labor Question" in the United States

Once upon a time, individual artisans produced goods and services using their own tools, perhaps with the help of a few servants.[4] For republican thinkers in early America, skilled artisans, along with yeoman farmers, were among the iconic citizens whose economic independence supplied the essential foundation for political independence and civic virtue.[5] That foundation began to crumble in the nineteenth century with the rise of the factory system, the separation of labor from ownership of capital, and the aggregation of capital in the corporate form. In hopes of retaining some modicum of autonomy, workers in the various trades began to organize associations. Through both political agitation and collective self-help, they sought through those associations not only to improve terms and conditions of employment but to control the pace and manner of production itself; for much of the nineteenth century, skilled workers resisted incorporation into the factory system as dependent "wage slaves."[6] But as wage labor and the factory system conquered the productive sphere, particularly after the Civil War and the end of slavery, and as labor was increasingly commodified and traded through labor markets, workers and their organizations converged around two main strategies—the legislation of minimum labor standards and collective self-help through trade unions—as means of improving their working lives and the rewards of work within the wage labor system.

Employers, for their part, resisted both regulatory and collective self-help initiatives, preferring to deal with workers as individuals, to control production, and to extract more of the returns for themselves. Through the early twentieth century, American employers found allies in the courts, and especially the federal courts, whose gospel of individual "liberty of contract" made little room for either workers' concerted action or minimum labor standards legislation.[7] The result was to delay and compress the process of enacting minimum labor standards and an industrial relations framework, and to intensify the conflict that preceded it.

A graphic depiction of the past century of labor conflict in the United States hints at just how complicated a story there is to be told here (if there were room to tell it). Figure 4.1 shows the number of workers involved in strikes each year from 1917 to 2014. (The black line represents participants in strikes involving over six workers, official data on which ended in 1980; the gray line represents participants in "major strikes"—over one thousand participants—data on which began in 1947.) I will refer back to this graph several times. But the first thing to note for now is that, in terms of workers affected, labor strife spiked to nearly the highest absolute level in the century in 1919—over four million workers—before dropping precipitously to its pre–New Deal low in 1930. This was a lull before the storm. The second thing to note is that in 1937, when the National Labor Relations Act (NLRA) was held valid, strike activity reached a peak, attaining a level not seen since 1919. Yet this peak was surpassed during and after World War II. Strike levels then declined through the early 1960s, spiked again during the tumultuous late 1960s and 1970s, and then began their steady decline. "Major strike" levels in the United States in the past decade are the lowest ever recorded in official government statistics.

We will return to some of the puzzles raised by these numbers below. But it is critical to keep in mind that the numbers do not tell the whole story. The magnitude of the labor unrest problem is not only about the number or size of strikes, but about the nature of strikes—especially their violence (or not) and their politicization (or not). So let us return to the story with all of this in mind.

By the early twentieth century, the trade unions, led mainly by the American Federation of Labor (AFL) and its base of skilled craft workers,

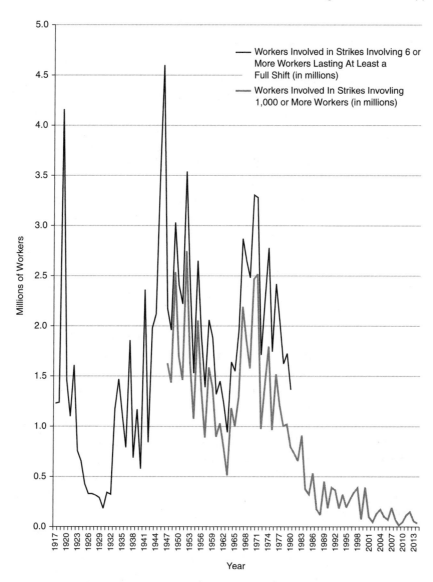

FIGURE 4.1 Workers Participating in Work Stoppages, United States, 1917 to 2014. *Note:* data for workers participating in stoppages involving 1000 workers or more was available only after 1947 while data for workers participating in stoppages involving 6 workers or more, lasting one full shift, was available only until 1980. *Sources:* Florence Peterson, *Strikes in the United States* 1880–1936; U.S. Bureau of Labor Statistics.

were engaged in intense organizing campaigns, strikes, boycotts, and other collective action aimed at pressuring employers to employ union members and to raise wages and other labor standards. Workers' efforts to bring collective economic pressure on private employers in these "interest disputes" were frequently met with employer and state repression—criminal sanctions, judicial injunctions, civil penalties, and the batons and bullets of local police and state and private militias. Not all employers fought unionization solely with "sticks"; some also deployed more sophisticated positive strategies to which we will return below. But employer resistance and violent repression of worker unrest were more severe in the United States than in many other industrialized nations, at least judging by the percentage of striking workers killed or injured during strikes.[8] The labor movement and its leaders were bruised, battered, and often weakened by these confrontations (and union membership and strike levels actually declined in the 1920s, as Figure 4.1 shows); but they were also hardened and, in some instances, radicalized.[9] Much of the political establishment seemed to have turned its back on workers and sided with the bosses.

The Great Depression both deepened economic misery and shook public confidence in capitalism and "free markets." Labor conflict grew more frequent and intense; and when it was met with private and especially public force, it also became more violent and more political.[10] In the early 1930s, several general strikes engulfed whole cities—Minneapolis and San Francisco in particular—and dramatically signaled the politicization of labor unrest. In the meantime, new industrial unions began to organize whole factories and industries, to demand wide-reaching structural reforms in the organization of industrial life, and to raise questions of class justice and the distribution of wealth.[11] Communist and socialist parties gained many adherents within the labor movement, especially in the industrial unions.[12] By the early 1930s, the "labor question," and the rising intensity and politicization of labor disputes, topped the domestic political agenda, and seemed to pose a dire threat to the political and economic order.

### The New Deal Answer to America's Labor Question

With the newly formed Congress of Industrial Organizations (CIO) in a leading role, workers and their allies began to press for a systemic solution to the "labor question" in the form of government support for union organizing and collective bargaining.[13] Structural reform of industrial relations—a settlement that would preserve the prevailing constitutional and capitalist system by reforming it—was a major plank of Franklin Roosevelt's New Deal platform when he won a resounding victory in

1932.[14] That victory, and America's New Deal, was built not only by political leaders from above but by industrial workers and their unions from
below. As historian Lizbeth Cohen has shown, the industrial unions, with
their deep roots in factories and working class neighborhoods, organized
workers and agitated for reform openly, creatively, and vigorously at the
local, state, and national levels.[15] CIO activists, through strikes, street-level
mobilization, mass media, and electoral politics, joined with political
leaders, intellectuals, and other social activists to mount a challenge to the
incumbent powers-that-be and to the conservative ideology that had held
sway, especially in the courts, for decades. (For China's leaders, the bottom-
up political agitation that helped to secure the New Deal labor reforms
may appear as fearsome as the reforms themselves.)

The first iteration of labor reform, part of the National Industrial
Recovery Act of 1933 (NIRA), reflected powerful corporatist impulses
that were in circulation at that low ebb of confidence in markets and capitalism.[16] The NIRA sought to integrate organized labor, alongside collectively organized employers and trade associations, into the cooperative
management of firms and of the economy as a whole; the aim was to
supplant "free competition" with "fair competition."[17] Had that model
taken hold, the U.S. economic system would have more closely resembled
those of Northern Europe, and would have made China's version of "state
corporatism" more recognizable to us.[18] It did not. Although the NIRA
helped to launch a wave of union organizing, it was already showing fatal
infirmities when it was struck down by the Supreme Court as unconstitutional in 1935.[19]

In the meantime, however, workers' political agitation and their votes
had helped to bring about a massive Democratic victory in the 1934 mid-
term congressional elections. That political groundswell, plus a growing
belief among elites in the justice of workers' demands, helped ease the way
for a new round of labor reform to legitimize unions and collective bargaining. A surge of strike activity in 1934 and 1935 underscored the case
for reform and helped to secure the enactment of the NLRA, or Wagner
Act, which set up the basic framework for union organizing and collective
bargaining that governs most of the U.S. private sector to this day.

In 1935, however, the NLRA's survival beyond its infancy was in much
doubt. Congress passed the statute just weeks after the Supreme Court had
struck down the NIRA on constitutional grounds that seemed likely to
doom the new law as well. Moreover, in the immediate wake of the NLRA's
enactment, strike levels spiked. Workers and unions, now fighting for and
backed by their newly granted federal rights, intensified their organizing
activity and their demands for recognition; yet many employers, convinced

that the Supreme Court would strike down the NLRA as unconstitutional, defied the law and refused to deal with unions representing large majorities of their workers.[20] The clash between newly emboldened workers and unions and recalcitrant employers contributed to the escalation of strike activity in 1936 and 1937, including "sit-in" strikes in major industries and general strikes in major cities.[21] When the Supreme Court surprised the nation by upholding the NLRA in 1937, it relied chiefly on the instrumental value of its structural reforms in securing "industrial peace" as the basis for its decision.[22]

Clearly "industrial peace" was not the only goal of the New Deal labor settlement.[23] The NLRA sought to promote justice, liberty, and democracy in industrial life, and to redress the "inequality of bargaining power" that unions and New Dealers believed was inherent in the relationship between individual workers and employers. The law's guarantee of basic freedoms of association and peaceful expression and self-help made workers into quasi-citizens of the workplace, and enabled them, by majority rule, to claim a role in industrial governance through collective bargaining. But those rights gained legal backing in the early 1930s, in both the legislature and the courts, partly because they came to be seen as essential to quelling industrial conflict and securing social order. In short, the goals of economic justice, freedom, and democracy and the votes of workers and their allies may not have been sufficient to secure either the NLRA's passage by Congress or its approval by the Supreme Court were it not for the waves of industrial unrest that underscored the link between a more just economic order and basic social and political stability.[24]

The salience of "industrial peace" in the New Deal settlement usefully reminds us of what is commonplace about China's current quest for "harmonious labor relations." All industrial societies have confronted serious labor disputes, and their leaders, whether elected or not, strive to keep those disputes from boiling over, threatening social order, and stalling the engines of economic growth. And so industrial unrest has often spurred policy makers to seek peaceful solutions to labor conflict—preferably structural solutions and not mere one-off settlements of particular disputes. Indeed, even in democratic societies, workers have rarely gotten major structural reforms—especially reforms that empower workers' organizations—without demanding them through agitation and escalation of conflict. So China watchers, as well as China's leaders, have good reason to ponder the means by which the New Dealers pursued and eventually achieved the goal of industrial peace.

With the NLRA of 1935, workers and their unions gained major structural reforms: Section 7 of the Act recognized workers' right to form independent trade unions and to engage in other collective action, including strikes, free from employer interference and reprisals. Although strikes were in one sense the problem that Congress was seeking to solve, it did so partly by legally *protecting* strikes, and curtailing the state and employer repression of workers' collective action that had proven so inflammatory and counterproductive. But protecting strikes was not enough; the Act also sought to attack the cause of most strikes by compelling employers to deal with unions. It created a basic legal framework for collective bargaining centered on employers' duty to recognize and bargain in good faith with a union that represented a majority of workers in an "appropriate bargaining unit" within the enterprise. And the law created a federal administrative agency, the National Labor Relations Board (NLRB), to oversee union representation elections and enforce the law.

The NLRA put the power of the federal government behind the right to form unions and to engage in collective bargaining. But the whole design of the law aimed to keep state intervention to a minimum, and to preserve a wide ambit for collective freedom of contract, in both the determination of substantive terms and conditions of employment and the resolution of collective disputes. The NLRA's framework for collective self-determination was touted as an alternative to direct government regulation of wages and working conditions.[25] Yes, Congress soon passed the Fair Labor Standards Act of 1938 (FLSA), which banned child labor and established a national minimum wage and a mandatory overtime premium for hours over forty per week. But in the core industries in which unions were active, Congress expected wages, hours, job security, and other matters to be set by the parties themselves. It was through unionization and collective bargaining that most workers and employers were expected to resolve most rights and interest disputes going forward. The prospect of costly but non-violent (and legally protected) economic conflict would lead unions and employers to compromise and reach collective agreements, which would in turn establish jointly administered procedures for the resolution of disputes during the term of the agreement.

The New Deal labor legislation did indeed lay the groundwork for resolving "the labor question" in the United States (though not initially by reducing strike levels). After 1937, employers grudgingly accepted the NLRA as the law of the land and began to bargain with unions that demonstrated majority support. Employers did not give up their opposition to the new labor regime. They plotted to roll it back in the future, and they persuaded the Supreme Court in several early decisions to tame the NLRA's "radical" potential for empowering workers and unions by limiting the scope of workers' statutory rights as against employer property

rights and managerial prerogatives.[26] Still, in that first decade, unions succeeded in organizing much of the core of the expanding industrial economy.
Collective bargaining became normalized and institutionalized, and wages
and benefits in the growing union sector rose.

The institutionalization of collective bargaining did not, however, mean
the end or even the immediate decline of strikes, as shown in Figure 4.1.
On the contrary, the law recognized that strikes and the prospect of strikes
were the main leverage by which unions secured concessions in collective
bargaining, and strike levels rose along with rising union density for well
over a decade, both during and especially just after World War II. But by
and large these were ordinary—if sometimes dramatic and disruptive—
interest disputes between employers and workers that were fought within
the new collective bargaining framework. Police and strikers no longer
engaged in extended street battles, and workers' grievances no longer escalated into "general strikes."[27] In short, after 1937, industrial unrest became
much less political and much less violent, and no longer posed an existential threat to the established political and economic order.[28]

This might be a pleasant place to conclude this comparative interlude,
and to draw a simple set of implications for Chinese reformers: Conflict is
a fact of industrial life, and its repression risks transforming ordinary
rights and interest disputes into political disputes. The solution to industrial conflict lies instead in structural reforms that empower workers to act
collectively through their own organizations and that channel conflict into
fair and peaceful procedures for collective bargaining, as well as into relatively contained and non-political industrial conflict. But there is more to
the story, and it will complicate the implications for China.

### The New Deal's Cold War Coda: Restrictions on Union Activity and the Rise of "Business Unionism"

The end of World War II saw a sharp uptick in labor conflict in the United
States: "The confluence of workers' determination to catch up with inflation through large wage increases and management's determination to
tighten up its control over the shop floor . . . provoked the largest strike
wave in the country's history; 4.6 million people walked off their jobs in
1946."[29] (Per Figure 4.1, that was the highest level of strike activity in the
whole century.) Some of these strikes stalled major industries and were
costly and disruptive to businesses, workers, and the wider public. Business
interests seeking to roll back the NLRA were emboldened by a growing
(though far from universal) sense that unions had become "too powerful"
and high-handed, as well as by the rise of conservative, anti-Communist

and anti-leftist political sentiment.[30] This coalition dealt organized labor a monumental defeat with the Taft-Hartley Act of 1947.[31] According to Alan Hyde (as of 1990), "[t]he Taft-Hartley Act was the last effective labor legislation in an advanced industrial economy which is wholly repressive of union power and contains no element of concessions to workers."[32]

The Taft-Hartley amendments did not undo the basic protections of the NLRA, but they recast the shape of national labor policy in crucial ways. Taft-Hartley shifted national labor policy away from overt encouragement of collective bargaining and toward the more neutral promotion of "employee free choice," and it expressly affirmed employers' freedom to oppose unionization (though not to threaten or coerce employees).[33] Most important, the law sharply reduced unions' power by outlawing some of their most effective tactics: It banned strikes or picketing aimed at "secondary" employers (those doing business with a "primary" employer whose labor practices were in dispute);[34] and it restricted some "top-down organizing" tactics that pressured employers to recognize and bargain with a union without proof of employees' majority support.[35] These restrictions on the scope of lawful collective action were buttressed by provisions for injunctions and monetary damages against unions in federal court.[36] In hindsight, and as a purely descriptive matter, one can say that the federal regulation of labor relations in the United States was carried out in two stages: first the Wagner Act legitimated and empowered unions, and then the Taft-Hartley amendments regulated and restricted them.

One more feature of the Taft-Hartley Act is worth noting: it effectively banned Communist Party members from serving as officers in labor unions that sought to use the NLRB's unfair labor practice process.[37] Cold War anxieties over the "Communist threat" to national security had led Congress to intervene in the internal affairs of labor unions to curb the influence of militant union leaders and to tame the most left-wing unions. I do not mean to equate this intervention with China's hierarchical control over its official unions; for one thing, the successor to this anti-Communist provision, like several other Cold War anti-communist enactments, was later struck down by the Supreme Court as unconstitutional.[38] But it is a reminder that encroachments upon labor union independence to curb union militancy and meet a perceived threat to political stability is not entirely foreign to American experience.

The Taft-Hartley amendments, and especially the restrictions on peaceful picketing, were furiously denounced by organized labor; in another time they might have provoked a major political backlash. But as the chilly political climate of the Cold War settled in, the major labor federations, the AFL and the CIO, succumbed to anti-Communist pressures, both legal and political, and purged many energetic and militant left-wing activists from their ranks.[39] After 1955, the newly merged AFL-CIO settled into the relatively sedate rhythms of "business unionism": unions bargained, often quite effectively, to increase their members' share of the growing economic pie, but they largely abandoned efforts to organize new sectors of the economy, to empower the working classes in general, or to challenge either managerial control of production or larger features of the "free enterprise system."[40] The unions got a seat at the table in national economic policy making, and their members got steadily increasing wages and benefits, job security, and a decent system of dispute resolution. Strikes continued to occur, but they were largely routine conflicts conducted within the post-1947 legal boundaries. They did not, and were not meant to, challenge the economic, political, or social order.

Stable industrial relations structures contributed in more quotidian ways to the productivity of the core unionized sectors of American industry. Turnover declined and long-term investment in skills increased as wages grew and seniority was rewarded, and as autocratic supervisory discretion gave way to fairer and more impersonal disciplinary and promotional processes. Well-paid and secure unionized workers became the core of the prosperous American middle class, while large swaths of the labor market were left unorganized and unions' share of the private sector work-force began its seemingly inexorable decline. (We will turn to those numbers soon.)

If we were to end our comparative interlude here, the potential implications for China would be quite different from those suggested by the New Deal history, and less encouraging to many proponents of collective bargaining. First, the benefits of collective bargaining are likely to accrue primarily to the workers in the core industries who have more market power to begin with, and who are most capable of exerting economic leverage in support of demands; the poorest workers who most need help may derive the least benefit from collective bargaining, and are likely to require much more direct forms of state support. Second, state protection of strikes and other concerted self-help is very likely to come with boundaries, and even with sharp edges that can cut into workers' rights and their gains. The edges were sharper in the United States than in many other democratic Western countries, but the boundedness of collective labor rights—limits on the timing, aims, and tactics of collective action—is endemic to modern industrial relations regimes, and it is part of how societies secure "industrial peace." Both of those cautionary notes might concern some advocates of collective labor rights and bargaining structures in China. But there is more of the story yet to come.

## One Last Round of Labor Law Reform and the Long Decline of Strikes and of Unions

In the late 1950s, unions were still powerful economic actors—powerful in relation to both employers and individual workers—in many regions and industry sectors. Another legislative coalition formed around an effort to address problems of corruption and mob influence in unions, as well as union suppression of internal dissent and internal democracy. The last set of problems is of particular interest here given the problem of unresponsiveness and lack of democratic accountability in the All-China Federation of Trade Unions (ACFTU). In the United States, the biggest threat to internal union democracy historically has been not outside interference from the state but *incumbent* suppression of internal dissent and control of elections for union leadership.[41] The Labor-Management Reporting and Disclosure Act of 1959 (LMRDA), with its "union members' bill of rights," set out in part to address that problem. It protects union members' freedom of expression and due process rights inside the union, and it regulates union election procedures to limit incumbents' ability to insulate themselves from democratic contestation and dissent.[42]

The U.S. law governing internal union affairs, including elections, both underscores and complicates a broad comparative point about the treatment of collective labor activity in "regulatory capitalism": Unions in the advanced Western democracies are self-governing associations of workers; they are not controlled by the state, but they are to varying degrees *regulated* by the state. In the United States, regulatory intervention even reaches into unions' internal governance in ways that are unusual in the West and that were very controversial when enacted (though that intervention is minimal as compared to the control that the Communist Party of China exercises over the ACFTU and its branches). One major legislative objective was to protect rank-and-file workers' ability to elect their preferred candidates in place of entrenched and (sometimes corrupt) incumbents. And indeed American unions may be more democratic than they were before the LMRDA was enacted.[43] They are also smaller and weaker.

The post-1950s slide toward single-digit union density in the United States was far from uneventful. In the late 1960s and early 1970s, rebellions of various shades shook much of the world, including Eastern and Western Europe and China. The American civil rights and anti-war movements both grew more intense—again partly in response to violent resistance. And after years of declining strike levels, labor unrest also began to surge. As David Montgomery describes it, "[t]he ensuing wave of strikes in America," from West Virginia's coal miners, to a national work stoppage at General Electric, to the strike at General Motors' factory in Lordstown, Ohio, "sharply challenged management's authority and rationality, and often that of established union practice and leadership as well."[44] Some of these strikes were led by newly energized unions responding to a wave of worker discontent with a dehumanizing factory regimen. But many were "wildcat" strikes by workers in defiance of union leaders whom they saw as staid and unresponsive. The complacent patterns of business unionism had left some workers without what they regarded as effective representation, and then collective action spilled outside of the legal boundaries that the unions were charged with enforcing.

In the United States, unlike in many Western European countries, no significant collective labor law reforms emerged out of this turbulent period.[45] The strike wave soon crested, and the onset of economic recession and the beginnings of "deindustrialization" put workers and unions on the defensive. In the 1970s and 1980s, America's post-World War II industrial dominance was eroding under growing competition from the rebuilt economies of Europe and Japan, and later from the developing world (including China). Unions' hard-won gains for industrial workers were part of the problem. In 1977, the average hourly wage in the U.S. iron and steel industry was $12.31, compared to $6.50 in Japan and $8.68 in West Germany.[46]

As American manufacturers fought for market share at home and abroad, they began to push back against high labor costs, to aggressively mechanize production, and to shrink or close the gigantic industrial plants that had powered U.S. economic dominance and organized labor's gains in the post-war period. America's unionized blue-collar workers in turn sought to defend once-secure jobs and generous wages and benefits against layoffs, factory closings, and employer demands for give-backs. But strikes were bound to be less effective in response to these new threats, especially as the U.S. employers themselves began to move production to cheaper jurisdictions or to outsource it to overseas suppliers. The strike threat was further muffled once employers in the 1980s grew more aggressive in exercising their long-recognized but little-used right under the NLRA to permanently replace economic strikers.[47] Strikes began to appear "suicidal" to unions in most cases, as they opened the door to permanent replacement of strikers, loss of majority support, and decertification of unions.

The mainstream U.S. labor movement eventually woke up to its dire predicament, and to the need to organize new groups of workers and find new ways of pursuing their economic and organizational objectives. But a variety of political and economic forces conspired to embolden and encourage managers to vigorously oppose union organizing—by legal and illegal means—and to resist dealing with unions or making concessions to them. And a peculiar constellation of political forces continued to block even the incremental reforms by which unions sought to strengthen their hand.[48]

Part of the challenge of organizing new groups of workers stemmed from the legal structure of union representation and bargaining under the NLRA: Workers in an "appropriate bargaining unit" within a single enterprise or facility choose by majority rule whether to be represented by a union; and if the union wins a majority, it becomes the "exclusive" representative of all workers in the unit. Gaining union representation thus requires an intense campaign for majority support, and the NLRA (with the First Amendment standing behind it) affords wide latitude for employers to mount a strong campaign in opposition.[49] Employer opposition is almost ensured in an enterprise-based bargaining system, for unionized employers must compete with non-union employers in the same market (unless the entire sector is organized and new entrants face barriers). That fuels strong employer resistance to both union organizing and bargaining demands.[50] By contrast, some advanced industrial democracies embrace the goal of taking labor costs out of competition, in part through sectoral bargaining.[51] In its strongest form, wage bargaining takes place at the national level between the dominant trade union and employer association in each major sector, and the results are extended throughout the sector. But American unions can take wages out of competition only by organizing across the sector—one workplace at a time, and usually in the teeth of strong employer resistance.

Employer resistance takes its toll in both organizing and bargaining. The NLRA is a regime of collective freedom of contract; it aims to redress "inequality of bargaining power" between workers and employers by allowing the former to organize and aggregate their bargaining power. But the law gives a wide berth to the "free play of economic forces" and to both sides' resort to "economic weapons," including permanent replacement of strikers. That commitment to collective freedom of contract has also constrained the employer's duty to bargain in good faith. Senator David Walsh, a leading sponsor of the original Wagner Act, expressed the NLRA's philosophy in stark, oft-quoted language: "When employees have chosen their organization, when they have selected their representative, all the Bill proposes to do is to escort them to the door of the employer and say, 'here they are, the legal representative of your employees.' What happens behind those doors is not inquired into, and the bill does not seek to inquire into it."[52] In language added by Taft-Hartley, the NLRA now explicitly provides that "such obligation does not compel either party to agree to a proposal or require the making of a concessions"; it does not require the employer to reach any agreement at all.[53] The Supreme Court has held that, even when the employer unlawfully refuses to bargain in good faith, the NLRB is not allowed to impose remedies that amount to the imposition of substantive terms of employment.[54] As a result, an employer that is committed to avoiding a collective agreement can generally do so as long as it is willing and able to take or break a strike.

The upshot is that the United States has now managed to secure "industrial peace"—and a remarkably low level of labor conflict—without a large labor movement or a large role for collective bargaining. By 2015, union membership in the private sector had fallen to 6.7 percent, and strike levels had fallen to levels not seen for well over a century: just twelve major work stoppages (those involving 1,000 or more workers and lasting at least one shift) affecting 47,000 workers in total. (By comparison, at the peak of union density in 1952, there were 470 major strikes affecting 2.75 million workers out of a much smaller labor force.)[55]

Meanwhile, workers' economic position has deteriorated and economic inequality has returned to pre-New Deal levels. Indeed, as Figure 4.2 shows, the rise and fall of union membership and strikes have been almost perfectly mirrored by the fall and rise of economic inequality, which has now reached the highest levels seen in the United States since the 1920s. According to leading economists, the decline of collective bargaining, and collectively bargained wage gains, accounts for one-fifth to one-third of the increase in economic inequality over the past decades.[56]

Recent years have seen flashes of worker militancy and new forms of labor organizing, especially at the bottom levels of the service sector in places like Wal-Mart, McDonald's, and Amazon.[57] These unconventional forms of labor activism have been crucial drivers in the surprisingly successful "Fight for Fifteen," which has resulted in several new state and local laws raising the minimum wage (over time) to fifteen dollars per hour.[58] But these mini-movements have thus far entailed almost no work stoppages or economic dislocation, and they have failed to produce new union members or collective bargaining as we know it.[59] Judged against the yardstick of the 1930s—or indeed most of the past century—these are small, almost symbolic insurrections. By all appearances, serious labor unrest is a very remote prospect in the United States today.

In the eyes of many labor activists and allies, the current era of labor peace evokes the "peace of the graveyard." Given the role that labor unrest has historically played in securing redistributive and democratizing reforms, it is hard to see how labor can make significant gains on the political front without making a bigger ruckus. Yet it is also hard to imagine how the

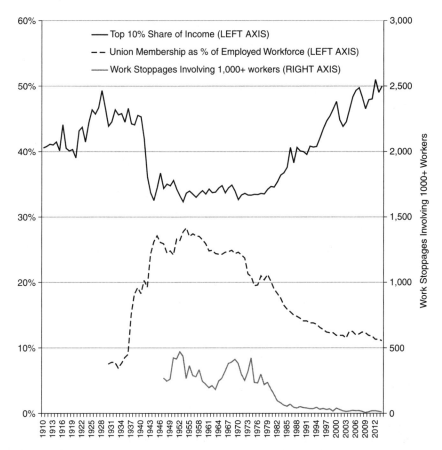

FIGURE 4.2 Income Inequality, Union Membership, & Work Stoppages in the United States, 1910–2014. *Sources:* U.S. Bureau of Labor Statistics; Thomas Piketty, Technical Appendix of the Book Capital in the 21st Century; World Wealth and Income Database; Gerald Mayer, "Union Membership Trends in the United States," Congressional Research Service; Unionstats.com.

current state of repose could have come about without both the swelling of independent labor activism and the basic redistributive labor reforms of the last century. Hence the challenge for China: Its leaders may look with envy on today's very low strike levels in the United States, and would desperately wish to get there from where they are without the intervening years of worker militancy, conflict and disruption. But as long as China's workers are taking to the streets in large numbers, China might have more to learn, or more cause for concern, from the tumultuous American experience of the 1930s and 1940s.

## *A Parallel Plot Line: Changing Modes of Management in the Non-Union Sector*

This brief history of U.S. labor and industrial relations has largely neglected the role of firms and managers, except as a source of resistance to collective bargaining. But there is a more interesting story line in the response of employers to the challenges of workforce management and of labor unrest in a modernizing economy. In the present context, it is a useful complement, or perhaps counterpoint, to the more conventional union-focused story line because of the lessons it might hold for those in China who are seeking to avert independent union organizing and collective bargaining, much as U.S. employers have long sought to do.

In the early twentieth century, a combination of union gains, labor conflict, tight labor markets, and the demands of wartime production led some employers to abandon their reliance on often-arbitrary foremen for hiring, firing, and control of workers, and to turn to more psychologically informed management methods administered by centralized personnel departments.[60] "Scientific management" sought to increase worker productivity by reengineering production (and minimizing control by both workers and low-level supervisors) and by adopting pay structures that aligned the economic interests of labor and management.[61] A competing model of workplace management, the "human relations" model, was based on the premise that more satisfied workers would be more productive. Organized labor responded with suspicion or hostility to both managerial strategies, as both sought to preserve managerial control by rationalizing it rather than by sharing control with workers through collective bargaining.[62] And indeed, the proponents of these new managerial strategies saw organized labor as an obstacle to effective workplace management, not as a partner. The notion that more satisfied workers would be less likely to turn to unions was hardly incidental for managers in the human relations vein.

The eventually dominant human relations school sought to discourage unionization through both "positive" tactics—"company-controlled employee representation programs and an expansion of pension, welfare, and profit-sharing programs"[63]—and "suppressive" tactics—strike breaking, firing and blacklisting union members, forcibly disbanding picket lines, and industrial espionage.[64] The combination of tactics proved to be a successful union avoidance strategy in the 1920s, and union membership declined sharply.[65] But the economic thunderclap of the Great Depression, and employers' resort to mass layoffs, dealt a hard blow to the positive pretensions of the human relations school, and indeed to public confidence in managers and markets generally. As we have already seen, the resurgence in union membership and in labor unrest was accompanied by demands for government intervention in support of collective bargaining, and set the stage for the New Deal industrial relations system. The collective bargaining model eclipsed the human relations model in the academy and in policy circles for several decades.[66] Indeed, the NLRA outlawed one of the cornerstones of the human relations model: employee representation plans that were dominated or supported by management were denigrated as "company unions" and outlawed.

Yet even as the NLRA institutionalized collective bargaining mechanisms for managing labor-management conflict, it did not mandate them or ensure their extension across the economy. In partially unionized or non-unionized firms and industries, personnel management methods were recast to comply (more or less) with the NLRA's constraints on employer conduct. Gone, for example, were the formal employee representation schemes outlawed by the NLRA. But managers continued to hone both the "positive" and the "suppressive" techniques of union avoidance through human relations management. Over the years it has become clear that the successors to the "human relations school" of personnel management, and both their positive and negative techniques, contributed mightily to the decline of unions, and came to overshadow unions as the dominant force in shaping the workplace environment.[67] The center of gravity in the labor field, in both the economy and the academy, has shifted decisively from industrial relations to human resource management (HRM), now the more prevalent term for workforce management methods in the non-union sector.

There are many ironies in this story. The earlier success of the collective bargaining paradigm in achieving peaceful industrial relations fostered the perception that it was no longer necessary, and that human resource managers could now handle the job.[68] Yet the more recent decline of collective bargaining now threatens to undermine the "human relations" paradigm as well. For while the human relations school posited that unions were not necessary to the advancement of employee well-being, union avoidance was a powerful motivating factor for employers that adopted their recommendations.[69] As the threat of unionization has receded, progressive personnel policies are receding as well, at least for workers without scarce skills and talents—the workers who once had turned to unions to improve their lot.

This history might suggest to China's policy makers that its labor pains could be greatly mitigated, and the need for dramatic structural reform of collective labor relations largely averted, if employers were to adopt better management methods along the lines of traditional "human relations" and modern HRM methods. Some Western companies often do bring relatively humane and legally compliant HRM practices from their home countries to their Chinese operations; but their supplier factories, many owned by domestic Chinese, Taiwanese, or Hong Kong-based firms, are widely seen as more harsh and autocratic in their management of workers.[70] Those practices can create a highly combustible workplace environment.

China's political leaders thus have every reason to sharpen the incentives of China's employers to adopt more humanistic and worker-friendly HRM policies. The focus of this book is on China's labor policies, not the management practices of companies operating there. But it is worth asking: what would motivate companies operating in China to invest in more worker-friendly management practices? Managers might conclude that more humane practices would help to avert strikes and other more subtle manifestations of worker discontent that impair productivity. Such practices might also help firms attract, retain, and motivate skilled workers, a growing concern in China as labor markets tighten. Companies that are part of global supply chains may find themselves pressured to improve labor practices by the brands they supply, and by the decades-long campaign for "corporate social responsibility"; Apple and its gigantic Taiwan-based supplier, Foxconn, provide a case in point.[71]

China's leaders directly control other levers of influence on management. Decent labor standards and the serious prospect of their enforcement through the legal system tend to go hand in hand with more worker-friendly management practices (in part by ruling out aspects of the harsh low-wage, long-hours, sweatshop strategy). A legal framework for real collective bargaining through unions that are accountable to workers can also induce companies to adopt more worker-friendly management practices, either through collective bargaining itself or as a means of union avoidance. So in examining the various reform strategies by which China seeks to address its "labor question" in the next four chapters, it will be worth reflecting on how those reform strategies may affect workplace management practices. If China's labor reforms do nudge companies toward the high road in workforce management, there will be less employee discontentment to fuel both workplace conflict and independent organizing. That would be an unmixed blessing for China's leaders, if not for those hoping for transformative industrial relations reforms.

## Collective Action as Leverage, Independent Unions as Its Regulators

It is tempting to look for "lessons" for China in the rise and fall of organized labor and of labor unrest in the United States, and in the industrial relations and management structures that shaped and were shaped by those developments. It is tempting to me in part because, in the course of many conversations, lectures, conferences, and classroom discussions over the past decade in China, I have been struck by the intense interest of my Chinese interlocutors in that U.S. history, precisely for the lessons that it might or might not hold for China's own "labor question." It is obvious that China is charting its own course through this stormy industrial relations period, and it is doing so in a world that is much changed from the twentieth-century world in which the United States charted its course. So (again) the main point of reviewing the U.S. experience is not to prescribe or predict China's path but to illuminate it. I aim to bring into sharper relief the preconceptions that may shape our own understanding—that of author and readers alike—of what is going on in China and where it is headed. Even so, it may be heuristically useful to consider possible "lessons" for China from the U.S. history of labor conflict and reform; they may serve as hypotheses to be reassessed, and perhaps rejected, as we delve into China's recent reforms in the chapters to come.

Let us begin with one rather well-tested hypothesis: Conflict of one kind or another is endemic to industrial life. What most workers want is not turmoil or revolution but decent work and rewards that are commensurate with the wider economy and their contributions to the enterprise. And most workers surely prefer compromise to conflict. But there is an inherent asymmetry, even in competitive labor markets, between individual workers and employers dealing with an entire workforce. Workers need some form of leverage—collective leverage, that is—to bring employers to the table and induce them to compromise over the distribution of rewards between labor and management. For most workers who lack scarce skills, the main leverage they have is their labor power and their ability to disrupt production by its withdrawal and to draw public attention and put pressure on employers by assembling and demonstrating. Employers may silently fold their hands and refuse to talk, but workers often have to shake things up by putting their bodies and voices on the street.

Once workers' discontent ripens into open conflict, the state response is crucial. State repression of labor conflict, even in the name of public order, is readily construed as taking the employer's side, for it strips workers of their most effective weapons in an unfair fight. When striking workers confront a government show of force, conflict often escalates, and becomes more violent, more political, or both. In the United States in the 1920s and 1930s, the state's efforts to forcibly suppress organizing and strikes helped to steer many union activists into socialist and communist politics that began to look like a threat to private property, market ordering, and even the "republican form of government."[72]

There is a logic in the escalation from ordinary to extraordinary labor disputes. Ordinary collective disputes may arise out of the violation of workers' legal rights (for example, unpaid wages or safety violations) or out of conflicting economic interests. These *rights disputes* and *interest disputes* between workers and their employers are endemic to industrial life, and are the daily fare of modern industrial relations structures.[73] If such structures are absent or inadequate, however, rights and interest disputes may be more disorderly, and may give way to *structural disputes* based on demands for institutional reforms that better enable workers to secure their rights and interests in the future.[74] And if workers' structural demands are not or cannot be accommodated within the existing political system, and especially if they are forcibly suppressed, labor disputes may turn into *political disputes* and even insurrection.

Intense labor conflict can thus be a catalyst for structural reforms that result in the recognition of collective rights and the formation of institutions through which workers can peacefully pursue their economic interests and resolve disputes with employers going forward. At some point— as in the tumultuous run-up to the New Deal in the United States—even dramatically redistributive reforms may become an acceptable price for economic elites to pay for maintaining the political and economic order. And once workers gain basic rights and fair ground rules for the resolution of their ordinary rights and interest disputes with employers, those ordinary disputes are far less likely to escalate into challenges to social order or political stability.[75]

In short, serious labor conflict has often preceded and helped to give rise to fundamental labor rights and fair labor relations structures; those labor relations structures in turn have helped to avert future labor conflicts. American workers won their rights to organize and bargain collectively *not* (or not only) by electing friendly legislators, or by persuading elites of the justice of their cause, but largely by making those rights the price of industrial peace—by creating a serious problem of labor unrest to which independent unions and collective bargaining became the solution. At a very general level, the pattern holds for many industrial relations regimes that took shape in the European and Anglo-American countries of the advanced capitalist world in the mid-twentieth century, both before and after the cataclysmic ruptures of fascism and war.[76] Even in societies in which labor-based political parties have held power, workers' votes alone did not produce the basic labor relations reforms of the mid-twentieth century. As Alan Hyde has put it, "sweeping legislative reform[] of labor law . . . [i]n advanced, Western economies . . . is most frequently a concession to a union movement or working class which is making trouble."[77]

To be sure, workers' votes and democratic political institutions may have been *necessary* to their gaining basic collective labor rights.[78] China's workers cannot vote for reforms, or for leaders who promise reforms. That is a huge caveat to any effort to extrapolate from the history of Western democracies to the future of China, and one that will occupy us going forward. But it is not clear that workers' votes were *sufficient* in the West, or at least in the United States, for organized labor to win the recognition, privileges, and powers embodied in modern industrial relations structures. That happened when workers and their organizations created a problem in the form of labor unrest, and "industrial peace" became a major policy priority for elites. Industrial peace is undoubtedly a policy priority for China's leaders, too; for while they cannot be voted out of office, they fear the consequences of unrest for economic growth and regime stability. That is what has moved them to consider reforming and rebalancing industrial relations, to make unions more responsive and collective bargaining more meaningful.

Let us probe a bit further, however, and ask *how* independent unions and collective bargaining brought about a tolerable level of labor peace in the United States. They did so partly by giving workers reasonable alternatives to ever-escalating agitation as a way to resolve their disputes with employers: collective bargaining enabled workers to resolve interest disputes, and grievance-arbitration mechanisms enabled them to resolve rights disputes under the collective contract. But that is not the whole answer. Strikes and agitation remained the energizing force in the collective bargaining process. Modern labor laws protected much of that collective activity and made it easier for unions to organize such activity. So what kept workers' collective action in check and within tolerable bounds? The answer, paradoxically, is "unions." The labor laws effectively interposed unions as intermediate regulatory institutions between workers and the state.

Once workers gain the organizational capacity and will to pursue shared economic interests through strikes and other forms of collective protest, direct state regulation of collective action has often proven to be costly and counterproductive. The use of force—armed police, criminal prosecutions, detentions, and jail sentences—tends to intensify and politicize the conflict by broadening the focus of workers' collective discontent from private employers to public officials and institutions.[79] The NLRA, like other modern labor laws, enables government to regulate workers' collective dissent indirectly through the intermediate institutions of trade unions—the very institutions that were leading workers' protests.

The labor law framework that took hold in the mid-twentieth century in the United States offered unions a tacit quid pro quo: Unions gained public legitimacy, a bundle of privileges and protections, and the ability to secure gains for workers through peaceful channels. But those gains were conditioned, more or less explicitly, on a corresponding set of restrictions on collective labor activity—restrictions on its timing, scope, and aims—and on the unions' acceptance of a regulatory role in securing industrial peace through collective bargaining.[80] In short, the government regulates unions, and unions regulate workers. (The labor laws also regulated employers, of course; and the laws' restrictions on employer self-help were also crucial to solving "the labor question.")

In the United States, the NLRA enabled workers to organize themselves into unions, and it enabled unions in turn to tap workers' collective power to disrupt production, to direct it into peaceful forms of economic conflict, and to strategically deploy that power to achieve instrumental ends. But unions could deploy workers' collective power as leverage only by regulating it—by being able to end or avoid strikes as well as to start them. Unions were induced to keep collective action within lawful bounds through a combination of rights and rewards (including better contracts, dues payments, and a seat at the table among policy makers) and punishments (including injunctions, fines, and damages awards against violent or other unlawful activity). The rights and rewards came with the Wagner Act in 1935, while the restrictions and sanctions were codified with the Taft-Hartley Act in 1947.[81]

American labor law is more heavy-handed than many Western industrial relations regimes in appointing unions as the chief regulators of workers' collective action, and American unions have arguably acceded to that regulatory role more fully than many Western labor movements have done.[82] But there is a deep logic to the basic quid pro quo embodied in the NLRA—for the offer of legitimacy, institutional support, and protection in exchange for the unions' role in regulating the timing, scope, and disruptiveness of strikes.[83] If workers basically trust their unions, and if the unions basically accept the legal rules of engagement, then the government can step back from the front lines of labor conflict and assume the status of neutral referee, policing both parties' respect for the lawful boundaries of conflict and administering the overall framework. The society can secure industrial peace, and avoid the politicization and escalation of labor conflict, by regulating unions and employers.[84] The mid-twentieth-century settlement of the "labor question" thus made independent unions central to the regulation of labor conflict.

In China, the notion that unions should regulate workers' collective action is self-evident and explicit; it is a central mission of China's official union. But here's the rub: Unions can regulate workers only if workers submit to union leadership. And workers will be led by the union only if they *trust* the union as their agent—accountable not to the state nor to employers but to them—and only if they can expect to improve their lot by working through the union rather than striking out on their own. Independent unions earn workers' allegiance in part by their performance— their ability to solve workers' problems and to deploy the threat of unrest strategically to advance workers' shared interests—and in part by the procedural legitimacy that stems from democratic accountability mechanisms. But when unions become passive, entrenched, or out of touch with workers' concerns, normal workplace disputes may break out into "wildcat strikes," as they have at times in the United States, and as they have been doing lately in China.

The problem for U.S. workers today—at least for those without specialized skills that fetch a good price on the market—is not unresponsive unions but no unions. Most of them face a future without union representation or collective bargaining, and without any alternative mechanism for lifting their wages and working conditions above what the (under-regulated) market will bear. It seems clear that the waning of serious labor conflict in the United States has tended to erode workers' power and their ability to make either economic gains through existing labor relations structures or structural reforms through the political process.[85]

China's leaders, observing the rise and fall of both unions and labor conflict in the United States, would surely prefer to leap over the tumult of industrial conflict and reform and go straight to the period of labor repose that may lie beyond it. (If that is their hope, they should find ways to encourage managers to improve and humanize their workforce management practices as well as raise wages.) But even if that is possible, those in the regime who worry about rising economic inequality should recall the conspicuous correlation throughout the twentieth century between economic equality and both union density and strike levels.


AMERICAN LABOR LAW will serve as a cautionary tale—for Western as well as Chinese readers—more than once in the chapters that follow. Some of its particulars are unusual in the West, including the severity and breadth of its restrictions on union activity.[86] We will take up a few of those particulars sparingly as they arise. But one exceptional feature of U.S. labor law is its sheer obduracy. The basic labor legislation for the private sector has undergone no major revision since 1947, and has been almost untouched since 1959.[87] Even if the law was well suited to the needs of employers and workers in 1959—and not, as many claim, skewed against organized labor—too much has changed in the American economy in the succeeding half century to imagine that it serves those needs now. Nobody should entertain the illusion that American labor law is a model for other countries. Still, the core principle that it shares with other Western labor law systems—that workers should be able to bargain collectively with employers through representatives that they choose and control—remains powerful, and a historically tested solution to the problem of serious collective labor unrest.

China's leaders are well aware of that history, but they also seek to make their own history within a radically different political system. The question for China's leaders is whether and how they can secure the industrial stability, broad-based prosperity, and political legitimacy that they aspire to without the independent labor activism that they fear. Reform is essential, but what kind of reform?

Let us now turn to four distinct aspects of labor reform by which China has sought to respond to the problem of labor unrest: Chapter 5 addresses the regulatory strategy, by which the state promises to deliver decent labor standards without resort to the messy business of collective activism. Chapter 6 turns to the rise of strikes and the distinctive forms of "collective bargaining" by which officials in China seek to resolve or avoid strikes. Chapter 7 takes up the related issue of union democracy, very limited forms of which have made it onto the agenda of both worker activists and reformers. Finally, Chapter 8 examines the tentative revival of a Maoist institution for "democratic management"—the "staff and worker representative congress"—and asks what it might mean for the future of China's workers and its "socialist market economy."

# CHAPTER FIVE

# Can China Regulate Its Way out of Labor Unrest?

## Rising Labor Standards and the Enforcement Gap

CHINA HAS SEEN much to envy and to emulate in the relatively peaceful, productive, and prosperous industrial economies that developed in Western capitalist democracies after World War II. Yet the history of independent labor activism that helped to bring about that peace, productivity, and prosperity is precisely what China's leaders want to avoid. They have sought to do that in part by reforming the official system of worker representation, and in part by repressing independent organizing efforts. But they have also sought to do so by mobilizing the state to address directly some of the underlying causes of labor disputes—to raise wages, improve working conditions, and curb the worst employer abuses.[1] In the words of President Xi Jinping in 2014, "protecting people's rights *(weiquan)* ought to be the foundation of stability maintenance *(weiwen).*"[2] In other words, stability maintenance is a major impetus for protecting rights.

That is not to say that China's leaders are motivated solely by political self-preservation, or that they have no genuine interest in improving workers' lives; the latter is surely part of the mix of motivations behind the policy shift toward raising labor standards and away from the pursuit of economic growth at all costs. Indeed, the desire to improve workers' lives was surely part of the motivation for the initial and continuing emphasis on growth itself. But both the aim of improving workers' living standards and the strategies for pursuing that aim have been strongly shaped by the overriding imperative of maintaining political stability and preventing social unrest from coalescing into political opposition, especially in the form of an independent labor movement.

The political imperative of forestalling independent labor organizing has ruled out the Western model of legitimizing workers' pursuit of their own economic goals through collective action and independent unions, and it has both postponed and constrained reforms designed to democratize unions and promote collective bargaining through the All-China Federation of Trade Unions (ACFTU), as we will see below. Instead, in dealing with rising labor unrest in the non-state economy, the regime's initial and pre-ferred strategy was to legislate higher labor standards and improve access to judicial and arbitral enforcement of individual workers' rights claims under the law. As observed in Chapter 4, employers' improvement of their own human resources practices could do much to mollify workers and quell discontent; mandating higher labor standards is perhaps the most direct way China's leaders can pursue that end. The legislature, judiciary, and administrative state have all been called into heavy duty in the push to enact and enforce new labor laws and regulations. Yet rights disputes have continued to spill out of overburdened agencies and adjudicative bodies and onto the streets, and "interest disputes," not amenable to legal resolu-tion, have risen to the fore since 2010 in the form of traditional and sit-down strikes.

This chapter briefly recounts the evolution of the regulatory approach to labor standards in China, and both its success—in drawing hundreds of thousands of rights disputes each year into legal channels of dispute resolu-tion and even in improving labor standards to some degree—and its failure to solve the problem of labor protest. Ironically, that failure stems in part from the regime's unwavering commitment to avoiding independent worker organizing. For that perceived political imperative not only steered China's leaders toward a regulatory strategy for improving labor standards; it also continued to shape some particulars of that regulatory strategy and to fore-close or curb some potentially fruitful strategies for effective regulation. Official worries about independent worker organizing outside the pre-scribed ACFTU structures are both driving and constraining China's strat-egies for containing labor unrest, including its favored regulatory strategy.[3]

## The Slow Road to Regulation in China's Factories

Decades of press accounts about China's hellish factories, and the stam-pede of global capital to avail itself of China's cheap labor supply, have fostered a widespread perception among casual Western observers that China has no labor laws—no minimum-wage laws or restrictions on working time, no health and safety regulations. The notion that wages and working conditions are unregulated in China is a gross misconception. But there is no doubt that China's poor migrant workers in the export-oriented non-state sector labored under horribly dangerous and abusive conditions in the wake of the "opening" to foreign capital, and that labor regulation got off to a slow start in China.

So let us begin with a puzzle flagged in Chapter 2: how can we make sense of the grossly under-regulated factory conditions that emerged in China out of what had been a comprehensively planned economy under Mao, and was supposed to be a "socialist market economy"? There is some kind of paradox, or at least anomaly, in the notoriously no-holds-barred exploitation of factory workers in the first few decades of China's non-state economy, and in its resemblance to the hypercapitalist era of laissez faire labor markets and "liberty of contract" in the United States. How did that happen in a nominally socialist society presided over by a powerful state?

China's slow start in regulating its newly emerging private sector may be traceable in part to the Cultural Revolution, which had largely destroyed legal and administrative institutions during the last decade of Mao's rule. The development of a regulatory state was hardly helped by the fact that, at Mao's death in 1976, there were no functioning law schools or courts and very few lawyers (about two percent as many per capita as in the United States).[4] On the other hand, the institutions that were destroyed in the Cultural Revolution were not the same ones that were needed once capitalism and markets came to China. For in the planned economy under Mao, while party-state *control* of economic activity was nearly total, *regulation* as we know it did not really exist.[5] That is a second and deeper explanation for why regulation of labor standards lagged behind economic development.

In the planned economy, all productive enterprises were owned and administered by the party-state, its local branches, and its appointed managers (as well as by the townships and villages and their corresponding Party officials). There was no separation between productive enterprises and the party-state itself, and no need for regulatory institutions as such. The need for a modern regulatory state grew along with the unleashing of market forces, the development of a private sector, and the privatization and "corporatization" of the state sector. This "double movement" toward both markets and their regulation is one of the great master trends of the last century and a half.[6] But the "double movement" in China has taken place at warp speed.[7] China has had just a few decades to construct modern regulatory institutions virtually from scratch – or from the historical traces of pre-revolutionary regulatory institutions, coupled with lessons from abroad.[8] China's development of a regulatory state has proceeded with impressive vigor on many fronts.[9] But its regulatory capabilities are still early in the making. Western critics of China's infamously bleak factory conditions perhaps make too little allowance for just how difficult it is to create a regulatory state.

On the other hand, it is clear that regulating labor conditions in the emerging private sector was not an early priority for the regime. Even after the enactment of labor standards in the early 1990s, enforcement remained sorely deficient, held back not only by lack of capacity but by lack of political will.[10] Hence a third reason for lagging regulation of labor standards: for the first two decades of "reform and opening," lagging labor regulation was a policy choice emanating from Beijing—a decision to free up market forces and capitalize on the comparative advantage of cheap labor in the interest of economic development. Local officials were rewarded and their careers advanced largely on the basis of success in promoting local growth and attracting foreign capital, and foreign capital was attracted above all by ample cheap labor.

A fourth reason for China's slow road toward decent labor standards lies in the nature of the economy that grew up in that early period of breakneck growth: an export-oriented, labor-intensive manufacturing economy in which many producers with little physical or financial capital competed ferociously for business by minimizing labor costs. Foreign brands took ruthless advantage of the profusion of competing sweatshops, playing suppliers off against each other, paying them far too little to support decent wages and labor conditions, and driving them to cut corners and to exact grueling hours of work in crowded and unsafe factories. In short, underregulation in the early years helped to foster a type of sweatshop economy that is notoriously difficult to regulate, as business survival depends on relentless exploitation of labor.

The decades of official emphasis on growth over decent labor standards (or environmental or product safety standards) also helped to foster a particular political economy at the local level, as local officials and local business owners cultivated close and varied ties. Many powerful Party cadres became business owners, sometimes acquiring enterprises from state or collective ownership on egregiously favorable terms; and business owners in turn were welcomed into the Party after a major ideological shift in 1992. For the first few decades after the opening, the intertwined interests of local officials and local businesses reinforced central policies that prioritized growth over regulation of wages and working conditions. But when central policy priorities began to shift toward higher wages and labor standards, those intertwined interests became an impediment to enforcement, which remained in local hands. That was especially true when local businesses were exploiting migrant workers from elsewhere.[11] So a fifth reason for lagging regulation of labor standards is "local protectionism," or foot-dragging by local officials charged with enforcement.

The problem of "local protectionism" highlights the complex relationship between the center and the localities in China. As already noted, China's size and diversity create a margin of de facto local autonomy; as the Chinese adage has it, "the mountains are high and the emperor far away." But China is not a federal system like the United States. Provincial and local governments have no separate powers and no formal autonomy or sovereignty; they administer national laws and policies subject to national supervision. This is not an invention of the Communist Party. At least since the foundation of the Qin Dynasty in 221 BC, says one scholar, "China has maintained a unitary framework in which the central laws are unlimited in competence and unconditionally superior to local regulations."[12] Of course, varying local conditions may call for policy variations, and local experimentation can be a source of national innovation; but local variation, experimentation, and innovation takes place at the sufferance of Beijing. That enables the central government to dictate *policy* more completely, but it has left *enforcement* in the hands of local party-state officials, who have often succumbed to the lures of appeasing and cultivating local businesses.

The ties and convergence of interests between Party officials and business owners, especially at the local level, help to explain why Chinese business owners tend to support the regime.[13] In China there seems to be little political dissent brewing among the business and commercial classes that have helped to topple autocratic regimes elsewhere. At the same time, however, business-Party ties have hampered the regime's ability to respond to popular discontent—that of workers as well as rural citizens displaced by development and victims of rampant pollution or unsafe consumer products. Those local business-Party ties and the resulting neglect of popular grievances often trigger protest, and thus threaten stability. This is part of what Eli Friedman calls China's "insurgency trap."[14]

So there is a long list of reasons why China got off to a slow start on the project of improving and enforcing labor standards, and why, even after labor regulation became a more serious priority, China faces an obstacle course largely of its own making. As a result, it has sometimes been hard to distinguish the "primary stage of socialism"[15] in China from a bare-knuckled version of capitalism. Conditions in the coastal factory areas grossly belied China's professions of socialist ideology, and earned China a reputation among labor advocates, especially in the West, as a global center of capitalist worker exploitation.

## Regulation Takes Hold in Chinese Labor Markets

Early in the post-Mao era, the grim factories of the new export-based economy stood in stark contrast to the as-yet-unrestructured state-owned enterprises (SOEs), whose workers were still protected by the "iron rice bowl" and the *danwei* system. For some time, then, China's "socialist market economy" looked like two separate economies, one socialist and one market-driven. Since the early 1990s, however, the two sectors have largely converged, and they have converged toward a seemingly familiar model, and toward rather familiar formal labor standards.

### China's Two Economies Converge toward Regulated Labor Markets

One half of the convergence—the "corporatization" of SOEs, the commodification of labor, and the smashing of the "iron rice bowl"—has been widely analyzed, perhaps most brilliantly by Professor Mary Gallagher.[16] The SOEs and their restructured and privatized successors clamored for the managerial freedoms (and profits) of the private sector, and that entailed a shift to commodified labor relations. The other half of the convergence—the shift in the non-state sector from virtual laissez faire toward regulation—began haltingly as noted above. Before 1994, "labor law" in China consisted of "a myriad of confusing and often contradictory laws, regulations, notices, directives and so on."[17] The Labor Law of 1994 was a breakthrough in its imposition of a single basic labor regime—one founded on regulated labor markets—across the state and non-state sectors.[18] It represented a major shift away from both direct administration of labor in the planned economy, and the near-hands-off approach to labor standards in the non-state sector that prevailed in the early period of liberalization.

The convergence toward regulated labor markets and labor contracts had sharply divergent implications for workers in China's two economies. In the SOEs, the Labor Law's embrace of the "labor contract system" formalized and furthered the demise of the *danwei* system and the "iron rice bowl," and the demotion of workers from "masters," or at least members, of the enterprise to mere employees under contract. But for rural migrant workers in the factories of the growing non-state sector, the Labor Law's regulation of labor contracts was a major step toward improving workers' legal rights and labor standards.[19]

In short, China's embrace of regulated labor markets represents a convergence both between China and the advanced economies of the world, and between China's two economies—one socialist and one market-driven—that coexisted in the period following its "opening" to capitalism. Once having made the dramatic shift toward regulated labor markets and labor contracts, China proceeded along a fairly well-trodden path toward higher minimum labor standards, regulatory structures, labor inspections, and avenues for adjudication of employment disputes. The official enactment of the Labor Contract Law (LCL), effective in 2008, was a big step along that path.

It surprises many Westerners to learn that the labor standards established by Chinese law on the books, apart from actual wage levels, track modern Western (especially European) labor standards rather closely in many respects.[20] But that is a surprise partly because it is so at odds with the occasional glimpses that Westerners get of actual factory conditions in China—as in the wake of a tragic fire, or the latest child labor scandal, or the multiple worker suicides at Foxconn factories. Professor Gallagher has aptly described China's labor standards regime as one of "high standards-low enforcement."[21] The "low enforcement" problem, already previewed above, will occupy much of this chapter. But the "high standards" part of the picture warrants a closer look. Let us first look at one particularly challenging labor standards issue: job security.

### Rising Labor Standards: The Case of Employment Protection

All modern legal systems protect some employees—at least "regular," non-fixed-term employees—against some kinds of discharge—arbitrary, unjustified, wrongful, or discriminatory. One might array national employment protection regimes along a spectrum from pure "employment at will" (terminable at any time for any reason whatsoever) to "lifetime" employment (never terminable by the employer). Nearly all actual legal regimes cluster in between those extremes: The great majority requires something like "good cause" for discharge of "regular" employees.[22] American law is an outlier in requiring no affirmative justification for discharge (absent a contractual promise of job security), but it prohibits a long list of discriminatory or retaliatory discharges based on protected traits or conduct.

Knowing the legally permissible and impermissible reasons for discharge in a particular country is not enough, however, to gauge employees' actual job security, for that depends on institutional details that are harder to encode along a single dimension (and are often ignored by comparative analysts): Which jobs are covered by protections against discharge, and how hard is it to get one of those protected jobs? What is the process for challenging a dismissal, how accessible is it, and how long does it take? Who bears the burden of proof of good cause or bad motive? What is the expected penalty or remedy for a wrongful dismissal? How much does the process cost both sides (in attorney fees and other costs), and who pays those costs? Even then, employees' actual *economic* security may depend not only on their protection from discharge but also on their ability to quit and find another job—and the latter may to some degree be inversely related to the former. So while the law on the books is not irrelevant, it may present a very partial and potentially misleading picture.

In the early post-Mao era—after the "opening" but before the "reform" of the SOEs—China's two economies occupied both ends of the spectrum. At one end, workers in the planned (or "socialist") economy enjoyed a kind of job security that might give job security a bad name. Workers were not mere employees, but permanent members of their work unit or *danwei;* except in rare cases, they could neither quit nor be fired. Workers in the *danwei* system had a kind of property right in their job, but work units also had "a form of property rights over their employees."[23] By contrast, in the foreign-invested and private sector that had begun to grow up in the wake of liberalization, many migrant workers were "temporary" and essentially terminable at will, while others were employed under written labor contracts that provided no real security against dismissal.[24]

With the 1994 Labor Law's adoption of regulated labor contracts, China brought all labor relations under a single legal umbrella and moved toward the international norm in extending modest job security for most Chinese workers—something in between the permanent membership of the *danwei* system and the disposability of the largely unfettered private sector. The Labor Law prohibited unjustified dismissals during the term of a labor contract, whether fixed or indefinite. But the law on the books did not correspond to reality on the ground. Apart from chronic enforcement difficulties, the Labor Law's version of job security was full of loopholes permitting summary dismissal, and was easily circumvented by employers' use of short fixed-term contracts.[25] One of the more ambitious objectives of the LCL was thus to shore up workers' job security. On paper, China succeeded: a 2013 Organisation for Economic Co-operation and Development (OECD) survey of employment protection legislation found that China's legislation ranked as the most protective of the forty-three countries surveyed![26]

The LCL sharply limited employers' use of fixed-term contracts: After two successive fixed-term contracts, employers must offer workers a written indefinite term contract, which in turn is terminable only for good cause (with the burden of proving cause on the employer). The law also sought to deter violations and to spur worker enforcement by providing for an award of double backpay for an employee who is unlawfully denied a continuing contract. At the same time, the 2008 reforms lowered the cost and procedural hurdles to bringing claims into the arbitration and judicial system. To be sure, many ordinary workers still lacked access to legal representation and effective legal recourse, and we will return to those hurdles. Still, the 2008 reforms brought a flood of claims into the formal adjudicatory system, and workers were winning a high percentage of them.[27] By 2009, employers in China were complaining about the stringent legal standards for dismissal, and looking for ways to get around the LCL's strict standards for dismissal and to recover staffing "flexibility."

Across the world, employers often respond to tough restrictions on discharge by shifting, if they can, to labor arrangements that fall outside the law's restrictions.[28] And China's employers did so, too. A popular device was to hire workers through a "labor dispatch" agency, which was then the responsible employer.[29] Even the lawful use of labor dispatch undermined the LCL's job security standards; in less scrupulous hands it became an outright evasion of the entire labor standards regime. Labor dispatch use roughly doubled after 2008, and reportedly included one-fifth of China's three hundred million urban workers by 2011.[30] The growth of labor dispatch parallels trends toward "casualization" of labor that are seen across the world—not only in China and not only in the wake of new labor regulations.[31] It is a form of what David Weil has called "the fissured workplace," which has wreaked havoc on labor standards in the United States and elsewhere.[32] But the explosion of labor dispatch in China after the LCL was too dramatic to be a coincidence.[33]

Chinese lawmakers responded with surprising alacrity to the explosion of labor dispatch by tightening the LCL's restrictions on the practice. The amendments restrict use of labor dispatch to "provisional, auxiliary, or substituting positions," and to no more than ten percent of the employer's total workforce—a drastic reduction for many employers. The amendments also aim to reduce employers' incentive to use dispatch workers and to mitigate the adverse impact of labor dispatch use on LCL compliance, mainly by requiring equal pay for regular and dispatch workers.[34]

Given worldwide trends toward casual and contingent forms of labor, it seems unlikely that China's European-style job security rights will take firm hold. Indeed, many European workers no longer enjoy "European-style" job security rights.[35] Some companies in China reportedly responded to tighter rules on labor dispatch by shifting to use of independent contractors,[36] or outsourcing some jobs altogether.[37] And other evasions, such as the use of "student interns" to perform factory work, persist.[38] Still, the labor dispatch story shows that China is getting more serious about regulating labor standards, and more savvy about how to do it.[39] Paradoxically, the very fact that so many employers in China sought lawful ways to circumvent the LCL's restrictions through labor dispatch, rather than simply ignoring them, is powerful evidence that labor law is becoming a serious constraint for private sector employers in China.

### The Puzzle of "High Standards" and the Persistent Enforcement Gap

In many respects, China's official labor standards—not only for job security but also for social insurance, working hours, and job safety—are comparable to those of the most advanced economies. (Minimum and actual wage levels have also risen in recent years, though they remain low by Western standards.) China's official labor standards are arguably higher than is sustainable given its current level of economic development (even apart from its level of political and legal development).[40] They are certainly higher than those that prevail on the factory floor. As Gallagher observes, China's model is one of "high standards-low enforcement."[41] We have seen a number of factors—both intentional choices and unintended consequences—that help explain the "low enforcement" part of that pattern. But the "high standards" part of the picture—a matter of intentional choice at the central policy making level—presents its own puzzles. Given the daunting enforcement challenges that China faces, why set nominal standards so high?

Professor Gallagher discerns a political logic in high standards at the national level: First, high standards that are enforceable mainly through individual legal complaints tend to benefit white-collar workers who have the resources to claim their legal rights and who are a crucial constituency for the regime. Second, high standards and individual enforcement create a "fire alarm" system that helps the center to monitor distant, errant local officials within China's fragmented government. Third, high standards on the books help to promote the legitimacy of the national party-state, reinforcing a deeply entrenched and useful popular conception of the central government as beneficent and public regarding, and of local officials, charged with enforcement, as corrupt. In short, "the central government . . . take[s] credit for good legislation, while shifting blame to lower levels for bad enforcement."[42] These dynamics are not limited to the labor arena. Benjamin Van Rooij, looking across multiple regulatory arenas, finds that "symbolic laws" are meant to shore up the legitimacy and stability of the party-state by assuring citizens that they are addressing risks that provoke unrest "even though they will likely be unable to reduce such risks in practice."[43]

Two other factors might help to explain the "high standards" puzzle in China. The first is a conception of law that has tended to be more aspirational and less prescriptive than in Western law.[44] That might have worked better in a planned economy in which law served to guide subordinate officials, including enterprise managers; it is bound to be less effective in regulating autonomous and opportunistic market-driven actors. Another factor lies in China's aspirations on the global stage. After a century of international isolation, foreign intervention, internal chaos, and poverty, China seeks a place among the great powers of the world. That sometimes counsels attention to international law. In the labor field, China essentially rejects some core international rights, particularly the freedom of association, as inconsistent with its political system. But the international standards that it accepts in principle, including most material labor standards, can play a surprisingly large role in shaping the law on the books.[45] China's aspirations for global leadership, coupled with a somewhat aspirational conception of law, may have helped to produce laws that nobody actually expects to be binding.

The LCL, as amended, represents a major move toward a more prescriptive form of law: its standards are relatively clear and detailed, and they have been coupled with some positive inducements to private enforcement.[46] It goes well beyond the symbolic, and attempts to wrestle with the problem of non-compliance.[47] After the LCL took effect, migrant workers were significantly more likely to have a written labor contract and social insurance coverage, and less likely to experience wage arrears.[48] This is real progress, though progress is measured against a very low baseline. Even after the enactment of the LCL, some 40 to 80 percent of migrant workers lacked one or another of the categories of social insurance provided by law, and over 37 percent did not have a written contract of any kind.[49] On another front, excessive working hours—above the maximum thirty-six hours *of overtime* per month—appear still to be endemic in manufacturing (partly because of legal loopholes that invite abuse).[50]

Whatever the logic of setting high labor standards at the national level, the gap between the law on the books and the law in action, and the grievances that fester in that gap, are a persistent source of protest and unrest.[51] At least one major purpose behind China's pursuit of the regulatory project, and the LCL in particular, has been to channel workers' discontent into "rights claims" and to steer those claims into official tribunals and out of the streets. At one level, the law has been a big success: 2008 saw a 93 percent rise in claims filed from 2007.[52] Surely some of the hundreds of thousands of rights disputes that poured into the legal system in the wake of the LCL would otherwise have spilled into the streets in the form of "mass incidents." On the other hand, some of those disputes probably only arose because of the LCL's higher labor standards, which widened the gap between rights and reality. Moreover, the flood of litigation has led to delays, shortcuts, and official pressure to settle, all of which risk sending dissatisfied claimants back into the streets.[53]

The reactions of Chinese workers to their mostly discouraging experiences with the legal system are surprisingly nuanced, as Mary Gallagher found in her study of legal aid plaintiffs in Shanghai. Many of those who lost in court, or who "won" but gained no tangible relief, said they were willing to sue again if necessary. They expressed disenchantment with the legal system, yet also more confidence in their own ability to work the system. Some became "little experts," passing on a hard-won understanding of the law to friends, family, and colleagues, and encouraging them to pursue legal claims as well.[54] The net effect of this growing body of first- and second-hand legal experience on social stability and political legitimacy is ambiguous: The spread of what Gallagher calls "informed disenchantment" with the legal system, if that is what results, can hardly be good news for China's rulers. And it is still unclear whether the resulting claims are substituting for or rather sparking more disruptive forms of disputation.

In short, China's regulatory strategy has not solved the problem of labor unrest, and in some ways it might have exacerbated the problem. Given workers' rising material expectations and their growing willingness to assert economic interests and not just legal rights, the regulatory strategy was bound to fall short of solving the whole labor unrest problem. Across-the-board minimum labor standards cannot deliver what China's skilled workers, and especially those in the more productive and profitable enterprises and sectors of the economy (like automotive and electronics), view as fair economic rewards. Historically, that has been a job for collective bargaining, and for reasonably responsive institutions for collective interest representation. We will return to this large topic in Chapters 6 and 7.

But it is not only interest disputes that are spilling onto the streets. Rights disputes—workers' complaints that they are not getting what the law prescribes—continue to spark disruptive protests. That is traceable to both halves of the "high standards-low enforcement" pattern—both the elevation of labor standards in 2007 and the egregious shortfall in enforcement. The Yue Yuen strike of 2014, described in Chapter 1, is illustrative: the law demands social insurance contributions of employers that are very high by international standards;[55] but local officials routinely look the other way when employers fail to make the payments. The gap between the law on the books and the reality on the ground was thus the immediate trigger for the largest strike in China's modern history.

When rights claimants do take to the streets, regulatory officials are under pressure from above to address their grievances. As Benjamin Van Rooij observes, again across multiple regulatory arenas, weak enforcement generates unrest, but "unrest also shapes enforcement," in part by drawing regulators' scarce time and resources toward the objects of unrest.[56] That often distorts regulatory priorities, but it also sends a perverse message to citizens: If you want your complaints addressed, you had better assemble a crowd, draw media attention, create a ruccus.[57] This dynamic—seen, too, in the response to strikes and collective interest disputes as described in Chapter 6—makes the party-state's response to unrest into yet another driver of unrest. As Van Rooij puts it, "the Party-state has institutionalized an incentive structure that is likely to create more rather than less unrest."[58]

## China's Dilemma in Rights Enforcement: The Crucial but Disquieting Role of Independent Worker Advocates

Many of the factors that slowed China's regulatory response to abusive labor conditions in the early years—including still-developing regulatory institutions and experience, local protectionism and cronyism, and the challenging dynamics of low-wage labor markets—are still a drag on enforcement. But some of the impediments to enforcement in China have their roots, ironically, in the very fear of labor unrest and independent worker activism that helped spur the effort to improve labor standards. Another brief comparative interlude will help to explain how this is so.

### The Regulatory Role of Workers and their Advocates

How do modern societies effectively regulate market-driven organizations? In particular, how do they maintain a decent floor on wages and working conditions? The question has bedeviled much of the industrial world, and certainly the United States, with its relatively freewheeling labor markets and large low-wage sector. Workers in the United States face an epidemic of "wage theft"—subminimum wages, unpaid overtime, and "off-the-clock" work—especially in sectors with a high portion of undocumented immigrant workers. As China seeks to upgrade labor standards and to regulate its own rather freewheeling labor markets, and as we seek to understand those efforts, Western regulatory experience and scholarship may be instructive. It might even be instructive to Chinese policy makers, for the how-to of labor standards regulation seems at first blush unlikely to meet deep-seated political resistance. It is a project to which China is committed in principle, and it seems much more technocratic than the intensely political matter of collective labor relations. Yet some of the key lessons that might be taken from Western regulatory experience run up against deeply illiberal attitudes and strictures regarding civil society in China. That is particularly true of the lessons associated with what is often called the "New Governance" school of thought (or "responsive," "reflexive," or "decentered" regulatory theory), which I find most persuasive.[59]

Regulatory experience across the globe and across the decades shows that institutions of public enforcement alone cannot enforce minimum labor standards across a large and diverse economy. No industrial society in the world employs enough government inspectors to do the whole job of enforcement—whether it is enforcement of labor standards, environmental laws, product safety, or any other regulatory regimes. That is true in an advanced economy and legal system like the United States, and it is certainly true in a huge and rapidly developing country like China. Given the endemic shortfall of public regulatory capacity, an effective system of regulation in any modern society must manage to stimulate both self-regulation by firms and private enforcement by affected citizens—in the present context, by workers.

Corporate self-regulation can do a bigger share of the regulatory work in large firms with sophisticated human resource and compliance departments, confidential reporting systems, in-house lawyers, and a valued reputation or "brand" that would be marred by serious or recurring legal complaints. Indeed, these internal compliance mechanisms, or self-regulation under the shadow of the law, encompass and explain much of modern human resource management. In smaller firms that lack those internal compliance structures and reputational incentives, workers' resort to external enforcement must play a larger role. But the two mechanisms—internal compliance structures and external enforcement mechanisms—are complementary: Even firms with elaborate compliance machinery are kept honest in part by the prospect of workers blowing the whistle or filing legal claims. And even small firms with none of that compliance machinery might be induced to avoid law breaking, and to take rudimentary precautions against infractions, if workers can readily trigger public scrutiny and sanctions.

The dichotomy between internal corporate self-regulation and external worker-triggered enforcement is too clean, even apart from their reinforcing one another. For one, workers who are well represented by an independent union may gain a voice in internal self-regulation. For another, "socially responsible" supply chain management—under pressure from external stakeholders and advocates—can extend the reach of large firms' regulatory capacity to the smaller firms that supply them. But let us stick for now with the simpler dichotomy.

Firms' self-regulatory structures and workers' access to external enforcement played complementary roles in improving compliance in the domain of equal employment opportunity in the United States. Major firms now tout their commitment to workforce diversity and inclusion, and the business imperatives that drive it. But the fear of damaging litigation reinforces managers' commitment to diversity and backs up internal safeguards against discrimination.[60] Individuals' ability to report unfair treatment internally, and to file a lawsuit if they remain aggrieved, is an essential driver of effective self-regulation. So, too, in the domain of workplace health and safety: corporate health and safety programs often go beyond compliance with applicable laws; they include joint worker-management committees and reporting procedures that are designed to tap into the pool of information that front-line workers have about safety hazards. Yet however proudly companies tout their internal "culture of safety," external pressures, such as legal liabilities for injuries and the higher insurance premiums that injuries may trigger, are among the crucial drivers in internal safety structures.

Workers thus supply essential regulatory resources—eyes and ears on the ground, and the ability to report problems, "blow the whistle," and trigger costly publicity, scrutiny, and sanctions—that can help to induce corporations to bring their own regulatory resources into play. But workers face major hurdles in enforcing their rights, especially fear of reprisals, including job loss. They also face collective action problems that are endemic to the workplace. When employer policies affect many workers at once, compliance is what economists call a "public good": both the benefits of compliance to workers as a group and its cost to employers far exceed what any one worker can hope to gain from enforcement efforts; as a result, no worker has enough incentive to invest the effort and take the risks entailed by enforcement efforts that would benefit all.[61] But if they have help in enforcing their rights, including mechanisms for collective voice, workers can do much of the job of monitoring compliance and triggering enforcement, thereby encouraging compliance by the firm.

So both workers and regulated firms supplement the chronically scarce enforcement capabilities of government regulators. No public system of labor standards regulation in a market economy can function adequately without those private inputs. That does not mean that private regulatory inputs can make up for any shortfall, however great, in public enforcement. Perhaps someday the dynamic field of "social regulation"— regulation through nongovernmental actors and nonlegal reputational sanctions—will become a robust and reliable replacement for public regulation. At least for now, however, public enforcement and sanctions are crucial in eliciting and backing up both firms' self-regulatory efforts and workers' self-enforcement activities. Most obviously, workers' ability to pursue legal claims is meaningless unless public adjudicators can process their claims and enforce judgments against law breakers. More broadly, a firm's incentive to avoid violations and to take precautions against unintended violations (through internal reporting mechanisms, for example) depends partly on the likelihood that regulators will detect and sanction violations. That simple deterrence logic ignores more complex dynamics that can encourage internalization of public values and cooperation between regulators and regulated organizations.[62] Still, a reasonably reliable threat of sanctions against cheaters and slackers—firms that violate the law either deliberately or due to inadequate precautions—is crucial to sustaining self-regulation by other firms lest they be undercut in the market by low-road competitors.

The regulatory challenge is most acute in low-wage, labor-intensive industries where firms compete for market share, or even survival, largely by minimizing labor costs rather than by innovating or improving productivity. State labor inspectors are chronically stretched far too thin to ensure that low-wage, low-road firms comply with minimum labor standards; yet both firms and workers contribute less regulatory resources than in more capital-intensive and technologically advanced sectors. Internal compliance incentives and structures in these firms are weak or absent. Workers are less able to assert their own rights because of poverty, lack of education, insecure legal status, and weak attachment to the firm: they are often easy to replace, and even in tight labor markets are more likely to switch jobs than protest.[63] Not surprisingly, labor standards violations are endemic in low-wage labor markets, both in China and in the United States. Low-wage workers in both countries need all the help they can get in enforcing their rights at work.

So where can workers, and especially low-wage workers, get that help? In the United States, they can turn to a reservoir of support within civil society. The best support might be independent unions, which enable workers to better enforce their legal rights as well as to bargain collectively over economic interests.[64] Unions can overcome both the collective action problems and the fear of reprisals that impede enforcement of workers' rights by pooling information, speaking up for individual workers who may remain anonymous, and protecting job security. Most workers in the United States do have the legal right to form and join independent unions, but in fact few workers manage to run the gauntlet that union organizing has become. Moreover, for a long time American unions neglected the most vulnerable workers at the bottom of the labor market.

Other worker advocacy organizations, such as worker centers, have grown up in the vacuum left by union neglect and decline; and in the meantime unions have awakened to the need to support low-wage workers, in part by supporting worker centers. Worker centers may file complaints or lawsuits or mount public campaigns—rallies, picketing, distribution of pamphlets, street theater—to pressure recalcitrant employers to comply with the law and remedy past violations.[65] In the United States, peaceful publicity and agitation is constitutionally protected against police or other government suppression, and is freely reported in independent media outlets with their own constitutional rights against censorship. Grassroots agitation coordinated by unions and worker centers has produced some major victories, as in ongoing state and local efforts to raise the minimum wage to fifteen dollars per hour.[66]

Lawyers in both non-profit organizations and private practice also play a critical supporting role. Lawyers may be willing and able to represent workers in their rights claims, even when individual workers cannot afford to pay lawyers' fees, because winning claims may nonetheless yield decent economic rewards: many U.S. employment statutes allow claimants to collect "reasonable attorney fees" if they prevail in their claims against errant employers. Some claims, especially under the wage and hour laws, can be pursued on an aggregate basis; if they succeed, they may yield a sizable "contingency fee" for lawyers even if each individual worker's recovery is too small to make litigation worthwhile. The combination of statutory attorney fee awards and contingency fees in the United States has fostered the growth of a sizeable plaintiff-side employment bar that represents workers in their rights claims.

Low-wage workers in the United States still face serious hurdles and enforcement deficits (including employers' ability to demand that workers submit employment claims to private arbitration versus litigation, and to do so on an individual basis rather than as a group[67]). Whatever hurdles U.S. workers confront in enforcing their rights, however, Chinese workers face more. To begin with, they face a more daunting economic environment, given the heavy reliance on low-wage labor, and a less capable regulatory state—one that is less developed and more compromised by local corruption and protectionism. Chinese workers need even more support from outside the state to successfully enforce their own rights. But that is where China's regulatory strategy for meeting workers' demands and quelling labor unrest collides with the regime's deep anxiety about organized collective activism that is outside of party-state control.[68]

### The Precarious Status of Independent Worker Advocates in China

It is no surprise to learn that China fails to protect the kinds of public protest by which workers and their organizations in the United States sometimes successfully pressure employers to comply with labor laws. Although China's constitution formally recognizes freedom of expression, that principle offers no refuge from police action or criminal prosecution under broad and vague proscriptions that may extend to any kind of public gathering. Protests do occur, of course, and they are sometimes quite disorderly—possibly more disorderly than they would be if the law protected peaceful protest activity. Such protection might constrain both protesters and police—inducing the former to stay within the boundaries of protection, and discouraging the latter from harsh tactics that can transform peaceful protest into unruly conflict. That is just one way in which the regime's preoccupation with social stability can be counterproductive.

What I found more surprising was the array of constraints on workers' effective redress through official judicial and arbitral channels. It is not that China has failed to appreciate the need to enable workers to enforce their own rights and labor standards. China's 2008 labor law reforms made a great leap forward, not only in raising labor standards but in enabling workers to pursue their own legal remedies. In particular, the double-wage remedy for workers who are wrongfully denied a continuing labor contract (under the LCL) and the near-elimination of filing fees (under its companion law, the Labor Dispute Mediation and Arbitration Law) were well-tailored to encourage workers to play their regulatory role, and to draw complaints about scofflaw employers into the courts and arbitral bodies. Yet China remains inhospitable to the independent, nongovernmental advocates—both individual lawyers and organizations—that can help workers pursue their rights claims; and it remains especially inhospitable to the adjudication of *collective* rights disputes—precisely the disputes that are most likely to trigger disruptive protest.

Workers can represent themselves, and many Chinese workers have attempted to do so, teaching themselves labor law from the Internet and using this knowledge to shape their demands.[69] But as the law becomes more complex, unrepresented claimants seem likely to fare relatively poorly in the legal system.[70] In order to play their part in the regulatory regime, workers need skilled advocates who are willing and able to pursue workers' rights claims. Higher-income claimants may be able to hire a lawyer from a commercial law firm. But workers who cannot afford to pay private commercial lawyers' fees have fewer options.[71] Not many private lawyers are willing and able to handle workers' rights claims, which have proliferated under the LCL.

Officially sanctioned legal aid clinics—most sponsored by courts, lawyer's associations, or local trade union branches—are able to help some worker-claimants.[72] China also maintains an official legal aid system administered through the Ministry of Justice, as well as legal aid offices administered through ACFTU branches; both have expanded in recent years.[73] But the official legal aid system falls short in both quantity and quality of representation: Many workers are either ineligible or confront serious hurdles to getting legal help (because they do not have a written contract, or their *hukou* is in another city, for example). And most accepted claims are not handled by the small paid staff but assigned out to private and non-profit volunteer lawyers, who are in short supply for reasons already noted and who often lack experience and expertise.[74] Despite an impressive ramping up of the official legal aid system, the net result is a significant "representation gap" between the number of claims by low-wage workers and access to affordable legal representation.[75]

The rise of labor nongovernmental organizations (NGOs) in China is a partly a response to that need; yet these independent advocacy organizations confront a hostile political and legal environment, previewed in Chapter 3. To the party-state, organized advocacy appears to be a short step away from organized dissent, and the independent leaders of worker advocacy organizations look like the potential leaders of independent labor activism. (To be sure, this fear of organized and collective advocacy is hardly confined to the labor arena; it takes a toll on civic organizations and legal advocates in other regulatory arenas as well.[76]) At least until recently, advocacy organizations that confined themselves to representing workers in "rights disputes" could sometimes achieve a measure of official legitimacy, including sponsorship by an official body—the ACFTU, the local labor department, or the local justice department—that is required under China's dual-registration regime. But even legal rights advocacy can raise official hackles, especially when rights claims are shared among groups of workers, as many workplace disputes are. And since 2014, the very concept of "rights protection" has come under a cloud of suspicion as a form of dissent.

As discussed in Chapter 3, the space for independent advocacy has clearly shrunk in recent years, especially since the beginning of the Xi administration. But while the envelope for acceptable advocacy has shrunk, China's workers and some of their advocates have also been pushing the envelope in recent years. Workers' demands have become more ambitious and their self-organizing capabilities more sophisticated, and rights advocacy has accordingly become more politically charged. The line between "rights disputes" and "interest disputes," although clear in principle, is often more fluid on the ground. As the Yue Yuen strike showed, a dispute that originates in a rights claim—unpaid wages or social insurance contributions—may blow up into a broader dispute over low wages or poor working conditions, or even over the inefficacy of official organs of worker representation.

Lawyers who represent workers in seemingly apolitical rights claims face suspicion and constraints that stem from the fear of independent organizing. Lawyers may raise political concerns because they stand between individual citizens and the state, shielding them from adverse government action or crafting their claims for government assistance. Most workers' rights claims are statutorily authorized and less sensitive than human rights claims that challenge existing law or official action, and most lawyers who bring workers' rights claims face less official hostility than do the intrepid "rights lawyers." Still, the risks of worker advocacy, along with its limited economic rewards, sharply limit the pool of lawyers who are willing to represent low-income workers. One lawyer who does so estimates that no more than twenty lawyers in all of China have a practice consisting solely of representation of workers![77] Workers who are unable to find a lawyer may turn to lay advocates, sometimes called "black lawyers" or "barefoot lawyers"; they are not formally trained or licensed, nor are they subject to political control through the bar association, but they face other restrictions.[78] (One may hear echoes of restrictions on the "unauthorized practice of law" in the United States; but those restrictions are not coupled with the deterrents that exist in China to the *authorized* practice of law in this area.)

It must be said that China is not only suppressing the supply of independent legal representation, but attempting to reduce the demand for such representation by expanding the official legal aid system. That is a constructive approach to the "representation gap," but it might also be part of the more nefarious effort to marginalize the labor NGOs that are not allied with the party-state. For if the party-state supplies legitimate and politically appropriate channels for legal aid (including through approved NGOs), that might suggest that the worker rights organizations that operate outside that network are up to something else—that perhaps they are not just non-governmental but anti-governmental organizations. In short, while the rise of labor NGOs is partly a response to a shortfall in access to legal aid, the recent expansion of state-sponsored legal aid might be partly a response to the rise of labor NGOs.

Constraints on the pursuit of labor claims extend beyond the restrictions on independent advocates. Political oversight of the courts also plays an important role, and keeps many cases from even being filed. Judges may simply refuse to accept lawsuits because they are politically "sensitive," because they are not authorized causes of action according to internal political guidelines, or because their size or complexity may depress the case-handling statistics that dominate performance reviews.[79] Claims under China's constitution and even some statutory claims may be off-limits under internal court guidelines, some of them emanating from the political officials who oversee courts.[80]

The political constraints on litigation are particularly salient as to collective litigation. Collective lawsuits are appealing to workers and the lawyers who represent them because they are comparatively efficient and because they may enable poor individuals to pool their resources and their recoveries, and thus pay enough to induce an attorney to represent them. Class actions or group claims are permissible as a formal matter in China, and they are not unheard of.[81] Initially after the LCL was enacted, the number of collective claims spiked along with the number of total claims; but the former dropped just as precipitously in the next few years, even as LCL claim rates remained very high.[82] That is partly because judges often reject group claims or break them up into separate claims.[83] And that, in turn, is said to reflect the fact that judges are judged (by their political superiors) partly on their numbers: how many cases have they resolved? A single lawsuit with many plaintiffs may entail a lot of work for one "case," and dividing that lawsuit into many individual cases boosts a judge's statistics.[84] Then again, judges sometimes informally aggregate formally separate claims in the interest of efficiency.

But bureaucratic gamesmanship is not the whole story. Group claims based on collective grievances—over pollution, land disputes, harmful products, or employer abuses—are politically "sensitive," and may spawn mass incidents. One might think that affording peaceful and efficient *legal* mechanisms for resolving those collective disputes would be a logical strategy for reducing social unrest. Yet organized collective activity outside the party-state—even a single attorney's representation of a group of plaintiffs in a single legal complaint—arouses anxiety and suspicion. It seems puzzling from an American perspective that even the rather denatured form of collective action that is embodied in a "class action" lawsuit sets off official alarm bells. (That very puzzle struck me during my first visit to

China in 2009, and began to open my eyes to the fascinating dilemmas that China faces in its effort to deal with the social spillovers of development while maintaining a stable one-party regime.) Collective litigation evokes the fearsome spectacle of a group of aggrieved individuals meeting, inside or outside the courthouse, under the leadership of an advocate whose primary loyalty is not to the state or the Party but to the group.

Consider the impact of these constraints on enforcement in the context of sex-based employment discrimination. Overt hiring discrimination based on sex is rampant in China; one study in 2010 found that 12.3 percent of job advertisements explicitly restricted openings to women or men only (with mostly clerical jobs reserved for women, and higher level jobs reserved for men).[85] In principle, Chinese law proscribes sex discrimination in hiring.[86] Until 2014, however, *there had not yet been a single judicial decision in China finding sex discrimination in hiring.* Courts resist accepting such claims for adjudication because they are both sensitive and difficult: Even when gender discrimination is overt, how is one to determine whether the particular plaintiff was rejected because of her sex? And what is an appropriate remedy for wrongful non-hiring? The difficulties are real, but courts elsewhere have overcome them, for refusing to do so effectively nullifies the ban on hiring discrimination. And that is what courts in China have done thus far by simply declining to consider these cases.

In the arena of employment discrimination law, there is some room for optimism. In 2014, the tiny community of gender equality advocates in China rejoiced when the first case of sex discrimination in employment was accepted by a court for adjudication, and resulted in a settlement.[87] The case represented a breakthrough even though the settlement was miniscule—30,000 yuan (about $4,800) and an apology. That victory was followed in 2015 by the first judicial finding of sex discrimination in employment: a woman who was denied a job as a courier with the Beijing Postal Service received a token compensation award of 2,000 yuan ($300).[88]

Unfortunately, these small breakthroughs in the courts have their very discouraging counterpoint in the episode of the "feminist five"—five feminist activists who were detained in Beijing in 2015 for planning to hand out leaflets about sexual harassment in the public transit system on International Women's Day.[89] This episode vividly illustrated the small and shrinking space for public advocacy in the era of Xi Jinping, even on not-very-political issues of sex discrimination that the courts have begun to reckon with.

The same official fears of collective contestation are curbing progress on combating discrimination in the courts—and consequently in China's workplaces. If courts were to begin accepting complaints plausibly alleging sex discrimination in employment, they could set in motion forces of "liability avoidance" within firms, encouraging internal precautions against biased decisions and countering ingrained habits of discrimination. But courts and policy makers in China appear to be moved less by the aim of combatting discrimination and more by the fear that serious treatment of discrimination claims would invite an unmanageable flood of litigation and even more disputation. For now, avoidance seems to remain the path of least resistance for most courts in "sensitive" cases, including discrimination cases.

Judicial reluctance in these cases reflects in part the fact that judges do not make these decisions entirely on their own, based on legal reasoning. For behind patterns of judicial avoidance lies China's rejection of the principle of "judicial independence" and the broader principle of "separation of powers"; both are contrary to the regime's founding commitment to Party leadership in all aspects of governance. That means that political officials can intervene in judicial decisions about which cases to accept and how to adjudicate them, and they evaluate judges' performance and determine their career advancement.[90] It matters a great deal how and how often political officials decide to exercise these powers, and the official word under Xi Jinping is that they mean to intervene less often going forward.[91] But political control of the judicial branch is a continuing fact of legal life in China. Sometimes it may lead officials to put a thumb on the scale for worker-claimants when the political situation seems to call for it. Probably more often it contributes to lagging enforcement against well-connected employers.

W HAT DOES ALL this mean for China's regulatory strategy for quelling labor unrest? It means that some potential regulatory actors—lawyers and advocacy groups that could help ordinary workers to enforce their rights and improve compliance—are either absent or severely restricted in their ability to play that role. Compared to low-wage workers and their allies in the United States, Chinese workers and worker advocates have much less freedom to pursue collective strategies to achieve compliance—peaceful agitation, petitions, consumer boycotts, or collective litigation—and much less access to legal assistance. To the extent that China's leaders had hoped to "solve" the problem of labor unrest through effective state regulation of wages and labor conditions, they have hobbled themselves by hobbling workers' efforts to enforce their own rights.

Labor NGOs and advocates are restricted not for nothing, of course, but for the threat they might pose to the same political imperative of stability that helped to spur regulatory improvements: independent worker advocates might help to promote stability by improving enforcement and channeling grievances into the legal system; but they might also provide a forum and a catalyst for collective action. They might articulate and amplify collective discontent that could eventually morph into a political challenge to one-party rule. China's leaders face a dilemma, and they have responded by conceding a limited, tenuous, and shrinking freedom of association and action to labor rights groups. We will return in Chapter 9 to the question of whether that response is a misguided overreaction, or instead reflects a well-founded assessment of the costs, risks, and benefits of greater associational freedom (though the latter would suggest that China is more of a tinderbox, and its people less content with CPC rule, than the regime likes to concede). Either way, China's response to workers' rights claims and advocates is emblematic of the challenges facing the rulers of this increasingly complex, dynamic, and demanding society.

# CHAPTER SIX

# Can China Secure Labor Peace without Independent Unions?

*Strikes and Collective Bargaining with Chinese Characteristics*

I F IT WAS NOT clear before the 2010 Honda strikes, it was certainly clear afterward: the regulatory response was not going to solve the problem of labor unrest. Even if China could improve regulatory and adjudicatory institutions, narrow the enforcement gap, and raise minimum labor standards, some workers would surely demand more. Especially skilled workers in the most advanced sectors—precisely the sectors that China hoped to expand—were bound to demand higher labor standards, and especially higher wages, than the government could possibly mandate across the whole labor market. And those demands were now breaking out into open conflict in a major industry. That kind of industrial relations challenge generally calls for collective bargaining, or so the history of industrialization across the world would suggest.

The Honda strikes also showed that workers were learning how to organize themselves to press their newly ambitious demands. A strike of any size and duration requires some measure of organization and cohesiveness. Far more than a spontaneous "mass incident," a strike requires leadership and lines of communication, a modicum of solidarity and group discipline among the workers, and some ability to formulate and present collective demands.[1] The level of self-organization and leadership that was evident in the initial Nanhai Honda strike and the ensuing wave of strikes at other factories was a new and, to China's leaders, alarming development in its private sector economy. If China's official labor institutions did not rise to the challenge, they were at risk of being swept aside by workers' own organizations.

China's new sense of urgency in finding ways to resolve collective interest disputes is motivated largely by the risk that localized outbursts of organized unrest could coalesce into an independent labor movement. But that same risk shapes and constrains China's approaches to reform, ruling out the sort of solutions to the labor question that took hold throughout the West during the twentieth century. Most important, fear of independent labor activism has so far ruled out a system of collective bargaining in which workers are represented by their own independent unions. With no democratic political process through which that judgment from on high can be challenged, the All-China Federation of Trade Unions (ACFTU) and its branches remain the only legitimate institutional vehicles of worker representation.

An aversion to conflict also constrains China's approach to industrial relations. A basic Maoist tenet holds that disputes among the people that do not challenge political stability or "resist the socialist revolution"— sometimes called "minor" or "non-antagonistic" contradictions—should be resolved through consultation and conciliation rather than through open adversarial conflict.[2] Hence the official preference for the term *jiti xieshang,* or "collective consultation," over the more combative-sounding *jiti tanpan,* or "collective bargaining," to describe negotiations between workers and managers over wages and other matters. "Collective bargaining" is gaining currency as the daily reality of strikes underscores the fact of conflict between labor and capital over basic distributional issues. But the notion that these interests inevitably conflict still meets resistance in official quarters, and that is partly because of China's socialist legacy, not in spite of it. The official view is still that in China's socialist market economy, unlike in capitalism, there is no basic conflict between the interests of labor and management, and thus no need for Western-style institutionalized adversarial contestation. Official discomfort with open labor-management conflict, with its deep historical and ideological roots, has left a deep imprint on the structure and conduct of the ACFTU and its branches, as well as on China's approaches to resolving collective interest disputes.

There is no single framework or legal structure for resolving collective interest disputes in China. Rather, there is what might charitably be called a "mixed strategy" that couples systemic and largely bureaucratic procedures for securing "collective agreements" —procedures that are virtually devoid of worker input—with reactive, ad hoc efforts to resolve active labor conflict. Modern collective bargaining systems in the West bring together the processes for avoiding and resolving labor conflict. But in

China the resistance to normalizing labor conflict and legitimizing strikes has impeded the integration of the two processes of resolving and avoiding conflict into a viable industrial relations system.

This is an arena of local experimentation, in part because levels of economic development vary dramatically across the country, and workers vary accordingly in their ability and inclination to pursue collective action. In Guangdong Province, for example, workers have become more experienced and savvy in group action and more ambitious in their demands. For many workers in China's non-state factories—rural migrants barely removed from the farms—industrial action was not part of their heritage. But more than thirty years of shared work and shared grievances in the factories, as one finds in Guangdong, create a very different medium for collective action from three or five years of such experience, as one finds in China's interior provinces. At the same time, what happens in Guangdong does not necessarily stay in Guangdong, as industry moves to less developed provinces and migrant workers and their networks and knowledge follow. So Guangdong may be a bellwether of industrial relations trends and a testing ground for solutions.

This chapter will begin with a brief sketch of how strikes come about and how officials respond to them, especially in Guangdong. It will then turn to the more systemic, bureaucratic efforts to address collective grievances and prevent unrest. It will then take up the interesting legal status of the "right to strike" in China and its impact on the rights of strikers—for the ambiguity and sensitivity of the strike issue is part of what stands in the way of an integrated system of industrial relations. The chapter will close with a brief account of the current Guangdong regulations on collective labor disputes, long in gestation and finally issued in 2014; these regulations represent the first tentative official reckoning with the reality of strikes and their role in collective bargaining.

## Strikes without Unions: How Do Strikes Start and How Are They Resolved?

The essence of a strike is simply a collective work stoppage: the concerted withdrawal of labor with an aim to protest or pressure the employer to meet workers' demands or address grievances. A work stoppage creates an economic problem for the employer—that is why it gives workers leverage—and in some measure, large or small, for the society. But striking workers invariably do more than cease work and stay home; they typically mount demonstrations, visibly and audibly expressing their discontent and their aims, in order to increase pressure on the employer and maintain workers' unity. Strikes are highly emotional and often tumultuous affairs. Workers are sacrificing their paychecks and potentially risking their jobs for their own and their co-workers' longer term well-being, and they do not do so lightly. The physical assembly of hundreds or thousands of agitated workers near a factory (or inside, in the case of a sit-in strike) presents a potential threat of social disorder or even violence.

In China the threat of disorder may be heightened—and management's practical ability to continue production using replacement workers constrained—because workers often live in dormitories on the factory grounds and gather inside the factory gates. That means that the striking workers are physically assembled for much of the duration of the strike (unlike in the United States, for example, when a rotating handful of workers usually man a picket line near the entrance to the establishment). The threat of disorder in China is also heightened because authorities target leaders and organizers for punishment and repression, and so leaderless and disorganized protests are the norm.

That leads to a more general point foreshadowed in Chapter 4: when a strike is led and organized by a union that can negotiate effectively with the employer, and that is bound by reasonable restrictions on the permissible scope of industrial action, the union can in turn "regulate" the workers, keeping them within legally prescribed boundaries. The union can tell the workers: "If you follow our lead, we will get you a better deal." And the union can get a better deal if it can credibly promise to end the strike on that condition. Genuinely representative unions thus stand at the core of Western collective bargaining systems: unions both enable workers to advance their economic interests and enable societies to regulate the scope and intensity of industrial action by serving as intermediate regulatory institutions. But unions can play that role only if they are seen by the workers as their faithful agents.

The official union in China is something quite different. It is supposed to represent workers' interests, but its various branches are controlled by the Party above the level of the enterprise, and its enterprise branches are largely controlled by enterprise management. There have been periodic efforts to make the enterprise trade unions more accountable to the workers; that is the subject of the next chapter. But as things stand, workers who are aggrieved, and who want to make demands on their employer, do not regard the union at any level as their faithful agent. The union cannot regulate the workers because the workers do not trust the union.

In particular, the official unions do not lead strikes. All strikes in China are what in the United States would be called "wildcat" strikes: they are not authorized or led by the union, but are organized from below by workers themselves. Indeed, it is often only when a strike is underway that the union and other party-state officials first get wind of a serious dispute. Wildcat strikes are problematic whenever and wherever they occur because there may be no organization or leadership that can credibly negotiate an end to the strike, or that can "regulate" workers' collective action and attempt to keep it within peaceful bounds. So even if the government aims only to enforce basic social order (as opposed to actively backing the employer), it is largely relegated to sending the police to the scene. Whatever limits the government seeks to impose on workers' collective action are backed up mainly by the threat of force against individual workers— arrests, detentions, police batons, or even bullets. A wildcat strike of any size or duration potentially puts workers in a direct face-off with police and creates some risk of escalating conflict and politicization.

Given the inability of the official union to play the kind of organizing and mediating role that unions play in the West, two questions arise: How do workers manage to organize a strike, or a credible threat of a strike, so as to put some clout behind their demands? And how do officials respond to strikes when they do occur? The main focus here is on the official response to labor unrest and what shapes that response. But that requires some attention to the workers' side of the equation: How do strikes take shape, and how do workers get their demands across, either before or during a strike?

The complex, varied, and fast-changing nature of collective labor activity in China deserves a much closer look than is offered here.[3] This is only a rough sketch to supplement the brief narrative of two pivotal strikes in Chapter 1. Even this glimpse of collective interest disputes and strikes, particularly as they have played out in Guangdong, will bring some focus to the ongoing debates and reforms around collective bargaining in China.

### Organizing Strikes without Unions

Many strikes in China are small in size and short in duration. Such strikes get little publicity, and many of them are probably missed by those who attempt to keep unofficial statistics on strikes.[4] Such strikes also take rather little organizing. Text messages from worker to worker, often based on "hometown" affiliations, may serve to spread the word of a walkout. Workers gather inside factory grounds (where they often live in dormitories) or perhaps even inside the factory. Among the assembled workers, informal leaders may emerge, and may even step up to "negotiate" with management over workers' demands (at considerable risk of reprisals, as described below). Larger and longer strikes—those that draw the greatest concern from officialdom—require more organizing. Formulation of collective demands and the collective decision to end a work stoppage also become more complex when hundreds or even thousands of workers are involved. How does that happen in the absence of an independent trade union to coordinate collective action?

One answer is technology (again). Modern social media technology offers a plethora of new tools for organizing, and China's workers have been quick to pick up new tools. Eighty-five percent of the Chinese population owns a mobile phone,[5] and even the inexpensive mobile phones that are ubiquitous among factory workers allow use of applications like Weibo (a Twitter analogue), WeChat and Weixin (for instant messaging and texting), and QQ (another social networking app).[6] Labor activists and ordinary workers use these platforms to organize strikes. The Nanhai Honda strike was reportedly organized mainly through text messaging; workers also created a QQ account entitled "Union is Strength" to disseminate news about the strike.[7] Workers at Yue Yuen used both QQ and Weibo to spread the word about the strike to fellow employees.[8] Strikers at a Zhongshan shoe factory in 2015 videotaped the strike and the management and police response, and posted the videos to the Internet.[9]

The use of social media not only facilitates organizing of strikes within one factory but also can convey information and inspiration to workers elsewhere, raising the risk of contagion that China's leaders most fear. So the government assiduously tracks social media for signs of unrest. Posts are often censored and posters are sometimes punished. Some activists have responded by developing complex codes, including homonyms, puns, and wordplay for which China's character-based language provides a rich medium, to sneak past censors.[10] At the other end of the technology spectrum, taxi drivers frequently use simple phone calls to organize; this frustrates government tracking, allows for immediate commitment, and mitigates the trust issue created by anonymity on the Internet.[11]

Still, leadership and experience is obviously useful in organizing an effective strike and formulating collective demands. In the chasm between the official trade union and increasingly demanding workers in Guangdong, a handful of independent grassroots activists and shoestring organizations have carved out a small and embattled space for coordinating workers' collective agitation and helping them to gain a collective voice. These worker activists do not foment discontentment or incite collective unrest; there is usually plenty of both by the time workers and activists find each other. They do not directly represent workers or lead them; but they help workers to identify and choose their own leaders. They sometimes train workers in how to elect leaders, how to articulate shared grievances and demands, how to carry out an organized and peaceful strike in support of those demands, and how to negotiate a satisfactory resolution. In China, nothing of this sort can take place without government officials knowing about it. And a handful of these activists' names recur in press reports about significant strikes. They have been continually monitored and harassed by security officials, but until 2015 they were rarely prosecuted or detained. The habitual forbearance, the routine harassment, and the recent turn toward harsher repression are all worth examining.

When asked (before the 2015 crackdown) why they were able to do what they do without being arrested, some activists maintained that it is because they were doing nothing illegal. There is no explicit criminal prohibition of strikes, and thus no basis for prosecution. (We will return below to the question of a legal "right to strike" in China.) They knew that local officials could and sometimes did prosecute activists for the rather amorphous crime of "provoking a disturbance," and could ensure a conviction if they chose to do so. China's courts are not independent of the party-state; its constitutional free speech guarantee is not enforceable or meaningful; and its criminal procedures offer little protection to defendants in politically sensitive cases.[12] Still, the criminal prosecution of individuals engaged in peaceful training and organizing of workers does have diffuse political costs. One activist opined that international opinion may play a role in discouraging repression. The prospects of bad press, an uproar from foreign human rights and labor activists, and diplomatic blowback from trading partners seem to inhibit routine use of the highly coercive and high-profile tools of criminal prosecution and imprisonment in these cases.

Some worker activists offered another reason for official forbearance and toleration, such as it was: the government needed them to help resolve industrial conflict. They have enough credibility with workers to help transform angry and spontaneous militancy into a relatively orderly process, with practical demands and peaceful tactics; and they help guide workers toward a peaceful end to a combustible confrontation. In effect, these activists help to fill the "representation gap" left by unaccountable, out-of-touch official trade unions, and to perform some of the industrial peacemaking functions that independent trade unions perform within a Western-type system of collective bargaining.

But whatever tenuous, grudging toleration these activists enjoy, they knew it was limited. If they were to overtly challenge Party rule, or to challenge the ACFTU's monopoly by declaring the formation of an independent trade union, they would cross into forbidden political territory, and neither the law nor international pressure would spare them from criminal punishment. So, too, if they were seen to be inciting the spread of strikes or building a network of worker activists across an industry or geographic area.[13] Even disseminating information about a strike could be criminalized, as it was when Yue Yuen activist Lin Dong was detained for posting an online update on the strike, as discussed in Chapter 1.

Even when grassroots activists steered clear of those red lines, they were hardly free from official scrutiny. Security officials, charged with avoiding collective unrest, do their best to monitor activists and to keep them off balance and aware of their precarious position. Pressuring landlords to evict activist organizations has been a favored police tactic. One labor rights activist reported in 2013 that he and his organization had been evicted, and compelled to find new quarters, ten times in a single year.[14] Obviously this sort of harassment limits how much organizing and educating these activists can do. It also serves as a constant reminder of the boundaries of official "toleration," if that is what one calls the sparing use of criminal prosecution and imprisonment. It signals that "we know who you are, where you are, and what you are doing."

One major figure in the Guangdong labor scene stood out for his high visibility in major strike episodes—again, at least until late 2015. Duan Yi is a lawyer who represents workers in collective disputes through his law firm, Laowei (which means roughly "worker protection"). A Chinese scholar called him "the concertmaster of China's labor movement" for his role both on the scene of many recent major labor disputes in Guangdong and in subsequent litigation over employers' dismissal of strikers and their leaders (on which more below).[15] Virtually alone among those who advocated for workers in collective disputes, he seemed to suffer no serious official harassment. Duan Yi's role in workers' collective interest disputes has been unique, but even just as a lawyer representing workers, he belongs to a very small category in China. Duan told me (and other informed observers agree) that there are no more than twenty lawyers in all of China whose practice consists solely of representation of workers. (Most lawyers who represent workers do so alongside a commercial law practice.) That is a stunning fact in a country of 1.4 billion people. It reflects China's illiberal policies toward advocacy organizations and lawyers, and it has ramifications for every aspect of China's efforts to meet workers' grievances through legal reforms.

Both Duan Yi's open, active, and vocal role in collective labor disputes and his singularity raised intriguing questions about the scope of official toleration for those who represent workers outside the official union structure. Duan was said to have some official support because he played a valuable role in coordinating workers' demands and helping to resolve disputes within the tumultuous Guangdong labor scene. But Duan's unusual insulation from official persecution was said to stem partly from his potent Party pedigree; as a child of a leading Party cadre, he had "spent his childhood among 'princelings' in an Army compound in Beijing."[16] Duan's insistent advocacy on behalf of workers, and his persistent criticism of the official union's inefficacy in collective interest disputes, may resonate to some degree within the top leadership; but the toleration that he enjoys does not seem to extend to the few others who seek to play a similar role. Indeed, by late 2015, even Duan Yi had begun to experience constraints: he was reportedly barred from representing Zeng Feiyang, the most prominent of the detained Guangdong labor activists, and was not permitted to leave the country to give talks in the United Kingdom.[17]

Zeng himself—not a lawyer, much less a princeling, but "one of the most experienced and trustworthy labour activists" in Guangdong—was in police custody and facing prosecution, largely for his role in a major strike at the Lide shoe factory in 2015. What was that role? According to workers, Zeng taught them about their "legal entitlements and how to get them," and about "how to negotiate with factory management." Far from "inciting workers to disrupt social order, Zeng and the other staff at the Panyu Centre had ensured that the workers always acted within the law: 'Zeng always told us to defend our rights in a legal way, not by blocking roads or smashing machines.' "[18] Without the role of Zeng and his colleagues, it seems likely the Lide strike would have been more chaotic, more violent, and much harder to resolve.

### The "Firefighting" Response to Strikes: Stability Maintenance as Industrial Relations

The typical response to strikes in Guangdong has been ad hoc, and it effectively reverses the chronology that is familiar in the United States: first a strike, then bargaining of a sort in its midst. The strike is invariably self-organized by workers outside any union structure; once alerted to the incident, if it is of any magnitude, local officials, including union officials, will swoop in to ascertain what the workers want and try to extract enough concessions from management to induce the workers to go back to work. This approach has been well described as a "firefighting" strategy: the strike sets off an alarm bell, and officials rush to the scene to try to put out the conflagration—to engineer some kind of deal that gets workers off the streets and back to work.[19] To some degree, this is just a variation on the "firefighting" response to all sorts of collective unrest or "mass incidents" in China. But the response to labor unrest, and strikes in particular, has some distinct features.

The union plays a key role in the "firefighting," not as the representative of the workers (though nominally it may play that role) but as more of a mediator, or go-between. In Chapter 4 I described independent unions in the United States as playing a mediating role, but that is in relation to the state and the workers; American unions do not purport to mediate between workers and employers in the resolution of labor disputes, as they do in China. Indeed, in China the neutral connotations of the term "mediator" might overstate the weight of workers' interests in the union's equation, for the union has typically performed this function on behalf of managers.

According to China's Trade Union Law, first enacted in 1992, in the event of an "outstanding incident" that interrupts production, "[t]he trade union shall assist the enterprise . . . in properly dealing with the matter so as to help restore the normal order of production and other work as soon as possible."[20] In 2001, amendments to that law tilted the scales slightly toward addressing workers' interests: in case of "work stoppages and slowdowns," the trade union should "present the opinions and demands of the workers and staff members, and put forth proposals for solutions," as well "help restore the normal order of production." (For its part, the enterprise "shall try to satisfy" the workers' "reasonable demands.")[21] An ACFTU official in 2007 described the law as "mandat[ing] that the union must intervene [in strikes], representing a negotiator between the workers and the enterprise. Under the precondition of satisfying reasonable requests of workers, we help the enterprise and state-run institutions restart their production sequence."[22] After the Honda strikes in 2010, the ACFTU's instructions to local unions, at least in Guangdong, were more explicit though less official: if five hundred or more workers were involved, the local union was required to intervene and to attempt to negotiate a settlement to end the strike.[23]

One might think that the local union's role would clash with that of the workers' own leaders—those who had helped organize the strike and who actually spoke for the workers. According to one knowledgeable source, however, union officials are generally content to allow informal worker representatives or worker committees, if they are on the scene, to take the lead and put in the work involved in negotiations (as long as they are seeking a resolution rather than an expansion of the strike).[24] But the official union in any case has to formally approve the results of collective negotiations, and the workers' unofficial representatives must accede to this symbolic assertion of the official union's authority.

One major problem with this ad hoc strategy is that it may do more to encourage than to prevent strikes: in the era of mobile phones and text messaging, workers at nearby factories quickly learn that a disruptive strike is the best way to secure a wage hike. Indeed, it might be the only way, since there is still no orderly system for collective bargaining under the shadow of a strike threat. There is no credible official representative of the workers, and often no de facto representative either, until a strike occurs. Moreover, Western observers must wonder what drives the parties to make a deal. What is the union's leverage, or the employer's incentive to make concessions, if the union can neither threaten a strike nor credibly promise to bring the strikers back to work? Seen through a Western lens, China's ad hoc "firefighting" approach to collective bargaining does not look like a viable industrial relations system.

As a stability maintenance strategy, however, the "firefighting" approach makes more sense. It allows authorities to keep most strikes quite short and confined to a single factory, and to keep unrest from spreading or intensifying to a dangerous degree, without having to open the door to independent unions. (They may be aided in this by the very high levels of turnover in China's factories, which make it very difficult to organize workers and keep them organized.[25]) After all, it is the escalation and spread of labor unrest that the government most fears.

As things stand, the number of strikes, while increasing, is not overwhelming. That is so even in Guangdong, where strikes are concentrated. In 2015, 414 collective labor incidents (many of them strikes, or work stoppages) were recorded in Guangdong by the *China Labour Bulletin,* widely regarded as the most reliable source on this matter in the absence of official statistics. Of those collective incidents, 265 were in manufacturing (many others involved construction or service workers), and 23 involved more than 1,000 workers.[26] That is enough to keep Guangdong's labor "firefighters"—mainly police and union officials—quite busy. But note that those strikes are spread across more than 1,000 smaller jurisdictions (cities, counties, and towns), 100 million residents, and an estimated 60,000 factories.[27]

Conditions could change quickly, much as an ill-timed wind in a dry spell can turn a campfire into a major conflagration (or, as they say in China, "a single spark can start a prairie fire"). But for now, the party-state's strategy of dealing with strikes one at a time on an ad hoc basis might do the job—the stability maintenance job, that is—for a long time before a more systemic solution is required, and certainly before China is forced to recognize and legitimize independent trade unions. That is partly because of the increasingly sophisticated arsenal that Chinese officials (and employers) can deploy to put out individual fires.

Fortunately for workers, part of that arsenal has been deployed against employers in the interest of appeasement and stability maintenance. Although the official union does not have the workers' trust, it does have the considerable clout of the party-state behind it in dealing with employers. Party-state officials have many levers of power that they may use—if workers need to be appeased—to pressure employers to grant concessions. In the context of a strike that is already putting substantial economic pressure on the employer, party-state involvement can supply enough added leverage to secure sizeable wage increases or lump sum payments when that is called for. Of course, not all worker demands can be satisfied with money; in particular, structural demands for greater control over the enterprise union— which are the most politically ambitious demands workers are making—call for a more delicate political calculation. Officials have sometimes been willing to grant those concessions, too, when the situation demands it, and with little risk of democracy running amok, as explored in Chapter 7.

Collective appeasement is only one facet of the official response to unrest, of course. Another option is individual appeasement or co-optation. Some grassroots leaders might be neutralized by being promoted into management or hired onto a local union staff. A Chinese labor scholar described this tactic as an application of Mao's advice on dealing with dissenters: "Mix with sand" *(chan sha zi)*.[28] Of course, grassroots worker activists in the West may also be co-opted by employers or entrenched union officials. But the temptation to succumb to such inducements is much greater in China. First, there is no alternative "career path" as a worker-leader within an independent union movement, as there is in the West (difficult though it may be). Second, workers who persist in their independent activism in China face a high risk of serious reprisals. For whether or not workers' collective demands are addressed, their leaders face a range of sanctions.

Sanctions come in many varieties. Strikers and their leaders are routinely fired, and courts accept participation in a work stoppage as a lawful reason for dismissal, as discussed below. But the risk of discharge pales beside the other risks that face China's worker activists. Activists who make connections across factories, or who openly encourage the spread of strikes, might be detained or relocated, or even criminally prosecuted. Even ordinary strikers can face such consequences. For example, in May 2014, over seventy workers protesting Walmart's modest severance payments in Hunan were detained without charges for a week, and eleven Guangdong security guards were convicted by a Guangzhou court for "disturbing public order" after a dispute with their employers.[29] Even if striking itself is not prohibited, attempting to publicize a strike or protest can readily run afoul of vague criminal prohibitions. For example, in August 2013, when hospital security guards hung a large banner from their Guangzhou clinic's roof to publicize their strike, they were arrested for "illegally gathering and disturbing the social order" and jailed for nine months.[30] In May 2015, nine striking bike light manufacturing workers were arrested by police for "disturbing public order."[31]

In short, Chinese officials have a range of repressive tools, poorly constrained by the "rule of law," that enable them to control the possible contagion of collective activity by disabling leadership. The harshest sanctions are rarely used, but their availability surely inhibits some potential leaders from stepping forward. And for those who do step forward, there are other sanctions—canceled leases and eviction, "visits" from the police, and the like—that may keep them off balance and on guard without provoking a heated backlash, either from workers or from the international community.

Genuine grassroots leaders and organizations can be useful to the regime and to employers in bringing an end to an industrial dispute; but they also increase the risk that strikes will spread from one factory to another, and that industrial activism will coalesce into something more politically consequential and dangerous. China's "firefighting" strategy for dealing with strikes seems to be well calibrated to keep strikes from spreading, in part by keeping potential leaders off balance, on guard, and scarce. But that strategy also ensures that strikes are usually chaotic and disorganized, and it impedes the emergence of a more lasting solution to industrial conflict. That is a trade-off that China's leaders appear willing to make for now, and perhaps for a long time.

## Collective Bargaining with Chinese Characteristics: Top-Down "Bargaining" at the Enterprise and Sectoral levels

China's ad hoc response to strikes is a far cry from a functioning industrial relations system in a modern economy, and its policy makers understand that. So let us turn from China's "firefighting" techniques to its "fire prevention" strategies.

### Bureaucratic Collective Bargaining at the Enterprise Level

The prevailing approach to collective bargaining in China, much like the prevailing approach to "union organizing" discussed in Chapter 3, is top-down, quota-driven, bureaucratic, and enterprise-based. Charged by their superiors with concluding large numbers of collective agreements, local unions proceed to fill their quotas by getting managers to sign agreements filled with boilerplate provisions, most of which merely repeat the law's mandatory labor standards.[32] After 2010, these agreements were somewhat more likely to provide for a modest wage bump above provincial-level minimum wages (which have themselves risen substantially in recent years). But workers rarely play any role in formulating the content of these agreements, or in agitating for their adoption. At best, managers may seek pro forma approval from the enterprise's Staff and Worker Representative Congress (SWRC), in accordance with the law's prescriptions. But the approval process, and the worker congress itself, is almost always just that: pro forma.

There are important exceptions to this pattern. Professor Mingwei Liu, among others, has documented instances of real collective bargaining of a sort—genuine interchange between employers and union officials in which workers ended up with significant improvements.[33] Especially in Guangdong, under the comparatively liberal regime of provincial party chief Wang Yang, there were glimmers of a more democratic bargaining process. Labor scholar Katie Quan, formerly a union organizer in the United States, has described several instances of collective negotiations since 2010 that she found reminiscent of real collective bargaining in the United States, in which the local union officials sought to engage the workers in formulating demands, and conducted multiple long and hard negotiating sessions with the employer in pursuit of a fair compromise.[34] Notwithstanding these encouraging exceptions, however, the norm for collective negotiations remains one of pro forma agreements arrived at through quota-driven, top-down processes.

It is hard to see this as a viable industrial relations model, but it might serve as a prophylactic complement to the "firefighting" model. With industrial peace as its overarching objective, China presumably aspires to a system of collective bargaining that can prevent disputes and not merely respond to them. If the official union can help push up wages without the immediate spur of industrial conflict, then workers may not feel the need to strike. They might even come to view the official union as a useful ally in their struggles for a decent livelihood.

A Western observer might be moved to ask again what induces employers to make concessions in this bureaucratic process. Even if strikes were officially sanctioned, union officials have too little connection to the workers to wield a credible strike threat, to assure employers that any particular deal will avoid a strike (or end one that is in progress), or perhaps even to predict the likelihood of a strike. But union officials do have other types of leverage, for the local party branch that stands behind it controls much of what local companies need to prosper. If employers believe that local party officials are serious in attempting to raise wages through collective agreements, that might enable the Party-backed union to exact concessions.

One thing is clear: Unlike the United States, and in spite of its partial conversion to the gospel of market ordering, China is not inhibited legally or ideologically from direct state intervention in determination of wages through the official trade union. Employers, who are actually embedded in markets, may well push back against active party-state involvement in wage setting, both in particular negotiations and at the policy level. And they may succeed, for employers still have plenty of pull behind the scenes with local party-state officials, and still hold the keys to the economic growth that remains central to the career trajectories of those officials. But employers in China cannot invoke any deep policy or doctrine or ideology of "collective freedom of contract"—of leaving the determination of the results of collective bargaining to the "free play of economic forces"—such as the National Labor Relations Act (NLRA) interposes in the United States as a barrier to official intervention in wage setting at the company level.[35]

The prevailing bureaucratic, quota-driven bargaining process is not well tailored to address the particularized worker grievances and demands that produce conflict. At best, it may produce modest wage increases with a diffuse tendency to allay discontentment. If it does that, it might be a small part of the solution to China's labor problems. Or it might encourage "rising expectations" and more ambitious demands on the part of workers who are able to mobilize a real strike threat of their own. Maybe the "firefighting" model can pick up where the bureaucratic model leaves off. Or maybe rising strike levels will eventually outstrip local "firefighting" resources.

A functional industrial relations system would integrate the procedures for resolving active labor disputes and for preventing labor disputes. It would link up the now-separate domains of union-led collective negotiations and worker-led industrial action, and channel workers' collective demands and energies into a regularized process of bargaining. Guangdong Province has recently taken some very modest steps in that direction in its 2014 Regulation on Collective Contracts for Enterprises, to which we will return below.

## *Sectoral Collective Bargaining*

A different approach to collective bargaining has gained traction in parts of Zhejiang Province, near Shanghai. Sectoral bargaining takes place at a higher level—between regional or industrial employer and union federations, instead of at the enterprise level. That approach holds some appeal in China because the sectoral and regional branches of the union are less dominated by management than the enterprise chapters. Sectoral bargaining has other potential advantages over decentralized enterprise-based bargaining. The latter, typified by U.S.-style collective bargaining, exposes employers to cost-based competition from non-union firms or from firms that strike a better deal with the union; that tends to stiffen employer resistance to union demands.[36] By contrast, sectoral bargaining, prevalent in much of Europe, holds out the promise of "taking wages out of competition" within a sector and making wage gains more sustainable. "Taking wages out of competition" is not always an advantage for workers, however, and it may not be an advantage for workers in its stronghold in Zhejiang, where it has been closely examined by Professor Eli Friedman.[37]

Zhejiang Province has long been a hotbed of domestic entrepreneurship in China. It was politically suspect under Mao, and was not much favored either by the policy makers who presided over China's "opening" or by the big foreign investors who poured into China in its wake. Still, Zhejiang's small entrepreneurs took advantage of the opening to private investment, and created a thriving economy of small- and medium-size businesses and of "local agglomeration economies"—clusters of similar factories, with economies of scale and active exchange of information amid competition for customers and workers.[38] The Zhejiang town of Yiwu, for example, produced three billion pairs of socks per year, nearly all for export.[39] Zhejiang also became home to relatively robust employer associations— rare in China, but crucial to effective sectoral bargaining.

Zhejiang's employers confronted a labor market problem that seemed to call for a sectoral solution. Competition for workers, especially skilled workers, was producing high turnover and rising wages. Sectoral wage bargaining offered employers a solution: uniform wages across firms would help to "stabilize" labor supply and reduce turnover. But is such "stability" good for workers? It all depends.

In tight labor markets, workers (especially those with scarce skills) can jockey for higher wages by forcing employers to compete for their services. In slack labor markets, employers can play workers against each other and keep wages low. Given their druthers, both workers and employers would prefer to constrain market dynamics by putting either a floor or a ceiling on wages. Despite the seeming symmetry, employers often hold the upper hand, in part because workers' labor power expires each day and cannot be saved up and sold at a more propitious time and price.[40] The "inequality of bargaining power" that generally prevails between workers and employers has led modern industrial societies to give greater legitimacy to workers' collective efforts to put a floor on wages—for example, through minimum-wage laws—than to employers' efforts to cap wages.[41]

Collective bargaining, and especially sectoral bargaining, can constrain wages at both the high and low ends. That is so even in democratic countries with independent labor movements. Nationally organized independent unions can take a long and broad view of workers' interests, and can bargain for a fair quid pro quo in exchange for "wage restraint" that benefits the economy as a whole. But unless workers are well represented, sectoral bargaining can become a vehicle for simple employer collusion—a way to cap wage levels below what the market would bear, and to limit employer competition in tight labor markets, without any future rewards for workers' forbearance. The risk of employer collusion is high in China, where the workers' official representatives answer to party officials, who are in turn often beholden to local businesses. Especially when multiemployer bargaining is a response to tight labor markets and rising wages, as in Zhejiang, one suspects it does more to restrain workers' bargaining power than to enhance it.

Friedman found that sectoral bargaining in Zhejiang, despite its appeal to employers seeking to restrain upward wage pressure, did not work out as planned. In short, employer associations were unable to bind employers to the sectoral deals that they had made.[42] Nonetheless, some scholars and policy makers in China have looked to sectoral bargaining as an appealing strategy for industry sectors and regions populated by many small- and medium-size employers, in which enterprise bargaining is an unwieldy and unlikely prospect.

Sectoral bargaining between Party-controlled trade unions and usually-Party-controlled employer associations is not collective bargaining as we know it in the West. But it could instead serve as a non-legislative mechanism for policymakers to set higher sector-specific minimum wage rates. That would be an innovative *regulatory* response to workers' demands for higher wages in the more productive sectors and might help to avert some disputes. It would still fall short of addressing many workers' demands, and it would not offer a way to resolve the disputes that do ripen into industrial conflict. Like quota-driven enterprise-level bargaining, however, it might be a useful prophylactic component of a mixed strategy for containing unrest.

One difference between enterprise-based and sectoral bargaining is more political than economic, and it may loom larger in China than in the West: Real sectoral bargaining requires organizing, solidarity, and collective action among workers across a sector. And that is anathema to China's leaders. As long as China remains committed to keeping labor mobilization and unrest localized and contained within particular enterprises, that commitment will constrain China's experimentation with what is currently a mix of enterprise-based and sectoral "collective bargaining" (albeit in forms that are barely recognizable to Western labor cognoscenti).

Sectoral bargaining is likely to remain confined to small niches of the economy unless and until China's employers form more robust associations for collective bargaining purposes. And sectoral bargaining, even where it exists, will not reliably serve workers' interests unless and until China's workers gain greater sway over their unions and gain the ability to organize and exert pressure across a sector. In those areas and industries where workers are themselves capable of mounting sizable strikes, neither bureaucratic, quota-based enterprise bargaining nor lopsided or fictitious sectoral bargaining is likely to solve China's problem of labor unrest.

### A Missed Opportunity: The 2014 Guangdong Regulations on Collective Bargaining

The current official methods of collective bargaining are not up to the challenges posed by newly demanding workers who are willing and able to organize collective action. Yet a new national framework for collective bargaining is not yet on the horizon, both because of the sensitivity of industrial relations and because of the dramatically different conditions of industrial relations in different parts of the country. Whatever happens at the national level, in the meantime provincial and municipal governments will have to find their own ways forward, "crossing the river by feeling the stones," as Deng Xiaoping once described the proper approach to economic reform.[43] Policy makers in Guangdong, who have been on the front lines of industrial conflict for over a decade, have been most acutely aware of the need for reform and have sought to craft a more realistic approach to collective labor relations.

Draft regulations were first released in 2010, and were viewed by labor advocates and scholars as promising. As Aaron Halegua explained, the draft law would have "made it easy for workers to request negotiations," and would have authorized fines against employers who "refused to negotiate, withheld information or negotiated in bad faith."[44] Crucially, the draft regulation "legitimised certain strikes," and barred the discharge of employees who struck in response to an employer's unreasonable actions. But sharp criticism, especially from the Hong Kong businesses that own many of Guangdong's factories, led to long delays and multiple rounds of revisions.

The final regulations, issued in September 2014 and effective on January 1, 2015,[45] fully satisfy nobody. It is fair to say they represent both the most advanced step so far in China's industrial relations development and a great disappointment to reform advocates. The final regulation made it harder for workers to demand negotiations; it eliminated penalties against employers who refused to bargain in earnest; and, most important, it retreated from the draft regulation's legitimation of strikes. The regulation explicitly prohibits workers from engaging in a strike or slowdown during negotiations, and it omits the draft law's protection for workers who strike in response to employers' bad faith bargaining. In other words, says Halegua, "the final regulation maintains the status quo," and "marks a missed opportunity to try to establish a functional collective bargaining system."[46]

## The "Right to Strike" and the Rights of Strikers

Collective bargaining of any kind depends on workers' ability to exert collective leverage against employers; historically that leverage has come in the form of a collective withdrawal of labor power—the strike. It is no surprise, then, that rising strike levels have both given China's workers greater leverage to demand concrete improvements and given momentum to reform efforts. Indeed, one focal point of reform efforts, as seen in the case of Guangdong, is the recognition of a legal "right to strike." As things stand, however, in Guangdong as throughout China, the legal status of strikes is highly ambiguous. China's constitution once proclaimed that workers had a right to strike; but since that clause was dropped in 1982, scholars and advocates must look elsewhere for the legal underpinnings of a right to strike.

Some Chinese legal scholars find a "right to strike" in China's ratification of the International Covenant on Economic, Social and Cultural Rights, effective in 2001, which calls upon signatories to "ensure . . . the right to strike, provided that it is exercised in conformity with the laws of the particular country."[47] They point further to China's Trade Union Law, amended that same year, which prescribes proper handling of "work stoppages and slowdowns": the trade union "shall, on behalf of the workers and staff members, . . . present [their] opinions and demands . . . and put forth proposals for solutions," and the enterprise "shall try to satisfy" the workers' "reasonable demands."[48] The law's neutral reference to work stoppages and its prescription of constructive responses leads some scholars to infer that strikes are lawful.[49] In addition, some invoke a principle that "everything that is not prohibited is allowed."[50] That is the spirit underlying the response of Duan Yi, the Guangdong attorney who has represented many strikers, to police when they warned Yue Yuen strikers that they were breaking the law: "Where is the law that says striking is illegal? If this activity is prohibited by the law, then you need to say so with crystal clarity. Which law is it?"[51]

The lack of a clear legal prohibition against strikes is important; it means that workers are rarely arrested or detained merely for joining a work stoppage. But if there is a legal "right to strike" in China, it is thin and fragile at best. In particular, it does not entail protection of strikers against dismissal. Recall from Chapter 5 that China's Labor Contract Law (LCL) protects most workers against unjustified dismissal. But one valid ground for dismissal under the LCL is "serious violation of the bylaws [or rules] of the employer."[52] And that includes employer rules against work stoppages, which are ubiquitous. The upshot is that employers are almost entirely free to dismiss workers based on their participation in a strike. That is not a "right to strike" as we know it in the West (but stay tuned).

Consider the findings of legal scholars Wang Tianyu and Fang Lee Cooke in their study of 897 court decisions from 2008 to 2015 reviewing the dismissal of workers based on organizing or participating in strikes, work stoppages, or slowdowns.[53] In 59 percent of the cases, the dismissal was upheld on the ground that the worker had violated an employer rule against work stoppages.[54] For example, in upholding the dismissal of workers who struck over allegedly improper calculation of overtime pay, one court wrote: "Workers should follow workplace rules . . . In the event of violation, employers may punish the workers concerned. Labor dispute, if any, should be resolved through established procedures and according to the law instead of by ceasing work, withholding performance, or any other improper and radical action to disrupt production, operation and management."[55] In most of the remaining cases, the dismissal was overturned on factual grounds—either the employer failed to prove that a work stoppage had occurred (29 percent), or the workers were found to have been "negotiating" rather than striking (7 percent). In 5 percent of the cases, the employer's rule against work stoppages was held invalid on procedural grounds (to which we will return). *Not one court questioned the substantive validity of an employer rule prohibiting strikes or work stoppages.*[56]

Perhaps these decisions, in allowing employers to prohibit strikes, are simply wrong as a matter of Chinese law. Professor Chang Kai, for example, argues that, for workers' violation of an employer rule to be a valid basis for dismissal, the rule must be both substantively and procedurally valid, and that a blanket rule against work stoppages is substantively invalid because it is contrary to the right to strike embodied in China's existing labor laws.[57] But so far that is not the view of China's courts. So while the law in China does not prohibit strikes, it gives effect to *employers'* prohibition of strikes.

The Wang and Cooke study found some consolation for workers dismissed for striking. Some courts were willing to delve into the facts; and some then found that what happened was "negotiation" with the employer rather than a work stoppage, or simply that the employer had failed to prove that a work stoppage had occurred.[58] When workers collectively submit requests or demands, and perhaps await a response from the employer, courts can and sometimes do construe this as a form of negotiating pursuant to the law. Recognizing a "right to negotiate" is not the same as a "right to strike," but it gives some breathing room to employees who are seeking to pressure employers in support of reasonable demands.

Also of interest are the cases examining the *procedural* validity of employer rules against work stoppages.[59] Among the five percent of cases holding the rule invalid on procedural grounds, a handful (two percent) relied on the employers failure to submit the rule for discussion or approval by the Staff and Workers' Representative Congress (SWRC). The SWRC is a key institution in what Chinese labor law calls "democratic management," and is the focus of Chapter 8. Both the Labor Law of 1994 and the Labor Contract Law require employer rules that bear directly on employee interests to be "submitted to the [SWRC] or all workers" for discussion.[60] This would seem to authorize or even require courts to inquire into the procedural background of rules that employers rely upon in justifying dismissal. But very few courts have done this in any serious way. We will return to this shortly.

In sum, Chinese workers may enjoy a "right to strike" in the sense that no criminal law prohibits them from collectively ceasing work. But the "right to strike" means more than that, at least in the West. In particular it means that employers are not allowed to prohibit strikes, or to punish workers for participating in a lawful strike. The courts in China clearly do not recognize a "right to strike" in that stronger sense.

The comparison becomes less stark, however, if we take a closer look at some limitations on the "right to strike" in the West, with the NLRA as our (not necessarily typical) example. To begin with, if strikers in the

United States were to gather and demonstrate on the employer's property, as Chinese strikers typically do, they would generally be subject not only to dismissal but to criminal prosecution for trespass. The NLRA protects both the right to strike and the right to demonstrate in support of a strike, but not the right to do so on the employer's property (unless workers live on the employer's premises—rare in the United States but common in China). Perhaps as another legacy of the *danwei* system, in which workers were members of the enterprise, Chinese strikers are more protected when they stay within the factory gates than when they venture onto public property. In the United States, by contrast, with its foundational commitment to private property rights, striking workers must leave the premises and retreat to public property, where they, unlike Chinese workers, have a constitutional and statutory right to gather and demonstrate. That makes it easier for U.S. strikers to draw media attention and public support, though harder for them to defend their jobs against the hiring of replacement workers.

Workers' right to strike is further limited in the United States by employers' right to *permanently replace* striking workers (unless the strike is in response to unlawful employer conduct).[61] Economic strikers are protected against discharge, and they might get their jobs back if vacancies later arise.[62] Still, most striking workers face a serious risk of long-term job loss. That contravenes what most Western and international labor law experts deem to be a "right to strike,"[63] is widely condemned by U.S. labor law scholars,[64] and has contributed to the difficulty of union organizing and declining union density in the United States.[65] But it remains the law.

A less controversial restriction on the right to strike is the "peace obligation," a version of which is found in many Western labor law systems.[66] Under the NLRA, workers who strike in violation of a "no-strike" clause of a collective bargaining agreement are usually not protected at all, and can be fired or ordered back to work.[67] In short, unions can and do waive employees' right to strike for several years at a stretch as part of the quid pro quo of collective bargaining. The logic is this: the main leverage unions have in seeking concessions from employers is their ability to strike—and their ability to credibly trade away the right to strike for the duration of a collective agreement. That theory highlights one large question hanging over China's attempts to reform collective labor relations: without either a legal "right to strike" or worker representatives that can deploy and channel the strike threat, it is unclear how collective bargaining is supposed to work. What leverage do Chinese workers have in pursuing their demands? Their "wildcat" strikes may give them de facto bargaining leverage, but that is hardly a stable industrial relations system.

The unprotected status of a strike in breach of a no-strike clause under the NLRA is also important because it highlights an analogy in Chinese labor law, and a potential avenue of reform. Chinese labor law allows dismissal of a worker who seriously violates employer rules, including a rule against work stoppages; but to be valid, such rules, as well as collective agreements, must be "submitted to the [SWRC] or all workers" for discussion and (arguably) approval.[68] For now, these "democratic management" institutions and procedures are pro forma at best in most private companies. But if courts gave them teeth by regularly overturning dismissals based on procedurally defective rules, *and* if the SWRCs were a forum for serious review of collective wage agreements and employer rules, then a properly approved and limited employer rule against work stoppages—one whose duration was tied to the collective agreement—would look less like a unilateral employer prohibition on strikes, as it is now, and a little more like a negotiated "no-strike" clause of a collective bargaining agreement.[69]

To be clear: there are many reasons to doubt that "democratic management" has a bright future in China, and we will explore them in Chapter 8. In the meantime, however, those courts that have been willing to look behind employer rules against work stoppages have hit upon a possible middle ground between those who assert there is a "right to strike" in Chinese labor law and those who find no such right. Even without new legislation, and without questioning the substantive validity of employer rules against work stoppages, courts could afford modest protection to strikers either by scrutinizing the procedural validity of such rules or by questioning their application to workers who were presenting reasonable demands to recalcitrant employers. This would be a far cry from a "right to strike" as it exists in Western labor law, but it would be a step toward a more balanced and realistic treatment of strikes in China.

Progress on the collective bargaining front may eventually require legislative protection of a "right to strike," among other reforms. But such legislation poses risks of its own. Some commentators in China have worried that any legislative declaration of a right to strike would inevitably come with sharp limits on the lawfulness of strikes—sharper and more restrictive than those found in the United States and elsewhere in the West. Such legislation might transform the "gray area" in which strikes currently take place into a "black and white" legal regime that puts strikers at *greater* risk.[70] That very fear has been realized in recent Guangdong legislation, reviewed above.

As things stand, workers who go on strike face a high risk of dismissal, with no legal recourse. That presumably inhibits some workers from participating in strikes. And that in turn may help to fortify the status quo against pressure for reform, and to discourage policy makers and courts from affording more forthright legal protection of the right to strike. That brings us back to the central thesis here.

On the one hand, the rising incidence of strikes has become a source of official anxiety and has highlighted the need for reform—for a more orderly structure for resolving collective labor disputes and preventing localized outbursts of worker unrest from multiplying and coalescing into a larger and more politicized independent labor movement. At the same time, however, that same objective constrains reform: It rules out the toleration of independent labor organizations, which could help bring order to collective unrest and facilitate genuine collective bargaining; and it inhibits efforts to put the "right to strike" on a firmer legal footing in China (for if workers had a "right to strike," there would probably be more strikes and more open organization of strikes). Seen through our Western-inflected lens, a reasonably robust "right to strike," coupled with effective procedures for collective bargaining through labor organizations that are trusted by workers, would lay the groundwork for more just *and* more peaceable industrial relations. But to China's powers-that-be, that path looks perilous and well-nigh unthinkable if it depends on the toleration of independent organizing.

VIEWED FROM WITHOUT, and especially from the West, China's jury-rigged approach to preventing and resolving collective labor unrest looks unsustainable. It has some familiar elements—trade unions, strikes, collective bargaining—but every one of those elements looks less familiar and problematic upon closer examination. China's official and only lawful trade unions bear little resemblance to the independent trade unions that are the central actors in Western industrial relations systems; most important, they are not accountable to workers at any level of the organization. The growing number of strikes are not organized by these official unions, nor by any organization that dares to call itself a union, but by workers themselves with limited support from a handful of embattled and marginalized worker advocates. "Collective bargaining" is usually a bureaucratic and pro forma process in which workers play no role, and occasionally an emergency response to workers' self-organized, nearly leaderless rebellions. It is not a system in which workers can present their demands and seek a peaceful resolution under the shadow of industrial conflict.

"And yet it moves." In spite of its seeming dysfunctionality as an industrial relations system, the amalgam of strategies and tactics, sticks and carrots, by which Chinese managers and officials have been responding to rising labor unrest has thus far managed to achieve several central goals of the industrial relations systems with which Westerners are more familiar. It has kept industrial conflict from either stalling the economy or seriously disrupting social or political order, and it has increased workers' incomes. And it has done this without compromising a central goal of China's regime—that is, without conceding any significant space for independent labor organizations. Those achievements pose a challenge to the broad consensus in much of the world outside of China (at least in principle) that the freedom of association, the right to form independent trade unions, and the right to bargain collectively through those unions must be the bedrock of any functional industrial relations regime.

For several years after the Honda strikes, China's leaders appeared to concede that collective bargaining was essential to the achievement of "harmonious" labor relations. Lately, however, some top leaders seem to be questioning the centrality of collective bargaining to the regime's larger goals. In his annual policy speech in March of 2015, Chinese Premier Li Keqiang dropped his usual reference to collective bargaining; the widely-noted omission was interpreted as reflecting concern over the impact of rising wages on China's growth rate.[71] And in a lengthy address in April 2015, Finance Minister Lou Jiwei depicted American and European experience with strong unions as a cautionary tale for China. He characterized sector-wide collective bargaining in particular as a "scary" prospect; that, he said, was how the United Auto Workers, bargaining with the "Big Three" American auto firms, had padded labor costs and contributed to the bankruptcy of the American auto industry.[72] In response to Lou's speech, a leading ACFTU official spoke out in support of collective bargaining as a "tried-and-tested process that's practiced by successful enterprises," and a key to stable labor relations.[73] It would appear that there is active debate within Chinese officialdom as to whether and in what form collective bargaining is a part of China's strategy for maintaining both economic growth and political power while "rebalancing" the economy in favor of ordinary workers. And experience in the West is clearly playing a role on both sides of that debate.

In the meantime, however, China's workers are still on the steep part of the learning curve in their ability to press collective demands and organize collective action. So alongside the "firefighting" and bureaucratic approaches to collective labor demands, reform of China's labor relations institutions continues in an effort to keep pace with workers' increasingly articulate and ambitious demands for a voice in their working lives. That brings us back again to the ACFTU, whose "uselessness" is a common, if perhaps overstated, refrain among workers and their advocates. What can be done to make the ACFTU and its millions of trade union affiliates more responsive to workers? Or, more to the point for China's leaders, what can be done to that end without the official trade unions spinning out of Party control?

# CHAPTER SEVEN

# What Does Democracy Look Like in China?

## Reforming Grassroots Union Elections

T HE WORLD WAS treated to a dramatic spectacle of popular demand for democracy in China in late 2011, when residents of the small village of Wukan, in Guangdong Province, rose up in rebellion against their corrupt and entrenched leaders and ran them out of the village. The resulting standoff between villagers and local police seemed likely to end badly for the villagers. But when provincial leaders intervened and granted the villagers' demand for democratic village elections, much of the world cheered this glimmer of hope for "grassroots democracy" in China.

Another election occurred a few weeks later and about a hundred miles to the west in a Shenzhen factory. Striking workers there demanded not only higher pay and fair pay structures but also election of new trade union officers through more democratic election procedures. Provincial trade union officials intervened and presided over a comparatively democratic election process that ejected incumbents and produced a new union chair who promised to stand with the workers. The election "was hailed at the time as a historic development in labour relations because for first time, a local trade union federation had responded favourably to demands from the workers themselves for trade union reform."[1]

This "tale of two elections," as well as the less uplifting aftermath of both elections, highlights some of the hopes and misgivings about the future of "grassroots democracy" in China's trade unions and beyond. Electoral democracy in some form is on the agenda, both of trade union and party leaders and of China's workers. But what does democracy mean in China, and when and why do democratizing reforms move forward or stall?

China's workers, especially migrant workers in the non-state sector, do not regard the official trade union as their own, dominated as it is by the Party and, within the enterprise, by management. A union that is useless to workers is also useless to the party-state in its struggle to dampen labor unrest. So the All-China Federation of Trade Unions (ACFTU) has come under pressure from above, below, and within to reform itself and become a more effective representative (and regulator) of China's unruly workers.[2] Party control of the ACFTU and its branches remains untouchable; and so it is management domination at the enterprise level that has come under pressure. That has led to proposals—not for the first time—for "direct election" of those officers by workers. But "direct election" turns out to be an exquisitely ambiguous term in China. "First selection, then election"—official selection or screening of candidates before election by constituents—is the norm for elections in China where and when they occur.[3] (That same norm was at the heart of the stormy contest in Hong Kong between mainland China and its allies and Occupy Central protesters over the form of future elections.[4]) Official control of nominations has left the door wide open for management domination of grassroots unions and union elections.

Lately, however, some workers have been pressing from below for a more open election process with a Chinese pedigree of its own. At least by 2012, some striking workers were demanding, and sometimes getting, so-called *haixuan,* or "sea elections"—in which workers nominate their own candidates—as part of the price of industrial peace. The *haixuan* concept is familiar to migrant workers because that is supposed to be the form of China's village elections. The law governing the latter has evolved since the 1980s away from "first selection, then election" and toward open nominations.[5]

*Haixuan* elections might seem to be the obvious antidote to the problem of unresponsive grassroots unions. But *haixuan* elections in the trade union setting look very risky to the powers-that-be in China's labor relations scene—employers as well as ACFTU and Party officials, local and national. They fear that workers might choose irresponsible or unqualified leaders, leading to wider conflict. That risk can sometimes be outweighed, however, by the vivid prospect of continued agitation from below. And so *haixuan* elections have become part of the bag of goodies, along with wage hikes, from which officials draw in their ad hoc responses to strikes. Some observers hope that *haixuan* elections will be more than a short-term, ad hoc fix, and a key to making unions more responsive and effective institutions in the future. Others doubt that *haixuan* elections have much of a future in the trade unions, "risky" as they are seen to be.

The pattern is by now familiar. As in other arenas of labor policy, reform of grassroots union elections is driven in part by official fears that worker unrest will build up, spread, and coalesce into independent labor organizations. Yet the space for reform is constrained by those same fears: "too much democracy," even within official institutions for worker representation, poses a risk that those institutions will spin out of official control. As a consequence, any democratization of union elections that does occur will likely be too cramped and constricted to work as a strategy for quelling labor unrest and forestalling independent activism.

Other fears may be at work, too. More democratic trade union elections might encourage demands for greater democracy in the polity. For most Americans, democracy is a self-evident entitlement, something any citizen of any society would wish for. Surely the experience of electing one's own leaders at any level, once sampled, would be contagious and hard to contain. In China, however, there may be antibodies and antidotes that keep demands for electoral democracy from spreading beyond the grassroots. Evidence for both the intuitive appeal of democracy and some of the Chinese characteristics that may check its spread can be found in the history of village elections.

Democratization is widely seen in China as a process that proceeds step by step—*yi bu, yi bu*—starting from the grassroots. Some of those steps are being taken by China's beleaguered workers. But the steps are likely to proceed slowly, and they are very unlikely to lead to what Westerners would regard as full-fledged electoral democracy.

## A Note on "Democracy"

"Democracy" sounds simple enough, but its definition is a complex and hotly contested matter. At bottom, democracy requires that those who govern gain the consent of the governed, not once but through periodic contests for political power.[6] A spare definition would call a system democratic if the governed choose their ultimate governors, and can displace incumbents, by some semblance of majority rule.[7] This definition slides over crucial questions, such as those about the proportion of the governed that can vote, restrictions on eligibility of candidates for elected office, the freedom of regime opponents to openly contest and campaign for power, and the scope of governmental authority exercised by elected leaders. All of the latter are matters of degree. The combination of these elements produces infinite possible permutations of more or less "democratic" systems, even among those that hold elections. Complications multiply when we consider the question of democracy not only within a nation but within workplaces, unions, private clubs, or towns within the nation.

China, for example, holds periodic elections for hundreds of thousands of public offices. Most of those are village elections, which are supposed to involve multiple candidates and secret ballots, and in which incumbent village officials theoretically risk being voted out of office by something like majority rule. Yet it would be a stretch to say that villages in China are governed democratically, even if those elections were free from manipulation, given that ultimate power in the village, as in the polity as a whole, resides in the Communist Party of China (CPC), whose cadres are not subject to popular election. Nor are officials at higher levels of the polity, who control much that matters for villagers, subject to popular election. (More on these matters below.) The result for China as a whole is nothing that Westerners would recognize as electoral democracy.

Lest American readers begin, however, with too self-satisfied a view of democracy in our own society, it is worth recalling that the vast majority of American workers has no democratic voice whatsoever within the workplace. Only a small minority participates in the distinct (and rather attenuated) form of industrial democracy that is achieved through collective bargaining. The great majority of workers is subject to a kind of managerial dictatorship, benevolent or otherwise, at work. They have a right to quit, or to exit, but no mechanism for "voice." And while Americans may take for granted the right of workers to choose their own union leaders, most American workers have no union in which to exercise that right. So Americans may judge harshly the institutional forms that "democracy" takes in China, but that judgment should be tempered, at least in the workplace setting, by the recognition that the *domain* of "democracy" in China is wider. It reaches a wider swath of industrial life than it does in the United States. (Another dimension of workplace democracy in China, the Staff and Worker Representative Congress (SWRC) system, is the subject of Chapter 8.) With that, let us return to the state of electoral democracy at the grassroots in China, both in the villages and in the enterprise trade unions.

## A Tale of Two Elections: Wukan and Ohms Electronics

We begin not in the factories this time but in the coastal village of Wukan in Guangdong Province. The story of Wukan—widely and well reported at the time in the Western press[8]—reminds us that China's migrant workers have carried lessons about both organizing collective action and electoral democracy back and forth between the villages and the factories, especially in Guangdong. The emergence of demands for open elections in the trade unions may owe something to the history of China's village election process, and in turn may affect the future of elections above and beyond the grassroots trade union chapters.

## The Siege of Wukan

The Wukan story began in a depressingly mundane way: faced with what they saw as illegal land grabs by corrupt local officials, villagers rose up in protest. Illegal land grabs are the single most prolific source of "mass incidents" in rural China. But this was no spontaneous outburst. The large-scale protest was spearheaded by a handful of "young men steeped in the migrant labor battles of the Pearl River Delta factory belt in southern Guangdong Province."[9] They called themselves "The Wukan Hot-Blooded Patriotic Youth League," and on September 21, 2011, after two years of organizing, investigating, petitioning, and even litigating, they managed to draw thousands of villagers to a protest march, loud but peaceful, under banners like "Return our Ancestral Farmland." The next day, "busloads of riot police cracked down . . . , beating men, women and school children with truncheons. Farmers and fishermen fought back with anything at hand—sticks, mops, brooms and rocks—along the main street of the village."[10] Several protest leaders were arrested.

Events in Wukan took an even more dramatic turn when one of the protest leaders died in police custody. Angry villagers effectively routed incumbent officials and police from the village and set up a blockade against their reentry. Police responded with their own blockade, preventing the entry of food and supplies. While the official Chinese press largely ignored the uprising, local villagers managed to publicize it through cell phone video clips and social media, and to draw the attention of the foreign press, which flooded into Wukan.

In the midst of the siege, things seemed likely to go badly for the protesting villagers, even as some of them expressed hope that higher-level officials, and the law, would come to their aid.[11] Eventually, however, provincial officials—led by Wang Yang, then Party chief of Guangdong, and a reputed reformer—intervened in support of the besieged villagers and their demands for an open secret-ballot election for village committee and a review of the land deals.[12] The election went forward on March 3, 2012, with great fanfare, and with international press coverage, and several protest leaders were elected to leadership positions in the village.

Consider a few points about the elections and how they came about. First, villagers began to challenge undemocratic and unresponsive village institutions only after their underlying complaints about corrupt land sales were repeatedly rebuffed without a fair hearing. Their complaints, however well-grounded in the law, probably would have been ignored by higher-ups but for the ruckus they caused. The pattern of escalation—from the assertion and frustration of particular rights and interests, often dressed up in legal garb, to demands for fairer and more democratic institutions for the pursuit of rights and interests in the future—echoes patterns seen in industrial conflict as well.

Second, both the extraordinary and ordinary features of the conflict together threatened to make it contagious. The villagers' unusual courage, the high drama of their standoff against local officials, and the international attention they gained, coupled with the ordinariness of their underlying complaint about land grabs, which have stirred protests all over rural China, were an explosive combination. Instead of repression, higher-ups offered a concession: open elections in exchange for ending the open rebellion. So the Wukan episode illustrates both the existence of grassroots demand for greater democracy in China and the potential, in the right circumstances, for securing it by making a ruckus.

Third, the villagers' demand for *haixuan* elections was in one sense very modest, for the laws governing village elections already prescribed *haixuan* elections, in which villagers could nominate candidates directly, and there were more candidates than positions.[13] But in many villages, as in Wukan at the time, nominations are still steered, screened, and manipulated by incumbents and CCP officials in the village or township.[14] The Wukan episode both highlights the role of elections in China's one-party political system and hints at the gap between having formal democratic rights on paper and actually being able to choose one's own leaders in the face of incumbents' resistance. Both are true on the labor front as well.

Unfortunately, the aftermath of the Wukan election was as depressing as its prologue: newly elected village leaders, who had entered office with high hopes and ideals, ended up resigning in frustration over their inability to unwind the land deals, or to change much of anything. They found that the elected village committee wielded little real power, hemmed in as it was by the unelected party-state officials above and around them.[15] This part of the story holds its own lessons, explored below, for the future of trade union elections.

## Ohms Electronics Workers Get Their Election

Just three weeks after the Wukan election, in late March 2012, over 600 of the 850 employees from the Japanese-owned Ohms Electronics factory, in Shenzhen, went on strike. They demanded, among other things, higher salaries and "democratic elections for a new trade union chairman."[16] The workers publicized the strike and their demands through the Internet, and especially Weibo (China's equivalent of Twitter), and they drew some attention, though the international press did not rush to the scene. Strikes had become fairly routine in Guangdong (though this was larger than most). The local police apparently did not confront the strikers directly. Instead, within a few days the Shenzhen ACFTU chapter, in accordance with the officially prescribed "firefighting" response to strikes, sent district-level union officials to negotiate an end to the strike. The resulting agreement was celebrated by many observers as a breakthrough: workers had demanded not just wage hikes but democratizing reforms, and provincial union leaders had agreed.[17] The workers returned to the factory on April 4, and preparations for the election began.

The election process, approved by the local ACFTU, was rather arcane. First, management conducted anonymous balloting in seven factory branches; that produced a committee of seventy-four representatives—most ordinary workers, some shift and team leaders—who presided over the rest of the election process.[18] The seventy-four elected representatives met and chose fourteen candidates, again by secret ballot. The incumbent union chair was eliminated in the first round. (He expressed surprise, but admitted that previous elections had not been very democratic.)[19] The list of candidates was submitted to the district trade union office for approval and was then posted. After a brief campaign featuring candidate speeches, on May 27 the election took place. But the workforce as a whole did not cast ballots. First, the fourteen candidates elected three of their own as candidates for union chair and vice-chair; then the seventy-four elected representatives voted on those candidates by secret ballot. The new chair, Zhao Shaobo, won with forty-nine out of seventy-four votes. Zhao was himself a manager, though at a lower level than his predecessor, and was said to have strong support from the rank-and-file workers. A few worker activists were also elected to union council positions, and all of the incumbent officers who were higher-level managers were voted out.[20] The workers celebrated their election and its outcome.

Unfortunately, the aftermath of the election at Ohms was no less discouraging than it was in Wukan. Chair Zhao, once elected, became "high-handed," according to one worker activist, siding with management and failing to consult with workers. The handful of worker-activists on the council "found themselves pushing up against a brick wall: 'It was useless. There was no point.'" Anger boiled over when management decided to terminate a group of sixty workers rather than convert them from fixed-term to indefinite-term contracts, and Zhao put up no fight; he reportedly said "this is nothing to do with us." Several of the affected workers climbed to the factory roof and threatened to jump in protest. They did not jump, but they did post a petition on the factory gate calling for Zhao's recall, and quickly garnered more than one hundred signatures. The recall demand was rejected by the factory union council. For his part, Zhao expressed frustration: The job was difficult, the workers' demands were sometimes unreasonable, and he had little experience and no real clout with the company that employed him.[21]

The fact that the Ohms election was hailed at the time as a breakthrough for democratic reform is itself revealing, considering the multiple filters through which workers expressed their preferences. Local ACFTU officials approved the list of candidates (though they apparently did not *disapprove* any candidates who were put forward), and few of the workers got to cast a direct vote for union leaders. Still, the procedure appeared to satisfy workers' demands for more democratic elections, and to follow ACFTU policy on selecting trade union chairs through "democratic electoral processes."[22] Though complex, the process was clearly more democratic than past union elections at Ohms, and more democratic than the vast majority of union elections. And even if it could have been more democratic along several dimensions, it was "democratic" in some threshold sense under the spare definition proferred above.

It is also interesting that workers elected a manager, albeit a lower-level manager than usual. (U.S. labor law excludes managers from the union altogether in view of the presumed conflict of interest with other employees.) Of course, manager Zhao was chosen not by the entire workforce, but by seventy-four elected representatives, including many shift and team leaders. There is nothing inherently undemocratic about choosing rulers through elected representatives. But why had the workers voted for shift and team leaders, rather than rank-and-file workers like themselves, to represent them in the nomination and voting processes? One worker activist later explained: "There were relatively few grassroots workers standing. People voted for who they knew. People are like this; apt to choose their own boss, because they think their workplace will benefit later, this is the mentality."[23] As for front-line workers' initial support for manager Zhao himself: "If we had chosen one of our workers, he would not have had any authority or prestige."[24] And that is what seems to matter: "authority or prestige" with management and officials rather than the power that might come (in Western unions) from the support of workers and the ability to lead a strike.

This is just one case, and perhaps one should not make too much of it. But it contains both encouraging and discouraging elements, some of them echoing the Wukan episode. For now let us back up and ask why and how democratizing reforms came to the fore in union elections.

## The Changing Role and Shape of Grassroots Trade Union Elections

As explored in Chapter 3, the basic structure of the ACFTU was forged in the planned economy, when enterprises were owned and controlled by the party-state through Party chapters and Party-appointed managers. Trade union officials were essentially adjuncts to management, and were chosen by the Party chapter through a "non-competitive, consultative proce-dure."[25] Much changed with the reform and "corporatization" of the state-owned enterprises (SOEs): Party cadres lost power relative to profit-oriented managers, and workers were demoted from members of the work unit to sellers of labor. But the basic mission and structure of the ACFTU did not change.

Even as market pressures and the primacy of profits drove a wider wedge between managers' and workers' interests, union officers were still typically appointed by managers and internal CPC cadres. That pattern held in SOEs and their privatized or reorganized successors, and it largely held within larger private and foreign-invested enterprises when the ACFTU began to organize chapters there. That followed in part from how those trade union chapters were organized, described in Chapter 3. Unlike union organizing in the United States, ACFTU "organizing" was a top-down affair; it did not depend on recruiting large numbers of active members, and it rarely pro-duced grassroots activists who might become union leaders. Rather, local ACFTU officials and Party cadres cajoled managers to accede to the estab-lishment of union chapters, which were expected, even promised, to sup-port management; and those same officials then joined with managers in choosing union officers, themselves usually managers.

These cozy arrangements predictably produced union officers with no organic connection to front-line workers and little motivation to assert their interests against the managers to whom they were both sympa-thetic and beholden. As such, the trade union was rather useless to the party-state in managing the surges of unrest that accompanied both the restructuring of the planned economy and the rise of the unplanned economy.[26] That raised the risk that workers would find other organizational outlets for pursuing their collective interests—in hometown associations or gangs,[27] or in independent worker organizations. That risk in turn led to efforts to make the official trade union chapters more accountable to workers. But that risk also constrained reform efforts.

### The Rise of "Direct Elections," Guided from Above

Already in the 1980s, some in the ACFTU pressed for "direct elections" for enterprise trade union leaders.[28] Yet the hope that more responsive elected leaders would help to allay unrest was always in tension with the fear that elected leaders would also be more militant and independent, and might stir unrest.[29] These conflicting impulses produced several "experiments" and "pilot projects" on direct elections in the 1980s, but little systemic reform. Pressure built up in the wake of Tiananmen, for the stirrings of independent worker activism in support of the student protests had been especially alarming to the regime.[30] But pressure for what—for democratization or for greater Party control? The answer was both—both more electoral accountability for "grassroots" ACFTU officials and greater Party control of the ACFTU hierarchy.

As a consensus formed in favor of elections at the enterprise level, attention turned to the form of elections. The overall goal, and the dilemma, remained the same: how to generate leaders who were responsive enough to workers to keep unrest from boiling over, but still subordinate to party leadership. These crosscurrents were reflected in the ACFTU's 2008 Method on Election of Trade Union Chairpersons, in both what was prescribed and what was not. The overall thrust of the policy was to reduce the formal role of managers and to increase the role of local ACFTU officials in the grassroots trade union. It put internal CPC cadres and "the trade union at the next higher level"—that is, the local Party-appointed ACFTU branch and its officials—in charge of overseeing the election process and nominating candidates, "based on the opinions of the members." The policy barred top managers and their close relatives from holding the position of union chair.[31] But many managers remained eligible (and were well represented among internal CPC cadres), and some of the qualifications prescribed for the union chair position—especially "educational background and knowledge of laws and regulations and production and business management"—seemed likely to screen out most non-managers.[32]

Like many dictates from Beijing, the policy left wide discretion over the form of elections to local officials. For example, would workers vote directly for officers or would the process be more filtered, with elected representatives casting the ultimate vote? ACFTU policy was to avoid direct elections in large companies or in the midst of active agitation, where "the risk of . . . militants being elected was too high."[33] The fear of electing "militants" perfectly captures the dilemma faced by the regime. Elections were embraced largely for their usefulness in enhancing responsiveness to workers and curbing unrest; but in the very places where that was most needed, democratic elections also risked catalyzing unrest and elevating militants into leadership roles.

The vagaries of the official line on elections, coupled with the discretion of local officials who were often inclined to indulge local businesses, left the door open to continued management manipulation on the ground. Some local officials conscientiously screened candidates for their competence and willingness to speak up for workers, but others simply deferred to management.[34] In effect, the same constellation of managers and internal Party cadres that had previously appointed union officers were overseeing the nomination and election process. Not surprisingly, those elections were not usually designed to elicit the genuine preferences of rank-and-file workers.

Some trade union "elections" did not look much like elections at all. In one large U.S. multinational firm as of 2011, managers would simply go to each working group or department and say, "We think workers X, Y, and Z would be good representatives of this group; anyone who disagrees please raise your hand." No one would disagree. The management-chosen electors would then vote on management-nominated candidates, and would eliminate the one or two lowest vote getters. Management would then assign union board positions to those who remained.[35]

Even when workers do get to vote, however, the election process is often designed to frustrate any serious challenge to the status quo. The aftermath of the Honda strikes at the Nanhai plant is instructive: What the workers had sought was direct elections; what they had by 2015 was quite different: "[W]orkers at Nanhai Honda . . . vote for the leader of their own working group . . . of about 20 to 30 people. These leaders then elect union delegates, and only the delegates get to vote for the union chairman."[36] This kind of tiered election process is typical at large establishments. Even without manipulation from above, it tends to muffle grassroots voices, especially if workers tend to look up to those with greater authority for their leaders.[37] According to one veteran of the 2010 strike, "the way workers vote actually turns the union into management's twin brother. Workers only vote for their group leaders, and group leaders only vote for their managers," so the union officers still end up being "mid-level and senior managers."[38]

Ironically, it was the Honda strikes in 2010 that led the ACFTU to advocate wider use of "direct elections," though still mainly in smaller companies. But what does "direct election" mean in China? It does not mean that workers choose their own leaders, for even "direct elections" almost invariably follow official screening and selection of candidates.[39] According to ACFTU officials, the nomination process is supposed to include consultation with workers; but workers' own preferences were just one set of inputs into a higher level process of selecting "qualified" candidates. As of 2013, the nomination process was still controlled by a familiar cast of characters: enterprise CPC cadres and local ACFTU officials, usually in consultation with management. This group—management friendly and often management-dominated—would nominate one or two more candidates than the number of positions available (e.g., nine candidates to fill seven or eight positions). Then workers would vote among these hand-picked nominees. In some elections, the winner became the union chair. In others the workers' vote only eliminated the lowest vote-getter; the leading group then proceeded to assign officer positions from among the "winners."

These modest reforms are not meaningless. Whenever there are more candidates than positions to fill, as there are supposed to be, even the least democratic of these "direct election" methods allows workers to eject an unpopular incumbent union chair. In 2008, the ACFTU's official website reported on one local experiment with direct elections: "[S]ince direct election was introduced in 2003, 13 trade union chairpersons have come up for re-election but not a single one of them got elected."[40] It turns out that even a little democracy can send a message to unresponsive incumbents. Still, none of the prevalent election procedures allows ordinary rank-and-file workers to choose their own leaders or to elect a candidate that is not approved by management. "First selection, then election" turns out to be the norm for elections—even "direct elections"—in China. But there are exceptions.

### The Rise (or Mirage) of Haixuan Elections

There is another type of direct election, the so-called *haixuan* or "sea-election," in which workers themselves choose the nominees, and can even nominate themselves. Strictly speaking, *haixuan* elections are both direct— the workers choose among candidates for office—and unmediated by official screening of candidates. True *haixuan* elections are deemed impractical in larger factories, which may require some intermediate role for worker-elected representatives. But it is mainly the departure from "first selection, then election" that is captured in the term *haixuan*. Actual election procedures vary in both their directness and their openness, but the Ohms Electronics election shows that it does not take much of either to be hailed as a democratic breakthrough in China.

*Haixuan* elections for trade union officials have been rare, though "pilot projects" and "experiments" have been reported over recent years.[41] In December 2011, when union reform was on the front burner, the official posture toward *haixuan* elections still remained cautious at best: They would surely not be required, and would continue to be rare; but they would be allowed in some cases if local officials deemed them appropriate.[42] That meant mainly small or "well-run" factories where the outcome was predictable and safe; it decidedly did not mean factories in which workers were aroused and in rebellion.

Yet events on the ground have sometimes run ahead of the planned scope of reforms. By May 2012, some striking workers in Guangdong were reportedly demanding and getting open *haixuan* elections for enterprise union officers. There were scattered reports of workers simply conducting their own elections and choosing their own leaders in the course of a strike, and of management and party or union officials acceding to the results.[43] These elections among mobilized and agitated groups of workers flew in the face of official guidelines on when direct (much less *haixuan*) elections were appropriate even on a pilot basis. But workers' demand for *haixuan* elections may have spurred a softening of official views. By 2013, pilot projects and experiments with *haixuan* elections could reportedly be found in most provinces in China, and especially in Guangdong.[44]

The idea of making unions more electorally accountable to workers, and even "pilot projects" to that end, have come and gone more than once in China's modern history when workers' collective agitation seemed to require that sort of concession.[45] For example, as of 2006, Tim Pringle reported that one small locality in Zhejiang Province, after "experimenting" with *haixuan* elections, was using them in nearly all grassroots union elections.[46] By May 2011, however, a Zhejiang trade union official told me that only a few teachers' unions were experimenting with *haixuan* elections.[47] So one may well wonder whether the recent flurry around *haixuan* elections represent a serious step toward institutionalizing more democratic elections in grassroots unions, or just another round in the recurring ebb and flow of reform proposals. The latter appears more likely: by 2016, these reform proposals had apparently returned to the back burner. Even so, over the longer run we might want to know more about why and when workers seek the right to choose their own leaders through more open elections. The answer may seem obvious to Westerners schooled from birth in the virtues of democratic self-governance. But it is worth asking why and when China's poor migrant workers would demand not just wage increases but institutional reforms like this.

Rising demand for *haixuan* elections appears to be largely instrumental—less a reflection of a sense of civic entitlement and more a response to frustration in pursuing ordinary, garden-variety demands for better wages and working conditions. This looks familiar from the history of industrial relations and reform elsewhere: When workers manage to organize themselves and take collective action, and are still unable to fairly resolve their "interest disputes," they may raise the stakes and demand structural reforms—better institutions for the resolution of future interest disputes. Some workers in China may reasonably conclude there must be a better way to deal with management than by repeatedly rousing coworkers, arduously organizing to carry out a strike—under the radar and under the threat of reprisals—and hoping that their demands draw more solicitude than antagonism from the official "firefighters" who rush to the scene. Far better to have above-board elected leadership that can carry demands to management and negotiate on their behalf before things boil over. A dose of democracy, in other words, may be instrumentally valuable in securing future material improvements.

If savvy, mobilized workers make electoral democracy part of the price of industrial peace, then *haixuan* elections could become, for anxious local officials, the "lesser of two evils," and a short-term tactic for fostering stability in localized arenas that have threatened to become unmanageable. Some officials and scholars take a longer view: Beyond the short-term benefit of ending a disruptive strike, democratically elected union officials could help reduce unrest and promote stability, and even shore up political legitimacy. (That was a major impetus for village elections, as we will see.[48]) There is a parallel "long view" among some enlightened managers, who believe that democratic trade unions will help cultivate a more engaged, loyal, and productive workforce with lower turnover and less turmoil. A handful of Northern European companies with a history of labor-management cooperation in their home countries were reportedly encouraging the use of *haixuan* elections before unrest broke out, as a good industrial relations practice.[49]

The longer view might gain traction if workers elect the "right" sort of leaders when they get the chance. Once workers gain the right to elect their own leaders and to bargain, they sometimes choose not the firebrands who first led them out on strike but more educated, skilled, and "responsible" leaders who seem better suited to dealing effectively with management.[50] (Strike leaders are often gone by the time of elections in any case.[51]) Of course this might reflect an ingrained respect for one's "superiors" that can prove self-defeating; or it might reflect workers' "adaptive preferences"— adaptive, that is, to managers' unwillingness to deal with more militant leaders. One way or another, real elections and real collective bargaining might help to nudge workers toward pragmatism and away from militancy. If that is so, *haixuan* elections will appear less risky and more useful to managers as well as union and party-state officials.

To Western ears, *haixuan* elections sound like not only just what is needed to make unions more responsive to workers, but also a harbinger of wider reforms, and eventually of real collective bargaining through independent trade unions. But that very fear is part of what keeps a tight lid on this particular reform, and ensures that the tide of democracy in China's trade unions ebbs as well as it flows. Most managers and local officials are just too nervous about giving up control over union elections. In the words of factory managers in Zhejiang, relayed to me by a union official: "We're most afraid that either we're not going to like their guys, or that they're not going to pick our guys."[52] "Our guys" might be defined in part by their intelligence, education, and appreciation of the realities of running a successful business—qualities that managers tend to see in their peers. "Our guys" are presumably also those who are not too aggressive, strident, or unyielding in their demands. Local union and CPC officials may not know individual employees as management does, but they share the goal of avoiding conflict, and are inclined to defer to managers' judgment on who is likely to help do that. Election procedures are designed to allow managers and officials to make those judgments.

The roots of the principle of "first selection, then election" run deep. Modern China's founding commitments to "democratic centralism" and CPC rule constrain both the form of elections, largely through guidance and screening of candidates, and the domain of elections, as discussed briefly below.[53] The principle of "first selection, then election" may sound to some Western readers like a thin theoretical cloak for the sheer desire to maintain power and its perquisites. But I have heard sincere and dedicated worker advocates in China defend the concept of "first selection, then election." They worry that unmediated, open *haixuan* elections would produce unqualified and ineffective leaders. Are ordinary rank-and-file workers qualified, they wonder, to do the work of a union chairperson, or even to recognize the qualities and skills that are needed to do the job? It may be fine in a small company, they say, but in large companies this is a very complex job. Many in China believe that, at least for now, party leaders and even managers can play a useful role in tempering the rash choices that uneducated workers might make if left unguided.

That is the best defense I have heard of the norm of "first selection, then election" in the union setting, and it did not sound to me to be a mere pretext for maintaining power. It sounded instead like a defense of meritocracy as a necessary counterweight to majoritarian democracy. To my American ears, the trust in top-down assessments of merit struck me, at the risk of trading in stereotypes, as very Chinese; it suggested too little confidence in the "quality" and self-governing capabilities of most ordinary uneducated citizens, and too little skepticism about the self-serving proclivities of those in power. But to my Chinese interlocutors, my profession of trust in workers' ability to choose good leaders seemed hopelessly naïve, very American, and based more on faith than experience. This, of course, was a discussion about the nature and merits of electoral democracy in general, and the prerequisites for successful democracy, to which we will return. Whatever its virtues, however, the prevailing norm of "first selection, then election" is being loudly challenged by some Chinese workers who are demanding or simply conducting *haixuan* elections for grassroots union officers. So let us table the very big questions about democracy for now, and return to the demand for *haixuan* elections.

In one sense, workers' demands are very modest. They have not sought openly to form a union that is independent of the ACFTU, nor to elect ACFTU leaders above the enterprise level—in the township or province, for example. Nor do workers openly contest the oversight role of the CPC over the union at each level, from the enterprise on up. Even if they harbored such wishes, open demands of that nature would be deemed a "political" challenge to the regime, and would be quickly quashed. By contrast, the demand for the right to elect "grassroots" leaders through open *haixuan* procedures is fairly safe—safe because it mainly challenges management control, not Party control, and because it has clear, politically correct precursors in the village election system. The experience of *haixuan*-type elections in the village may be easing the way for grassroots demands for greater democracy in the trade unions. That experience may offer further clues to what Chinese workers want, what they are likely to want in the future if *haixuan* elections catch on, and what they are likely to get.

## Clues to the Future of Trade Union Elections from the History of Village Elections

One-party rule by the CPC is inscribed in China's constitution, and Party leaders are not popularly elected. That is not a democracy by Western lights. The official view in China, however, is that China is a democratic society under the leadership of the CPC, and that CPC rule and democracy go hand in hand. Deng Xiaoping explained that "China would be in great chaos . . . if democracy is not put under the leadership of the CPC, and there would be no democracy if there is political instability."[54] In his book entitled *Democracy is a Good Thing,* leading CPC theorist Yu Keping elaborates in more modern terms: Chinese democracy, he argues, is embodied not in contested multi-party elections but in a variety of mechanisms by which the people's interests and opinions inform and shape public policy.[55] (More recently, as discussed in Chapter 9, Yu has emphasized the importance of contested elections, though still not multi-party elections, as part of China's democratic development.)

### The Role of Elections in "Democracy with Chinese Characteristics"

Popular elections do have a role in China's version of "consultative democracy." But both the ambit and the form of elections have been sharply constrained by the overriding premise of CPC leadership. Popular elections do not extend to the CPC itself, where ultimate power resides; and *direct* popular elections do not extend above the bottom-most level of government, in the so-called "grassroots" social units that are closest to the citizens—villages, neighborhoods, workplaces. For example, the National People's Congress (NPC), the highest legislative body in China, consists of a few thousand delegates chosen through a multi-tiered election process: NPC delegates are elected by provincial people's congress members, who in turn are elected by lower-level assemblies, and so on down to the village committees and their urban counterparts. Only the last are directly elected by the people. Through the many tiers of elections, candidates who are not approved by the Party, even if they can get elected at the lowest level, get weeded out through official or unofficial screening processes; none can realistically reach the NPC itself. Moreover, the NPC's legislative powers are subordinate to unelected Party structures. So it is that "the NPC has never voted down a piece of legislation put in front of it" by the unelected party-state organs that are authorized to propose legislation.[56]

Even so, one dimension of "democracy with Chinese characteristics" is the use of direct elections at the bottom-most levels of the polity, or the "grassroots." China's most ambitious venture into electoral democracy began in 1987 with the introduction of direct elections in the villages, the smallest and lowest level of the polity in rural China.[57] The 1982 constitution had called for village committees (VCs) to serve as "mass organizations of self-management at the grassroots level" in rural areas (still under Party supervision).[58] But "self-management" did not necessarily mean open, direct elections. Reform-oriented officials at the Ministry of Civil Affairs, with varying degrees of support from above, below, and abroad, pressed vigorously for direct village-wide elections.[59]

The arguments for and against direct elections prefigured debates in the union setting. Proponents argued that direct elections would promote political stability by improving village governance and villagers' cooperation with higher levels of government from the townships on up, and with the Party, whose village branches were still powerful and still unelected. Skeptics worried that even this modest dose of decentralization and democratization would be destabilizing and would undermine implementation of central government policies. They predicted conflict between elected village officials and party-appointed officials both at the village level and at the township level and above. Proponents largely prevailed, but they had to settle for gradual implementation of elections.

In the beginning, "first selection, then election" was the general rule in village elections as elsewhere. That, along with the law's ambiguity, allowed local officials to manipulate election procedures, restrict nominations, and suppress campaigning by unapproved candidates.[60] But experience helped to generate support in some quarters for more democratic elections, and paved the way for the 1998 Organic Law, which mandated direct village elections nationwide, and clarified some issues of election administration and voter eligibility.[61] Most importantly, the 1998 law called for both secret ballot voting and *haixuan*-type primary elections, with open nominations, throughout rural China. Over time, clearer direction from above, pressure from villagers themselves, and growing support among mid-level officials has tended to produce cleaner and more open elections. One recent assessment by Professors Gunter Schubert and Anna Ahlers found "a steady improvement in *election quality*" since 1987, with greater use of secret ballots and less "blatant manipulation."[62]

To be sure, village elections are still organized and "guided" by unelected Party officials at the village and township levels. Guidance often verges into interference in the nomination and campaign process even when *haixuan* elections are officially required; the habit of "first selection, then election" is hard to shake, given its advantages to incumbent officials. Villagers rarely fight back, Wukan-style, to claim their democratic rights. On the other hand, not all villagers want to fight Party control: Schubert and Ahlers found that 60 percent of villagers accepted the Party's role in conducting and guiding village elections, and only 12 percent did not.[63] That could mean that Party oversight is generally seen as light-handed and fair, or that even more heavy-handed efforts to screen out "troublemakers" or "unqualified" candidates are accepted by many rural citizens.

One thing is clear: village elections are popular. They have garnered strong enthusiasm and high levels of participation from villagers.[64] The 80 percent participation rate in the Wukan election was not out of the ordinary. Whatever villagers' initial reasons for wanting or participating in elections, they now see voting as a political *right*, a civic entitlement. The village election experience might hold some lessons for the future of grassroots union elections on several fronts.

## Are Haixuan Elections Likely to Become the Norm in the Union Setting?

The pattern of increasingly regular, orderly, and democratic village election procedures might encourage cautious optimism about the prospects for moving from scattered ad hoc experimentation toward greater institutionalization of open *haixuan* elections in grassroots union chapters. But progress is not inevitable, and backsliding is possible. Even after over two decades of progress in village elections, there is still plenty of interference and manipulation from sources with close analogies in the union context. Much as VCs and VC elections are vulnerable to interference from unelected officials—both village party chiefs and party-state officials in the township and above—elected grassroots union leaders face a similar constellation of unelected officials both in the enterprise (CPC cadres) and above it (local ACFTU and CPC officials). Those officials have formal power over elections, nominations, and campaigns. And that is apart from company managers, who have direct power over elected union officers and a direct economic interest in controlling them. So grassroots union officers may face even more pressure than elected VCs.

Moreover, *haixuan* elections in the trade unions thus far lack strong champions in Beijing. The relatively happy story of village elections is a testament to the role of the Ministry of Civil Affairs as an early and consistent champion of reform. By contrast, the ACFTU still appears committed to "first selection, then election" and skeptical of *haixuan* elections (or any election process that does not screen candidates). So progress toward democratic elections in the trade unions would take even more powerful and articulate demands from below—from workers themselves.

Growing demand for *haixuan* elections in the trade union setting appears to be concentrated among migrant workers of the coastal south, and might be partly rooted in experience with *haixuan* elections in the villages. Much as the Wukan Hot-Blooded Patriots seem to have carried lessons in organizing collective protest from the factories to the villages, they might carry lessons in electoral democracy from the villages to the factories. They might also carry those lessons from factory to factory. Turnover—much higher in the factories than in village populations—cuts both for and against continued reform. On the one hand, it dampens workers' interest in factory-specific reforms and makes reforms harder to sustain: a workforce that secures a *haixuan* election in the wake of a strike might turn over almost completely over the course of a year or two.[65] On the other hand, high turnover might also accelerate the "contagious" effect of grassroots elections as workers carry experiences with elections from one factory to another.

So the forecast for expansion of direct and open elections, and especially *haixuan* elections, is partly cloudy with a chance of thunderstorms. But to whatever extent more democratic elections do take hold, what will be the consequences? Will they improve the responsiveness and performance of the grassroots unions, and get workers more of what they want? And will the experience of democratic elections at the grassroots level spur demand for elections or soften official resistance to elections at higher levels of the union or in the still-dominant Party chapter in the enterprise?

### Are Elected Grassroots Leaders More Effective and Responsive?

Allowing workers to elect their own grassroots leaders should make the unions more effective representatives (and regulators) of the workers, and should help to make collective bargaining a mechanism for avoiding strikes and improving industrial relations, and not just a way to put out fires after they have flared up. Democratically elected union leaders should be better at addressing the grievances that lead workers to organize and strike. That appears to be what workers are after in demanding the right to elect their own leaders, and that is why some far-sighted officials and managers are willing to grant those demands. That was the hope for elected village leaders, too. Rural unrest was already a concern in 1987, and elections were to be part of the answer. They would resolve incipient grievances by making the decision making process more transparent and responsive, and they would promote cooperation with the Party and higher-level officials— "buy-in," as we might say.

The aftermaths of the elections in Wukan and Ohms Electronics are rather discouraging on that score. In both cases, entrenched and ineffectual incumbents were tossed out, and new officials were elected in their place, with enthusiastic support from rebellious citizens and through reasonably democratic processes. In both cases, however, the newly elected officials were still surrounded by unelected powers-that-be—CPC officials in the firm or village, party-state and union officials at the township level, and, in the factories, the workers' own bosses. When those powers-that-be proved recalcitrant, or determined to pursue their own contrary interests, the elected officials succumbed, perhaps after fighting the good fight.

Behind these two discouraging stories are structural constraints that are endemic to both VCs and grassroots trade union chapters: Both are subordinate to, and operate under the supervision of, unelected CPC cadres at the same level, and of unelected local officials at the next level up. That might be one explanation for the Schubert and Ahlers' rather mixed empirical findings on the contribution of elected village committees to villagers' assessment of their material well-being or the quality of village governance.[66] (It is also possible that villagers who elect their own leaders are more engaged and more critical of their performance.)

Other evidence suggests that elected VCs have not been wholly successful either in addressing villagers' grievances or in achieving social harmony. A high proportion of rural "mass incidents" stem from the sort of land sales that triggered the Wukan rebellion, in which local officials sell off rights to valuable farm land to favored developers, often illegally, and award villagers a small fraction of the sale price in compensation.[67] The institution and reform of village elections has been a constructive, maybe even a necessary, response to rural unrest; things might be much worse but for those reforms. But the reforms have not been sufficient to address some of the most stubborn problems in rural governance, partly because so little real power resides in the elected VCs.

For some of the same reasons, there is reason to doubt that democratically elected grassroots union officials will be able to deliver dramatically better results for workers. What they might be able to do is to sound the alarm earlier, and summon the more powerful (and still unelected) institutional actors that can address grievances before they boil over. That is not nothing, but it is not much either.

### Will the Experience of Elections Spread above and beyond the Grassroots?

One might assume—or at least most Americans, with their civic faith in electoral democracy, might assume—that the experience of electing union (or village) leaders would foster a wider sense of entitlement to self-rule. One might assume that citizens would be especially eager to elect the leaders with real power—in the CPC and at the township or even the provincial level—if their elected union (or village) leaders were running into resistance from those unelected officials.[68] But is that the case in China? Will the experience of grassroots elections spur demand or build official support for elections at other levels of the union (or the polity)? The history of village elections suggests that it will do so slowly at best. Over thirty years of experience of limited village democracy appear to have generated little popular demand and even less official support for its extension, either horizontally to the position of village party secretary or vertically to township officials.

In the early days of village elections, many scholars and especially foreign observers of China expected those elections to lead to elections for township officials, and perhaps further up the party-state hierarchy. Some officials shared those expectations. One 1999 study found that some township cadres "clamored for direct elections at their own administrative level in order to relieve them of their difficult limbic status between the villages and the upper-ranking county government."[69] During the late 1990s, several localities, especially in Sichuan and Guangdong Provinces, did in fact hold open nominations and direct elections for township director.[70] But this spate of democratic experiments was brought to a halt in early 2002, when the CPC Central Committee declared direct elections of township directors to be *unconstitutional,* as they derogated from the constitutionally prescribed leadership role of the Party in selecting local officials.[71]

The idea of popularly electing township or higher-up officials is not currently on the agenda in China, but it is thinkable. By contrast, the idea of popularly electing Party officials is barely thinkable in China. That is crucial, for just as the ACFTU is subordinate to the corresponding Party branch at every level, all the way down to the enterprise chapters, the CPC hierarchy parallels the government hierarchy, and dominates the corresponding government bodies, at every level from Beijing on down to the villages. While greater "intraparty democracy"—or competitive elections held among Party members—is quietly discussed in China, direct popular elections for Party positions are almost unimaginable.

One might have expected popular pushback against the confinement of elections to the least powerful governing entity at the lowest level of the polity. Yet decades of experience with electoral democracy in the villages do not seem to have generated broad support for direct elections either higher up the party-state hierarchy or for Party officials themselves. Some support, yes; but mixed and hardly irresistible. Schubert and Ahlers found that 38 percent of villagers supported direct elections for township director, while 34 percent opposed it. (Given the consistently higher levels of approval that most Chinese citizens express for provincial and especially national levels of the government, it seems fair to suppose that support for elections above the township level was even lower.) The same study found that 48 percent of villagers supported election of village party secretary, but 29 percent opposed such a reform.[72] The mixed verdict is striking, given the nearly universal support for the current practice of electing village committees.

Some readers may be surprised that more citizens do not express a desire to elect their own leaders at higher levels of government or in the Party. Others might just not believe the survey results, given the political sensitivity of the subject. Undoubtedly, surveys on such matters should be taken with a grain of salt. But these numbers are less surprising to Chinese observers, who point to a long history and a deeply ingrained habit in China of looking upward, rather than toward one's fellow citizens, for wise governance.[73] Moreover, many (especially rural) citizens seem to think that the Party, and especially the central party-state, has done rather well for them in the past three decades.[74] And on many measures of well-being, they are clearly right. Ironically, villagers' satisfaction with village elections seems to have bolstered support for overall Party rule, as many rural citizens credit the central CPC with giving them elections at the grassroots. According to Schubert and Ahlers, "village elections do much more (for the time being) to reinforce one-party rule than to democratize the Chinese political system."[75]

A simple extrapolation to the union setting would suggest that elections at the grassroots might do more to quell than to stoke demands for greater voice in the union (and the polity), and might shore up both social stability and the political legitimacy of Party rule. But things may not be so simple. Migrant factory workers might be more demanding, civically speaking, than rural villagers both because of their urbanization and because of their migrant status.

Urbanization may or may not be linked generally with greater political awareness, political skills, and demand for political voice.[76] At least in China, the conventional wisdom holds that rural citizens are less demanding of a political voice and more accepting of authority than urban citizens. (They are also poorer, older, and less educated, and those differences might drive urban-rural differences in political attitudes.)[77] But migrant workers might confound these beliefs. They are younger and less bound to village authority structures than rural residents, yet they are marginalized in their urban environment by a combination of social prejudice and discrimination, some of it still grounded in the official *hukou* or household registration system.[78] Marginalization, along with experience in urban labor markets and factories, might dispose these workers less to acquiescing in Party control and more to demanding a voice of their own. Party leaders are clearly worried about migrant workers' marginalization and its role in promoting unrest, and some ongoing reforms take aim at the problem. In the meantime, it is debatable—and, it seems, actively debated in policy

circles—whether facilitating and institutionalizing worker voice by democratizing grassroots union chapters will do more to quell or to stir up unrest.


IN CRITICALLY ASSESSING the state of union democracy in China, I do
not mean to imply that American unions are paragons of autonomous and
democratic self-governance. Various unions at various times have been
plagued by corruption, mob influence, racial exclusion, segregation and
discrimination, suppression of internal dissent, and incumbent entrench-
ment against democratic accountability. Moreover, electoral democracy is
a complicated business everywhere. Even apart from the wide array of
structural arrangements that bear on "democratic-ness," elections are vulnerable to many forms of manipulation by insiders or outsiders with power
within or over the entity.[79] The U.S. experience suggests that the law can
be a tool to mitigate those threats, reduce manipulation, and reinforce
democratic practices—if that is the goal of those who make and enforce
the laws. For now, however, China's leaders appear to be ambivalent at
best about the project of enhancing the accountability of grassroots unions
to their constituents.

The debate over the shape of union elections, and particularly over the
principle of "first selection, then election," is to some extent a microcosm
of debates over democracy versus meritocracy in China. In conversations
that I have had with Party-friendly Chinese intellectuals on these issues,
they ask: Does it really make sense to rely on ordinary citizens to judge and
choose their leaders? Why not rely (instead, or at least more than we in the
United States do now) on those above and around would-be leaders to
judge them based on their merits—their training, experience, and past performance? Yes, of course, ordinary citizen voters could and should choose
based on those very qualities. But do they? And are they the best judges of
those qualities? Or are they unduly swayed by superficial appeals, ground-
less claims, empty promises, or clever slogans? (Point taken, even before
the 2016 presidential election campaign.)

On the other hand, we may ask (as I did): Without a popular electoral
check on leadership, what is to prevent incumbents from entrenching their
power by choosing underlings and fellow leaders who will not rock the
boat? What is to counter the temptation to cloak self-interest in self-serving
assessments of merit? (Some in the Party would answer: The survival of
CPC rule and the future of China depend on countering that temptation,
rooting out corruption, and putting honest and competent public servants in
charge of the organs of government.) Even apart from such pragmatic considerations, however, don't the people have a right to decide for themselves

who they want to lead them and how they want to be led? Aren't popular elections, even with all the imperfections of any actual election system, essential to ensure the consent of the governed? And isn't the consent of the governed essential to political legitimacy in the modern world?

Those questions run through or underneath debates within China over the scope of popular electoral democracy in the trade unions as well as in the polity generally. The disagreements are deep, but the conversation is worth having. It may be unsettling for thoughtful defenders of American-style democracy as well as for thoughtful defenders of China's system of governance. Unfortunately, in the current environment in China, those debates take place largely behind closed doors—among well-vetted participants under Party supervision, within the gated confines of foreign campuses, or more furtively, in private settings or through coded references on social media—rather than openly in mass media outlets and academic journals. That is a shame, and a loss for China and the world. Yet there is more to say on these larger questions, and we will return to them in Chapter 9.

# CHAPTER EIGHT

# Will Workers Have a Voice in the "Socialist Market Economy"?

## The Curious Revival of the Worker Congress System

IN MUCH OF THE WORLD, "industrial democracy" has another facet beyond collective bargaining through trade unions—some kind of institutionalized mechanism for workers' representation and participation in workplace governance. The United States stands virtually alone in its hostility to workers' collective representation outside the context of bargaining through independent unions, which now reaches less than seven percent of the private sector workforce. China instead stands with much of the world in maintaining officially sanctioned institutions beyond the trade unions through which workers are represented, and are to participate in governance, within the workplace. The Staff and Worker Representative Congresses (SWRCs),[1] which bear a family resemblance to European and especially German "works councils," are official vehicles of "democratic management" through which all employees of an enterprise are meant to participate in its governance.

In the planned economy, the SWRCs, operating in conjunction with the trade union chapters, were the embodiment of workers' supposed authority as "masters of the enterprise," but their actual role varied widely from firm to firm. With the reform and opening of China's economy, the SWRCs' role waned within the newly corporatized SOEs, and was largely absent within the growing non-state sector. More recently, however, the SWRCs seem to be experiencing a modest revival. In the wake of the campaign by the All-China Federation of Trade Unions (ACFTU) to organize union chapters in large private enterprises, policymakers have begun to press for the establishment of SWRCs in those enterprises as well. The move might prove to be little more than symbolic; for now, China's SWRCs are generally feeble and ineffectual. But symbols can be portentous, and change may be in the air.

The revival of SWRC system—if that is what is afoot—may be another facet of China's broad effort to keep workers' grievances from boiling over and coalescing into cross-factory activism. As in the other arenas of labor reform canvassed so far, China's approach to social stability creates a dilemma: Leaders might wish to make the SWRCs more effective vehicles for addressing worker grievances before they boil over; yet doing so might risk making them more effective vehicles for independent worker activism. Then again, the SWRC system might appear to be a relatively safe reform in this vein.

This Chapter traces the evolution of the SWRCs, and begins to ask what their tentative revival means: What does it mean for China's workers and for companies operating in China? What goals and impulses lie behind the effort to rehabilitate an apparent vestige of the planned economy? And what might it suggest about the emerging shape of the "socialist market economy"? China's leaders surely do not mean to reinstall workers in their former role as "masters of the enterprise" within the state-owned enterprises (SOEs), much less within the private firms operating in China. But some Chinese leaders might well aim to give workers a larger role in enterprise governance. Having first "corporatized" the enterprises of the planned economy to resemble the capitalist enterprises of the developed market economies, some in the regime may aim to "socialize" the capitalist enterprises operating in China to this modest degree. That is a hypothesis whose elaboration will have to await the final chapter.

## The Fall and Rise of "Democratic Management" and the SWRCs

In the 1960s, on the cusp of the Cultural Revolution, Deng Xiaoping described the SWRC as "a good means of broadening democracy in the enterprises, of recruiting workers and staff to take part in the management and of overcoming bureaucracy," as well as being "an effective method of correctly handling contradictions among the people."[2] That last objective may be a major clue to the recent revival of the SWRCs. But first let us review what it is that is being revived.

## Democratic Management in the Twilight of the Planned Economy

China's SWRCs were originally conceived in the 1950s to engage workers directly in the constitutionally prescribed "democratic management" of the state-run enterprises of which they were the official "masters."[3] Despite its constitutional bona fides, the "democratic management" system was embattled under Mao. Many saw both the trade union and the SWRC as ideologically suspect rivals to the authority of the Party and the Party-appointed factory directors. Then came the Cultural Revolution, which decimated China's political institutions, including the SWRCs and the ACFTU. So, paradoxically, the SWRCs first gained a firm foothold within the SOEs under Deng Xiaoping early in the era of "reform and opening." The reform of China's planned economy lagged behind the growth of the unplanned, non-state economy, and its institutions were restored before they were restructured (and weakened) in the move to market ordering.[4] Deng thus announced in 1980 that SWRCs "will be introduced in all enterprises and institutions. That was decided long ago. The question now is how to popularize and perfect the system."[5] Deng's statement characteristically invoked Mao's legacy while glossing over the rupture of the Cultural Revolution.

The SWRC was supposed to represent the workforce as a whole and enable workers to enact their role as "masters of the factory." According to Deng's 1980 statement, "These congresses . . . have the right to discuss and take decisions on major questions of concern to their respective units, to propose to the higher organizations the recall of incompetent administrators, and to introduce—gradually and within appropriate limits—the practice of electing their leaders."[6] The revival of this workplace democratization project in the early days of economic liberalization might have signaled limits to the project of liberalization, or only its postponement in the SOEs. Or perhaps the SWRCs were meant to help legitimate and facilitate the disruptive changes that were soon to come with SOE reform.[7]

As a formal matter, the SWRCs stood above factory management. But their formal powers were compromised by institutional design from the outset. Most SWRCs met just once or twice a year, while their day-to-day functions were to be carried out by the enterprise trade union, usually dominated by management. And all of those actors within the enterprise were clearly subordinate to Party cadres.

Two aspects of the SWRCs—their selection and composition, and their formal functions—bear closer scrutiny. Deng's suggestion in 1980 that the SWRCs were supposed to "democratize" enterprises without necessarily entailing elections may puzzle many Westerners, but not those familiar with Chinese (and Leninist) conceptions of "democratic centralism": Party guidance in the selection of grassroots representatives promotes democracy, for the Party is held to embody the people's will.[8] From a Western perspective, however, the democratic character of the SWRCs lay chiefly in their composition: These were large bodies made up of about ten percent of the workforce, with tiers of representation from the production line up to management.[9] Any member of an enterprise could be a representative; leading cadres or managers were supposed to make up no more than twenty percent of the SWRC, and women and younger workers were to constitute a "suitable" proportion.[10]

By 1986 the law did call for elections. Depending on the size of the enterprise, SWRC representatives were to be directly elected from either individual work units or entire factories and workshops.[11] As in trade union elections, that did not foreclose guidance from above, but there was a good deal of variation on the ground in how SWRC members were chosen, as found by Professor Joel Andreas in his close study of "democratic management" in the SOEs before (and after) their restructuring:

> In some factories . . . , the process of selecting representatives was relatively democratic—small teams nominated candidates and workshops then convened meetings to elect representatives from among the small teams' nominees. More often, elections were "guided from above" *(yindao)*, with workshop party leaders asking workers to select from a list of nominees with one or two more names than the number of representatives required from their workshop, and in some factories, the party secretary simply named the representatives.[12]

However they were selected, "representatives were generally people on whom the party organization felt it could rely"—employees "who cooperated with the factory leadership and conscientiously took responsibility for factory affairs."[13] Managers were overrepresented, and shift supervisors and team leaders held many of the positions reserved for workers. Said one former SWRC representative: "Even though there are elections, people vote for the candidates the leaders support. Most representatives are common people, but they agree with what the leaders want."[14]

On paper the SWRCs enjoyed broad powers. The 1988 law governing SOEs contained a long list of the SWRCs' "functions and powers," including the formal power to "evaluate and supervise" and even remove factory directors (subject to the approval of Party authorities).[15] That power seemed to give real bite to the SOE workers' official standing as "masters of the enterprise," and it backed up the SWRCs' other powers, such as "the right to know virtually everything about the enterprise . . . and participation in decisions on anything related to workers' wages, benefits, and welfare, distribution of housing."[16] The SWRC had more formal powers than the union, though it was dependent on the union to exercise those powers; the SWRC met only when convened by the trade union, and between meetings its functions were delegated to the union.[17]

Did the SWRCs actually empower workers in the SOEs of the planned economy? The picture is mixed.[18] SWRCs usually served as little more than a "rubber stamp" for management.[19] But sometimes workers were able to use their formal participation rights to influence a range of managerial decisions.[20] According to Andreas: "In some factories, congresses were held irregularly and were simple events with perfunctory reports and votes. In others, congresses were convened at least twice a year and were protracted and elaborate events."[21] SWRCs were fairly active in selecting and supervising shop floor leaders.[22] When it came to evaluating factory directors, the SWRCs' role was usually "perfunctory" but occasionally decisive: "There were some instances . . . in which employee representatives—or the entire workforce—voted to remove a leader, and in some cases candidates for leadership positions competed for votes. Several informants recounted listening to several candidates make speeches outlining their qualifications and plans before large meetings of employees, and the winner was not always the candidate preferred by higher level leaders."[23] These outbursts of workplace democracy took place within limits determined from above—that is, the Party. Voting over the factory director position, for example, "could only be organized by higher level authorities," and might have "simply provided democratic cover for decisions already made at higher levels." At times, however, "authorities arranged such votes in response to dissatisfaction from below."[24]

Andreas concludes that the system of democratic management afforded a measure of power to ordinary workers by virtue of their permanent "membership" in the enterprises of the planned economy: Because workers were permanently assigned to their *danwei,* and could rarely either quit or be fired, managers and Party cadres had to attend to workers' views, cultivate their loyalty, and select leaders for whom they were willing to work diligently. It was their permanent "membership" in the *danwei,* says Andreas, more than the formal institutions of "democratic management," that modestly empowered workers in a Party-managed economy.[25]

## *The Decline of Democratic Management in the Era of "Corporatization"*

As reform proceeded and the SOEs were "corporatized," the SWRCs lost clout relative to more profit-driven managers.[26] The 1994 Company Law was a watershed: It still purported to require democratic management pursuant to the constitution and "relevant laws," but it recast many of the SWRCs' functions in permissive terms and reassigned their most conspicuous legal power—the power to "appraise and supervise the cadres and elect the director of the enterprise"—to a corporate board of directors and supervisory committee.[27]

At the same time, the SWRCs' informal power was undercut as workers gradually lost "membership" in the enterprise; those who were not laid off became mere employees by contract. Andreas finds that workers and managers alike linked workers' loss of power to their loss of job security (especially in enterprises that were effectively privatized). Said one retired factory director: "If a worker complains you can just let him go. So, if they have a complaint—the workshop doesn't have air conditioning, the labor law isn't being implemented, . . . wages are low, the boss took revenge against me, he treated me unfairly—who dares to say anything? . . . If you complain, I'll cut your bonus or make you go home."[28] A worker in a privatized factory agreed: "Now they can fire you on the spot . . . [T]he workers are more docile."[29] Another worker contrasted the late 1980s to the present: "Back then, when workers attended meetings, if they had something to say, they just said it . . . . Now, [i]t's more dictatorial . . . They can fire you, take your wages, you won't have anything to eat."[30]

With the loss of job security and the growing power of shareholders and managers, the influence of the SWRC steeply declined. And when SOEs were wholly or partially privatized, democratic management structures were often "undermined, if not completely forgotten" along the way.[31] Andreas reports that, in privatized former SOEs, "any suggestion that employees might have a say in their selection or removal would be seen as ridiculous."[32] Even in the remaining SOEs, "the ideas, institutions, and practices of 'democratic management' are widely regarded as anachronistic relics of a bygone era, not suited for a modern corporate environment."[33] The form of the SWRC remained in the SOEs and their successor firms, but in most it became an empty shell.

There were exceptions. Anita Chan and her colleagues report that SWRCs continued to influence the fate of factory directors and managers into the late 1990s. In one province, "more than 2300 [SOE] managers . . . were dismissed or demoted after failing to obtain the necessary 60 percent of the votes" of their SWRCs.[34] Some SOEs retained a more paternalistic culture, and trade unions were able to use the SWRCs and their powers to improve workplace health and safety,[35] or to fairly distribute new housing benefits.[36] So while the SWRCs were often powerless, active trade unions could sometimes put their formal powers to use on workers' behalf, at least when management was not antagonistic.

In the burgeoning non-state sector, however, most companies lacked even the formalities of democratic management.[37] Oddly, the law conferred powers on the SWRC if it existed, but did not clearly require its existence.[38] It was the job of Party and union cadres to set up the SWRC, and that task lagged behind the push to organize Party and ACFTU chapters in large private and foreign-invested enterprises.[39] It was big news in 2006 when Wal-Mart agreed to create an SWRC, after lengthy negotiations with the newly organized ACFTU chapter, and later when the Nanjing Wal-Mart's SWRC, at its first meeting, approved a collective contract that provided for annual raises for all workers.[40] But these appear to have been rare events.

Even the Labor Contract Law (LCL) of 2008—a major advance in the *regulation* of employment relations—did little to clarify the shape of "democratic management" in the non-state sector. Like the 1994 Labor Law, the LCL provided that changes to certain corporate by-laws, company rules, and collective contracts for both state and non-state enterprises must "be submitted to the workers representative assembly *or all workers.*"[41] Initially most private and foreign companies either ignored the LCL's worker consultation provisions altogether or sought to circumvent them. For example, some lawyers advised managers to notify "all workers" of changes to by-law or collective contract provisions by posting them on an employee bulletin board or handbook, and to treat employee inaction in the face of such notice as assent.[42]

In short, the SWRCs have not been much of a factor in Chinese labor relations in recent decades, especially in the non-state sector. They have been widely viewed as "useless" and as a "rubber stamp."[43] At a conference in 2010, a Chinese labor scholar's prediction that the SWRCs might enhance protection of worker rights was met with laughter.[44]

### Are the SWRCs Staging a Comeback?

Perhaps that is changing. Some signs come from the Chinese academy. In a 2012 essay, Professor Tongqing Feng, a senior scholar at the China Institute of Industrial Relations, the academic arm of the ACFTU, endorses SWRCs as still-important vehicles of "democratic management," and find new interest on the part of workers.[45] While "workers' congresses established top-down are prone to becoming mere rubber stamp organizations," those that are established "bottom-up are often highly energetic,"[46] and "a powerful weapon in [workers'] participation in reform."[47] Feng maintains that that "workers' congresses in China can have a bright future" if the trade unions become more democratic and responsive, and if they do more to support SWRCs on the ground.[48]

Similarly, Professor Xie Zengyi of the Chinese Academy of Social Sciences (CASS) argued recently that "[n]ot only is the use of SWRCs justified, it is also feasible and essential." He maintains that "China should not abandon SWRCs, but rather should support and perfect them."[49] Aiming to recast democratic management for the contemporary era, Xie contends that "the basis for establishing SWRCs is not that workers are 'masters of the enterprise,' " but rather that workers' participation will have economic and political benefits in both state and non-state enterprises.[50] To be sure, Xie (like Feng) appears to focus chiefly on the still-large state sector, where the SWRCs have a longer legacy; yet his arguments echo those of many Western proponents of worker participation in private firms. Xie argues that SWRCs will not only "mitigate worker subjugation," but also "increase the flow of information between managers and employees," raise employee morale and productivity, and "strengthen oversight of corporate operations."[51] Xie maintains that the SWRCs' consultative role in decisions that touch on employee interests is entirely compatible with the managerial structure and overall managerial power contemplated by the Company Law.[52] Far from supplanting the authority of corporate managers, he argues, SWRCs can supplement it; and he cites positive experience with SWRCs at the provincial level, as well as with works councils in capitalist Europe.

In the meantime, official bodies have acted to bolster the SWRCs' powers, including in the non-state sector.[53] A few courts have given sharper teeth to the LCL requirement that company rules must be submitted to the SWRC (if one exists). For example, a 2009 court ruling overturned an employee's discharge because it was based on new rules that had not been approved by the company's SWRC.[54] At the same time, officials have begun to prod companies to establish SWRCs. Both Shanghai and Zhejiang Province have issued regulations requiring the establishment of SWRCs in all public and private enterprises.[55] As of March 2013, roughly 81 percent of the organizations, public and private, that had a trade union chapter—over four million organizations—had established a worker congress.[56]

The ACFTU joined the chorus with its 2012 Provisions on the Democratic Management of Enterprises, which call for the establishment of SWRCs in private enterprises nationwide.[57] The Provisions are not legally binding on companies, but they do govern the trade union chapters that are charged with convening the SWRCs.[58] And once SWRCs are established, binding national laws define their formal powers. The Provisions mostly track those laws in describing the SWRCs' powers: they are to put forward opinions and suggestions on an enterprise's development plans and operation, "deliberate the bylaws . . . on important matters formulated," "deliberate and adopt collective contract drafts," and "examine and supervise the enterprise's implementation of labor laws and regulations."[59] Notably, the Provisions purport to empower SWRCs to elect supervisors and directors, as well as the enterprise's business managers, although the latter only "upon authorization."[60] Depending on the import of that cryptic qualification, this provision might be either a gloss on the law or an overreach in some tension with the Company Law's reallocation of these supervisory powers to the corporate board.

The ACFTU Provisions represent a major official intervention in an ongoing debate on "democratic management": Is a robust role for the SWRCs consistent with the Company Law and its management- and shareholder-centered vision of corporate governance? On the other side of that debate are most major companies operating in China, along with some powerful allies in government. We will return to this critical debate about the role of workers in China's "socialist market economy."

The Provisions also underscore the SWRCs' potential to represent the workforce as a whole—as well as the potential for management domination. No more than one-fifth of the members can be upper- or mid-level managers,[61] and members are to be directly elected or removed by their work unit at a meeting at which two-thirds of the members are present.[62] But representatives may be nominated by the trade union, managers, or employees, and actual practices vary.[63] In short, nothing in the law nor in the ACFTU Provisions ensures that the SWRCs' make-up will reflect the genuine choices of rank-and-file workers, nor that they will act more vigorously or be taken more seriously than has been the norm in recent years.[64]

Still, the SWRCs do supply a legally sanctioned vehicle for enterprise-level worker participation that is larger and less management-heavy than grassroots trade union officers. And scattered reports show that they can afford workers a politically safe vehicle for a measure of democratization *when they have mustered their own collective power.* In one account, workers used the SWRC "to fight against a private enterprise's attempts at swindling state-owned assets out of the factory."[65] In 2007, workers of a city-owned paper mill managed to organize through the mill's SWRC to reverse its privatization.[66] And in 2011, when workers at a machine parts factory learned that they would not be receiving year-end bonuses, the enterprise's twenty-two-member SWRC helped to both lead the strike action and successfully negotiate an end to the strike.[67] These appear to be rare episodes. But they show that where and when workers themselves manage to marshal enough collective economic power to stand up to management, the SWRC might be a viable, politically safe conduit for worker voice. That could entail risks as well as gains to the regime. Some of the same concerns that constrain democratization of the enterprise trade unions might end up constraining the rejuvenation of the SWRCs.

### A Note on SWRCs and Employee Committees in Multinational Corporations

In recent decades, multinational corporations have been under pressure from stakeholders to maintain "socially responsible" supply chain practices, and to engage workers in the enforcement of their rights under external law and private codes of conduct. That ordinarily means allowing workers to freely form unions—to exercise the "freedom of association" that is prescribed as a "core" labor right by the International Labor Organization (of which China is a member). In China, however, workers do not have that freedom, and they do not choose or control the only unions they are allowed to have. Among the many firms that are unwilling to forego operating in China in the face of this conflict, some have turned to SWRCs as a way to engage workers in enforcement of their rights. McDonalds,[68] KFC,[69] and, as noted above, Walmart are among the multinational companies with SWRCs in some of their China-based locations.[70] Informed observers have reached varying views on the efficacy of SWRCs in enforcing companies' legal and social responsibility commitments.[71]

But SWRCs are not the only enterprise-based vehicles of employee participation in China. Some multinational companies and their major suppliers have voluntarily set up democratically elected Employee Committees to engage employees in workplace governance.[72] These committees have no legal status, no legal powers, and no formal connection to the Party or the ACFTU. Employee Committees are most common in Northern European companies (or their major suppliers), whose managers have favorable experience at home with democratic unions and works councils. Those companies tend to pay relatively well and to take a proactive approach to labor relations; they see little risk of workers going into opposition against management. Even so, the impetus for the creation of Employee Committees often comes from outside—from stakeholders or unions at home urging the engagement of workers in achieving compliance with labor standards.

Perhaps because of their independence from officialdom, and in spite of their creation by management, these Committees can occasionally serve as vehicles of grassroots worker empowerment when employees do mobilize. When the Foshan Honda strikers in 2010 elected their own representatives to negotiate with management, they reportedly did so under the auspices of an Employee Committee, not the SWRC (and certainly not the trade union).[73]

For now, Chinese officialdom appears to be leaving Employee Committees alone. They are seen as creatures of management, neither part of the official structure for worker representation nor a threat to it, and they pose little risk of spreading worker activism from one enterprise to others. If officials become more committed to the role of SWRCs in these foreign companies, the Employee Committees might begin to look like rivals, and might incur greater official scrutiny. And if the SWRCs do end up functioning as genuine mechanisms of worker participation, the Committees might begin to look redundant.

## Contrasting Views of "Democratic Management" from Both Sides of the Atlantic

For Western observers seeking to make sense of the SWRCs and their possible revival, it may be helpful to compare them to more familiar institutions of worker participation. American observers, for their part, may need a comparative layover in Europe, where the concept of "democratic management" has a resonance that it lacks in the United States, and where works councils have long served as a second channel of employee participation in enterprise governance.

### American Labor Law's Hostility to Non-Union Employee Representation

U.S. labor law may be unique in the world for virtually barring institutions of employee participation other than collective bargaining through independent unions. There is no analogue to the officially prescribed SWRC, and a voluntarily constituted, management-sponsored Employee Committee would be an illegal "company union." This is just one dimension of the "American exceptionalism" that so often shows its face in the law of the workplace.

Under the National Labor Relations Act (NLRA), an employer and a union presumably can, through collective bargaining, jointly create an employee representation structure that resembles a works council or an SWRC (provided that the union itself is independent, not employer-dominated). But that rarely happens, for American trade unionists have traditionally regarded such structures as unwelcome rivals of the union, while American employers may regard them as extensions of the union. The United Auto Workers (UAW) and Volkswagen (VW) thus broke new ground in agreeing to establish a works council in the event workers in VW's Chattanooga, Tennessee, plant chose to be represented by the union.[74] But the workers' February 2014 vote against union representation—a serious blow to the UAW—at least postponed the innovative VW experiment.[75]

In the non-union workplaces occupied by over 93 percent of private sector employees in the United States, there is almost no legal space for employee representation committees. Such committees were a linchpin of the "human relations" managers' positive approach to union avoidance in the run-up to the New Deal, and were anathema to the proponents of independent unions and collective bargaining. Hence the NLRA's sweeping ban on anything resembling a "company union," enacted in 1935 and still the law today. The law makes it unlawful for management to "dominate" or "interfere with," or "contribute financial or other support" to a "labor organization"; and the latter is defined in turn to include any representative structure through which employers "deal with" employees on terms and conditions of employment.[76] It is almost impossible for a non-union employee committee structure to operate without employer support and involvement of a sort that the law prohibits. The prohibition holds even if employees embrace the representation scheme, and even absent any anti-union motive on the employer's part.[77]

The peculiar union-or-nothing system of worker representation in the United States has generated two sharply different regimes, each of which affords a single channel for both the resolution of "distributional conflict" over wages and the potentially cooperative pursuit of mutual gains: either collective bargaining through independent trade unions, or unfettered managerial discretion. In the small union sector, that means that the cooperative pursuit of mutual gains is at least periodically disrupted by distributional conflict; and in the much larger non-union sector, it means that workers have no institutionalized collective mechanism to ensure that gains from cooperation will be mutual.

Still, American firms are not immune from the challenges of human resource management that have led to the rise of employee participation schemes elsewhere. So while old-style "company unions" and formal non-union employee representation plans have been largely extinct since the 1930s, informal representation schemes are surprisingly common—surprising, that is, given that nearly all are illegal. In one recent study, 34 percent of non-union employees reported that their employers had established a system in which employee representatives met with management to discuss workplace issues.[78] Most employees were quite satisfied with these representation schemes, virtually all of which appear to violate federal law.

So China's informal, unregulated, management-sponsored Employee Committees do have their U.S. analogues, albeit under a shadow of illegality. This sort of illegality carries no onerous sanctions, and usually none at all, as enforcement can be triggered only by a complaint to the NLRB, and no one is likely to file one. Still, the law has consequences. These informal representation schemes operate under the radar without public scrutiny, regulation, or support. They neither reflect nor reinforce public norms of industrial democracy, a concept that remains exclusively identified with unions, shrinking and beleaguered as they are.

The illegality of nonunion representation schemes complicates the U.S. perspective on China's SWRCs. On the one hand, the view of worker representation that is embodied in U.S. labor law might lead one to dismiss the SWRCs, like the trade unions that stand behind them, as "company unions"—not merely less effective than independent union representation but illegitimate. On the other hand, one suspects (and survey data suggest) that most U.S. workers would take a different view of an SWRC-like body—as better than nothing, and perhaps even better than an independent union that has to fight management every step of the way.[79]

### Comparing SWRCs to German Works Councils

In sharp contrast to the United States, the rest of the developed world allows, encourages, or even mandates non-union forms of employee participation in workplace governance. In particular, China's SWRCs have an obvious kinship with European works councils (WCs), which have their roots in early twentieth-century efforts to promote industrial democracy (alongside of and often in competition with the trade unions).[80] China's SWRCs fit a prominent scholarly definition of WCs as "institutionalized bodies for representative communication between a single employer and the employees of a single plant or enterprise,"[81] and in most respects would fit comfortably within a typology of WCs, which vary widely within Europe.[82]

In particular, China's SWRCs and its system of "democratic management" are analogous to Germany's WCs and its "co-determination" system. The latter system is recognized as a prototype within Europe, and is the product of over a century of institutional development (though it had to be restored in the wake of World War II and Nazi rule).[83] That long institutional history sets the German WC system apart from its counterparts within Europe as well as from China's SWRCs.[84] Moreover, the German and Chinese systems are obviously intertwined with a raft of differences between the two countries' legal, political, and industrial relations systems. Still, the comparison will highlight some crucial features of the SWRCs and their institutional context.

The German WCs are also unusual within Europe in their formal legal prerogatives. The WCs have not only rights to *information* and *consultation* over a broad range of management decisions, but also *codetermination* rights—the right to demand third-party resolution in case the WC does not agree with management—and even *veto* rights over some topics. Roughly speaking, the prerogatives of the WC cover the full range of employees' concerns as employees, but they lose strength as they approach core managerial and strategic concerns. Specifically, German WCs have *veto* rights over some individual staff movements; *co-determination* rights over many personnel and work-related matters that do not affect the basic scope or strategy of the enterprise; weaker but still meaningful *consultation* rights regarding other aspects of the work environment and job-related decisions (including new technology); and still-weaker yet meaningful rights to *information* on financial matters and structural decisions that might affect workers.[85]

The German WCs are designed to enable workers to participate in enterprise decisions that affect workers directly and that affect productivity. Crucially, however, the WCs have no role in wage-setting and no right to strike.[86] In Germany, as in much of Europe, collective wage bargaining takes place mainly at the sectoral level; that is the domain of the trade unions. The logic of the system is to hive off the potentially cooperative pursuit of mutual gains from sharp distributional conflict over economic terms; and that logic is reflected in both the powers of the WCs and in their formal separation from the trade unions.[87]

But the formal separation of the unions and WCs is not fully borne out on the ground. Over the years, the unions have found the WCs to provide a useful workplace-level structure for engaging and protecting union members, and have used consultation and co-determination rights to influence managerial decisions on working conditions and job security. Unions have exercised informal power in and through the WCs, for example, by running candidates for positions on the WCs.[88] The German WCs became stronger and more effective in the postwar era partly because of the trade unions' gradual shift from skepticism to pragmatic support to what one leading German scholar describes as a "symbiotic relationship" with the WCs.[89] The trade unions' tighter embrace of the WCs in recent decades may reflect in part the unions' declining power outside the WC system.[90]

The role of the union is only one of several variables that affect the actual functioning of a WC. Managerial "culture" and posture toward workers and WCs matters as well, and can determine, together with the role of the trade union, whether WCs are marginalized or engaged, cooperative or combative, conventional or creative.[91] It turns out that even a clear and well-entrenched legal framework does not produce uniform or uniformly effective institutions on the ground.

Returning to China: If we were to compare the rights and powers of German WCs and Chinese SWRCs on paper, we would observe that, before the 1990s, the SWRCs (at least in the SOEs) had formal decision-making power in some areas in which the German WCs have rights of co-determination or less. In particular, they had the power to approve some major business decisions and even to replace management. But those powers were rarely exercised even then, and have been much diluted since 1994. Today the SWRCs' powers are both vaguer and weaker, even on paper, than those of the WCs. In one respect, however, the SWRCs' formal powers are broader than those of the WCs: The SWRCs have a formal role in approving collective contracts, including wage levels. That difference between SWRCs and WCs goes hand-in-hand with another: the SWRCs are formally intertwined with the trade union, which is charged with carrying out the day-to-day functions of the SWRC in between its infrequent meetings. In short, China's system combines the economic issues over which management and workers are most likely to be at odds with other issues on which workers' participation might contribute to a more productive enterprise; and it deals with both through linked institutions—the trade union and the SWRC—that managers almost invariably dominate.

Whatever the formal powers of the SWRCs, it is clear that, at least since their heyday in the waning years of the planned economy, they have in fact rarely exercised any power on workers' behalf, especially in non-state enterprises. On the whole, though to varying degrees, German WCs have had a much, much greater impact on both management and workers than the SWRCs.[92] One might even say this: Germany's version of social democracy looks a lot more "socialist," at least in respect of worker power and participation within enterprises, than does China's "socialist market economy."

## Constraints on Democratic Management in China, and the Outlook for Change

Several dimensions of the SWRCs and their institutional context seem crucial to the SWRCs' efficacy. One dimension, diffuse but important, is the vagueness of Chinese law on the SWRCs' powers, structure, and composition, which gives workers far less traction against managerial power than the more specific and detailed legal provisions of German law. The difference is partly a reflection of the Chinese legal system in general, and it raises larger issues of judicial independence and legal development. Considering that China began constructing a modern legal and regulatory system virtually from scratch just a few decades ago, continued progress on this front seems quite possible.

Another point of comparison lies outside the SWRCs and WCs as such, but has been highlighted by Andreas: employees' job security. In addition, the role and nature of both the trade union and state—in the SWRCs and in China—command our attention. On each of these dimensions, the current state of affairs tilts against Chinese workers' prospects for a real voice at work through SWRCs, especially as compared to German workers and their WCs. But on each dimension, we can discern possible signs of a shift in workers' favor in China.

### *Job Security and Job Tenure*

Andreas's claim that the decline of "democratic management" follows from workers' loss of job security may strike a chord with American legal scholars, including myself, who have argued that freedom from unjustified dismissal is a necessary predicate for workers' ability to exercise any rights that they enjoy on paper.[93] If that is so, then the fate of the SWRCs may turn partly on whether the Labor Contract Law can accomplish one of its more ambitious objectives of conferring greater job security on Chinese workers. On paper, China has arrived: recall that the Organisation for Economic Co-operation and Development (OECD) rated China's legislation as the most protective in the world![94]

To be sure, the LCL makes no effort to restore what Andreas calls "membership" in the enterprise—or what Walder characterized as the *danwei*'s property rights over their employees.[95] The permanency of those work relationships surely helped to *motivate* workers to speak up and managers to listen; but it is not coming back. The LCL does attempt to *enable* "indefinite term" workers to speak up by requiring employers to justify their dismissal or else to compensate them. That is roughly the kind of job security that is enjoyed by most formally employed workers in the developed world, including Germany, and by the small fraction of U.S. workers who are covered by a collective bargaining agreement. If that is the kind of security workers need to exercise their democratic participation rights, then the LCL would seem to be just the ticket.

On the other hand, the Chinese courts' treatment of strikers, reviewed in Chapter 6, suggests a formalistic approach to violations of employer rules that might make it quite easy to dismiss any worker who speaks up for group concerns. Even a rule violation that is in fact a pretext for retaliation might nonetheless provide a legal basis for dismissal; the law offers no clear warrant for contesting an employer's factually accurate grounds for dismissal based on pretext or motive. Without clearer legal protection of employee rights to speak up and participate in "democratic management," the LCL may do little to protect worker voice.

Even if workers were protected against dismissal, however, they might continue to rely more on "exit" than "voice" to find what they are looking for at work. Collective workplace-based mechanisms of "voice" require a measure of continuity and an investment of energy from both sides. At least for now, high turnover in China's non-state enterprises is a major hurdle to improving institutions of workplace participation. It is also a major hurdle to improving productivity, and is drawing a great deal of concern from employers. Therein may lie some hope for a more participatory workplace environment in China's future.

## The Nature and Role of the Trade Unions and the State

Two other major areas of difference between the SWRCs and the German WCs—the role and nature of both the trade union and the state—are more intractable because they are closer to the heart of China's one-party system of governance. In contrast to the German WCs, which are formally separate from the trade unions, SWRCs are formally linked to, and their functions generally exercised by, the enterprise trade union. Yet German trade unions do much more to empower workers through the WCs than the Chinese trade unions do through the SWRCs.[96] German unions are relatively strong, independent of both management and the state, and democratically accountable to workers, while China's trade unions and their umbrella organization, the ACFTU, are subject to domination by the Party and, within the enterprise, by management. Unions in China have rarely strengthened workers' hand in the SWRCs or made use of their powers vis-à-vis management. To a great extent, then, the future of the SWRCs may depend on reform of the ACFTU, and that will be a long, uphill battle at best.

Intertwined with the role of the trade union is the role of the state. In Germany as in China, the state creates the legal framework for WCs/SWRCs and defines their powers. In both countries, the trade unions play a large role, formal or informal, in the WCs/SWRCs. And in both countries, the dominant trade unions are affiliated with political parties, including some that exercise state power—permanently as in China or from time to time as in Germany. But these similarities cannot obscure the chasm beneath: multiparty democracy and associational freedoms make all the difference. German trade unions are chosen and ultimately controlled by their worker-members, not by the political parties with which they are affiliated; and those political parties have to compete for citizens' votes in periodic multi-party elections. In China, one political party controls the state and the trade unions, potentially all the way down to the enterprise level. That does not mean that Party leaders in Beijing call the shots; party-state power is "fragmented,"[97] and much of it is devolved down to local officials. But that does little good for the workers, for, at the enterprise level where the SWRCs operate, it is managerial power that holds sway.

With all of these institutional limitations—a vague legal framework, workers' vulnerability to reprisals, enterprise unions' domination by management, and the party-state's undependable posture toward workers—it is hard to see how the SWRCs could offer workers an institutional voice in workplace governance. The SWRC structure might still occasionally prove to be a useful and politically safe mechanism of voice for workers who muster their own collective power, as noted above. But for the broad run of workers, the formal proliferation of SWRCs in private-sector firms will do little or nothing by itself to democratize industry. It is possible to imagine a future with clearer laws, stronger employment protections, more responsive unions, and a stronger party-state commitment to delivering improvements to workers. Unless and until that happens, however, SWRCs and China's constitutional commitment to democratic management appear doomed to irrelevance.

## Why Revive the SWRCs?

That brings us to a final set of questions about the SWRCs: Why are (some) policy makers pressing to revive an institution with enfeebled roots in the planned economy? What do they hope to accomplish and what future do they envision? The SWRC's revival, if it becomes more than words on paper, would modestly constrain managerial power within the corporate enterprise. But to what end? Here I am left to surmise.

One end could be the consolidation of Party power. On this view, the establishment of SWRCs, like the Party and ACFTU organizing drives that preceded it, is meant to extend the reach of Party power within non-state enterprises. The consolidation and extension of Party power in the society certainly appears to be a major goal of the CPC, especially under Xi

Jinping. But the SWRC system would seem to be an oddly attenuated way to pursue that goal. The SWRCs are one step further removed from the Party than is the ACFTU, and their composition and conduct is less easily controlled by the Party. If the SWRCs are intended to consolidate Party power, they must do so indirectly by accomplishing other aims.

The SWRCs could also be part of China's regulatory modernization project. As discussed in Chapter 5, effective regulation cannot be a wholly top-down affair; it requires involvement by stakeholders both inside and outside regulated organizations.[98] That is a major tenet of what is often called the "New Governance" school of thought regarding regulation. Similarly, worker advocates have long argued that corporate commitments to comply with labor laws and improve labor standards in the supply chain, to be credible, must involve workers in monitoring. The SWRC could be a way to do that. It might seem odd to suggest that the revival of this vestige of China's planned economy might be part of a forward-thinking regulatory project. "New Governance" is not a prominent part of the Chinese lexicon. Indeed, as discussed in Chapter 5, the signature "New Governance" emphasis on bottom-up enforcement by stakeholders and civil society organizations runs headlong into China's authoritarian approach to social control. But the SWRCs might be seen as safe vehicles for engaging workers in the regulatory project—safe because they are part of the official system of "democratic management," confined to a single enterprise, and under the watchful eye of management.

Improving enforcement of workers' rights would also serve the central policy priority of maintaining stability. Recall Deng's characterization of the SWRC system as "an effective method of correctly handling contradictions among the people."[99] If more robust SWRCs can help resolve workplace disputes inside the enterprise, they would promote social stability both in the short term by preventing those disputes from spilling into the streets, and in the longer term by preempting independent labor activism. For if workers can resolve their rights and interest disputes inside the enterprise and through official channels, they are less likely to turn to unofficial and independent forms of activism.

If SWRCs can do all those things, then it is no wonder that they are being revived. But of course they can do none of those things unless they become more than paper institutions—unless they actually empower workers to address their concerns at work. That will be challenging.

The central goal of maintaining stability and promoting "harmonious labor relations" is hardly unique to China. "Labor peace"—reducing the incidence and intensity of industrial conflict—has been a major goal of all industrial nations, and is essential to a productive advanced economy.

China is of course determined to pursue that goal while preventing the rise of independent unions, which have been the central actors in Western industrial relations systems. Given that determination, reviving the SWRCs might look like the safest way forward—safer by far than democratizing the official trade unions. And yet even this relatively safe and modest way of empowering workers poses risks: Enabling workers to assemble and discuss their goals and grievances might crystallize conflict and facilitate collective action if management is unresponsive. The revival of the SWRCs might be yet another reform that is both *motivated* and *constrained* by the overriding objective of preventing the rise of an independent and potentially political labor movement.

All in all, there are several overlapping and compelling reasons for China's leaders to press forward with the project of making the SWRCs work at least modestly well for workers. That project might also offer clues about some Chinese leaders' conception of the "socialist market economy." It might suggest that they mean to go beyond expanding the role of capitalist enterprises in the Chinese economy, and beyond mimicking them within the state sector. The SWRCs suggest something new— an effort to reform those capitalist enterprises by giving workers a greater voice in workplace governance. The *reasons* for doing so would be those already discussed: improving legal compliance, resolving and containing workplace disputes, and avoiding collective unrest and organizing outside the enterprise. At least some of China's leaders may perceive a need to empower workers inside the enterprise in order to accomplish those ends.

On this view, the SWRCs would be analogous to the German WCs, but with a different support system—not an independent trade union, but the party-state itself. If workers are to exercise meaningful influence within powerful transnational corporations in the modern global economy, they will need powerful outside support. In the West, independent trade unions sometimes provide that support, and they sometimes provide that support through WCs as well as through collective bargaining. But trade unions' power ultimately stems from workers' own collective economic power, and that is waning across the world. In a world where capital and managers are gaining ground against workers and their unions, stronger state and legal backing might be needed to give workers a real voice in workplace governance. The Chinese model *potentially* supplies affirmative state backing to workers and SWRCs through CPC and ACFTU chapters within the enterprise as well as the other forms of leverage that the party-state exercises from outside the enterprise.

"Potential" is the key, of course. The ACFTU has largely failed to perform this function given its multiple conflicting missions, its lack of accountability to workers, and its coziness with managers inside the enterprise and at the local level. But there is no doubt that the party-state has enormous leverage that could be, and sometimes has been, deployed in the interest of workers, at least when they noisily demand it. So *if* the party-state is determined to give workers more clout within private firms, and *if* that determination filters down to the local level, then the SWRCs could actually help to democratize workplace governance. Those are, of course, big "ifs."

There are other "ifs" as well. For if the party-state in China overcomes its discouraging history of local protectionism and cronyism, and gives real teeth to measures that empower workers and constrain management discretion, employers are likely to push back, and perhaps even flee (or threaten to flee) to friendlier shores. There are obviously limits to the ability of any jurisdiction to impose costly conditions on private firms that can choose to operate elsewhere. But China—with its skilled workforce, its gigantic and growing consumer market, and its impressive infrastructure—might have the latitude to impose conditions that other countries do not.[100] If compelled to live with these measures, employers could even discover that meaningful worker participation can stabilize and improve workplace governance.[101]

IN THE END, China's tentative moves toward reviving the SWRCs probably reflect a mix of motives and aims that are both ideological and pragmatic, both public-regarding and self-serving. But part of the mix may be a genuine desire to empower workers as China moves toward the next phase of "socialism with Chinese characteristics." That aspiration is often proclaimed, and often contradicted on the ground, but it has a following within the CPC. The recent "democratic management" measures may represent a small victory by, or a concession to, those in the Party who seek to restore what they regard as the salutary side of Mao's legacy—the egalitarian and pro-worker commitments that were shunted aside during the first decades of economic liberalization. And to that degree, those measures may be meant in part to enhance the regime's legitimacy among citizens who share those values.

Even if one is convinced, however, that China's official ideology is nothing but a veneer for a single-minded determination to maintain power, it still matters both how and why the regime seeks to maintain power. If China's leadership is seeking to perpetuate its hold on political power in part by better living up to its pro-worker ideology, and enhancing the voice and improving the lives of discontented workers, then employers and workers of the world, and those who care about their fate, will have to take another look at China, and perhaps reenvision the future that China is shaping.

# CHAPTER NINE

# Conclusion

WILL THERE BE a New Deal for China's workers? It cannot help but strike the reader that the title of this book and of nearly every chapter takes the form of a question. One aim of this book is to add color, complexity, and depth to the fairly nebulous view of China's labor landscape that is held by most Americans, and indeed most Westerners, who think, read, and write about labor issues. But some of the basic questions posed here become only harder to answer from a more informed point of view. Aristotle's maxim that "the more you know, the more you know you don't know" is nowhere more true than in China.

In this final chapter I will, with due regard for the perils of the undertaking, venture a provisional answer to the titular question. But first I will briefly address two other overarching questions: First, how might the more textured account of China's labor scene that is offered here change or challenge prior understandings of American labor law and policy (and even American democracy)? Second, what might this account tell us about what the "socialist market economy" will mean for Chinese workers and their employers? After all, it is a "socialist market economy," not an American-inspired New Deal, that China's rulers themselves claim to be building.

## Looking Back at the American Labor Scene from China: What Looks Different?

After two decades of teaching, researching, and writing in the field of American labor and employment law, with just an occasional sortie into comparative and international territory, I spent much of the next decade, starting in 2009, studying China's labor and employment scene. My foray into China quickly took me beyond superficial preconceptions about China's lawless sweatshop economy, and the analogy to America's late nineteenth- and early twentieth-century laissez faire political economy. (I am struck by how often a one-sentence description of what I am working on elicits the response, "China has labor laws?") It took me beyond my initial perception of similarities to America's pre- and early New Deal period—the rising unrest, the surge of union "organizing," the enactment of labor standards, and the sheer salience of labor issues on the national agenda—that first kindled my interest in China. And it took me beyond the sheer indignation that China's brutal denial of workers' freedom of association evokes among many Western democrats and labor advocates. My own close look at China has taken me beyond a recognition of similarities and differences with the Western and American labor law and history that I know better, and has exposed some of the paradoxes, ironies, and contradictions that helped to shape this book. I say "beyond" even though strains of those early impressions, as well as the indignation, still ring true, albeit in more complex chords, after several years of research and reflection.

Close study of China has also caused me to reflect back on the United States, especially but not only on the law and policy governing work and industrial relations. Although my past writings have often been critical of the American law of work, most of that criticism has judged legal and practical realities against an internal benchmark of the law's own aspirations and objectives. Some of the basic underpinnings and animating principles of American labor and employment law remained beyond my critical compass, and implicitly shaped my view of other systems, including China's. I have devoted this book largely to examining China's labor question and the official responses to it, and to using the labor question in turn as a window on the Chinese political and economic landscape, mainly for the edification of Western and especially American readers. But in this conclusion I want to pass through that window and look back at the system I know best.

Let us begin with the regulatory side of the equation. Sadly, as I have observed more than once here, the United States has ample experience, past and present, with low-wage labor markets. Absolute wage levels and standards of living at the bottom are higher, of course, in the much richer United States—no small matter, but no excuse for the rampant illegality that characterizes low-wage labor markets in the United States as well as in China. Low-wage work typically means not only low wages but widespread violation of minimum labor standards. Outright failure to pay wages is far more prevalent in China, and still far and away the most frequent cause of strikes.[1] But "wage theft" in other forms—failure to pay the full amount of wages required by law under the circumstances—is shockingly common in the United States. In both countries, a major problem is employers' efforts to evade legal responsibility (by misclassifying employees as independent contractors or, in China, by failing to offer a written contract). And in both countries, the low-wage labor market is heavily populated and perpetuated by large numbers of poor workers with second-class or tenuous legal status (migrant workers in China, undocumented immigrants in the United States). Even as American worker advocates celebrate recent victories in the fight to raise state and local minimum wages, they are facing up to the daunting enforcement challenges that will follow.[2]

One crucial advantage that American low-wage workers have over their Chinese counterparts (beyond higher absolute wage levels) is access to independent nongovernmental advocates—lawyers, worker centers, sometimes (though rarely) unions—and the freedom to peacefully protest violations and appeal for public support. Sometimes independent advocates help workers gain access to the well-developed and independent (but cumbersome) U.S. court system, and the credible threat of a costly lawsuit presumably induces some employers to comply with the law. But the prevalence of noncompliance at the bottom of the labor market suggests that too few low-wage workers actually have a credible threat of going to court, and those who do often find that they cannot collect on a judgment.[3]

In the end, arguably the best thing that can be said for the U.S. law governing low-wage work, comparatively speaking, is that it leaves workers to their own devices—free to seek out help from others or to muster their own collective responses to widespread illegality. Workers' advocates and associations can operate openly and without fear of official harassment (even if individual workers, and especially undocumented immigrants, are vulnerable to a range of reprisals). Freedom of speech and association, and an independent and entrepreneurial bar, are worth celebrating for many reasons. But it is discouraging that labor standards remain so egregiously underenforced at the bottom of the U.S. labor market, given how long we have been at the regulatory project. (It is also striking how comparatively little social conflict has arisen in the United States over the yawning "enforcement gap.")

When we look just at the law on the books, at least at the national level, China has done far more than the United States since 2007 to improve formal labor standards for poor workers. (Too much, perhaps, given the corrosive consequences of the yawning enforcement gap.) In part that stems from an ideological embrace of market ordering in the United States that is wider, and puts a heavier burden of persuasion on the proponents of regulation, than one finds in China (or in most of the world, for that matter). That is a big part of the story of "American exceptionalism," familiar but cast into sharp relief when seen from China.

Another obvious reason for the lack of national legislation in recent years extends beyond the labor field: divided government and a gridlocked, polarized political process—in other words, our current version of multiparty democracy. There is much to regret there. Seeing that problem from a Chinese perspective has added, for me, a sense of chagrin, even embarrassment, that American democracy has performed so poorly in recent years. In scores of conversations with Chinese interlocutors, both one-on-one and in groups, about the virtues of multiparty democracy, I have felt obliged to try to explain away or apologize for the dysfunctionalities on display lately in the United States. More on that shortly.

The lack of legislative action on the American labor front is even more striking when we shift our focus from regulation of labor standards to collective labor relations. The U.S. labor movement has mounted several major campaigns for labor law reform in Congress over the past several decades, and has achieved nothing. That failure stems not only from political dysfunction and gridlock, but also from American workers' relative quiescence. Recall Alan Hyde's claim that major labor reform is usually a concession to a labor movement that is "making trouble."[4] American workers and their unions have not been making a lot of trouble lately, either in the workplace or on the streets. Major strikes are at their lowest level in over a century, and the smaller job actions that have been popping up over the past decade, mainly in fast food and retail, have done little to disrupt employers' operations, much less the economy or public order. American workers are far from content. But they seem to be in more of a funk than a fury over deepening inequality and erosion of living standards and economic security, and more inclined to blame those below them on the economic ladder than those at the top. That bodes ill for the political prospects of labor law reforms, large and small. And that brings me to another set of reflections on the state of American labor law and industrial relations that my exposure to China has provoked or sharpened.

American workers, unlike Chinese workers, have a legal right to form independent unions, bargain collectively, and strike. American employers, for their part, have the means, the motivation, and ample legal latitude to oppose and discourage the actual exercise of those rights. The path to unionization is strewn with obstacles and perils, and the right to strike is spiked with risks. That is part of the reason why private-sector workers in the United States are not much more likely than workers in China to actually participate in a system of collective bargaining through independent unions. And for the overwhelming majority of American workers who do not have union representation, the National Labor Relations Act's all-or-nothing model of employee representation, discussed in Chapter 8, virtually precludes any other institutionalized role in workplace governance.

Of course the legal right to form an independent union has value, both intrinsic and instrumental, even when it is not exercised. In times and places where the "threat" of unionization is alive to employers, it has motivated not just opposition to unions but concessions to workers—not just sticks but carrots—to induce them to stay on board with the default non-union regime of unilateral managerial control.[5] Today, however, there are rather few industries where that threat is real. Some employers still have to compete for skilled workers, and to cultivate the loyalty of the workers they have. But workers also compete with each other for jobs; many have to take what they can get, and what many workers can get these days is less remunerative and less secure than what was available to their parents' generation in unionized and union-influenced blue-collar jobs.

That is not just a coincidence. The decline of unions and the virtual demise of the "union threat effect" are responsible, according to leading mainstream economists, for much of the wage stagnation below the top of the income distribution, and for a fifth to a third of the increase in economic inequality over the past decades.[6] Obviously there are factors other than union decline behind wage stagnation and growing inequality, just as there are factors other than employer opposition and weak labor laws behind union decline. But the bottom line is that American workers have gotten little mileage lately out of their right to form unions, and that has contributed to their faltering economic fortunes.

China's workers, by contrast, lack a legal right to form independent unions, to bargain collectively through them, or to strike in support of bargaining demands—not to mention the right to vote for their political leaders. But they *are* making trouble. And they have gained real concessions, given the government's deep fear of organized dissent and the risks of escalation and loss of legitimacy entailed by sheer repression of protest that is based on shared grievances. Just since 2007, Chinese workers have gotten higher labor standards—some real, some only on paper—and higher wages, along with some very tentative steps toward trade union democracy within the All-China Federation of Trade Unions (ACFTU) and toward a voice in workplace governance. In essence, a version of the familiar "union threat effect" is operating on China's authoritarian government: the threat of independent labor organizing is pushing policy makers who are anxious to avoid that fate to mollify workers in other ways.

And there are other ways. For most workers most of the time, independent unions are means to other ends—better wages and working conditions, job security, and fair dispute resolution structures, for example. Most Western labor advocates hold that, at least for workers at the middle and bottom of the labor market, independent unions are the best or most reliable means to those ends; that bodes ill for American workers as well as Chinese workers who lack such union representation. But evidently unions are not the only means to those ends. In recent years, China's workers have been getting real mileage out of their relatively unorganized agitation even without its culmination in independent union organizing. Indeed, they have arguably gotten more mileage out of that agitation than American workers are currently getting out of independent unions and the legal right to form unions. That is a sobering thought.

Let me be very clear: I do not mean to cast doubt on the intrinsic value of the freedom of association and solidarity and democracy that unions both depend on and foster. Nor do I mean to suggest for a moment that U.S. workers would or should want to trade places with Chinese workers, in part (and only in part) because the latter's progress is measured from a much lower baseline. But the recent trajectory for China's workers is comparatively promising along several fronts, while American workers and their advocates are casting about for strategies to forestall further decline. Even in the growing economy of 2016, workers face growing fragmentation and insecurity of workplace arrangements, deterioration in real wages, shifting of market risks from employers to workers, and movement toward what some call a "winner-take-all" economy.[7] That reflects in part what I have called the "race to the rising bottom" in a global economy.

The role of independent unions is changing, and is undeniably shrinking, in a post–collective bargaining era. Privatized industrial self-governance through lightly regulated collective bargaining—the New Deal model that was meant to spread through most of blue-collar and white-collar employment alike—now seems unlikely to survive beyond a few entrenched but shrinking niches of the labor market. And no new strategy that is yet visible on the horizon promises anything like what collective bargaining in its heyday achieved for many American workers.

In the meantime, China's leaders are surely taking note that a robust collective bargaining system and an independent labor movement are not inescapably necessary for "industrial peace"; we in the United States have had the latter but not the former for a good many years. To be sure, it is unlikely that we could have gotten from the labor turmoil of the early twentieth century to the quiescence that prevails today without the grand New Deal settlement that institutionalized collective bargaining and incorporated independent unions into the process of workplace governance. But some in China are surely hoping to move past the current period of rising labor unrest directly into a period of labor peace without going through the intervening phase of contentious collective bargaining, threatening as that is for China's one-party regime. Whether China can indeed reach a sustainable settlement with its workers—one that promotes the broader prosperity that China credibly claims to be seeking—without allowing them to organize real unions remains the critical question running throughout this book.

There is another reason, however, for U.S. observers to attend closely to the determined effort of China's leaders to develop mechanisms other than independent organizing and collective bargaining to enable workers to improve their lives and resolve their problems at work: It is possible that we might learn something from those positive policy initiatives in our own effort to forge a decent *post*–collective bargaining regime. Those initiatives should not replace but might supplement existing rights and freedoms.

Of course, those who believe workers' only hope lies in the revival of the collective bargaining paradigm will object that anything we learn from China's efforts to avoid independent organizing is likely to serve that same end here. That objection taps into a real concern, but it proves too much. It would condemn American unions' longstanding commitment to improving mandatory minimum labor standards, and anything else that promises to make workers' lives better even without their forming a union. Unions and their allies do and should support reforms that benefit all workers, even if they allay some of the anger that might otherwise lead to union organizing. That is particularly true when just seven percent of the U.S. private-sector workforce has union representation, and when there is no realistic prospect for even doubling that number. In seeking to discourage union organizing, China's rulers (and American employers) do many things that are repugnant; but that should not condemn their efforts to satisfy workers' demands and help them solve their problems at work. With that in mind, let me suggest three disparate points on which China's recent labor reforms might be worth pondering in the American context.

First, consider China's response to the flood of claims under the Labor Contract Law (LCL): Hoping to speed the resolution of rights claims and stem the tide of litigation, and drawing on China's long history of favoring mediation over formal adjudication,[8] policy makers launched a massive expansion of mediation outlets for labor disputes. For those in the United States who are similarly concerned about too much employment litigation, too little access to justice for workers with legitimate but low-value claims, or both, greater investment in mediation is worth a close look. Mediation is hardly unknown in the United States,[9] nor is it a panacea.[10] But a significant expansion of mediation, if done right, would be preferable to the current reign of mandatory arbitration, which has been the American answer to concerns about too much litigation.

Many U.S. employers require employees, as a condition of employment, to waive their right to litigate future legal claims and to submit them instead to a private system of arbitration. Arbitration takes place in private (when it takes place at all), and decisions are usually cursory, with little or no elaboration of reasoning. Under an aggressive and anachronistic reading of the pre–New Deal Federal Arbitration Act, the Supreme Court has closed off nearly all avenues for challenging those arbitration "agreements," even when they are unilaterally imposed by the dominant party in a contractual relationship.[11] Clearly there is a need for cheaper, faster, and fair alternatives to litigation, and arbitration could be just that if it were fairly implemented.[12] But the law now gives employers too much latitude to devise arbitration procedures that deliberately skew outcomes and choke off claims (especially group claims). Recent data suggest that mandatory arbitration is doing far more to close off than to open up avenues for adjudication of employee rights claims.[13] In short, mandatory arbitration in its current form undermines both employee rights and "rule-of-law" values served by public adjudication of legal claims.

Some have made strikingly similar claims about China's turn toward mediation. Mediation norms and procedures in China leave much to be desired from an American "rule-of-law" perspective; outcomes appear too often coerced and inattentive to legal merits. Indeed, Carl Minzner has argued that China's sharp turn toward mediation and away from litigation—evident across the civil justice system by 2010—was part of a wider turn away from principles of legality.[14] Still, we should not be too quick to dismiss the virtues of mediation as such. An expansion of *voluntary* mediation, in which the unimpaired right to litigate drives the parties toward compromise, might be a better way to promote fair and efficient resolution of employment disputes than the existing employer-dominated process of mandatory arbitration. As compared to the latter, it would be more even-handed and more respectful of the principle of legality that should guide our own law reforms as well as China's.

Two other aspects of China's recent employment law reforms reflect an audacious and perhaps doomed effort to shore up twentieth-century patterns of stable jobs and cohesive workplaces in the face of global trends that are transforming the organization of work. Consider China's embrace of job security protections in the LCL and its amendments, explored in Chapter 5. The point here is not that China is doing anything different or better than the great majority of countries around the world that still proscribe arbitrary dismissals. But the LCL's enactment in the face of strident predictions of economic doom and gloom, especially from the American Chamber of Commerce,[15] solidifies an international normative consensus favoring protections against arbitrary dismissal and some economic layoffs, and underscores America's status as an outlier with its formal employment-at-will presumption.

In enacting the LCL, and in doubling down on its employment protections by restricting the use of labor dispatch, China is swimming against both a modest liberalizing current in parts of the developed world and deeper trends toward declining job tenure, splintering of work organizations, outsourcing of production, and contingent work arrangements.[16] The continuing slide from long-term employment within integrated firms toward a "gig" economy, though celebrated by some, has potentially dire consequences for workers who risk losing the entire panoply of rights, protections, and benefits that twentieth-century reforms had attached to the employment relationship. But China is seeking to defy that trend, and to shore up job security and stability. Perhaps the *danwei* concept retains some residual hold over policy makers' conception of the proper relationship between workers and firms even in the era of commodified labor. Or perhaps the prospect of unmooring ever more workers from the security and discipline of stable workplace communities is more unsettling to China's one-party authoritarian regime than it is in a pluralist democracy.

Of course, it remains to be seen whether China can resist trends toward the disintegration of work and workplaces, and whether its newly fortified job security protections can actually take hold. Most American labor economists would predict that new legal restrictions on staffing flexibility would trigger a new round of evasive measures or reduced employment levels. It is too early, and there is too little reliable data, to know whether they are right. But for those who believe, as I do, that stable workplace communities have served as a foundation not only for greater economic security for individuals but also for greater social solidarity and stronger communities, China's concerted if quixotic effort to resist their demise evokes a certain admiration. The goal if not the particular means might be worthy of emulation.

The attempt to institutionalize "democratic management" in private firms—partial and halfhearted though it appears to be thus far—might also be part of an effort to shore up stable workplace communities. (Or it might only reflect a failure to reckon with the disintegration to which they are doomed.) As in the case of job security, China has lots of company across the world in promoting enterprise-based worker representation, and there are better models available elsewhere. But China's effort to build up the Staff and Workers Representative Congresses (SWRCs) bolsters the claim that institutions such as European works councils (WCs) reflect global norms of good workplace governance. As with other such global norms, China is thus far falling short in realizing its formal principles of worker representation. But it is jarring to conclude, as I do, that China's laws on this particular matter may offer a better model than U.S. law. There is ample evidence to suggest that many American workers would welcome an institution like the SWRC if it did what it was supposed to do.[17] Our policy of all or nothing, and mostly nothing, with regard to collective worker participation, even on core issues of health and safety, is yet another embarrassment of sorts. I can understand both its origins and its endurance.[18] But I cannot justify it, and would not recommend it to policy makers anywhere.

Here again some American union proponents will object: If the SWRCs are part of China's strategy to avert independent organizing, as they likely are, that should only strengthen the case against an analogous policy change in the United States. My answer is foreshadowed above: Unions should not be opposing reforms that could benefit many non-union workers, even if those reforms might also drain off some of the discontent that fuels union organizing. But a more specific response is also in order: Germany's experience suggests that, where independent organizing is also possible (as it is not in China), the impact of WCs on unions depends a great deal on unions' strategy for engaging with them. American experience is not all to the contrary: some unions in the 1930s were able to use "company unions" as platforms for independent organizing.[19] Of course, fear of that very result in China is likely to hold back efforts to make the SWRCs as robust as they would need to be to serve their appointed functions. That brings us to the next big question on the table.

## What Will the "Socialist Market Economy" Mean for China's Workers?

China claims to be building a "socialist market economy." From the beginning of China's opening to private capital, it has often been hard to distinguish its version of socialism from a bare-knuckled version of capitalism. Conditions in the new factory areas grossly belied the regime's professions of socialist ideology, and earned China a reputation among labor advocates and others in the West as a center of capitalist exploitation of workers. Yet China's leaders are not galloping down a path of continued economic liberalization and privatization.[20] For one thing, they appear committed to maintaining, not shrinking, a large state-owned sector with monopolies or protected positions in several strategic or highly lucrative industries.[21] That is among the central features of the Chinese political economic model that some observers describe as "state capitalism."[22] But is that what China means by a "socialist market economy"?

If we focus on China's policy toward the governance of the enterprises that populate its mixed economy, a different picture emerges—one of considerable convergence over time between the state-owned enterprises (SOEs) and the larger non-state enterprises, as well as between China's economy and our own. In the early "reform and opening" period, China maintained two largely distinct industrial economies: a still-planned, state-owned socialist economy, whose workers were protected by the "iron rice bowl," and a new private market economy with its grim and nearly unregulated factories. Since the early 1990s, however, trends in the two sectors have converged, as Mary Gallagher and others have shown. One half of the convergence entailed the "corporatization" of the SOEs, the commodification of its labor, and the smashing of the "iron rice bowl," sketched in Chapter 2. The other half of the convergence—the extension of state oversight to the non-state sector—began in the 1990s.[23] The Labor Law of 1994 was a watershed in its imposition of a single regulatory regime across the state and non-state sectors, with sharply opposing implications in the two sectors: The law's embrace of the "labor contract system" formalized and furthered the decline of job security in the state sector; but its regulation of that system began to improve standards in the non-state sector.[24] The rise of labor standards, regulatory structures, and avenues for adjudication of rights disputes continued with the LCL of 2008.[25] Enforcement still lags for many reasons explored here, but the trend toward greater regulation is clear and steady.

Most elements of the emerging regime suggest a convergence not only between China's two economies, but also between China and the developed world, toward a model of regulatory capitalism. But among the important differences is one explored in this book: In the developed regulatory capitalist economies of the West, both organized labor and organized capital are relatively autonomous from the state—regulated to varying degrees, but not directly managed by the state. In China, as we have seen, these two halves of the market economy are treated quite differently.

On the side of capital, the state now acts less as its direct proprietor and more as a regulator of semi-autonomous productive entities, public and private. Even SOEs function fairly independently (though the mechanisms of state control are complex and often opaque[26]). Private capital for its part is comparatively free to aggregate and organize itself into corporations that conduct their own affairs, subject to regulatory constraints (and the risk of political interference). But China has not made the parallel shift with regard to collective labor activity. Rather than allow workers to form their own labor organizations, subject to regulatory constraints (on violence, or on the timing and scope of work stoppages, for example), China's leaders are still trying to manage collective labor activity directly through the party-state and its labor arm, the ACFTU. The official trade unions enjoy less autonomy from the party-state than SOEs and their managers; and, in contrast to the relative freedom of organized capital, independent organized labor outside the ACFTU structure is still harshly suppressed.[27]

But there is a countercurrent—what I call here a "socialization" story—that qualifies the story of growing autonomy of organized capital and its managers (though not that of continued control of organized labor). The socialization story begins with the establishment of Party chapters within large private and foreign-invested companies;[28] that facilitated the ACFTU's drive to organize trade union chapters, and in turn the recent press to establish SWRCs, in those companies. The net result has been to reproduce in the market economy the forms, though not the substance, of both Party authority and worker representation that originated in the planned economy. The SWRCs in particular are touted as vehicles of democratic management, and they could serve the regime's interests in short-term and long-term stability maintenance by creating an official channel for conflict resolution and rights enforcement within the enterprise. Crucially, however, the SWRCs can only serve those objectives if they actually help workers address their grievances, and empower them vis-à-vis employers, at least to a modest degree.

The attempted resurrection of the SWRCs, if it takes shape on the ground and not only on paper, suggests that China intends not only to regulate enterprises and their labor practices through external imposition of labor standards, but to shift their internal modes of governance in a pro-worker direction. In short, after "corporatizing" the SOEs, and restructuring them to largely mimic the capitalist firms of the West, China (or at least some of its leaders) might now be seeking to dial back a notch or two, and to modestly "socialize" the capitalist firms operating in China—to mandate structures that give workers a greater role in governance. That would resonate with the regime's own rhetoric and its invocation of "democratic management" as an integral part of China's pro-worker ideology, ensconced in the constitution and sprinkled throughout its legislation and policy documents.[29]

I return to the SWRCs in this final chapter because they capture several of the "Chinese characteristics" of the emerging regime for governance of labor. Everything about the SWRCs—the potential to resolve conflicts early, inside the enterprise, under the eye of management, and through an officially sanctioned, Party-supervised entity—make the SWRC an appealing mechanism from the regime's standpoint for addressing workers' grievances and diverting them from independent organizing. For now, the SWRCs are unlikely to work well or often, given the weight of management domination and the absence of independent worker organizations. But the SWRCs and the principle of democratic management are among the most interesting elements of China's eclectic repertoire of responses to labor unrest, and could lend some substance to the concept of the "socialist market economy" and distinguish it from a regulated market economy with a large state sector.

## A New Deal for China's Workers? Concluding Thoughts on Labor Unrest and Democracy

Will China's workers get their own New Deal? If the question is whether they will get the right to engage in concerted self-help and collective bargaining through autonomous, freely chosen, and reasonably democratic trade unions, the answer is surely no, not within the foreseeable future. For now, China's leadership appears both unified in its determination to avoid that outcome and capable of foreclosing it, though not without costs and difficulties explored here. China's leaders are intensely focused on "stability maintenance"—on avoiding large-scale, contagious, disruptive mass protest—and on preempting any political challenge to Party rule. In the labor context, that means preventing the rise of independent, organized labor activism outside the Party-approved and Party-controlled trade union structure. That determination, as we have seen, shapes every facet of China's response to labor unrest, reformist and repressive alike.

The determination to prevent the rise of independent labor organizing underlies recent efforts to improve minimum labor standards and access to legal remedies for rights violations, but it also underlies restrictions on labor NGOs and even collective litigation that might promote workers' enforcement of their rights. That determination underlies efforts to defuse strikes by pressuring employers to grant economic concessions, but it also underlies official resistance to genuine collective bargaining under the shadow of a strike threat. That determination underlies efforts to make the official enterprise unions more accountable to workers through "direct elections," but it also cabins and even cripples those efforts lest too much democracy compromise Party control of the trade unions. That same determination to forestall independent worker organizing underlies efforts to shore up and extend the official SWRC system, but it also forecloses the deeper reforms, including the independent labor organizations, that may be necessary to empower workers to use that system.

Finally, that same determination to prevent the rise of independent and contagious labor activism underlies both the use and the avoidance of repression—both the parsimonious deployment of police forces against most strikes and the more surgical yet systematic suppression of any glimmer of independent organizing across factories. Sadly, it became increasingly clear in 2015 that the Xi regime had veered toward greater use of repression—still surgical rather than broad gauged, still aimed chiefly at the tiny group of activists involved in multiple strikes rather than the average striker. But the goal remains the same: to avoid the coalescing of dissent into an independent labor movement.

In short, China's leaders are determined to suppress both the demand for independent union representation that might challenge Party rule, and the supply of such representation. Can they succeed? Can China resolve its labor troubles (or keep them from derailing social, political, and industrial progress) without allowing workers to organize independently and bargain collectively? Those who believe it is impossible for China to skip past that highly contentious phase of industrial relations must reckon with the unprecedented course of China's development thus far. China's rapid economic transformation has telescoped processes of economic development, industrialization, and urbanization that unfolded over a much longer period of time in the West. China's post-Mao experience of mass industrialization, and the integration of millions of poor farmers into an urban industrial economy, has overlapped with the development of a vibrant consumer culture and service economy, growing individualism, and other trends typically associated with late- or post-industrial development. Some of those trends may favor the development of an independent labor movement, but others may undermine it.

The upsurge of collective activism that is unaccompanied and uncontained by organized institutional vehicles is a defining feature of contemporary Chinese labor relations. The New Deal reference point might suggest that there is a pressing need for a more institutionalized system for resolution of disputes, one in which independent unions play a necessary role. Independent unions both mobilize and organize workers; they make it easier to undertake collective action, but they can also keep it within peaceful and lawful bounds and avert open conflict through negotiations. When I began my foray into China, I believed that systemic reform along Western lines was necessary if not imminent given the rise of serious labor unrest. But I have come to doubt that this is so. China's leaders see organized mobilization as a much greater threat than disorganized and chaotic unrest. And they are making a calculated trade-off in resisting the organized mobilization that independent labor organizations might bring.

The regime's preference for disorganized unrest over organized mobilization must surely depend partly on the magnitude of the former. But I have also come to doubt that the problem of labor unrest is as serious and salient to China's leaders as it would have to be to push them toward dramatic reforms that risk organized mobilization. With few exceptions, strikes in the past decade—that is, since the large-scale protests over SOE reform and layoffs—are localized protests directed at a single employer, largely unrelated to each other in either their inspiration or their instigation (apart from workers' growing awareness that strikes are often efficacious in gaining concessions). What China's rulers most fear, and most vigorously repress, is any sign of contagion and organization across factories. Those risks appear fairly small and repressible thus far, given the relative sparsity of strikes, and especially of long or large strikes, across China's vast territory and population.[30] With strike levels rising each year in recent years, the party-state cannot afford to be complacent. But vigilance and persistence rather than dramatic systemic reform may look like the safest response.

One experience that drove home to me the relative sparsity of strikes was observing a day-long conference in 2014 in Shenzhen on "China's changing workforce" for several hundred representatives of firms doing business in China's electronics industry, including major Western and Asian brands and suppliers. The two dozen or so presenters sought to impart various dimensions of a longer and broader perspective on the practical staffing problems that these firms faced in China. There was much talk of turnover and labor shortages in jobs requiring skill and education, and of changing workforce demographics, demands, and aspirations beneath the surface of those daily realities. Those were pressing strategic concerns for employers. I heard no mention, however, of strikes or collective unrest, either by presenters or by participants in their questions.[31] It was as if, for any one employer, being hit by a major strike was like being hit by lightning—a potential calamity if it occurs, but too unlikely to serve as a major impetus for firm policy and planning.

Curiosity led me to attempt to compare the sheer volume of strikes in the United States and in China—in particular between the U.S. in the 1930s and China in recent years. Quantitative comparisons are risky if not foolhardy here, given the quality of the available data and vast differences in historical and national context. Still, the differences are stark and suggestive. Figure 9.1 compares estimated percentages of the working-age populations that were involved in strikes in the United States from 1920 to 1937 (that is, in the run-up to the New Deal labor reforms) and in China from 2011 to 2015 (the years for which some strike data are available).[32] The striker estimates for China are very rough. There is no official data comparable to that in the United States; and the available data (from the China Labour Bulletin's Strike Map) both understate and overstate the incidence of strikes, or concerted work stoppages,[33] and gives the number of participants only in broad ranges. But the estimates in Figure 9.1 aim to err on the side of overstating the number of strikers in China (and thus understating the differences between China and the United States).[34]

The data in Figure 9.1 suggest that, even at the lowest ebb of pre-New Deal strike activity in 1930, the share of the U.S. working-age population that was involved in strikes was more than double the roughly comparable share in China at the peak (so far) of strike activity in 2015. (If we were to focus on Guangdong Province, which has experienced much higher strike levels than China as a whole, the percentage of strikers does approximate those at the low ebb of strikes in the United States; but of course the percentage of strikers in the hotbeds of labor unrest in the United States in the 1930s were much higher as well.) These numbers would suggest that China's labor problem, significant as it is in the Chinese context, is of a different order of magnitude—far less massive and less disruptive, as well as less political—than the labor unrest that shook the floorboards of 1930s America and helped usher in the New Deal.

To be sure, even apart from the vagaries of the data, one might spin this quantitative comparison in the opposite direction: For one thing, it is impressive that strike levels are as high as they are in China despite a more repressive environment and the inability of strike organizers to operate openly with the help of unions. Moreover, the U.S. data remind us that the low ebb of strike activity in 1930 was followed within a very few years by the dramatic upsurge in strikes that helped to prod policy makers into structural reforms. Things can change fast. But they would have to change a great deal in China to rival the labor unrest that produced the New Deal.

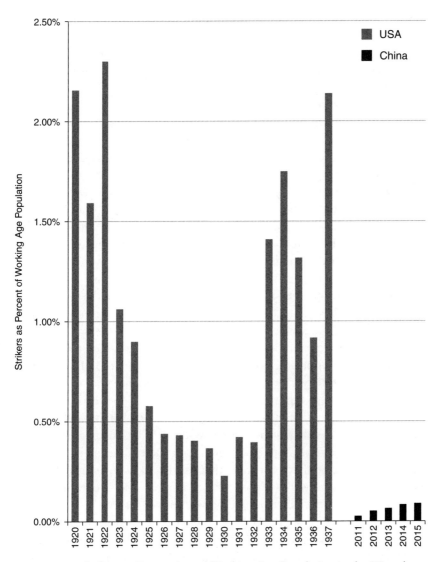

FIGURE 9.1 Strikers as Proportion of Working Age Population in the US and China, 1920–1937 and 2011–2015. *Sources:* National Population Estimates by Age, Sex, and Race, U.S. Census Bureau, Population Division, available online at https://www .census.gov/popest/data/national/asrh/pre-1980/PE-11.html; Florence Peterson, Strikes in the United States 1880–1936; U.S. Bureau of Labor Statistics, Monthly Labor Reports; World Development Indicators, The World Bank, available online at http://databank.worldbank .org/data/reports.aspx?source=world-development-indicators; China Strike Map, China Labour Bulletin (CLB), available online at http://strikemap.clb.org.hk/strikes/en#. *Note:* China strike map data is unlikely to be exhaustive, so when estimating strikers in China, several assumptions were made to correct for this. For more detail, see note 34.

Hence my tentative conclusion: Looking at the labor scene alone, it appears likely that China's leaders can keeping labor unrest within manageable bounds, while giving no quarter to independent union-like organizing, for the foreseeable future. The regime's laser-like focus on the goal of avoiding political challenges to Party rule (in the labor arena and beyond), and the growing sophistication of its tactics for doing so, suggest to me a long life expectancy for the current ad hoc, seemingly dysfunctional approach to industrial relations. That would not be all bad news for China's workers, for the regime's prophylactic strategy requires continuing improvements to workers' standard of living, along with modest reforms. But it will not entail the kind of deep structural reforms that Western labor advocates and labor organizations have long hoped for in China. We might call it a "New Deal with Chinese characteristics," but aficionados of America's New Deal would justifiably object to the analogy even with the (admittedly clichéd) qualifier.

There are many big "ifs" lurking behind this tentative prediction of continuing stability and very modest reform. One concerns the behavior of party-state officials, especially at the local level: Can they be counted on to do their part in appeasing workers by putting party-state power behind their reasonable demands, despite a long history and a lucrative habit of indulging local businesses? Or will they instead resort too often to blunt and counterproductive forms of stability maintenance that inflame and politicize conflict (as Eli Friedman shows they have long tended to do)?[35] While some in China have called for a more "flexible" approach to maintaining stability based on greater freedom, democracy, and procedural fairness,[36] Chinese officials, top to bottom, appear determined to maintain the flexibility to use tools of coercion that are poorly constrained by "due process of law," as well as tools of appeasement and cooptation. Local officials may be especially tempted to overuse the former.

The biggest "ifs" lie in the larger economic and political context, and in the nature and resilience of China's system, which have drawn close attention from many quarters as China has outlasted other one-party Communist regimes. For many years, some American observers maintained that political liberalization and democratization were inevitable in the wake of economic liberalization, or with the formation of a sizable middle class, or in the age of the Internet.[37] China's defiance of those predictions, and its success in combining economic development and stable one-party rule, has in turn generated a cottage industry of scholarship on the "new model" that China might represent. "Fragmented authoritarianism,"[38] "consultative," "responsive," or "deliberative authoritarianism,"[39] and "resilient" or "adaptive authoritarianism"[40] are all terms that aim to encapsulate explanations for the surprising staying power of China's distinctive political economy. Each couples "authoritarianism," denoting unelected one-party rule, with some evocation of dynamism and flexibility of a sort not previously associated with such regimes. All of those features of China's system—its authoritarianism as well as its fragmented, consultative, responsive, resilient, and adaptive dimensions—are on display in its response to labor unrest.

Yet stability on the labor front and beyond depends on continuing growth and material improvements for China's citizens. That is one reason why recent economic turmoil is causing palpitations in Beijing. Indeed, one leading scholar of modern China, Minxin Pei, predicts (in the title of a recent essay and in a forthcoming book) "the twilight of Communist Party rule in China," in large part because the stalling of China's economy, which he traces to structural and not cyclical forces, spells the end of the rising living standards that have been the single biggest source of legitimacy for China's rulers.[41] Pei argues that China has reached the limits of growth, resilience, and adaptability, and is descending into a death spiral of economic stagnation, growing repression, elite in-fighting, and loss of legitimacy. Pei's deeply informed diagnosis of "the exhaustion of the regime's post-Tiananmen survival strategy" has many moving parts. In his own summary, "[s]everal critical pillars of this strategy—such as elite unity, performance-based legitimacy, co-optation of social elites, and strategic restraint in foreign policy—have either collapsed or become hollow, forcing the CPC to resort increasingly to repression and appeals to nationalism to cling to power."[42] The increasing resort to repression of labor activism, seen here, may be the tip of an iceberg that could, on Pei's account, sink the Titanic.

Pei's diagnosis of systemic decay and impending collapse in China would cast a very dark shadow over China's labor landscape, and over my tentative conclusion that China's current labor troubles are, by themselves, probably "manageable" by a regime that is determined to manage them. But Pei's pessimism is not shared by all. Other well-informed observers point to sources of resilience and popular legitimacy that may allow its leaders to weather the current storms and continue China's development, if not at the breakneck pace of the recent past.[43] One commentator summed up the bullish view in late 2014:

> Here's the truth: the Chinese state is not fragile. The regime is strong, increasingly self-confident, and without organized opposition. Its economic management is competent and pragmatic. Its responsiveness to social pressures on issues such as the environment is imperfect, but well-informed by research and public opinion surveys. It derives real legitimacy from its consistent demon-

strated ability to raise living standards, provide a growing range of public goods, and maintain a high level of order while mostly letting people do what they want in their daily lives (unless what they want is to organize against the government).[44]

The resolution of these debates is well beyond the scope of this book and of my expertise. Suffice it to say that China has defied predictions of doom before. In case China manages to do so again, at least for another decade or two, it remains worthwhile to examine how things are likely to play out in this one field of social unrest. It is worthwhile as well to reflect on the light that China's recent history in the labor field and beyond might cast on the United States.

My time in China has coincided with some of the worst polarization and dysfunctionality in American politics in my lifetime. I confess to moments of admiration toward the ability of China's leaders to get things done. While its system is riddled with flaws, including many that kick in at the implementation stage and some that might prove fatal, the Chinese regime has been able to move policy initiatives forward—not only labor reforms but also improvements in legal and regulatory institutions, infrastructure, education, and health.[45] The material progress that China has made since the late 1970s—in large part through experimentation and collectively deliberated policy judgments, but without either the accountability or the distraction of democratic contestation—unsettle any easy faith in democracy as a universal imperative.[46]

The principle of democratic governance through contested popular elections is self-evident and inviolable for Americans and others throughout the world. However, insofar as people need an *effective* government and all the benefits it can bring, democracy in its modern American form has both merits and flaws. In some ways, it has performed less well in delivering the goods—especially the public goods that only government can deliver—than China's post-Mao authoritarian system. It might be too easy for American democrats to insist that the principle of democratic self-rule, as embodied in contested multiparty elections, trumps those instrumental and material considerations for still-developing economies.

More deeply troubling than the regime's obdurate resistance to electoral democracy are the tightening restrictions on civil society and especially foreign-sponsored NGOs, the arrests and detentions of "rights lawyers" and labor activists, and the effort to suffocate intellectual debate on democracy, civil liberties, and human rights. The last was underscored in a Party communique, "Document 9," that was circulated quietly through Party channels in universities and elsewhere in the spring of 2013.[47] The document warned against promotion of "Western" ideas about civil society, constitutionalism, "universal values," and the role of media; it was an unusually explicit effort to mark such ideas as subversive and chill their open discussion even in academic settings.

Some Party defenders argue that the control of civil society and suppression of dissent are still-necessary conditions of China's "governability" and continued development.[48] When I first heard those claims, I was inclined to reject them out of hand as mere self-serving pretexts for fortifying the Party's hold on power for its own sake. Over the years I became convinced of the good faith of at least some of those claims: I think many CPC leaders and their academic allies genuinely believe that a wide-open, liberalized sphere of public discourse and a much freer civil society could undermine one-party rule, and that stable one-party rule is still essential for China's people to fulfill their most pressing needs and aspirations. In other words, they might say, free speech is an unaffordable luxury for those who are still aspiring to a level of material security and well-being that many Americans take for granted.

But what if those beliefs are not only sincere but well-grounded in China's reality? And what if the great majority of China's citizens themselves would be unwilling (if given a choice) to imperil the stability and progress they have experienced for the past forty years in exchange for greater freedom to criticize the regime they credit with bringing about that stability and progress? Is there not some all-too-American hubris in the conviction that we know better what China needs? In short, I found that some of the liberal and democratic certainties with which I began my exploration of China were shaken.

The crackdown on peaceful dissenters, free thinkers, and human rights defenders since 2015 has pulled me back a few steps from that place of doubt. A regime that claims to have the near-universal support of its citizens cannot be so fragile that it cannot tolerate those critical voices, and a regime that is that fragile needs to find other ways to reclaim the support of its citizens.

The problem is that the prophecy of dissent leading to chaos is not only self-serving, but self-fulfilling in two ways: First, if outlets for peaceful dissent are closed, pressure is likely to build up and take more chaotic and insurrectionary forms (unless popular grievances are somehow magically dissolved—unlikely in a modern but undemocratic society). Imagine a steam engine in which too many pressure valves are closed tight; an explosion is likely to follow. Second, if peaceful opposition is outlawed, and defined as disloyal, then there is no chance for the development of a loyal opposition, or an alternative leadership structure. Those who argue that there is no viable alternative to unified CPC rule are right insofar as suppression of critical voices has ensured that there are no non-CPC leaders-in-waiting. One potential solution, much debated among Chinese intellectuals, is to allow greater and more open *intraparty* disagreement and democratic contestation.[49] But even intraparty debate is aggressively policed lest a challenge to the current leadership gain standard bearers; some argue that was a major impetus behind the anti-corruption campaign—its choice of targets if not the campaign itself.[50]

The prospects, virtues, and risks of liberalism and democracy are hotly debated among China watchers and Chinese intellectuals.[51] For it is not only Westerners who believe that "Democracy Is a Good Thing."[52] That is the title of a book by Yu Keping, a leading political thinker and occasional advisor to the government in China, and one of those who, despite a chillier environment for political debate, continue to press the case for political democracy. Yu responded in a 2016 essay to the fear that democracy will cause unrest.[53] "Those who are against democracy often use this possibility to frighten their audience. The truth is that there is much evidence to show ... [j]ust the opposite: over the long term, it is only democracy and the rule of law that will provide for the long-lasting peaceful rule of the nation."[54] Citing Sun Yat-sen, he says: "The movement towards democracy everywhere is a political trend that cannot be reversed. China is no exception."[55] Democracy, along with the rule of law, should come sooner rather than later, for it is essential and integral to "the political development of socialism with Chinese characteristics," and to the fight against corruption and declining public trust.[56] As for what democratization entails, Yu is very clear that it requires competitive elections, as well as other forms of popular responsiveness and accountability: "Our democracy will naturally be one with Chinese characteristics. But democracy cannot be separated from elections and competition."[57] Although Yu does not go so far as to call for *multi-party* competitive elections, it is encouraging that respected Chinese intellectuals can advocate electoral competition—not only abroad and in English but in official media within China.[58]

Clearly the future of China's political model will be shaped by global and domestic economic trends, changing information technology, nationalism and regional and international relations, and environmental degradation and reforms, and other issues barely touched on in this book. Yet a close look at China's "labor question" reveals a thick slice of the challenges the regime faces and the strengths and weaknesses it brings to the task of addressing those challenges. China's effort to contain labor unrest is both emblematic, and a crucial test, of its ability to modernize while avoiding deeply liberalizing and democratizing political reforms. And what we have seen on that front in the past few decades suggests that China's political system has greater staying power, dynamism, and functionality than most outsiders had believed possible.

That staying power depends in part on Chinese workers. What do they really want, and what they will want going forward as China continues to develop? Even if future growth in China allows for continuing wage hikes, will workers be content with wage increases and better material labor standards, or will they hold out for deeper structural reforms, and greater freedom of association, collective autonomy, and democracy? China's leaders hope to build a harmonious and "moderately prosperous society" by climbing the global production ladder, out of mass manufacturing based on low-wage labor and into more technologically advanced and profitable phases and sectors of production. Yet a more educated workforce whose basic material needs are met might be a more demanding workforce, one that is less willing to trade away rights for wages.

China's workers are very unlikely to get anything that we would recognize as a New Deal. That is partly because they do not have, and are very unlikely to get, the right to elect their leaders or the other civil rights and liberties that we rightly treasure. But they are having some success in pushing their unelected rulers to find other ways to address many of their legitimate grievances. They have begun to make more calculated and concerted use of the ability to stall the machinery of production and create a ruckus—vital to workers' struggles to improve their lot throughout the history of industrialization. As widespread hunger, misery, and chaos have receded into the past, workers' vision of the future has expanded to encompass choice and change, entitlements and aspirations, dreams and ambitions.[59] It seems only fitting to end this book with one last unanswerable question: What will China's workers do with those gains?

# Notes

## Preface

1. Cynthia L. Estlund and Seth Gurgel, "Will Labour Unrest Lead to More Democratic Trade Unions in China?," in *China and ILO Fundamental Principles and Rights at Work,* ed. Roger Blanpain, Ulla Liukkunen, and Yifeng Chen Kluwer Press, 2014.
2. Cynthia L. Estlund, "Will Workers Have a Voice in China's 'Socialist Market Economy'? The Curious Revival of the Workers Congress System," *Comparative Labor Law and Policy Journal 36* (2014): 1.

## 1. Introduction

1. "Towards the End of Poverty," *Economist,* June 1, 2013, http://www.economist .com/news/leaders/21578665-nearly-1-billion-people-have-been-taken-out -extreme-poverty-20-years-world-should-aim.
2. Albert O. Hirschman, *Exit, Voice, and Loyalty: Responses to Decline in Firms, Organizations, and States* (Cambridge, MA: Harvard University Press, 1970).
3. Mitali Das and Papa N'Diaye, "The End of Cheap Labor," *International Monetary Fund Finance and Development 50,* no. 2 (June 2013), http://www .imf.org/external/pubs/ft/fandd/2013/06/das.htm.
4. The "one-child generation" is a handy shorthand for a more complicated story of declining birthrates in China. See Chapter 2.
5. "Rising Labor Costs Trigger Industrial Relocation," editor's note, *China Daily,* July 6, 2010, http://www.chinadaily.com.cn/bizchina/2010-07/06/content

_10069557.htm; Keith Bradsher, "Gift-Bearing Officials Try to Lure Chinese Factories Inland," *New York Times,* August 27, 2014.

6. In spite of recent economic turmoil in China, many business experts remain bullish on China's long-term growth prospects. "Buffett: I'm Bullish on China, It Has Long-Term Potential," interview with David Westin, *Bloomberg News,* September 8, 2015, http://www.bloomberg.com/news/videos/2015-09-08/buffett -i-m-bullish-on-china-it-has-long-term-potential; Leslie Shaffer, "Goldman: Still Bullish on China, Despite Slashing Target," CNBC, October 8, 2015, http://www.cnbc.com/2015/10/08/goldman-still-bullish-on-china-despite -slashing-target.html. Others think China is headed toward an economic downturn. Greg Bresiger, "Chicago Economists Bearish on China," *Financial Advisor,* January 15, 2016, http://www.fa-mag.com/news/chicago-economists -bearish-on-china-24639.html. Even China's finance minister, Lou Jiwei, has said that China has a "greater than 50%" chance of falling into the mid-dle-income trap, an economic term for a developing country that reaches a plateau at which growth stagnates. "Nation Must Be Alert to Middle-Income Trap," *China Daily,* April 28, 2015, http://www.chinadaily.com.cn/opinion /2015-04/28/content_20559900.htm. The IMF takes a middle ground, calling the recent slower growth rate the "new normal," but more sustainable and stable. *People's Republic of China,* IMF Country Report no. 15/234 (Washington, DC: International Money Fund, August 2015), http://www.imf.org/external /pubs/ft/scr/2015/cr15234.pdf.

7. Compare Ronald B. Davies and Krishna Chaitanya Vadlamannati, "A Race to the Bottom in Labor Standards? An Empirical Investigation," *Journal of Development Economics* 103 (July 2013): 1-14 (finding that countries may enforce labor laws less strictly in order to draw foreign investment), with Ajit Singh and Ann Zammit, "Labour Standards and the 'Race to the Bottom': Rethinking Globalization and Workers' Rights from Developmental and Solidaristic Perspectives," *Oxford Review of Economic Policy* 20, (2004): 101 (finding little evidence to support the race-to-the-bottom theory), and Layna Mosley and Saika Uno, "Racing to the Bottom or Climbing to the Top? Economic Globalization and Collective Labor Rights," *Comparative Political Studies* 40 (August 2007): 923-48 (finding that FDI inflows positively affect workers' rights while trade competition generates downward pressure).

8. Stephanie Clifford, "U.S. Textile Plants Return, with Floors Largely Empty of People," *New York Times,* September 19, 2013.

9. The World Bank, "The State of the Poor: Where are the Poor and where are they Poorest?," April 17, 2013, http://www.worldbank.org/content/dam /Worldbank/document/State_of_the_poor_paper_April17.pdf.

10. Greg Knowler, "Sourcing Report Reveals Scale of China's Rising Labor Costs," *Journal of Commerce,* April 15, 2015, http://www.joc.com/international -logistics/sourcing-report-reveals-scale-china%E2%80%99s-rising-labor -costs_20150415.html.

11. In 2010 and 2011, annual hikes were as high as 20 percent in some provinces. Sarah Biddulph, *The Stability Imperative: Human Rights and Law in China* (Vancouver: University of British Columbia Press, 2015). That said, rates of

increase have slowed of late. The average increase year over year from 1990 to 2009 was over 10 percent; from 2013 to 2014 it was less than 6 percent. Chinese nominal wages from http://www.tradingeconomics.com/china/wages (last visited 5/3/16). Chinese inflation deflator from *Chinese Statistical Yearbook 2014*, http://www.stats.gov.cn/tjsj/ndsj/2014/indexeh.htm. Calculations by Ellen Campbell under the author's supervision.

12. "Nation Must Be Alert to Middle Income Trap."

13. The advantage of lower labor costs elsewhere—as much as 30 percent lower than in China—is often offset by disadvantages such as poor infrastructure. "The End of Cheap China: What Do Soaring Chinese Wages Mean for Global Manufacturing?," *Economist*, March 10, 2012, http://www.economist.com/node/21549956. .

14. Beverly J. Silver and Giovanni Arrighi, "Polanyi's 'Double Movement': The *Belle Époques* of British and U.S. Hegemony Compared," *Politics and Society* 31 (June 2003), 325-55; Mosley and Uno, "Racing to the Bottom or Climbing to the Top?"

15. David H. Autor, David Dorn, and Gordon H. Hanson, "The China Shock: Learning from Labor Market Adjustment to Large Changes in Trade," NBER Working Paper No. 21906, January 2016, http://www.ddorn.net/papers/Autor-Dorn-Hanson-ChinaShock.pdf.

16. Layoffs can have long-term negative effects, even on workers' children. See Austin Nichols, Josh Mitchell, and Stephan Lindner, *Consequences of Long-Term Unemployment* (Washington, DC: Urban Institute, 2013), 10–11, http://www.urban.org/sites/default/files/alfresco/publication-pdfs/412887-Consequences-of-Long-Term-Unemployment.PDF.

17. See David Weil, *The Fissured Workplace: Why Work Became So Bad for So Many and What Can Be Done to Improve It* (Cambridge, MA: Harvard University Press, 2014); and Thomas Piketty, *Capital in the Twenty-First Century* (Cambridge, MA: Harvard University Press, 2014).

18. Michael B. McElroy, Chris P. Nielsen, and Peter Lydon, *Energizing China: Reconciling Environmental Protection and Economic Growth* (Cambridge, MA: Harvard University Press, 1998).

19. David Whitford, "Where in the World Is Cheap Labor?," *Fortune*, March 22, 2011, http://archive.fortune.com/2011/03/22/news/international/fair_labor_china.fortune/index.htm (quoting Auret van Heerden).

20. James A. Hagerty and Mark Magnier, "Companies Tiptoe Back towards 'Made in the U.S.A.,' " *Wall Street Journal*, January 13, 2015.

21. "Senior Chinese Officials Acknowledge Rising Social Unrest, but Rule Out Political Liberalization," Congressional-Executive Commission on China, August 1, 2005, http://www.cecc.gov/publications/commission-analysis/senior-chinese-officials-acknowledge-rising-social-unrest-but-rule; "In 2005, Incidents of Social Unrest Reached 87,000,"*Asia News*, January 20, 2006, http://www.asianews.it/news-en/In-2005,-incidents-of-social-unrest-hit-87,000–5169.html.

22. "Protecting Workers' Rights or Serving the Party: The Way Forward for China's Trade Unions," *China Labour Bulletin*, March 2009, p. 6, http://

www.clb.org.hk/sites/default/files/archive/en/share/File/research_reports
/acftu_report.pdf.

23. "China's Spending on Internal Police Force in 2010 Outstrips Defense Budget,"
    *Bloomberg News,* March 6, 2011, http://www.bloomberg.com/news/2011
    -03-06/china-s-spending-on-internal-police-force-in-2010-outstrips-defense
    -budget.html (citing sociology professor Sun Liping).

24. One study estimates 45 percent of such incidents arise from labor disputes.
    Yanqi Tong and Shaohua Lei, "Large-Scale Mass Incidents in China," East
    Asia Institute, April 15, 2010, http://www.eai.nus.edu.sg/publications/files
    /BB520.pdf. Another finds that 31 percent of incidents reported in mass media
    from 2011 to 2013 were labor related. Hou Liqiang, "Report Identifies
    Sources of Mass Protests," *China Daily,* April 9, 2014, http://www.chinadaily
    .com.cn/china/2014-04/09/content_17415767.htm.

25. "Nearly 1,000 People Dispersed following Wage Protest in SW China,"
    *People's Daily Online* (English), October 12, 2010, http://english.peopledaily
    .com.cn/90001/90776/90882/7164113.html.

26. Grzegorz Ekiert and Jan Kubik, *Rebellious Civil Society: Popular Protest and
    Democratic Consolidation in Poland, 1989–1993* (Ann Arbor: University of
    Michigan Press, 1999), 5.

27. Andrew Walder and Xiaoxia Gong, "Workers in the Tiananmen Protests: The
    Politics of the Beijing Workers Autonomous Federation," *Australian Journal
    of Chinese Affairs* 29 (January 1993), 1-29.

28. Youwei, "The End of Reform in China," *Foreign Affairs,* May/June 2015,
    https://www.foreignaffairs.com/articles/china/end-reform-china. "Youwei" is
    a pseudonym for a Chinese scholar. A scholar's perceived need for a pseudonym
    speaks volumes about the state of academic freedom in China.

29. David Shambaugh, *China's Communist Party: Atrophy and Adaptation*
    (Washington, DC: Woodrow Wilson Center Press, 2008).

30. Youwei, "End of Reform in China."

31. Weiwei Zhang, "The Five Reasons Why China Works," *Huffington Post,*
    February 26, 2014, http://www.huffingtonpost.com/zhang-weiwei/the-five
    -reasons-china-works_b_4859899.html.

32. "Avid Young Reader of Mao Zedong's Poetry from the Post-1980s Generation
    Leads the Honda Strike," *China News Weekly,* June 2, 2010, translated by
    China Labor News Translations, http://www.clntranslations.org/article/56
    /honda ("Avid Young Reader").

33. "Strike Breakers: Strikes Are as Big a Problem for the Government as They Are
    for Employers," *Economist,* July 3, 2010, http://www.economist.com/node
    /16282233.

34. Kevin Gray and Youngseok Jang, "Labour Unrest in the Global Political
    Economy: The Case of China's 2010 Strike Wave," *New Political Economy*
    20, no. 4 (2015), doi: 10.1080/13563467.2014.951613.

35. "Avid Young Reader," 10. Wage disparities between regular Nanhai Honda
    workers and long-term "interns" on the same line also exacerbated worker
    discontent.

36. Anita Chan, "Labor Unrest and Role of Unions," op-ed, *China Daily,* June 18,

2010, http://www.chinadaily.com.cn/opinion/2010-06/18/content_9987347 .htm.

37. David Barboza, "In China, Unlikely Labor Leader Just Wanted a Middle-Class Life," *New York Times,* June 13, 2010.

38. Beverly J. Silver, *Forces of Labor: Workers' Movements and Globalization since 1870* (Cambridge: Cambridge University Press, 2003).

39. Both China's politicians and its businessmen carefully study history. Ronald Herman Huisken and Meredith Christine Thatcher, *History as Policy: Framing the Debate on the Future of Australia's Defence Policy* (Canberra: ANU E Press, 2007), 61–65; Cheng Zhu, "What We Can All Learn from China's Business Leaders," *Forbes,* January 26, 2011, http://www.forbes .com/2011/01/24/china-america-business-lessons-leadership-managing-ccl .html.

40. Chris King-Chi Chan and Elaine Sio-Leng Hui, "The Dynamics and Dilemma of Workplace Trade Union Reform in China: The Case of the Honda Workers' Strike," *Journal of Industrial Relations* 54 (2012): 658–659, doi: 10.1177 /0022185612457128.

41. Gregory T. Chin, *China's Automotive Modernization: The Party-State and Multinational Corporations* (New York: Palgrave Macmillan, 2010), 2, 145.

42. "China's Union Facing Restructuring Because of Labor Disputes, Some Regions Trial Elections," *China News Weekly,* June 1, 2010, translated by China Labor News Translations, http://www.clntranslations.org/article/56 /honda.

43. Zeng was a "redhat" businessman, among those who were welcomed into the CPC after 2001 when capitalism was officially brought under the socialist umbrella. Kellee S. Tsai, *Capitalism without Democracy: The Private Sector in Contemporary China* (Ithaca, NY: Cornell University Press, 2007).

44. "Avid Young Reader," 9.

45. Ibid.

46. "Strike Breakers."

47. "Avid Young Reader," 7. Other reports indicate that the thugs were actually police wearing union badges so that they could enter the factory grounds; police have been largely barred from entering foreign factories from early in China's romancing of foreign capital.

48. "Strike Breakers."

49. Chan, "Labor Unrest and Role of Unions."

50. "Yue Yuen Strike Is Estimated to Cost $60 Million," *Wall Street Journal,* April 28, 2014. ("Labor-rights activists have estimated that the back payments Yue Yuen needs to make would total 100 million to 200 million yuan.")

51. "Thousands of China Workers on Strike," *BBC News,* April 17, 2014, http://www.bbc.com/news/business-27059434.

52. "Defeat Will Only Make Us Stronger: Workers Look Back at the Yue Yuen Shoe Factory Strike," *China Labour Bulletin,* May 22, 2014, http://www.clb .org.hk/en/content/defeat-will-only-make-us-stronger-workers-look-back-yue -yuen-shoe-factory-strike.

53. Echo Hui, "Labour Advocate Helping Dongguan Factory Strike Arrested over

WeChat Message," *South China Morning Post,* April 29, 2014, http://www
.scmp.com/news/china/article/1500074/labour-advocate-helping-dongguan
-factory-strike-arrested-over-wechat.

54. "Yue Yuen Workers Won't Cry," China Labour Net, April 28, 2014, translated by China Labour Net, http://www.worldlabour.org/eng/node/674.

55. Kam Wing Chan and Will Buckingham, "Is China Abolishing the Hukou
System?," *China Quarterly* 195 (September 2008): 600–601.

56. "Defeat Will Only Make Us Stronger."

57. "Chinese Trade Group to Mediate Shoe Factory Strike," *CBS News,* April 18,
2014, http://www.cbsnews.com/news/chinese-trade-group-to-mediate-shoe
-factory-strike/.

58. "Defeat Will Only Make Us Stronger."

59. Ibid.

60. "Strike Map," *China Labour Bulletin,* accessed January 16, 2016, http://
maps.clb.org.hk/strikes/en. The rate of increase probably reflects in part
greater reporting over time, especially through social media; on the other
hand, the absolute numbers of strikes and collective protest are almost certainly higher in reality, given restrictions on reporting of all kinds. These questions are explored in greater detail in Chapter 9.

61. Similar patterns are observed by Sarah Biddulph in her recent account of
China's "stability management" approach to labor unrest and by Eli Friedman
in his account of China's "insurgency trap." Biddulph, *Stability Imperative,*
chapter 2; Eli Friedman, *Insurgency Trap: Labor Politics in Postsocialist China*
(Ithaca, NY: Cornell University Press, 2014). Friedman emphasizes tension
between central and local governments, as local officials who are inordinately
responsive to local businesses undermine central government efforts to quell
unrest through restraint and reform. In addition to that important dynamic, I
emphasize ambivalence at the center, where an overriding commitment to stability cuts in contradictory directions.

62. Qingjun Wu and Zhaoyang Sun, "Collective Consultation under Quota Management: China's Government-Led Model of Labour Relations Regulation,"
*International Labour Review* 153, no. 4 (2014): 609–633.

63. This was not the first appearance of worker demands for more democratic
elections. Anita Chan, "Challenges and Possibilities for Democratic Grassroots
Union Elections in China: A Case Study of Two Factory-Level Elections and
Their Aftermath," *Labor Studies Journal* 34 (2009): 293–317.

64. Edward S. Steinfeld, *Playing Our Game: Why China's Rise Doesn't Threaten
the West* (Oxford: Oxford University Press, 2010).

65. This point remains in controversy. Chinese leaders claim that China is not
capitalist but is in the primary stage of socialism. Alan R. Kluver, *Legitimating
the Chinese Economic Reforms: A Rhetoric of Myth and Orthodoxy* (Albany:
State University of New York Press, 1996), 71–72.

66. Bruce J. Dickson, *Red Capitalists in China: The Party, Private Entrepreneurs,
and Prospects for Political Change* (Cambridge: Cambridge University Press,
2003).

67. The reference is to Francis Fukuyama, *The End of History and the Last Man*

(New York: Free Press, 1992), which argued that Western liberal democracy had proven its superiority over competing forms of government and would eventually take hold across the world. Fukuyama later became more pessimistic about the triumph of democracy, in part because of patterns of political decay in established democracies like the United States, a theme he explores in Francis Fukuyama, *Political Order and Political Decay: From the Industrial Revolution to the Globalization of Democracy* (New York: Farrar, Straus and Giroux, 2014).

## 2. The Rise of China, and of Labor Protest, in the Reform Era

1. During the Cultural Revolution, revolutionary committees took control of the state-owned enterprises (SOEs), leading to "unified management" by the Party. For further analysis, see Barry Naughton, "Danwei: The Economic Foundations of a Unique Institution," in *Danwei: The Changing Chinese Workplace in Historical and Comparative Perspective,* ed. Elizabeth J. Perry and Xiaobo Lu (Armonk, NY: M. E. Sharpe, 1997), 169–194. On the Cultural Revolution's destructive impact on the Chinese educational system, see Zhong Deng and Donald J. Treiman, "The Impact of the Cultural Revolution on Trends in Educational Attainment in the People's Republic of China," *American Sociological Review* 103, no. 2 (September 1997): 400–401.

2. The impact of "reform and opening" on labor is elaborated by Mary E. Gallagher, *Contagious Capitalism: Globalization and the Politics of Labor in China* (Princeton, NJ: Princeton University Press, 2007); Ching Kwan Lee, *Against the Law: Labor Protests in China's Rustbelt and Sunbelt* (Berkeley: University of California Press, 2007); Tim Pringle, *Trade Unions in China: The Challenge of Labour Unrest* (New York: Routledge, 2011); and, with a particular focus on SOE reform, William Hurst, *The Chinese Worker after Socialism* (Cambridge: Cambridge University Press, 2009).

3. Walder describes this as a system of "organized dependency" in Andrew G. Walder, "Organized Dependency and Cultures of Authority in Chinese Industry," *Journal of Asian Studies* 43 (1983): 51. Dependency was mutual, given managers' need to coax productivity out of an essentially permanent workforce. Andrew G. Walder, "Factory and Manager in an Era of Reform," *China Quarterly* 118 (1989): 242, 247.

4. Walder, "Factory and Manager," 249. Walder was describing the system in the late 1980s, in the early stages of "reform" and restructuring of the SOEs.

5. Walder, "Organized Dependency"; Eli Friedman and Ching Kwang Lee, "Remaking the World of Chinese Labour: A 30-Year Retrospective," *British Journal of Industrial Relations* 48 (2010): 507–508.

6. Friedman and Lee, "Remaking the World of Chinese Labour," 516.

7. Gallagher, *Contagious Capitalism,* 106–107.

8. Robert Michael Field, "The Performance of Industry during the Cultural Revolution: Second Thoughts," *China Quarterly* 108 (December 1986): 625.

9. David Bray, *Social Space and Governance in Urban China: The Danwei System*

*from Origins to Reform* (Stanford, CA: Stanford University Press, 2005): 131, 155.

10. Andrew Tylecote, Jing Cai, Jiajia Liu, "Why Are Mainland Chinese Firms Succeeding in Some Sectors and Failing in Others? A Critical View of the Chinese System of Innovation," *International Journal of Learning and Intellectual Capital* 7 (January 2010): 123. For the original source, see Zhonghua Renmin Gongheguo Gongsi Fa [Company Law of the People's Republic of China] (promulgated by the Fifth Session of Standing Committee of Eighth National People's Congress, December 29, 1993, effective July 1, 1994), chapters 89–119 (Lawinfochina) (China).

11. Yasheng Huang, *Capitalism with Chinese Characteristics: Entrepreneurship and the State* (Cambridge: Cambridge University Press, 2008), 73–77.

12. In the words of the great twentieth-century writer Lu Xun, the peasants' fate was "to suffer until they become stupefied" or "to devote all their energies to dissipation." Lu Xun, *My Old Home* (1921), https://www.marxists.org /archive/lu-xun/1921/01/x01.htm.

13. Gallagher, *Contagious Capitalism*, 45–61.

14. Edward S. Steinfeld, *Playing Our Game: Why China's Rise Doesn't Threaten the West* (Oxford: Oxford University Press, 2010). At the same time, the state retained effective control of many nominally privatized enterprises through a variety of mechanisms, some of them decidedly non-transparent; as a result, both the line between private and state-owned enterprises and the size of the remaining state-owned (or state-controlled) sector is somewhat obscure. Huang, *Capitalism with Chinese Characteristics,* 13–19; Richard McGregor, *The Party: The Secret World of China's Communist Rulers* (London: Penguin Books, 2010).

15. On the staging and mechanisms by which capitalism took hold in China, and the key role played by foreign direct investment, see Gallagher, *Contagious Capitalism.*

16. In the early years of reform, many managers felt compelled to distribute more or less equally the higher revenues that were intended to incentivize performance in order to buy workers' cooperation and avoid conflict. Andrew G. Walder, "Wage Reform and the Web of Factory Interests," *China Quarterly* 109 (1987): 22; Gallagher, *Contagious Capitalism,* 74.

17. Pringle, *Trade Unions in China,* 25–28, 77–81; Hurst, *Chinese Worker after Socialism,* 37–59.

18. Lee, *Against the Law.*

19. Hurst, *Chinese Worker after Socialism,* 108–132: Pringle, *Trade Unions in China,* 68–81.

20. Workers who had bypassed higher education for an SOE job were particularly hard hit—more likely to be laid off and less likely to find a new job. See Shunfeng Song, "Policy Issues of China's Urban Employment," *Contemporary Economic Policy* 21 (April 2003): 258-269.

21. Barry Bluestone and Bennet Harrison, *The Deindustrialization of America: Plant Closings, Community Abandonment, and the Dismantling of Basic Industry* (New York: Basic Books, 1982).

22. Gallagher, *Contagious Capitalism*, 77. Ching Kwan Lee tells the illustrative story of an unemployed, low-skilled, middle-aged former SOE worker. Lee, *Against the Law*, 69–70. Laid-off women also had more trouble finding new work. Hurst, *Chinese Worker after Socialism*, 100. Some workers who were laid off or unemployed suffered "long-term psychological scars." Yu Xie and Jia Wang, "Feeling Good about the Iron Rice Bowl: Economic Sectors and Happiness in Post-reform China," *Social Science Research* 53 (2015): 203-217.

23. Minxin Pei, *China's Trapped Transition: The Limits of Developmental Autocracy* (Cambridge, MA: Harvard University Press, 2006).

24. Roger E. Backhouse, "The Rise of Free Market Economics: Economists and the Role of the State since 1970," *History of Political Economy* 37 (2005): 355-392.

25. Pringle, *Trade Unions in China*, 68–84; Lee, *Against the Law*; Eli Friedman, *Insurgency Trap: Labor Politics in Postsocialist China* (Ithaca, NY: Cornell University Press, 2014); "Going It Alone: The Workers' Movement in China, 2007–2008," *China Labour Bulletin*, July 2009, http://www.clb.org.hk/sites /default/files/archive/en/share/File/research_reports/workers_movement _07-08_print_final.pdf; Hurst, *Chinese Worker after Socialism*, 108–132.

26. Pringle, *Trade Unions in China*, 38.

27. Hurst, *Chinese Worker after Socialism*, 108–132; Lee, *Against the Law*, 69–122; Pringle, *Trade Unions in China*, 77–81.

28. "No Way Out: Worker Activism in China's State-Owned Enterprise Reforms," *China Labour Bulletin*, September 2008, 3–4, http://www.clb.org.hk/sites /default/files/archive/en/File/research_reports/no_way_out.pdf.

29. Ching Kwan Lee, "The 'Revenge of History': Collective Memories and Labor Protests in Northeastern China," *Ethnography* 1 (2000): 217, 226.

30. Kai Chang and William Brown, "The Transition from Individual to Collective Labor Relations in China," *Industrial Relations Journal* 44 (March 2013): 102-21.

31. Pringle, *Trade Unions in China*, 80, 84. Pringle points out that once workers are laid off, their ability to affect the productivity of the firm, and thus their power and influence, are limited.

32. Friedman, *Insurgency Trap*, 51.

33. Friedman and Lee, "Remaking the World of Chinese Labour," 516. Reforms to the *hukou* system have been partial and halting, and still encounter resistance from both local officials and urban citizens. Fang Cai, "Hukou System Reform and Unification of Rural-Urban Social Welfare," *China and World Economy* 19 (2011): 33-48.

34. Tania Branigan, "China Reforms *Hukou* System to Improve Migrant Workers' Rights," *Guardian*, July 31, 2014. The policy of mass urbanization puts additional pressure on the *hukou* system. Ian Johnson, "China's Great Uprooting: Moving 250 Million into Cities," *New York Times*, June 15, 2013.

35. Huang, *Capitalism with Chinese Characteristics*; McGregor, *Party*, chapter 7. Just one source of leverage lies in the vesting of ultimate title to all land in China in state or "collective" ownership; there is still no private ownership of

land. Some private leases and use rights are fairly secure while others—especially those of rural residents—are notoriously insecure. Eva Pils, "Land Disputes, Rights Assertion, and Social Unrest in China: A Case from Sichuan," *Columbia Journal of Asian Law* 19 (2005): 235–292; Frank Upham, "From Demsetz to Deng: Speculations on the Implications of Chinese Growth for Law and Development Theory," *Journal of International Law and Policy* 41 (2009): 585–591.

36. Gallagher, *Contagious Capitalism,* 14, 105–110.

37. Gallagher, *Contagious Capitalism,* 103–107; Sean Cooney et al., "China's New Labour Contract Law: Responding to the Growing Complexity of Labor Relations in the PRC," *University of NSW Law Journal* 30 (2007): 788–803. We will return to the paradox of Dickensian working conditions in the "socialist worker state" in Chapter 5.

38. Shen Tan, "Private Conversations among Working Women: An analysis from Hundreds of Letters Collected from the Remnants of the Zhili Toys Factory in Shenzhen," *China Academy of Social Sciences* (2012), http://csen.cssn.cn/Publications/Publications_Articles/201208/t20120822_1976045.shtml.

39. B. Drummond Ayres, Jr., "Factory Fire Leaves Pall over 'All-American City,' " *New York Times,* September 5, 1991; Chris Buckley, "Over 100 Die in Fire at Chinese Poultry Plant," *New York Times,* June 3, 2013.

40. On the latter, see William E. Forbath, "The Ambiguities of Free Labor: Labor and the Law in the Gilded Age," *Wisconsin Law Review* (1985): 767-817; and Friedman and Lee, "Remaking the World of Chinese Labour," 507–508.

41. "Wage theft" is the illegal withholding of wages (or benefits) that are rightfully due an employee; it includes both outright failure to pay promised wages as well as a variety of violations of wage and hour laws that result in underpayment.

42. Kim Bobo, *Wage Theft in America: Why Millions of Working Americans Are Not Getting Paid—and What We Can Do about It* (New York: W. W. Norton, 2009); Steven Greenhouse, *The Big Squeeze: Tough Times for the American Worker* (New York: Alfred A. Knopf, 2008); Annette Bernhardt et al., eds., *The Gloves-Off Economy: Workplace Standards at the Bottom of America's Labor Market* (Champaign: University of Illinois at Urbana-Champaign, 2008).

43. Jérôme Gautié and John Schmitt, eds., *Low-Wage Work in the Wealthy World* (New York: Russell Sage Foundation, 2010), 5.

44. Naixin Chen, Jianbing Lou, and Mei Chen, "The New Thinking of Stipulating the Right to Strike into the Constitution" (paper presented at Labor Relations Conference, Renmin University, 2011): 98.

45. For a collection of media accounts, letters, and interviews concerning poor factory conditions and workers' responses to them, mainly in the 1990s, see Anita Chan, *China's Workers under Assault: The Exploitation of Labor in a Globalizing Economy* (Armonk, NY: M. E. Sharpe, 2001).

46. See discussion in Chapter 1.

47. Jeremy Goldkorn, "Legal Daily Report on Mass Incidents in China in 2012," *Danwei,* January 6, 2013 (citing *Legal Daily,*法治日报, 2012 Mass Incident

Research Report [2012年群体性事件研究报告]), http://www.danwei.com
/a-report-on-mass-incidents-in-china-in-2012/.

48. "China Celebrates Deng Centenary," *BBC News,* August 22, 2004.

49. The retirement age for white-collar workers is fifty-five for women and
sixty-five for men. China plans to gradually raise the retirement age. Owen
Haacke, "China's Mandatory Retirement Age Changes," U.S.-China Business Council, April 1, 2015, https://www.uschina.org/chna%E2%80%99s
-mandatory-retirement-age-changes-impact-foreign-companies. On the 4-2-1
issue, see Mu Mian, "4-2-1 Phenomenon: New Partnership Explores Aging in
China," *Social Impact,* Winter 2007, http://brownschool.wustl.edu/Documents
/China%20Aging.pdf. On rising life expectancy, see "World Databank: World
Development Indicators," World Bank, http://databank.worldbank.org/data
//reports.aspx, accessed on July 19, 2015. On retirement age, see "Paying
for the Grey," *Economist,* April 5, 2014, http://www.economist.com/news
/china/21600160-pensions-crisis-looms-china-looks-raising-retirement-age
-paying-grey.

50. Albert O. Hirschman, *Exit, Voice, and Loyalty: Responses to Decline in Firms,
Organizations, and States* (Cambridge, MA: Harvard University Press, 1970).

51. The "one-child policy" formally began in 1980, but the decline in birthrate
began in the 1970s with Mao's shift to coercive family planning policies, and
was in part a familiar consequence of economic development. Martin King
Whyte, Wang Feng, and Yong Cai, "Challenging Myths about China's One-
Child Policy," *China Journal* 74 (July 2015): 144-159. The recently announced
relaxation of the one-child policy will have little effect on labor markets until
at least 2030, and is not currently expected to have a large effect even then.
Minxin Pei, "China's One-Child Policy Reversal: Too Little, Too Late,"
*Fortune,* November 2015.

52. For an early report of labor shortages in China in the *Wall Street Journal,* see
Yiping Huang, "A Labor Shortage in China," *Wall Street Journal,* August 6,
2004. For a more recent account of labor shortages in China's official English-
language newspaper, see Qihui Gao, "What Is behind the Labor Shortage?,"
*China Daily,* February 25, 2010.

53. Keith Bradsher, "Defying Global Slump, China Has Labor Shortages," *New
York Times,* February 26, 2010; Tingting Zhao, "China's Salaries to Increase
139% in Five Years," *China Business News,* January 7, 2011, http://www
.chinadaily.com.cn/bizchina/2011-01/07/content_11811112.htm.

54. See Mary E. Gallagher, "Mobilizing the Law in China: 'Informed Disenchantment' and the Development of Legal Consciousness," *Law and Society Review*
(December 2006): 793–796. See also Benjamin van Rooij, "Pufa: Legal Education Campaigns" (unpublished manuscript, 2003);

55. Gallagher, *Contagious Capitalism,* 98; Lee, *Against the Law,* 157–203.

56. Gallagher, *Contagious Capitalism,* 114–116; Gallagher, "Mobilizing the Law
in China."

57. Mary Gallagher highlights the saga of Du Linxiang, whose case was featured
on a popular television show. Although he won his suit for severance pay, a
year later he had yet to receive any money from the suit. Yet the visibility of his

win encouraged many other workers to seek legal redress for their claims. Gallagher, "Mobilizing the Law in China," 796.

58. On many hurdles to recovery of unpaid wages in China, see Aaron Halegua, "Getting Paid: Processing the Labor Disputes of China's Migrant Workers," *Berkeley Journal of International Law* 26 (2008): 254-322.

59. Sean Cooney, "Making Chinese Labor Law Work: The Prospects for Regulatory Innovation in the People's Republic of China," *Fordham International Law Journal* 30 (2006): 1050-1097; Halegua, "Getting Paid," 270; Virginia Ho, "From Contracts to Compliance? An Early Look at Implementation under China's New Labor Legislation," *Columbia Journal of Asian Law* 23 (2009): 35-107.

60. Halegua, "Getting Paid."

61. The centrality of law in pre-LCL labor disputes is elucidated in Gallagher, *Contagious Capitalism;* and Lee, *Against the Law.*

62. Kevin J. O'Brien and Lianjiang Li, *Rightful Resistance in Rural China* (New York: Cambridge University Press, 2006).

63. See Carl F. Minzner, "Xinfang: An Alternative to Formal Chinese Legal Institutions," *Stanford Journal of International Law* 42 (2006): 103-179.

64. Bobo, *Wage Theft in America.*

65. These protests exemplify what Benjamin Sachs calls "employment law as labor law." Benjamin Sachs, "Employment Law as Labor Law," *Cardozo Law Review* 29 (2008): 2685-2748; Benjamin Sachs, "Revitalizing Labor Law," *Berkeley Journal of Employment and Labor Law* 31 (2011): 333-347.

66. Xin He and Yang Su, "Street as Courtroom: State Accommodation of Labor Protest in South China," *Law and Society Review* 44 (August 11, 2009): 157-184.

67. Ibid.

68. Conversations with Chinese labor scholars, May and December 2011. All interviews were conducted in confidentiality, and the names of interviewees are withheld by mutual agreement.

69. Mao Zedong, "On the Correct Handling of Contradictions among the People," *Selected Works of Mao Tse-Tung* (Beijing: Foreign Language Press, 1977), 5:384–421.

70. "Wealth Gap Tops List of Concerns ahead of China's Political Meetings," *China Real Time Report* (blog), *Wall Street Journal,* February 27, 2015. A recent Peking University study found China's GINI coefficient to be 0.49, the third highest among the world's top twenty-five economies, and much higher than the United States (0.41). Gabriel Wildau and Tom Mitchell, "China Income Inequality among World's Worst," *Financial Times,* January 14, 2016, http://www.ft.com/intl/cms/s/0/3c521faa-baa6-11e5-a7cc-280dfe875e28 .html#axzz3xFnm5EI8.

71. Beverly J. Silver, *Forces of Labor: Workers' Movements and Globalization since 1870* (Cambridge: Cambridge University Press, 2003); Beverly J. Silver and Lu Zhang, "China as an Emerging Epicenter of World Labor Unrest," in *China and the Transformation of Global Capitalism,* ed. Ho-fung Hung (Baltimore, MD: Johns Hopkins University Press, 2009), 174-187.

72. Jason Dean and Ting-I Tsai, "Suicides Spark Inquiries: Apple, H-P to Examine Asian Supplier after String of Deaths at Factory," *Wall Street Journal,* May 27, 2010.

73. Margaret Heffernan, "What Happened after the FoxConn Suicides," *CBS News,* August 7, 2013.

74. Widespread coverage within China ceased after a few days of the Honda strike.

75. Anita Chan, "Labor Unrest and Role of Unions," op-ed, *China Daily,* June 18, 2010, http://www.chinadaily.com.cn/opinion/2010-06/18/content _9987347.htm.

76. Eli Friedman discusses the ACFTU's response to Tiananmen Square, which was to reaffirm its commitment to oppose any independent worker organizations. Friedman, *Insurgency Trap,* 47. For a translation of the relevant provision of the Trade Union Law of the People's Republic of China, see Trade Union Law of the People's Republic of China (adopted April 3, 1992, at the Fifth session of the Seventh National People's Congress, amended October 27, 2001), article 27, http://english.mofcom.gov.cn/aarticle/policyrelease/internationalpolicy /200703/20070304475394.html: "The trade union shall assist the enterprise or institution in properly dealing with the matter so as to help restore the normal order of production and other work as soon as possible."

77. "Strike Map," *China Labour Bulletin,* accessed May 5, 2016, http://maps.clb .org.hk/strikes/en.

78. "Strike Map."

79. "China Saw a Dramatic Increase in Wage Arrears Protests in Run Up to New Year," *China Labour Bulletin,* Feb. 3, 2016, http://clb.org.hk/content/china-saw -dramatic-increase-wage-arrears-protests-run-new-year (accessed May 5, 2016).

## 3. Who Speaks for China's Workers?

1. "ACFTU Seeks to Organize All Workers into Unions," *All-China Federation of Trade Unions,* http://en.acftu.org/28739/201405/23/140523150246365 .shtml; Stanley Lubman, "The New Challenge of the Strikes Won't Go Away," *Wall Street Journal,* July 11, 2010.

2. For an example, see Anita Chan, "Labor Unrest and Role of Unions," op-ed, *China Daily,* June 18, 2010, http://www.chinadaily.com.cn/opinion/2010 -06/18/content_9987347.htm.

3. For rich empirical accounts of the ACFTU, and of variations along regional, sectoral, and even enterprise lines, see Eli Friedman, *Insurgency Trap: Labor Politics in Postsocialist China* (Ithaca, NY: Cornell University Press, 2014); Tim Pringle, *Trade Unions in China: The Challenge of Labour Unrest* (New York: Routledge, 2011); Mingwei Liu and Chunyun Li, "Environment Pressures, Managerial Industrial Relations Ideologies, and Unionization in Chinese Enterprises," *British Journal of Industrial Relations* 52 (March 2014); Mingwei Liu, "Union Organizing in China: Still a Monolithic Labor Movement?," *Industrial and Labor Relations Review* 64 (October 2010): 30-52.

4. The fledgling trade union soon became the target of political adversaries. After a massacre and a crackdown in 1927, the ACFTU became less a trade union federation and more an arm of the CPC, useful, for example, in mobilizing members for war. Lai-To Lee, *Trade Unions in China: 1949 to the Present* (Singapore: Singapore University Press, 1986), 20.

5. Pringle, *Trade Unions in China.*

6. On the "transmission belt" function of the ACFTU, see Jude A. Howell, "All-China Federation of Trade Unions beyond Reform? The Slow March of Direct Elections," *China Quarterly* 196 (2008): 849; Richard McGregor, *The Party: The Secret World of China's Communist Rulers* (London: Penguin Books, 2010).

7. Elizabeth J. Perry, "Shanghai's Strike Wave of 1957," *China Quarterly* 137 (March 1994): 17–19.

8. For a concise overview of the history and structure of the ACFTU, see "Protecting Workers' Rights or Serving the Party: The Way Forward for China's Trade Unions," *China Labour Bulletin,* March 2009, http://www.clb.org.hk/sites /default/files/archive/en/share/File/research_reports/acftu_report.pdf.

9. Ibid., 11–12.

10. "Going It Alone: The Workers' Movement in China, 2007–2008," *China Labour Bulletin,* July 2009, 70–71, http://www.clb.org.hk/sites/default/files /archive/en/share/File/research_reports/workers_movement_07-08_print _final.pdf. For a concise account of the changing relationship between the ACFTU and the CPC, see Bill Taylor and Qi Li, "Is the ACFTU a Union and Does It Matter?," *Journal of Industrial Relations* 49 (2007): 411-428.

11. For more detail on the Trade Union Law's 2001 revisions, see Pringle, *Trade Unions in China,* 53.

12. Simon Clarke, Chang-Hee Lee, and Qi Li, "Collective Consultation and Industrial Relations in China," *British Journal of Industrial Relations* 42 (2004): 235-254, 241.

13. "Union Accepts Migrant Workers," China Daily, Sept. 3, 2003, http://www .chinadaily.com.cn/en/doc/2003-09/03/content_260707.htm.

14. Kai Chang and William Brown, "The Transition from Individual to Collective Labor Relations in China," *Industrial Relations Journal* 44 (March 2013): 102-121.

15. Ching Kwan Lee, *Against the Law: Labor Protests in China's Rustbelt and Sunbelt* (Berkeley: University of California Press, 2007), 57–59. Strictly speaking, only the national organization is called "All-China"; others are identified by region or industry (e.g., the Guangdong Federation of Trade Unions). But for the sake of readability, I refer to them as ACFTU or ACFTU branches.

16. "Labor dispatch" workers are directly employed by labor dispatch agencies, and "dispatched" to work for other companies. In the early 2000s and especially after the enactment of the LCL, both private firms and SOEs increasingly used dispatch workers to avoid some of their legal obligations. "The Dispatch Labor System in China Questioned," China Labor News Translations, September 29, 2011, http://www.clntranslations.org/article/64/dispatch-labor -questioned.

17. Taylor and Li, "Is the ACFTU a Union and Does It Matter?," 707–708.

18. Yongnian Zheng, *De Facto Federalism in China: Reforms and Dynamics of Central-Local Relations* (Hackensack, NJ: World Scientific, 2007).

19. Howell, "All-China Federation of Trade Unions beyond Reform?"

20. Friedman, *Insurgency Trap*, 5–6.

21. Yu Juan Zhai, "Thoughts on the Labor Side of China's Collective Consultation," (paper presented at Labor Relations Conference, Renmin University, 2011): 606.

22. All firms with more than twenty-five employees, foreign or domestic, are supposed to establish a labor union under the ACFTU umbrella. Mary E. Gallagher, *Contagious Capitalism: Globalization and the Politics of Labor in China* (Princeton, NJ: Princeton University Press, 2007), 44, 76. However, in many of these unions, a manager is concurrently the union cadre and a Party representative. Lee, *Against the Law*, 59.

23. Zhai, "Thoughts on the Labor Side of China's Collective Consultation"; Lubman, "New Challenge of the Strikes."

24. Clarke, Lee, and Li, "Collective Consultation and Industrial Relations in China, 242–243. The mode of selecting enterprise union officials is the central focus of Chapter 6, and we will return to it.

25. Ibid., 237.

26. Elaine Sio-Ieng Hui and Chris King-Chi Chan, "The 'Harmonious Society' as a Hegemonic Project: Labor Conflicts and Changing Labour Policies in China," *Labor, Capital, and Society* 44 (2011), http://www.lcs-tcs.com /PDFs/44_2/7%20Hui%20and%20Chan.pdf.

27. Andreas Lauffs and Jonathan Isaacs, "Responding to the Unionization Drive," Baker and McKenzie, accessed July 25, 2015, http://www.bakermckenzie .com/RRChinaRespondingToTheUnionizationApr10/.

28. Jianhua Feng, "Unions Target Foreign Firms," *Beijing Review,* January 11, 2009, http://www.bjreview.com.cn/nation/txt/2009-01/11/content_174156 .htm.

29. This "unionization timeline" was recounted in numerous interviews with international law firms in Shanghai and Hong Kong. All interviews were conducted in confidentiality, and the names of interviewees are withheld by mutual agreement.

30. Confirmed in discussions with district and municipal labor union leaders.

31. Cynthia L. Estlund, "The Ossification of American Labor Law," *Columbia Law Review* 102 (October 2002): 1527-1612.

32. Ibid.

33. Liu, "Union Organizing in China."

34. "Union Chair Resigns over the Imposition of Collective Contracts at Wal-Mart," *China Labour Bulletin,* September 23, 2008, http://www.clb.org.hk /content/union-chair-resigns-over-imposition-collective-contracts-wal-mart.

35. Esther Wang, "As Wal-Mart Swallows China's Economy, Workers Fight Back," *American Prospect,* April 23, 2013.

36. Ibid.

37. Informal employee representation schemes are, however, surprisingly common given their probable illegality. See Chapter 8.

38. Yanfeng Qian, "Collective Contracts Sought for Worker's Rights," *China Daily,* July 9, 2010, http://www.chinadaily.com.cn/china/2010-07/09/content _10084430.htm.

39. Howell, "All-China Federation of Trade Unions beyond Reform?," 854–862.

40. "Protecting Workers' Rights or Serving the Party," (citing "Unions: The Gap between Ideal and Reality," *Sino-Foreign Management* 10 [2006]: 28–29).

41. Prominently, Professor Kai Chang, now retired from Renmin University. Kai Chang, "Lun Zhongguo de Tuanjie Quan Lifa Jiqi Shishi" [Associational rights in China: Legislation and implementation], *Dangdai Faxue* [Contemporary Law Review] 121 (2007).

42. The Trade Union Law, chapter 2, article 9, bans relatives of executives from serving as trade union chairs. Zhonghua Renmin Gongheguo Gonghuifa [Trade Union Law of the People's Republic of China] (adopted April 3, 1992 at the Fifth session of the Seventh National People's Congress, amended October 27, 2001) (hereinafter Trade Union Law) (China), original at http:// www.gov.cn/banshi/2005-08/05/content_20697.htm; translation at http:// www.china.org.cn/english/DAT/214784.htm.

43. The exclusion of supervisors from union representation and collective bargaining in the United States is more controversial and more reflective of management's desire to maintain control of the workplace than of unions' suspicion of supervisory loyalties.

44. Gerald Mayer and Jon O. Shimabukuro, *The Definition of "Supervisor" under the National Labor Relations Act* (CRS Report no. RL34350) (Washington, DC: Congressional Research Service, 2012). See also ILO Convention 87, which states that workers and employees, without distinction, have the right to organize unions as support for international law. "Human Rights Watch Expresses Deep Concern about Recent U.S. National Labor Relations Board 'Supervisor' Ruling," Human Rights Watch, October 22, 2006, https://www .hrw.org/news/2006/10/22/human-rights-watch-expresses-deep-concern -about-recent-us-national-labor-relations.

45. "All workers doing physical or mental work in enterprises, public institutions and government organs ... who earn their living primarily from wages shall have the right to participate in and form trade union organizations pursuant to the law." Trade Union Law, article 3. For further support, see Zhongguo Gonghui Zhangcheng [Constitution of the Chinese trade unions] (adopted at the Fifteenth National Congress of Chinese Trade Unions, October 2008, amended at the Sixteenth Meeting of the Standing Committee of the National People's Congress, October 22, 2013), article 1 (China), http://www.acftu.org /template/10001/file.jsp?aid=81124.

46. "Trade unions shall organize and conduct education among workers and staff members in order that they shall, in accordance with the provisions of the Constitution of the People's Republic of China and other laws, give play to their role as masters of the country and participate in various ways and forms in the administration of State affairs, management of economic and cultural undertakings and handling of social affairs." Trade Union Law, article 5.

47. For a powerful divergent view, see Jianrong Yu, "Holding Tight and Not

Letting Go: The Mechanisms of 'Rigid Stability,' " *Global Asia* 5 (June 2010): 28-39. Yu argues that "flexible stability," including greater protection of worker rights and associations, will secure more durable stability.

48. Among nonunion, nonsupervisory employees in the United States, 30 to 40 percent say they would like to have a union. Richard Freeman and Joel Rogers, *What Workers Want,* 2nd ed. (Ithaca, NY: ILR Press, 2006), 87. But over 80 percent say they prefer jointly run employer-employee committees (of a sort that violates federal labor laws). Ibid., 84. Indeed, if forced to choose between an organization with which management cooperated and an organization that had more power but that management opposed, employees chose the former by a margin of nearly three to one (63 to 22 percent). Ibid., 84–85.

49. Chan, "Labor Unrest and Role of Unions." For further support, see Jonathan Soble and Tom Mitchell, "Toyota Affiliate Hit by Strike in China," *Financial Times,* June 18, 2010.

50. Nelson Lichtenstein, *State of the Union: A Century of American Labor* (Princeton, NJ: Princeton University Press, 2002).

51. See, for example, the description of wage bargaining in France in Christophe Vigneau, "Labor Law between Changes and Continuity," *Comparative Labor Law and Policy Journal* 25 (2003): 129–135.

52. For examples, see Curtis J. Milhaupt and Wentong Zheng, "Beyond Ownership: State Capitalism and the Chinese Firm," *Georgetown Law Journal* 103 (2015): 665-722; Curtis Milhaupt and Katharina Pistor, *Law and Capitalism: What Corporate Crises Reveal about Legal Systems and Economic Development around the World* (Chicago: University of Chicago Press, 2008); and Edward S. Steinfeld, *Playing Our Game: Why China's Rise Doesn't Threaten the West* (Oxford: Oxford University Press, 2010).

53. Bruce J. Dickson, *Red Capitalists in China: The Party, Private Entrepreneurs, and Prospects for Political Change* (Cambridge: Cambridge University Press, 2003).

54. That principle requires member states to guarantee workers' ability to form and join organizations that are "free to draw up their own constitutions and rules, to elect their representatives in full freedom, to organize their administration and activities, and to formulate their programmes." Convention on the Freedom of Association and Protection of the Right to Organize (no. 87), International Labor Organization, July 9, 1948, 68 U.N.T.S. 17.

55. For further detail, see Sarah Ashwin, "Social Partnership or a Complete Sellout? Russian Trade Unions' Responses to Conflict," *British Journal of Industrial Relations* 42 (March 2004): 24-46; and Sue Davis, "Russian Trade Unions: Where Are They in the Former Workers' State?," in *Russian Civil Society: A Critical Assessment,* ed. Alfred. B. Evans (Armonk, NY: M. E. Sharpe, 2006), 197-208.

56. Paul W. Kuznets, "An East Asian Model of Economic Development: Japan, Taiwan, and South Korea," *Economic Development and Cultural Change* 36 (April 1988): S28.

57. Eli Friedman, " 'Change to Win' Delegates Visit China," *China Labor News Translations,* June 18, 2007, http://www.clntranslations.org/article/18/change-to-win-delegates-visit-china.

58. Taylor and Li, "Is the ACFTU a Union and Does It Matter?," 712.
59. Ibid., 709.
60. Ibid., 711.
61. Anita Chan, *China's Workers under Assault: The Exploitation of Labor in a Globalizing Economy* (Armonk, NY: M. E. Sharpe, 2001).
62. Chan, "Labor Unrest and Role of Unions."
63. That was the question that Earl Brown, of the AFL-CIO's Solidarity Center, posed to me on the eve of my first research trip in China in 2010. The point was not that the ACFTU was actually serving as a vigorous voice for workers, but that its ability to do so might depend more on support from the government than on independence from it.
64. Anita Chan, "China's Trade Unions in Corporatist Transition," in *Associations and the Chinese State: Contested Spaces,* ed. Jonathan Unger (Armonk, NY: M. E. Sharpe, 2008), 69–85.
65. Karla W. Simon, *Civil Society in China: The Legal Framework from Ancient Times to the "New Reform Era"* (Oxford: Oxford University Press, 2013).
66. Regulation on Registration and Administration of Social Organizations [Shehui Tuanti Dengji Tiaoli] (issued by State Council, effective September 25, 1998), article 3 (China), original and translation at http://www.lawinfochina.com /display.aspx?lib=law&id=5613&CGid=.
67. Jonathan Unger and Anita Chan, "Associations in a Bind: The Rise of Political Corporatism in China," in Unger, *Associations and the Chinese State,* 48–68.
68. Simon, *Civil Society in China.*
69. Jo Freeman, "The Real Story of Beijing," *Off Our Backs* 26, no. 3 (March 1996): 1, 8–11, 22–27, available at http://www.jofreeman.com/womenyear /beijingreport.htm.
70. Shawn Shieh and Guosheng Deng, "An Emerging Civil Society: The Impact of the 2008 Sichuan Earthquake on Grassroots Civic Associations in China," China Development Brief, November 1, 2011, http://chinadevelopmentbrief .cn/articles/an-emerging-civil-society-the-impact-of-the-2008-sichuan -earthquake-on-grassroots-civic-associations-in-china/.
71. "NGO Law Monitor: China," International Center for Not-for-Profit Law, February 25, 2015, http://www.icnl.org/research/monitor/china.html. Beijing has allowed public-interest associations to register directly with the Ministry of Civil Affairs without the need for a party-state sponsor since April 2013. Tongshu Quan, Xiayue qi shehui zuzhi ke zhijie dengji wuxu guakao zhuguan danwei [Next month social organizations can directly register without official authorizing body], *Xinhua,* March 29, 2013, http://www.bj.xinhuanet.com /bjyw/2013-03/29/c_115204807.htm. Other localities liberalized registration requirements earlier and more fully, at least for the least politically sensitive NGOs. Dan He and Yuli Huang, "NGOs Get Boost from Shenzhen Register Reforms," *China Daily,* August 21, 2012, http://usa.chinadaily.com.cn/china /2012-08/21/content_15690983.htm.
72. Simon, *Civil Society in China.*
73. Isabel Hilton, Carl Minzner, Teng Biao et al., "The Future of NGOs in China:

A ChinaFile Conversation," *ChinaFile,* May 14, 2015, https://www.chinafile .com/conversation/future-ngos-china.

74. Early reactions to the final law are collected in Sebastian Heilman, Thomas Kellogg, Christina Ho, William C. Kirby, Charlie Smith, Zhou Dan, and Francesco Sisci, How Should Global Stakeholders Respond to China's New NGO Management Law?, ChinaFile, May 5, 2016, https://www.chinafile .com/conversation/how-should-global-stakeholders-respond-china-new-ngo -management-law. See also Edward Wong, "Clampdown in China Restricts 7,000 Foreign Organizations," *New York Times,* April 28, 2016.

75. Ira Belkin and Jerome A. Cohen, "Will China Close Its Doors?," *New York Times,* June 1, 2015.

76. For a sampling of U.S. commentary on the draft law, see ibidi; Andrew Jacobs, "Foreign Groups Fear China Oversight Plan," *New York Times,* June 17, 2015; Stanley Lubman, "China Asserts More Control over Foreign and Domestic NGOs," *China Real Time Report* (blog), *Wall Street Journal,* June 16, 2015, http://blogs.wsj.com/chinarealtime/2015/06/16/china-asserts-more -control-over-foreign-and-domestic-ngos/; "Uncivil Society: A New Draft Law Spooks Foreign Non-profit Groups Working in China, " *Economist,* August 22, 2015.

77. See, for example, Thomas Kellogg's comment in the ChinaFile conversation cited above.

78. Shaoming Zhu, "The Chinese Communist Party in Chinese NGOs" (August 24, 2015): 1, http://www.thecpe.org/wp-content/uploads/2013/05/The-CCP -in-Chinese-NGOs.pdf.

79. For a defense of China's model, and the idea that "political rights . . . should be seen as privileges to be negotiated based on the needs and conditions of the nation," see Eric Xi, "Why China's Political Model Is Superior," *New York Times,* February 6, 2012.

80. Beijingshi Gaoji Renmin Fayuan 2010 Gaoxing Zhongzi Di 64 Hao Xingshi Caidingshu [The Beijing Municipal High People's Court appeal decision in Liu Xiaobo's case] (Beijing Superior People's Court, February 9, 2012) (China), http://www.hrichina.org/cht/content/3308; translation at http://www.hrichina .org/en/content/3211.

81. Zhiyong Xu, "The New Citizens Movement in China," *China Change,* July 11, 2012, http://chinachange.org/2012/07/11/china-needs-a-new-citizens-movement -xu-zhiyongs-许志永-controversial-essay/.

82. Andrew Jacobs and Chris Buckley, "China Sentences Xu Zhiyong, Legal Activist, to 4 Years in Prison," *New York Times,* January 26, 2014.

83. Andrew Jacobs and Chris Buckley, "China Targeting Rights Lawyers in a Crackdown," *New York Times,* July 22, 2015.

84. Jane Perlez, "Chinese Rights Lawyer, Pu Zhiqiang, Is Given Suspended Prison Sentence," *New York Times,* December 21, 2015.

85. Jenkin Chan Shiu-Fan, "The Role of Lawyers in the Chinese Legal System," in *Law in the People's Republic of China: Commentary, Readings, and Materials,* ed. Ralph Haughwout Folsom and John H. Minan (Dordrecht, Netherlands:

Martinus Nijhoff, 1989), 216, 217; Youxi Chen, "A Tale of Two Cities—The Legal Profession in China," *International Bar Association's Human Rights Institute Thematic Papers No. 2* (March 2013): 6–7, 18.

86. Austin Ramzy, "Human Rights Lawyers on Defense in China," *Time,* April 22, 2010. The lawyers' licenses expired, and "their renewal applications—usually considered a formality—were blocked, which the lawyers said was meant to prevent them from doing their jobs. Nearly one year later, at least six of those lawyers . . . [were] still trying to get their licenses renewed by the Beijing Lawyers Association." Ibid.

87. Norbert C. Brockman, "The History of the American Bar Association: A Bibliographic Essay," *American Journal of Legal History* 6, no. 3 (July 1962): 269-285, 282.

88. "Another Underground Priest Arrested in Fujian," *Asia News,* March 24, 2010, http://www.asianews.it/news-en/Another-underground-priest-arrested -in-Fujian-17965.html.

89. Tom Phillips, "China's Christians Angry as Removal of Church Crosses Continues," *Guardian,* August 7, 2015.

90. David Brion Davis, "Some Themes of Counter-Subversion: An Analysis of Anti-Masonic, Anti-Catholic, and Anti-Mormon Literature," *Mississippi Valley Historical Review* 47, no. 2 (September 1960): 205-224.

91. "Worker Activist Sentenced to Three Years in Jail—Scholars Demand Release," *China Labour Bulletin,* October 22, 2010, http://www.clb.org.hk/content /worker-activist-sentenced-three-years-jail-%E2%80%93-scholars-demand -release.

92. Simon, *Civil Society in China.*

93. Labor NGOs in Beijing were "reminded" in 2009 of their obligation to register. In 2010 and 2011, those in Guangzhou were invited to meet with local ACFTU officials, who touted the advantages of formal affiliation but did not demand it. In Shanghai, sources indicate that no independent labor NGOs have managed to operate for any significant period of time.

94. Ching Kwan Lee and Yuan Shen, "The Anti-solidarity Machine: Labor NGOs in China," (working paper presented at The Changing Face of Chinese Labor and Employment conference, Cornell ILR, Ithaca, NY September 26–28, 2008); Jennifer Hsu, "A State Creation? Civil Society and Migrant Organizations," in *China in an Era of Transition: Understanding Contemporary State and Society Actors,* ed. Reza Hazmath and Jennifer Hsu, (New York: Palgrave Macmillan, 2009) 132.

95. "Leading Cases," Beijing Legal Aid Office for Migrant Workers, accessed July 25, 2015, https://sites.google.com/a/chinapilaw.org/blaomw/leading-cases.

96. "Legal Aid," Congressional-Executive Committee on China, accessed July 25, 2015, http://www.cecc.gov/legal-aid.

97. "Guangyu Guangdongsheng 'Zhiye Gongmin Dailiren' Wenti de Diaoyan Baogao" [Investigative report on the question of "professional citizen legal agents" in Guangdong Province], Guangdong Provincial Communist Party's Committee on Policy and Law, January 2009, translation at http://www .clntranslations.org/article/51/citizen-agents.

98. Fiona Tam, "Guangdong Shuts Down at Least Seven Labour NGOs," *South China Morning Post,* July 27, 2012, http://www.scmp.com/article/1007829 /guangdong-shuts-down-least-seven-labour-ngos.

99. "Labour Activist Lin Dong Released after 30 Days Detention in Dongguan," *China Labour Bulletin,* May 22, 2014, http://www.clb.org.hk/en/content /labour-activist-lin-dong-released-after-30-days-detention-dongguan.

100. Edward Wong, "China Releases Five Women's Rights Activists Detained for Weeks," *New York Times,* April 13, 2015.

101. Andrew Jacobs, "China Raids Offices of Rights Group as Crackdown Continues," *New York Times,* March 26, 2015.

102. "Chinese Labor Activists Detained en Masse," LaborNotes, December 9, 2015, http://www.labornotes.org/blogs/2015/12/chinese-labor-activists-detained -en-masse.

103. Alexandra Harney, "China Labor Activists Say Facing Unprecedented Intimidation," Reuters, January 15, 2015.

104. "World Report 2015: China," Human Rights Watch, https://www.hrw.org /world-report/2015/country-chapters/china-and-tibet.

## 4. How Did the New Deal Resolve the American "Labor Question"?

1. This pattern of ameliorative labor reforms in response to serious labor unrest is brilliantly explored in Alan Hyde, "A Theory of Labor Legislation," *Buffalo Law Review* 38 (1990): 383-464.

2. The term "regulatory capitalism" is meant to describe the prevailing political order of the advanced industrial world; specifically, "a capitalist order in which actors, both state and non-state, use a wide array of techniques to influence market behaviour." Peter Drahos, "Regulatory Capitalism, Globalization and the End of History," *Intellectual Property Law and Policy Journal* 1 (2014): 1. For a fuller exposition, see John Braithwaite, *Regulatory Capitalism: How It Works, Ideas for Making It Work Better* (Cheltenham, UK: Edward Elgar, 2008).

3. Walter Korpi finds, based on data from eighteen Western nations, that liberal or left party control of government promotes redistributive government policies and reduces unemployment and therefore reduces industrial conflict. In short, favorable political conditions for labor allow industrial conflict to shift from the labor market (and the streets) to the political arena. Walter Korpi, *The Democratic Class Struggle* (Boston: Routledge, 1983), 159–183.

4. See David Montgomery, *Workers' Control in America* (New York: Cambridge University Press, 1979), 11–15.

5. See William Forbath, "The Ambiguities of Free Labor: Labor and the Law in the Gilded Age," *Wisconsin Law Review* 1985 (1985): 767-816.

6. Montgomery, *Workers' Control,* 10.

7. See William Forbath, *Law and the Shaping of the American Labor Movement* (Cambridge, MA: Harvard University Press, 1991), 60–66; and Melvyn Dubofsky, *The State and Labor in Modern America* (Chapel Hill: University of North Carolina Press, 1994), 44–48.

8. See Forbath, *Law and the Shaping,* 105–118; see also Michael Wachter, "The Striking Success of the National Labor Relations Act," in *Research Handbook on the Economics of Labor and Employment Law,* ed. Cynthia L. Estlund and Michael L. Wachter (Cheltenham, UK: Edward Elgar, 2012), 432–434.

9. For a contemporary view of the relationship between state repression and radicalization, see Selig Perlman, *A Theory of the Labor Movement* (New York: Macmillan, 1928).

10. For an excellent account of this tumultuous period, see Irving Bernstein, *The Lean Years: A History of the American Worker, 1920–1933* (Cambridge, MA: Riverside Press, 1960).

11. Lizbeth Cohen, *Making a New Deal: Industrial Workers in Chicago, 1919–1939* (New York: Cambridge University Press, 1990), 292.

12. According to Philip Taft, "by 1938 the Communists were in major strategic positions in the CIO [Congress of Industrial Organizations]. They were influential, if not in control of the legal and publicity departments, and were either a strong minority or in full control of a dozen unions." Philip Taft, *Organized Labor in American History* (New York: Harper and Row, 1964), 620.

13. Cohen, *Making a New Deal,* 304–305.

14. See Bernstein, *Lean Years,* 505–513.

15. Cohen, *Making a New Deal,* 304–305.

16. See Ira Katznelson, *Fear Itself: The New Deal and the Origins of Our Time* (New York: Liveright, 2015). The idea of governing in part through intermediate organizations—corporations, unions, and trade and professional associations—had roots in both American and European reflections on how to govern an increasingly complex industrial society. James Q. Whitman, "Of Corporatism, Fascism, and the First New Deal," *American Journal of Comparative Law* 39 (1991): 761–764. Although corporatism was neither historically nor logically allied with fascism, that association took hold in the American mind in the 1930s and helped to curb the "corporatist" impulse in the United States thereafter. *Ibid.,* 754–755, 777–778.

17. Wachter, "Striking Success."

18. See discussion below of "varieties of capitalism."

19. Wachter, "Striking Success." The NIRA contained no legally binding rules regarding union organizing and bargaining, but it did encourage both, and the NIRA's "symbolic but unenforceable acknowledgement of workers' right to organize" both spurred labor activism and heightened "pressure for more coercive legislation." See Cohen, *Making a New Deal,* 303.

20. "Workers probably understood that for the moment, at least, business had lost control of the state. Consequently, labor militancy surged in 1936 and 1937 ... more than half the strikes were over the demand for union recognition under the terms laid out in the Wagner Act." Frances Piven, *Poor People's Movements: Why They Succeed, How They Fail* (New York: Vintage Books, 1979), 133; see also Wachter, "Striking Success," 435.

21. Wachter, "Striking Success," 435.

22. NLRB v. Jones & Laughlin Steel Co. 301 U.S. 1 (1937). See James Pope, "The Thirteenth Amendment versus the Commerce Clause: Labor and the Shaping

of American Constitutional Law, 1921–1957," *Columbia Law Review* 102 (2002): 85–92.

23. See generally James Atleson, *Values and Assumptions in American Labor Law* (Amherst: University of Massachusetts Press, 1983); Karl E. Klare, "Judicial Deradicalization of the Wagner Act and the Origins of Modern Legal Consciousness, 1937–1941," *Minnesota Law Review* 62 (1978): 265-349; and Pope, "Thirteenth Amendment," 18.

24. For a sampling of the debate over the goals of the Wagner Act, see Atleson, *Values and Assumptions;* James A. Gross, "Worker Rights as Human Rights: Wagner Act Values and Moral Choices," *University of Pennsylvania Journal of Labor and Employment Law* 4 (2002): 479-492; Klare, "Judicial Deradicalization"; Theodore J. St. Antoine, "How the Wagner Act Came to Be: A Prospectus," *Michigan Law Review* 96 (1998): 2201-2211; and Wachter, "Striking Success," 430.

25. See Thomas A. Kochan, Harry C. Katz, and Robert B. McKersie, *The Transformation of American Industrial Relations* (Ithaca, NY: ILR Press, 1994), 24–25.

26. See NLRB v. Fansteel Metallurgical Corp. 306 U.S. 240 (1939); and NLRB v. Mackay Radio and Telegraph Co. 304 U.S. 333 (1938). See generally Atleson, *Values and Assumptions,* 20; and Klare, "Judicial Deradicalization," 20.

27. See Wachter, "Striking Success," 436–437.

28. See Clark Kerr et al., *Industrialism and the Industrial Man* (Cambridge, MA: Harvard University Press, 1960); see also Montgomery, *Workers' Control,* 163.

29. Montgomery, *Workers' Control,* 166; see also Thomas A. Kochan and Harry C. Katz, *Collective Bargaining and Industrial Relations,* 2nd ed. (Homewood, IL: Richard D. Irwin, 1988), 38.

30. See Kochan and Katz, *Collective Bargaining,* 38.

31. The unions might have been able to help shape a more moderate set of restrictions if they had not simply refused to discuss any amendments to the Wagner Act. See James Gross, *Broken Promises: The Subversion of U.S. Labor Relations, 1947–1994* (Philadelphia: Temple University Press, 1995), 5–8.

32. Hyde, "Theory of Labor Legislation," 443–444.

33. It also imposed a sixty-day "cooling-off" period for strikes in national emergencies, prohibited "closed-shop" agreements that limited employment to union members, began to regulate unions' internal affairs, required union officers to sign "non-Communist" affidavits, and outlawed campaign contributions by unions. On the range of union activities outlawed by the Taft-Hartley Act, see John Paul Jennings, "The Right to Strike: Concerted Activity under the Taft-Hartley Act," *California Law Review* 40 (1952): 22–23. Many of these restrictions were decried by organized labor as unconstitutional, but those arguments gained little traction in the courts. See Pope, "Thirteenth Amendment," 101.

34. See National Labor Relations Act, U.S. Code 29 (2006), § 158(b)(4)(b).

35. See ibid., § 158(b)(7)(c), limiting "recognitional" picketing (picketing to pressure an employer to recognize a union) to a reasonable period of time not to exceed thirty days, unless an election petition is filed before that period expires.

36. Congress did not invent those restrictions on collective labor activity in 1947; precursors could be found in state law, and the Wagner Act did not clearly outlaw all of those restrictions. (To those who attacked the Wagner Act as "one-sided," Senator Wagner responded that existing state restrictions on unions were "sufficient," and that the present need was to regulate employer conduct.) The unions contended after 1935 that many of those state restrictions were invalid because they conflicted with workers' new federal rights. But the courts had only begun to address those conflicts when Taft-Hartley codified a rather fulsome version of the state restrictions into federal law.

37. Taft-Hartley added Section 9(h) to the NLRA, which required all of a union's officers to attest by affidavit that they were not members of or affiliated with the Communist Party as a prerequisite to that union's participation in NLRB proceedings involving matters of representation and unfair labor practices. In 1959, Congress replaced section 9(h) with a criminal prohibition on current or recent members of the Communist Party serving as an officer or employee (unless engaged in exclusively clerical or custodial duties) of a labor union. 29 U.S.C. § 504.

38. See United States v. Brown 381 U.S. 437 (1965).

39. On the role of communists and socialists in the U.S. labor movement, see generally Nelson Lichtenstein, *State of the Union: A Century of American Labor* (Princeton, NJ: Princeton University Press, 2002); and Judith Stepan-Norris and Maurice Zeitlan, *Left Out: Reds and America's Industrial Unions* (New York: Cambridge University Press, 2003).

40. The unions' adoption of "business unionism" was arguably a rational strategic response to the incentives set up by the NLRA's system of collective bargaining. See Joel Rogers, "Divide and Conquer: Further Reflections on the Distinctive Character of American Labor Laws," *Wisconsin Law Review* 1-147 (1990).

41. See generally Seymour Martin Lipset, Martin Trow, and James Coleman, *Union Democracy: The Internal Politics of the International Typographical Union* (New York: Free Press, 1956); and James B. Jacobs, "Is Labor Union Corruption Special?," *Social Research* 80, no. 4 (Winter 2013):1057–1086.

42. For example, it prohibits rules that unduly restrict eligibility for union office, such as a requirement of attendance at four union meetings in the past year, where that would disqualify 97 percent of union members, and all but current insiders, from running for union office.

43. See John L. Holcombe, "Union Democracy and the LMRDA," *Labor Law Journal* 12, no. 7 (July 1961)-604.

44. Montgomery, *Workers' Control*, 6.

45. Hyde, "Theory of Labor Legislation," 392.

46. Steel Panel Commission on Technology and International Economics and Trade Issues of the Office of the Foreign Secretary, Commission on Engineering and Technical Systems, Division on Engineering and Physical Sciences, National Academy of Engineering, and National Research Council, *The Competitive Status of the U.S. Steel Industry* (Washington, DC: National Academy Press, 1986), 58.

47. Employers' ability to permanently replace economic strikers was assumed by the Supreme Court, though it was not at issue, in NLRB v. Mackay Radio and Telegraph Co., 304 U.S. 333 (1938). But permanent replacements were not common for several decades, presumably because of their poisonous effect on labor-management relations. See generally Michael H. LeRoy, "Regulating Employer Use of Permanent Striker Replacements: Empirical Analysis of NLRA and RLA Strikes 1935–1991," *Berkeley Journal of Employment and Labor Law* 16 (1995): 169-208. A turning point occurred in 1981 when the federal air traffic controllers, led by their union, PATCO, went on strike in defiance of the no-strike provision of the law governing federal labor relations (not the NLRA). President Ronald Reagan fired and gradually replaced all the strikers and decertified their union. This was widely seen as legitimizing the permanent replacement of strikers even in the private sector, where strikes were lawful. See Kochan and Katz, *Collective Bargaining*, 44.

48. See Cynthia L. Estlund, "The Ossification of American Labor Law," *Columbia Law Review* 102 (2002): 1542–1544.

49. Employers may not "coerce" or threaten employees, but they may vigorously publicize and explain their preference for remaining nonunion, and they may commandeer employees' work time in "captive audience" meetings to advance their cause. In part, that stems from the "employer free speech" provisions of the Taft-Hartley amendments. For an early analysis of those provisions and the likely impact on workplace organizing, see Archibald Cox, "Some Aspects of the Labor Management Relations Act, 1947," *Harvard Law Review* 61 (1947): 15-20.

50. See Rogers, "Divide and Conquer," 29–30.

51. For a comparative analysis of the collective bargaining systems of North America and Europe, see Roy Adams, *Industrial Relations under Liberal Democracy: North America in Comparative Perspective* (Columbia: University of South Carolina Press, 1995); and Clyde Summers, "Worker Participation in Sweden and the United States: Some Comparisons from an American Perspective," *University of Pennsylvania Law Review* 133 (1984): 175-225. The variety of industrial relations systems is at the core of the "varieties of capitalism" outlined in Peter A. Hall and David Soskice, "An Introduction to Varieties of Capitalism," in *Varieties of Capitalism: The Institutional Foundations of Comparative Advantage,* ed. Peter A. Hall and David Soskice (New York: Oxford University Press, 2001), 1-68. In particular, the United States is the prototypical "liberal market economy," while the "coordinated market economy," with its corporatist and sectoral industrial relations structures sketched below, is typified by Germany and by Scandinavian countries.

52. Senator Walsh, speaking on the Wagner Act, *Congressional Record of the U.S. Senate,* vol. 79 (1935), 7660.

53. National Labor Relations Act, § 158(d).

54. See H. K. Porter Co. v. NLRB 397 U.S. 99 (1970).

55. For union affiliation data, see Bureau of Labor Statistics, "Table 3. Union Affiliation of Employed Wage and Salary Workers by Occupation and Industry," accessed May 14, 2016, http://www.bls.gov/news.release/union2

.to3.htm. For work stoppage data, see Bureau of Labor Statistics, "Table 1. Work Stoppages Involving 1,000 or More Workers, 1947–2015," accessed May 14, 2016, http://www.bls.gov/news.release/wkstp.to1.htm. The modern low point in work stoppages was 2009, when there were just five major work stoppages affecting 13,000 workers.

56. Bruce Western and Jake Rosenfeld, "Unions, Norms, and the Rise in U.S. Wage Inequality," *American Society Review* 76 (August 2011): 513-537.

57. See, e.g., Steve Greenhouse, "Hundreds of Fast-Food Workers Striking for Higher Wages Are Arrested," *New York Times,* September 5, 2014; and Hiroko Tabuchi and Steven Greenhouse, "Walmart Workers Demand $15 Wage in Several Protests," *New York Times,* October 17, 2014.

58. See Steven Greenhouse, "How the $15 Minimum Wage Went From Laughable to Viable," *New York Times,* April 1, 2016.

59. See Steven Greenhouse, "How to Get Low-Wage Workers Into the Middle Class," *The Atlantic,* August 19, 2015.

60. Kochan and Katz, *Collective Bargaining,* 32–33.

61. Ibid. For critical perspectives on scientific management, see Harry Braverman, *Labor and Monopoly Capital: The Degradation of Work in the Twentieth Century,* 2nd ed. (New York: Monthly Review Press, 1998); and Montgomery, *Workers' Control,* 9–27.

62. See Kochan and Katz, *Collective Bargaining,* 32–33.

63. Ibid., 34.

64. Ibid.

65. Union membership fell from 12.1 percent of the labor force in 1920 to 7.5 percent in 1930. The number of union members fell by over 3.5 million between 1921 and 1931.

66. Kochan and Katz, *Collective Bargaining,* 34.

67. On the role of better management methods in declining labor unrest and organizing, see Wachter, "Striking Success," 457. On the role of more "suppressive" forms of union avoidance, both lawful and unlawful, in union decline, see Robert J. Flanagan, "Has Management Strangled U.S. Unions?," in *What Do Unions Do? A Twenty-Year Perspective,* ed. James T. Bennett and Bruce E. Kaufman (Picastaway, NJ: Transaction, 2007), 459–488; and Robert M. Smith, *From Blackjacks to Briefcases: A History of Commercialized Strikebreaking and Unionbusting in the United States* (Athens: Ohio University Press, 2003).

68. Wachter, "Striking Success," 457.

69. Ibid., 447.

70. For a rough comparison, see "The 2015 ITUC Global Rights Index: The World's Worst Countries for Workers," International Trade Union Confederation, http://www.ituc-csi.org/IMG/pdf/survey_global_rights_index_2015_en.pdf.

71. Connie Guglielmo, "Apple's Supplier Labor Practices in China Scrutinized after Foxconn, Pegatron Reviews," *Forbes,* December 12, 2013, http://www.forbes.com/sites/connieguglielmo/2013/12/12/apples-labor-practices-in-china-scrutinized-after-foxconn-pegatron-reviewed/.

72. Irving Bernstein, *The Turbulent Years: A History of the American Worker, 1933–1940*, (New York: Houghton Mifflin, 1969).

73. On the basic taxonomy of rights and interest disputes, see John Spielmans, "Labor Disputes on Rights and Interests," *American Economic Review* 29 (1939): 299-312, http://www.jstor.org/stable/pdfplus/1803627.

74. See generally Bruce Kaufman, *The Global Evolution of Industrial Relations: Events, Ideas and the IIRA* (Geneva: International Labor Organization, 2004), 24–32.

75. See Richard Hyman, *Strikes*, 4th ed. (Hampshire: Macmillan Press, 1989).

76. See Colin Crouch, *Industrial Relations and European State Traditions* (New York: Oxford University Press, 1993); and Hall and Soskice, "Introduction to Varieties of Capitalism," 18–21.

77. Hyde, "Theory of Labor Legislation," 384, 432.

78. See Theda Skocpol, "Political Response to Capitalist Crisis: Neo-Marxist Theories of the State and the Case of the New Deal," *Politics and Society* 10 (1980): 200. Skocpol argues powerfully that the U.S. industrial working class was not strong enough in the 1930s to achieve positive change through economic disruption alone, but also depended on electoral mobilization and support from the federal government and the Democratic Party.

79. It may also draw public sympathy and political support to the workers' cause, as happened in the United States in the 1930s. See Piven, *Poor People's Movements*, 29.

80. The distinctive shape of the quid pro quo in U.S. labor law is explored in Cynthia L. Estlund, "Are Unions a Constitutional Anomaly?," *Michigan Law Review* 114 (2015): 169-234.

81. See generally George W. Taylor, *Government Regulation of Industrial Relations* (New York: Prentice-Hall, 1948), 252–263.

82. See Rogers, "Divide and Conquer," 33.

83. See Estlund, "Ossification."

84. See Piven, *Poor People's Movements*, 155–173; see also Piven explaining that "unionization also ritualizes and encapsulates the strike power, thus limiting its disruptive impact on production, and limiting the political reverberations of economic disruptions as well." Piven, *Poor People's Movements*, 175.

85. Making unions responsible for bringing about industrial peace requires a delicate balance, as Gerald Friedman has noted: "[T]o the extent that pacification succeeds, it risks undermining popular militancy until employers conclude that there is no longer a threat of unrest and they can abandon dealing with the union. But if pacification fails, if workers reject the narrow gains of collective bargaining and there is renewed labor militancy, employers conclude that the union cannot restrain labor unrest and there is no gain in dealing with the union." Gerald Friedman, *Reigniting the Labor Movement: Restoring Means to Ends in a Democratic Labor Movement* (Florence, KY: Routledge, 2007), 56.

86. See Forbath, *Law and the Shaping*, 10–36.

87. See Estlund, "Ossification," 1532–1533.

## 5. Can China Regulate Its Way out of Labor Unrest?

1. Concern over social unrest, and the aim of securing stability, has been a major driver across several regulatory arenas, including food safety, environmental protection, property rights, and labor rights. See Benjamin Van Rooij, "Regulation by escalation: unrest, lawmaking and law enforcement in China," in *The Politics of Law and Stability in China*, ed. Susan Trevaskes, Elisa Nesossi, Flora Sapio, and Sarah Biddulph (Cheltenham, UK: Edward Elgar, 2014), 83-106, 86-89.

2. Wen-Ti Sung, "Is Xi Jinping a Reformer?," *Diplomat,* March 5, 2014, http://thediplomat.com/2014/03/is-xi-jinping-a-reformer/.

3. Sarah Biddulph observes a similar pattern in the response to labor protest. Sarah Biddulph, *The Stability Imperative: Human Rights and Law in China* (Vancouver: University of British Columbia Press, 2015), 36–38.

4. Victor Li, *Law without Lawyers: A Comparative View of Law in China and the United States* (Westview Press, 1978); Timothy A. Gelatt, "Lawyers in China: The Past Decade and Beyond," *New York University Journal of International Law and Politics* 23 (1991).

5. See Van Rooij, "Regulation by escalation," 86.

6. See Karl Polanyi, *The Great Transformation: The Political and Economic Origins of Our Time* (Boston, MA: Beacon Press, 1957).

7. See e.g., Shaoguang Wang, "Double Movement in China," *Economic and Political Weekly* 43 (2009): 51–59, http://www.jstor.org/stable/40278334.

8. See Sean Cooney, Sarah Biddulph, and Ying Zhu, *Law and Fair Work in China* (New York: Routledge, 2012).

9. See Dali Yang, *Remaking the Chinese Leviathan* (Stanford, CA: Stanford University Press, 2004).

10. On the development of China's labor regulatory framework, see Cooney, Biddulph, and Zhu, *Law and Fair Work;* and Mary E. Gallagher and Baohua Dong, "Legislating Harmony: Labor Law Reform in Contemporary China," in *From Iron Rice Bowl to Informalization: Markets, Workers, and the State in a Changing China,* ed. Sarosh Kuruvilla, Ching Kwan Lee, and Mary E. Gallagher (Ithaca, NY: ILR Press, 2011).

11. See Mary E. Gallagher, " 'Time is Money, Efficiency is Life': The Transformation of Labor Relations in China," *Studies in Comparative International Development* 39 (2004): 23.

12. See Qianfan Zhang, *The Constitution of China: A Contextual Analysis* (Oxford, UK: Hart, 2012), 84.

13. See Bruce J. Dickson, *Wealth into Power: The Communist Party's Embrace of China's Private Sector* (New York: Cambridge University Press, 2008), 171–172.

14. See Eli Friedman, *Insurgency Trap: Labor Politics in Postsocialist China* (Ithaca, NY: Cornell University Press, 2014). See also Christian Gobel and Lynette H. Ong, *Social Unrest in China* (London: Europe China Research and Advice Network, 2012), 19, http://www.chathamhouse.org/sites/files/chathamhouse/public/Research/Asia/1012ecran_gobelong.pdf.

15. The preamble to China's constitution states that "China will be in the primary stage of socialism for a long time to come." Xianfa [Constitution of the People's Republic of China] preamble (2004), http://www.gov.cn/english /2005-08/05/content_20813.htm. The phrase is notoriously flexible, however, and has been put to various uses by Chinese leaders in response to the changing economy. See Alan R. Kluver, *Legitimating the Chinese Economic Reforms: A Rhetoric of Myth and Orthodoxy* (Albany: State University of New York Press, 1996), 72.

16. See Mary E. Gallagher, *Contagious Capitalism: Globalization and the Politics of Labor in China* (Princeton, NJ: Princeton University Press, 2007); William Hurst, *The Chinese Worker after Socialism* (Cambridge University Press, 2009); and Tim Pringle, *Trade Unions in China: The Challenge of Labour Unrest* (New York: Routledge, 2011), 56–86.

17. See Susan Leung, "China's Labor Contract System from Planned to Market Economy," *Journal of Law, Ethics, and Intellectual Property* 3 (2012): 2. http://www.scientificjournals.org/journals2012/articles/1519.pdf.

18. Gallagher and Dong, *Legislating Harmony*.

19. Ibid., 39.

20. See generally Cooney, Biddulph, and Zhu, *Law and Fair Work*; Gallagher and Dong, *Legislating Harmony*.

21. Mary E. Gallagher, "China's Workers Movement and the End of the Rapid-Growth Era," *Daedalus* 143 (2014).

22. See Samuel Estreicher and Jeffrey M. Hirsch, "Comparative Wrongful Dismissal Law: Reassessing American Exceptionalism," *North Carolina Law Review* 92 (2014): 343-480, 347.

23. See Andrew G. Walder, "Organized Dependency and Cultures of Authority in Chinese Industry," *Journal of Asian Studies* 43 (1983): 56.

24. See Leung, "China's Labor Contract System," 2–3.

25. See Gallagher and Dong, "Legislating Harmony"; Leung, "China's Labor Contract System," 2–3.

26. See "OECD Indicators of Employment Protection," Organisation for Economic Co-operation and Development, 2013, http://www.oecd.org/employment /emp/oecdindicatorsofemploymentprotection.htm.

27. In 2008, the number of labor-related cases doubled to over six hundred thousand, and that number has stayed relatively steady since then. In 2011, workers won almost two hundred thousand of the cases they brought, whereas employers won less than seventy-five thousand. *Zhongguo Laodong Tongji Nianjian* 2012 [China Labor Statistical Yearbook 2012] 368, tbl. 9–1.

28. See Lars W. Mitlacher, "The Role of Temporary Agency Work in Different Industrial Relations Systems—a Comparison between Germany and the USA," *British Journal of Industrial Relations* 45 (2007): 584–586; David H. Autor, "Outsourcing at Will: The Contribution of Unjust Dismissal Doctrine to the Growth of Employment Outsourcing," *Journal of Labor Economics* 21 (2003): 32.

29. See Virginia E. Harper Ho and Qiaoyan Huang, "The Recursivity of Reform: China's Amended Labor Contract Law," *Fordham International Law Journal*

37 (2014). The LCL had regulated the use of labor dispatch, but its provisions were vague and easy to evade.

30. Ibid., 982, 996n97. In Dongguan, a southern manufacturing center in Guangdong Province, the number of labor dispatch agencies increased by at least 500 percent after 2008. Ibid.

31. See generally Kuruvilla, Lee, and Gallagher, *From Iron Rice Bowl*, 1–7.

32. David Weil, *The Fissured Workplace: Why Work Became So Bad for So Many and What Can Be Done to Improve It* (Cambridge, MA: Harvard University Press, 2014).

33. Arguably the LCL's treatment of dispatched labor actually legitimized the practice, and the "indeterminacy" of its rules helped "open . . . the door for an over-expansion of labor dispatch." See Ho and Huang, "Recursivity," 17.

34. Labor Contract Law of the People's Republic of China (2012 Amendment) (promulgated by the Standing Committee of the National People's Congress, December 28, 2012, effective January 1, 2008) (hereinafter Amended LCL) (Lawinfochina) (China). The law also requires "equal pay for equal work" between dispatch and regular workers, and requires labor dispatch agencies to be licensed, to have a minimum amount of registered capital and facilities, and to comply with labor laws (article 57). The 10 percent restriction, set by authoritative (draft) regulations issued in January 2014 (Laowu Paiqian Zanxing Guiding [Interim provisions on labor dispatch] [promulgated by the Ministry of Human Resources and Social Services, January 24, 2014, effective March 1, 2014], article 4 [China], http://www.mohrss.gov.cn/gkml/xxgk/201401/t20140126_123297.htm), does not apply to Chinese representative offices of foreign entities. Ibid., article 25. Laowu Paiqian Ruogan Guiding (Zhengqiu Yijian Gao) [Draft provisions on labor dispatch (seeking comments)], Legislative Affairs Office of the State Council P. R. China, August 8, 2013, http://www.chinalaw.gov.cn/article/cazjgg/201308/20130800389847.shtml.

35. Manfred Antoni and Elke J. Jahn, "Do Changes in Regulation Affect Employment Duration in Temporary Help Agencies?," *Industrial and Labor Relations Review* 62 (2009): 226–228.

36. 2015 saw a large increase (38.7 percent) in "labor service disputes" involving "independent contractors" (some of which are "quasi-employment" relationships). Data from the Supreme People's Court on 2015 Labor/Employment Disputes, Supreme People's Court Monitor, March 27, 2016, https://supremepeoplescourtmonitor.com/2016/03/27/data-from-the-supreme-peoples-court-on-2015-laboremployment-disputes/.

37. Yuanyuan Zhang, "Yu Guibi Xin Laodongfa Xiangguan Xianzhi Qiye Laowu PaiqianTubian 'Laowu Waibao' " [To circumvent new labor law restrictions, companies replace dispatch labor with "outsourced labor"], June 24, 2013, http://finance.youth.cn/finance_gdxw/201306/t20130624_3413854.htm.

38. Earl V. Brown and Kyle A. deCant, "Exploiting Chinese Interns As Unprotected Industrial Labor," *Asian-Pacific Law and Policy Journal* 15 (2013): 150–94.

39. See Ho and Huang, "Recursivity."

40. "In terms of labor protection, few countries have moved as aggressively as

China in recent years." Mary E. Gallagher, "China's Workers Movement," 14–15.

41. See ibid.

42. Mary E. Gallagher, "Authoritarian Legality: Law, Workers, and the State in Contemporary China" (unpublished manuscript chapter 2, p. 43, accessed May 8, 2016, https://www.academia.edu/15249101/Authoritarian_Legality _Law_Workers_and_the_State_in_Contemporary_China_draft_book _manuscript_.

43. Van Rooij, "Regulation by escalation," 90.

44. Some point to roots in Confucianism. Margaret Y. K. Woo, "Conclusion: Chinese Justice from the Bottom Up," in *Chinese Justice: Civil Dispute Resolution in China,* ed. Margaret Y. K. Woo and Mary E. Gallagher (Cambridge: Cambridge University Press, 2011), 388.

45. Biddulph, *Stability Imperative,* 36–38; Cooney, Biddulph, and Zhu, *Law and Fair Work,* 144.

46. Ho and Huang, "Recursivity," 10–18.

47. Van Rooij, "Regulation by escalation," 91.

48. See Richard B. Freeman and Xiaoying Li, "How Does China's New Labor Contract Law Affect Floating Workers?" (working paper no. 19254, National Bureau of Economic Research, Cambridge, MA, 2013): 18, http://www.nber .org/papers/w19254.pdf?new_window=1.

49. See ibid.

50. See Cooney, Biddulph, and Zhu, *Law and Fair Work,* 114–115.

51. Van Rooij, "Regulation by escalation," 92.

52. "Cases Soar as Workers Seek Redress," *China Daily,* April 22, 2009, http:// www.chinadaily.com.cn/china/2009-04/22/content_7701725.htm.

53. Mary E. Gallagher, "Mobilizing the Law in China: 'Informed Disenchantment' and the Development of Legal Consciousness," *Law and Society Review* 40 (2006): 783-816.

54. For example, Gallagher cites machine operator Yao, who lost his case, but was soon advising friends and colleagues about the importance of getting the proper proof and evidence. Ibid., 801.

55. See Johanna Rickne, "Labor Market Conditions and Social Insurance in China" Research Institute of Industrial Economics, 2012): 5, http://www.ifn .se/wfiles/wp/wp924.pdf.

56. Van Rooij, "Regulation by escalation," 92-93.

57. Ibid., 97. See generally Yongshun Cai, *Collective Resistance in China: Why Popular Protests Succeed or Fail* (Stanford: Stanford University Press, 2010).

58. Van Rooij, "Regulation by escalation," 99.

59. I explore these issues at length in Cynthia L. Estlund, *Regoverning the Workplace: From Self-Regulation to Co-regulation* (New Haven, CT: Yale University Press, 2010).

60. See Frank Dobbin, *Inventing Equal Opportunity* (Princeton, NJ: Princeton University Press, 2011); Estlund, *Regoverning.*

61. Ibid., 143.

62. Ian Ayres and John Braithwaite, *Responsive Regulation: Transcending the Deregulation Debate* (New York: Oxford University Press, 1992).

63. Shannon Gleeson, "Brokered Pathways to Justice and Cracks in the Law: A Closer Look at the Claims-Making Experiences of Low-Wage Workers," *Journal of Labor and Society* 18 (2015): 80.

64. Charles B. Craver, "Why Labor Unions Must (and Can) Survive," *University of Pennsylvania Journal of Labor and Employment Law* 1 (1998): 15–23; Alison Morantz, "Coal Mine Safety: Do Unions Make a Difference?," *Industrial and Labor Relations Review* 66 (2013); Robert J. Rabin, "The Role of Unions in the Rights-Based Workplace," *University of San Francisco Law Review* 25 (1991): 172–173.

65. See Janice Fine, *Worker Centers: Organizing Communities at the Edge of the Dream* (Ithaca, NY: ILR Press, 2006).

66. See Patrick McGeehan, "New York Plans $15-an-Hour Minimum Wage for Fast Food Workers," *New York Times*, July 22, 2015, http://www.nytimes.com/2015/07/23/nyregion/new-york-minimum-wage-fast-food-workers.html.

67. With a green light from the U.S. Supreme Court, many U.S. employers require workers, as a condition of employment, to agree to arbitrate future employment disputes and to do so on an individual basis. See Lauren Weber, "More Companies Block Employees from Filing Suits," *Wall Street Journal*, March 31, 2015, http://www.wsj.com/articles/more-companies-block-staff-from-suing-1427824287. Arbitration must formally preserve the substance of workers' legal claims, but may muffle or defeat those claims by barring aggregate proceedings, reducing recoveries, and minimizing publicity. For a recent empirical assessment of mandatory employment arbitration, see Alexander J. S. Colvin and Kelly Pike, "Saturns and Rickshaws Revisited: What Kind of Employment Arbitration System Has Developed?," *Ohio State Journal on Dispute Resolution* 29 (2014): 59-84.

68. On a variety of limitations on private enforcement of labor rights and the relationship to stability concerns, see Biddulph, *Stability Imperative*, 57–58.

69. Jean-Philippe Béja, "The New Working Class Renews the Repertoire of Social Conflict," *China Perspectives* 2 (2011): 6, http://chinaperspectives.revues.org/pdf/5535; Gallagher, "Mobilizing the Law in China."

70. Mary E. Gallagher, "Use the Law as Your Weapon! Institutional Change and Legal Mobilization in China," in *Engaging the Law in China: State, Society, and Possibilities for Justice*, ed. Neil Jeffrey Diamant, Stanley L. Lubman, and Kevin J. O'Brien (Stanford, CA: Stanford University Press, 2005), 47 n17 (citing Ming'an Jiang, *Zhongguo xingzheng fazhi*). Additionally, Chinese labor law issues tend to be quite complex, exacerbating the need for a lawyer. "Xiao Weidong, a legal aid lawyer in Beijing, found . . . 962 national-level laws and regulations relating to labor, in addition to countless local laws, regulations, and guidelines, all riddled with contradictions and inconsistencies between them. As Xiao explained, '[a] lawyer would need quite a considerable amount of time to become clear on all these rules, let alone a migrant worker.' " Aaron Halegua, "Getting Paid: Processing the Labor Disputes of

China's Migrant Workers," *Berkeley Journal of International Law* 26 (2008): 271–272.

71. Ibid. at 281–282. Ethan Michelson found ample evidence that most lawyers actively shunned cases from poor claimants. Ethan Michelson, "The Practice of Law as an Obstacle to Justice: Chinese Lawyers at Work," *Law and Society Review* 40, no. 1 (2006): 17.

72. Halegua, "Getting Paid," 281–282; Ching Kwan Lee, *Against the Law: Labor Protests in China's Rustbelt and Sunbelt* (Berkeley: University of California Press, 2007): 184; Pringle, *Trade Unions in China,* 144–146.

73. Aaron Halegua, "Protecting the Legal Rights of Chinese Workers: A Mapping of Legal Issues and Avenues for Recourse in Several Chinese Cities, " April 1, 2016 (unpublished paper on file with author).

74. Ibid.

75. Ibid.

76. Van Rooij, "Regulation by escalation," 98.

77. See Chapter 6.

78. Aaron Halegua, "China's Restrictions on Barefoot Lawyers Could Backfire, Leading to More Unrest," *South China Morning Post,* March 30, 2015, http://www.scmp.com/comment/insight-opinion/article/1748592/chinas -restrictions-barefoot-lawyers-could-backfire.

79. Jerome A. Cohen, "Struggling for Justice: China's Courts and the Challenge of Reform," *World Politics Review,* January 14, 2014.

80. Keith Hand, "Resolving Constitutional Disputes in Contemporary China," *University of Pennsylvania East Asia Law Review* 51 (2011): 61n37.

81. "Class Action Litigation in China," *Harvard Law Review* 111 (1998): 1523–1525.

82. Biddulph, *Stability Imperative,* 46.

83. Jing-Huey Shao, "Class Action Mechanisms in Chinese and Taiwanese Contexts—a Mixture of Private and Public Law," *Emory International Law Review* 28 (2014): 255.

84. Carl Minzner, "Judicial Disciplinary Systems for Incorrectly Decided Cases: The Imperial Chinese Heritage Lives On," in Woo and Gallagher, *Chinese Justice,* 64.

85. See Timothy Webster, "Ambivalence and Activism: Employment Discrimination in China," *Vanderbilt Journal of Transnational Law* 44 (2011): 656. See also Xun Zeng, "Enforcing Equal Employment Opportunities in China," *University of Pennsylvania Journal of Business Law* 9 (2007): 999.

86. Such provisions can be found in China's constitution, article 14 of the Labor Law; and most importantly in chapter 3 of the PRC Employment Promotion Law enacted in 2007. See Jiefeng Lu, "Regulating Employment Discrimination in China: A Discussion from the Socio-legal Perspective," *Michigan State International Law Review* 23 (2015): 440–442.

87. "Plaintiff Obtains 30,000 Yuan in China's First Gender Discrimination Lawsuit," *China Labour Bulletin,* January 9, 2014, http://www.clb.org.hk/en /content/plaintiff-obtains-30000-yuan-china%C3%A2%E2%82%AC%E2

%84%A2s-first-gender-discrimination-lawsuit. The defendant, Juren Academy in Beijing, had advertised positions for men only, and the plaintiff was manifestly qualified for the position.

88. "Woman Successfully Sues Beijing Postal Service in Gender Discrimination Case," *China Labour Bulletin,* http://www.clb.org.hk/en/content/woman -successfully-sues-beijing-postal-service-gender-discrimination-case.

89. Didi Kirsten Tatlow, "Police Remove Bail Conditions on 5 Chinese Feminists Detained Last Year," *New York Times,* April 13, 2016.

90. Jerome A. Cohen, "China's Legal Reform at the Crossroads," *Far Eastern Economic Review* (2006): March, http://www.cfr.org/china/chinas-legal -reform-crossroads/p10063.

91. Willy Wo-Lap Lam, *Chinese Politics in the Era of Xi Jinping: Renaissance, Reform, or Retrogression?* (New York: Routledge, 2015), 117–118.

## 6. Can China Secure Labor Peace without Real Unions?

1. On the distinctive impact and import of strikes, as compared to other forms of protest, see Elizabeth Perry, *Shanghai on Strike: The Politics of Chinese Labor* (Stanford, CA: Stanford University Press, 1993), 6–8.

2. Mao Zedong, "On the Correct Handling of Contradictions among the People," speech, Eleventh Session (Enlarged) of the Supreme State Conference, published in edited form in the *People's Daily,* June 19, 1957, available at https://www .marxists.org/reference/archive/mao/selected-works/volume-5/mswv5_58.htm.

3. For more in-depth accounts of the emerging shape of collective interest disputes and the role of the ACFTU, see Eli Friedman, *Insurgency Trap: Labor Politics in Postsocialist China* (Ithaca, NY: Cornell University Press, 2014); Tim Pringle, *Trade Unions in China: The Challenge of Labour Unrest* (New York: Routledge, 2011); Mingwei Liu and Chunyun Li, "Environment Pressures, Managerial Industrial Relations Ideologies, and Unionization in Chinese Enterprises," *British Journal of Industrial Relations* 82-111 (March 2014); and Mingwei Liu, "Union Organizing in China: Still a Monolithic Labor Movement?," *Industrial and Labor Relations Review* 30-52 (October 2010).

4. *China Labour Bulletin*'s "Strike Map" is the leading source. "Strike Map," *China Labour Bulletin,* accessed January 7, 2016, http://maps.clb.org.hk /strikes/en.

5. Jun Liu, "Calling for Strikes," *Georgetown Journal of International Affairs* 15 (2015): 15.

6. Chinese netizens surpassed 591 million in 2013, of which 464 million were mobile users. Social media is particularly popular among China's youth. "Sina Weibo User Demographic Analysis in 2013," ChinaInternetWatch, January 9, 2014, accessed July 12, 2015, http://www.chinainternetwatch.com/5568 /what-weibo-can-tell-you-about-chinese-netizens-part-1/.

7. Jean-Philippe Béja, "The New Working Class Renews the Repertoire of Social Conflict," *China Perspectives* 2 (2011), http://chinaperspectives.revues.org /pdf/5535.

8. Paul Mason, "China's Workers Are Turning from Analogue Slaves to Digital Rebels," *Guardian,* September 14, 2014, http://www.theguardian.com /commentisfree/2014/sep/14/china-analogue-slaves-digital-rebellion.

9. Chuang, "Yet Another Shoe Factory Revolt: Strike of 10,000 Suppressed in Zhongshan," *Chuangcn.org* (blog), Chuangcn.org, March 28, 2015, http:// chuangcn.org/2015/03/zhongshan-xinchang-shoe-strike/.

10. Mary Kay Magistad, "How Weibo Is Changing China," *YaleGlobal Online,* August 9, 2012, http://yaleglobal.yale.edu/content/how-weibo-changing -china.

11. Jun Liu, "Calling for Strikes," 21.

12. China's legal system has vastly improved since the Cultural Revolution's chaos. Chenguang Wang, "From the Rule of Man to the Rule of Law," in *China's Journey toward the Rule of Law,* ed. Chenguang Wang and Dingjian Cai (Leiden: E. J. Brill, 2010), 1–50. However, many issues remain, especially in cases that directly affect the interests of the party-state. For example, judges are reliant on the support of local cadres to maintain their positions. Pierre Landry, "The Institutional Diffusion of Courts in China," in *Rule by Law: The Politics of Courts in Authoritarian Regimes,* ed. Tom Ginsburg and Tamir Moustafa (Cambridge: Cambridge University Press, 2008), 209. Additionally, judicial decisions "are often reviewed and amended by committees chaired by Party officials . . . before going into effect." Pitman Potter, *China's Legal System* (Cambridge: Polity Press, 2013), 2. Finally, in criminal cases, China continues to rely on confessions coerced through torture. Ira Belkin, "China's Tortuous Path toward Ending Torture in Criminal Investigations," *Columbia Journal of Asian Law* 24 (2011): 273-301.

13. For an example, see Criminal Judgment Suiyun faxing chuzi no. 125 (2014), by The Baiyun District People's Court of Guangzhou, Guangdong Province on April 14, 2014.

14. Conversation with labor activist, June 18, 2014.

15. John Ruwitch, "Labor Movement 'Concertmaster' Tests Beijing's Boundaries," Reuters, December 6, 2014.

16. Ibid.

17. Tom Mitchell and Lucy Hornby, "China Lawyer Trial Begins amid Crackdown on Labour Rights Groups," *Financial Times,* December 14, 2015.

18. "Workers Speak Out in Support of Detained Labour Activists in Guangdong," *China Labour Bulletin,* January 5, 2016, http://www.clb.org.hk/en/content /workers-speak-out-support-detained-labour-activists-guangdong.

19. Tim Pringle, "Trade Union Renewal in China and Vietnam?" (paper 26th International Labour Process Conference, University College, Dublin, March 18–20, 2006), http://web.warwick.ac.uk/fac/soc/complabstuds/russia/ngpa /Trade%20Union%20Renewal%20in%20China%20and%20Vietnam.doc.

20. Zhonghua Renmin Gongheguo Gonghuifa [Trade Union Law of the People's Republic of China] (adopted April 3, 1992, at the Fifth session of the Seventh National People's Congress, amended October 27, 2001) (hereinafter Trade Union Law), article 25 (China), http://www.lawinfochina.com/display.aspx ?lib=law&id=452&Cgid.

21. Trade Union Law, 2001 Amendment, article 27.
22. Jun Guo, director of the ACFTU's "democratic management" department, quoted in "After the Passage of the Labor Contract Law, Can the Unions Extend their Power?," *Southern Weekend,* July 4, 2007, http://www.infzm .com/content/7939 (translated for author).
23. Conversation with Chinese labor scholar, August 13, 2013.
24. Ibid.
25. Turnover rates as high as 100 or 200 percent were reported in some factories in the past. Jass Yang, "Turnover Rates in Chinese Factories," *CSR Asia Weekly,* August 11, 2005, http://www.csr-asia.com/weekly_news_detail .php?id=4788. A more recent and systematic study in the Pearl River Delta electronics manufacturing industry estimated an average annual turnover rate of 36 percent, said to approximate the overall rates for China. Pamela Hartmann, Daniel Schiller, and Frauke, "Workplace Quality and Labour Turnover in the Electronics Industry of the Pearl River Delta, China," *Zeitschrift für Wirtschaftsgeographie* 56 (2012): 66, http://www.wigeo .uni-hannover.de/uploads/tx_tkpublikationen/ZfW-Hartmann-Schiller -Kraas_2012.pdf. This compares to an average annual turnover rate of about 24 percent in U.S. manufacturing between 2011 and 2015. United States Department of Labor, Bureau of Labor Statistics, Current Employment Statistics Survey 2005–2015, Manufacturing Employment, Series ID: CES3000000001; Department of Labor, Bureau of Labor Statistics, Job Openings and Labor Turnover Survey 2005–2015, Manufacturing Separations, Series ID: JTS30000000TSL.
26. "Strike Map," *China Labour Bulletin,* accessed May 18, 2016, http://maps .clb.org.hk/strikes/en.
27. "China-Labour Relations in Guangdong," Foreign and Commonwealth Office [UK], January 30, 2015, https://www.gov.uk/government/publications/china -labour-relations-in-guangdong/china-labour-relations-in-guangdong.
28. Conversation with Chinese labor scholar, January 11, 2014.
29. Tom Mitchell and Demetri Sevastopulo, "China Labour Activism: Crossing the Line," *Financial Times,* May 7, 2014; Tom Mitchell, "China Crackdown on Labor Activism Bolstered by Court Ruling," *Financial Times,* April 15, 2014, http://www.ft.com/intl/cms/s/0/aa194620-c46d-11e3-8dd4-00144feabdco .html%20-%20axzz33DRg9BJL.
30. Mimi Lau, "Guangdong Collective Bargaining Proposal Seen as Bellwether for China," *Southern China Morning Post,* July 6, 2014.
31. Elaine Hui, "Chinese Bike Light Strikers Occupy Factory, Face Firings and Arrests," *LaborNotes,* May 20, 2015, http://labornotes.org/2015/05/chinese -bike-light-strikers-occupy-factory-face-firings-and-arrests.
32. Liu and Li, "Environment Pressures."
33. Ibid.; Liu, "Union Organizing in China"; Pringle, *Trade Unions in China,* 123–132.
34. Katie Quan, "One Step Forward: Collective Bargaining Experiments in Vietnam and China," in *Chinese Workers in Comparative Perspective,* ed. Anita Chan (Ithaca, NY: Cornell University Press, 2015), 174-192.

35. H. K. Porter Co. v. NLRB, 397 U.S. 99 (1970); Machinists v. Wisconsin Employment Relations Comm'n, 427 U.S. 132 (1976); Golden State Transit Corp. v. Los Angeles, 475 U.S. 608 (1986). This is discussed briefly in Chapter 4.

36. Michael L. Wachter, "Labor Unions: A Corporatist Institution in a Competitive World," *University of Pennsylvania Law Review* 155 (2007): 581-634.

37. Friedman, *Insurgency Trap,* 99–118.

38. C. Cindy Fan and Allen J. Scott, "Industrial Agglomeration and Development: A Survey of Spatial Economic Issues in East Asia and a Statistical Analysis of Chinese Regions," *Economic Geography* 79 (2003): 302, http://www.sscnet .ucla.edu/geog/downloads/597/208.pdf.

39. Pringle, *Trade Unions in China;* Quentin Sommerville, "The Rapid Rise of China's Sock Town," *BBC News,* September 29, 2005.

40. Cynthia Estlund, "Just the Facts: The Case for Workplace Transparency," *Stanford Law Review* 63 (2011): 351–407.

41. The latter is hardly unheard of, and was common in preindustrial or early industrial societies. For example, in Western Europe after the Black Death, the aristocracy and clergy attempted to enforce a wage cap on peasant labor. Robert S. Gottfried, *The Black Death* (New York: Free Press, 1983), 94–103.

42. Friedman, *Insurgency Trap,* 115–118.

43. Satya J. Gabriel, "Economic Liberalization in Post-Mao China: Crossing the River by Feeling for Stones," China Essay Series, no. 7, Mount Holyoke College, October 1998, https://www.mtholyoke.edu/courses/sgabriel/economics /china-essays/7.html.

44. Aaron Halegua, "China's New Collective Bargaining Rule Is Too Weak to Ease Labour Conflicts," *South China Morning Post,* February 25, 2015, http:// www.scmp.com/comment/insight-opinion/article/1723213/chinas-new-collective -bargaining-rule-too-weak-ease-labour.

45. Standing Committee of the Twelfth People's Congress of Guangdong Province Public Notice (no. 21), Guangdong Provincial Regulation on Collective Contracts for Enterprises, September 25, 2014 [English translation], http://laborcenter.berkeley.edu/pdf/2014/guangdong-regulation-collective -contracts.pdf.

46. Halegua, "China's New Collective Bargaining Rule."

47. International Covenant on Economic, Social and Cultural Rights, December 16, 1966, 993 U.N.T.S. 3, December 16, 1966, article 8.1(d), ratified by China March 27, 2001. China attached no qualifications or reservations to its ratification of this section of the covenant's article 8. By contrast, as to article 8's provision for the right to form and join trade unions "of one's choice," China declared that its application "shall be consistent with the relevant provisions" of China's constitution, Trade Union Law, and Labor Law.

48. Trade Union Law, 2001 Amendment, article 27.

49. Kai Chang, "Guanyu Bagong Hefaxing Jiqi Falu Guizhi (On Legitimacy and Laws of Strike)," *Dangdai Faxue (Contemporary Law Review)* 5 (2012), 109–17; Bulei Cheng, "Bagongquan de Shuxing, Gongneng, Jiqi Duoweidu Fenxi Moxing (Nature, Function and Multi-dimensional Analysis

Model of the Right to Strike)," *Yunnan Daxue Xuebao (Faxueban) (Journal of Yunnan University)* (Law Edition) 5 (2006), 7-14.

50. Chang, "Guanyu Bagong Hefaxing Jiqi Falu Guizhi (On Legitimacy and Laws of Strike)," 111; Quanxing Wang and Xiongfei Ni, "Lun Woguo Bagong Lifa He Bagong Zhuanxing de Guanxi (The Relation between Legislation on Strike and Transformation of Strike)," *Xiandai Faxue (Modern Law Science)* 188 (July 2012), 187–93; Yongkun Zhou, "'Jiti Fanhang' Huhuan Bagongfa (Returned Planes Call for Legislation on Strike)," *Faxue (Law Science)* 1 (2008), 3–11.

51. Ruwitch, "Labor Movement 'Concertmaster.' "

52. Zhonghua Renmin Gongheguo Laodong Hetongfa (Labor Contract Law of the People's Republic of China) (promulgated by the Standing Committee of National People's Congress, June 29, 2007, effective January 1, 2008) (hereinafter Labor Contract Law), article 39 (LawInfoChina) (China). See also Zhonghua Renmin Gongheguo Laodong Fa (Labor Law of the People's Republic of China), Article 25 (permitting dismissal when workers "seriously violate labor discipline or the rules or regulations of the employer).

53. Tianyu Wang and Fang Lee Cooke, "Striking the Balance in Industrial Relations in China? An Analysis of 308 Strike Cases (2008-2014)," working paper on file with author, December 2015). Note that the paper was revised to include 897 cases through 2015; but this change had not yet been reflected in the title of the paper.

54. Ibid., table 7.

55. (2013) Min Min Yi (Min) Chu Zi no.15805, no. 15801, no. 15803, no. 15810, no. 15804, no. 15812, and no. 15778.

56. Wang and Cooke, "Striking the Balance?"

57. Chang, "On Legitimacy and Laws of Strike."

58. Wang and Cooke, "Striking the Balance?"

59. Wang and Cooke found courts making no such inquiry in 26 percent of the cases, and in most others (45 percent) they asked only whether the employer had informed workers of the rules. Ibid., table 9.

60. The Labor Contract Law, article 4, states that, when considering rules or decisions "which have a direct bearing on the immediate interests of workers, . . . the employing unit shall, after discussion by the conference of workers or all the workers, put forward plans and suggestions and make decisions after consulting with the trade union or the representatives of the workers on an equal footing." China's Labor Law of 1994 provides that new workplace rules "shall be submitted to the [SWRCs] *or all the employees* for discussion and passage." [emphasis added], Labor Law, article 33.

61. NLRB v. Mackay Radio and Telegraph Co., 304 U.S. 333 (1938). Employers do not have the right to permanently replace workers who are striking in response to an unfair labor practice by the employer. NLRB v. Thayer Co., 213 F.2d 748 (1st Cir. 1954), cert. denied, 348 U.S. 883 (1955).

62. Laidlaw Corp., 171 NLRB 1366 (1968), aff'd, 414 F.2d 99 (7th Cir. 1969), cert. denied, 397 U.S. 920 (1970).

63. Human Rights Watch, *Unfair Advantage: Workers' Freedom of Association in*

*the United States under International Human Rights Standards* (New York: 2000), https://www.hrw.org/reports/pdfs/u/us/uslbro08.pdf.

64. For example, see Julius Getman, *The Betrayal of Local 14* (Ithaca, NY: ILR Press, 1998), 224–228; William B. Gould IV, *Agenda for Reform* (Cambridge, MA: MIT Press, 1993), 185–188, 202–203; and Paul C. Weiler, *Governing the Workplace: The Future of Labor and Employment Law* (Cambridge, MA: Harvard University Press, 1990), 264–269.

65. Julius Getman and Thomas Kohler, "The Story of *NLRB v. Mackay Radio & Telegraph Co.*: The High Cost of Solidarity," in *Labor Law Stories,* ed. Laura Cooper and Catherine Fisk (New York: Foundation Press, 2005), 13.

66. Michael Wallerstein and Bruce Western, "Unions in Decline? What Has Changed and Why?," *Annual Review of Political Science* 3 (2000): 355-377.

67. Boys Markets, Inc. v. Retail Clerks Local 770, 398 U.S. 235 (1970).

68. See note 60 above.

69. A no-strike clause in the United States lasts only as long as the collective bargaining agreement; employer rules in China may last indefinitely until the employer seeks to change them. That enables employers to rule out work stoppages that aim to secure a better agreement. But if one can imagine the SWRCs (or the trade unions) serving as genuine vehicles of worker empowerment, one can certainly imagine the few tweaks that would be required to facilitate periodic renegotiation of collective contracts.

70. "Should China Create a Law on Strike?," China Labor News Translations, July 20, 2011, http://www.clntranslations.org/article/62/strike+law.

71. Chun Han Wong, "Not Part of the Bargain: Chinese Premier's Speech Omits Key Phrase for Workers," *China Real Time Report* (blog), *Wall Street Journal,* March 6, 2015, http://blogs.wsj.com/chinarealtime/2015/03/06/not-part-of -the-bargain-chinese-premiers-speech-omits-key-phrase-for-workers/.

72. "Activism on the Rise in 'World's Workshop,' " *Japan Times,* May 28, 2015, http://www.japantimes.co.jp/news/2015/05/28/business/activism-rise-worlds -workshop/#.Vprvo1MrKCR. A transcript of the speech is available at http:// www.sem.tsinghua.edu.cn/portalweb/sem?__c=fa1&u=xyywcn/69292.htm.

73. Chun Han Wong, "Bargaining with Chinese Characteristics: Labor Group Defends Practices," *China Real Time Report* (blog), *Wall Street Journal,* March 13, 2015, http://blogs.wsj.com/chinarealtime/2015/03/13/bargaining -with-chinese-characteristics-labor-group-defends-practices-2/.

## 7. What Does Democracy Look Like in China?

1. "Workers' Voices: Learning the Hard Way about Trade Union Elections," *China Labour Bulletin,* May 9, 2013, http://www.clb.org.hk/en/content/learning -hard-way-about-trade-union-elections.

2. Tim Pringle, *Trade Unions in China: The Challenge of Labour Unrest* (New York: Routledge, 2011), 168–170.

3. Qianfan Zhang, *The Constitution of China: A Contextual Analysis* (Oxford: Hart, 2012), 250–253.

4. For a discussion of recent election reform proposals in Hong Kong, see "China: Hong Kong's Democracy Debate," *BBC News,* June 18, 2015, http://www.bbc .com/news/world-asia-china-27921954; Dylan Loh Ming Hui, "Hong Kong Election Reform: Will It Happen?," *RSIS Commentary,* April 29, 2015, http:// dr.ntu.edu.sg/bitstream/handle/10220/25850/CO15103.pdf?sequence=1.

5. Gunter Schubert and Anna L. Ahlers, *Participation and Empowerment at the Grassroots: Chinese Village Elections in Perspective* (Lanham, MD: Lexington Books, 2012).

6. Bernard Manin uses the term "renewed popular consent." Bernard Manin, *The Principles of Representative Government* (Cambridge: Cambridge University Press, 1997), 176.

7. This definition combines the element of majoritarian rule through elections by the governed (emphasized in, e.g., Robert A. Dahl, *How Democratic Is the American Constitution?* (New Haven, CT: Yale University Press, 2001), 50–51), and the possibility of displacing incumbents through such elections (emphasized in Adam Przeworski, Michael E. Alvarez, Jose Antonio Cheibub, and Fernando Limongi, *Democracy and Development: Political Institutions and Well-Being in the World, 1950–1990* (Cambridge: Cambridge University Press, 2000), 18, 23).

8. For a brief account of the Wukan rebellion and its electoral aftermath, see Andrew Jacobs, "Residents Vote in Chinese Village at Center of Protest," *New York Times,* February 1, 2012.

9. James Pomfret, "Freedom Fizzles Out in China's Rebel Town of Wukan," Reuters, February 28, 2013.

10. Ibid.

11. Michael Wines, "Revolt Begins like Others, but Its End Is Less Certain," *New York Times,* December 16, 2011 (quoting the village's then de facto leader as saying, "I do have concerns [over the lack of progress,] [b]ut I do believe this country is ruled by law, so I do believe the central government will do whatever it has to do to help us").

12. Wang Yang's unusually tolerant approach to social conflict both in Wukan and in the factories earned him favorable attention from some quarters, but some observers believe it slowed his rise within the Party leadership. Mimi Lau, "Guangdong Chief Wang Yang Dodges Questions on Promotion," *South China Morning Post,* November 10, 2012.

13. Organic Law of the Villagers Committees of the People's Republic of China (promulgated by the Standing Committee of the National People's Congress, November 11, 1998, effective November 11, 1998), article 14 (Lawinfochina). ("For election of a villagers committee, the villagers who have the right to elect in the village shall nominate candidates directly. The number of candidates shall be greater than the number of persons to be elected.")

14. Schubert and Ahlers explain that article 3 of the Organic Law, which defines the role of the village party branch as the " 'leading nucleus' . . . in village self-government, leaves no doubt as to who has the final say in village affairs." They argue that the village party branch "steers the process of implementing elections." Members of the party branch are also encouraged to run for seats on the village council, while village council members, once elected, are recruited

to the party branch—a phenomenon known as *yijiantiao,* or "two posts on one shoulder." Schubert and Ahlers, *Participation and Empowerment at the Grassroots,* 165, 87, 134.

15. Pomfret, "Freedom Fizzles Out in China's Rebel Town of Wukan."
16. Dongfang Han, "A Chance to Help Build Grassroots Democracy in China," *China Labour Bulletin,* July 5, 2012, http://www.clb.org.hk/content/chance-help-build-grassroots-democracy-china.
17. Ibid.
18. "Workers' Voices: Learning the Hard Way"; Jiangsong Wang, "Luoshi Gongren Jieshe Ziyou Fangzhi Qiye Gonghui Zhixuan Chengwei Xin de Zhengzhi Huaping" [Giving workers freedom of association can prevent direct union elections from becoming just another political showcase], 6 *Jiti Tanpan Zhidu Yanjiu* [*Collective Bargaining Research*]: 14 (2012), translated by *China Labour Bulletin,* July 25, 2012, http://www.clb.org.hk/en/content/prescription-workplace-democracy-china.
19. Tianming Sun, "Oumu Qian Gonghui Zhuxi Lishizhong: Luoxuan Shuoming Xuanju Wanquan Minzhu" [Former Ohms union chairman Li Shizhong: My loss means election entirely democratic"], *Nanfang Wang* [Guangdong News] http://www.oeeee.com/a/20120529/1056001.html.
20. "Oumu Gonghui Zhuxi Zhixuan Beihou" [Behind the scenes of Ohms's direct election for union chairman], *Nanfang Ribao* [Southern Daily], June 5, 2012, http://epaper.nfdaily.cn/html/2012-06/05/content_7090697.htm; "Workers' Voices: Learning the Hard Way."
21. "Workers' Voices: Learning the Hard Way."
22. ACFTU, Zhonghua Quanguo Zonggonghui Guanyu Jinyibu Jiaqiang Qiye Gonghui Gongquo Chongfen Fahui Qiye Gonghui Zuoyong de Jueding [Decision of the ACFTU on further strengthening the work of enterprise trade unions and putting enterprise trade unions to full use], http://acftu.workercn.cn/c/2010/08/10/100810160211243329553.html. Paragraph 4 of the decision refers to the Measures for the Election of the Trade Union Chairman of an Enterprise and to selecting the trade union chair through "democratic electoral process" *(minzhu xuanju chengxu).*
23. "Workers' Voices: Learning the Hard Way."
24. Ibid.
25. Pringle, *Trade Unions in China,* 160.
26. Ibid., 160–162.
27. Ibid., 106, 142.
28. Jude A. Howell, "All-China Federation of Trade Unions beyond Reform? The Slow March of Direct Elections," *China Quarterly* 196 (2008): 845-863; Pringle, *Trade Unions in China,* 160.
29. Pringle, *Trade Unions in China,* 161–162, 167; Howell, "All-China Federation of Trade Unions beyond Reform?," 853.
30. Pringle, *Trade Unions in China,* 161.
31. Method for the Election of Trade Union Chairpersons of an Enterprise (for Trial Implementation) (promulgated by the All-China Federation of Trade Unions, effective July 25, 2008), articles 4, 6 (Lawinfochina).

32. According to the Method for the Election of Trade Union Chairpersons of an Enterprise, "a leading group composed of the representatives of the trade union at the next higher level, the Party organization of the enterprise and the members," was to oversee the process. Ibid., article 7. Candidates were to be "deliberated and recommended by branches or groups of the trade union, or recommended in secret ballot by all the members, and the trade union committee in the last term, the trade union at the next higher level or the trade union preparatory group [would] propose a list of candidates based on the opinions of the members." The list needed to have at least one more candidate than positions to be filled, and was to be reviewed and approved by the trade union at the next higher level, which would "make adjustments on those who did not satisfy the conditions for office," as prescribed by article 5. Ibid., articles 5, 8, and 9.

33. Pringle, *Trade Unions in China,* 168. Another reason to avoid direct elections was the risk of electing "gangsters"; some "place-of-origin" or hometown associations for migrant workers are involved in criminal activity. Ibid.

34. Pringle, *Trade Unions in China,* 171–172.

35. This procedure was described in an interview in June 2011. All interviews were conducted in confidentiality, and the names of interviewees are withheld by mutual agreement.

36. "Five Years On, Nanhai Honda Workers Want More from Their Trade Union," *China Labour Bulletin,* May 15, 2015, http://www.clb.org.hk/en /content/five-years-nanhai-honda-workers-want-more-their-trade-union.

37. The role and nature of voter preferences in Chinese elections (and perhaps more widely), is not entirely distinct from election structures, but it does play an independent role to which we will return.

38. "Five Years On"; "Plans for Election of Union Chair at Nanhai Honda," *Takungpao,* June 14, 2010, translated by China Labor News Translations, http://www.clntranslations.org/file_download/118.

39. Pringle similarly cites an ACFTU researcher saying that "the key issue is not the staging of elections, but whom members are permitted to elect, and, even more importantly, whom they are not permitted to elect." Pringle, *Trade Unions in China,* 180.

40. This information about union elections in Dalian, in northeast China, appeared in an item, "Direct Elections for Union Leaders," posted on the English-language website for the ACFTU on April 10, 2008 (emphasis added). But the item has since been removed.

41. Conversation with Chinese labor scholar, May 6, 2013.

42. Conversation with Chinese labor law scholar, December 17, 2011.

43. Conversations with Chinese labor law scholars, December 2011 and May 2012.

44. Pringle, *Trade Unions in China,* 165.

45. Howell, "All-China Federation of Trade Unions beyond Reform?"

46. Pringle, *Trade Unions in China,* 172–175. In larger enterprises, workers first elected representatives (in essentially a *haixuan* process), and those representatives then elected officers. This appears to be similar to the process used at Ohms Electronics.

47. Conversation with provincial union official, June 4, 2011.

48. Schubert and Ahlers, *Participation and Empowerment at the Grassroots*.

49. Conversation with Professor Shi Xiuyin, Chinese Academy of Social Sciences, Beijing, May 26, 2012.

50. Ibid.

51. See Chapter 6.

52. Conversation with Professor Shi Xiuyin.

53. Zhang, *Constitution of China*, 104–105, 250–252.

54. Keping Yu, "Toward an Incremental Democracy and Governance: Chinese Theories and Assessment Criteria," *New Political Science* 24 (2002): 184–185, http://www.tandfonline.com/doi/pdf/10.1080/07393140220145207.

55. Keping Yu, *Democracy is a Good Thing: Essays on Politics, Society, and Culture in Contemporary China* (Washington, DC: Brookings Institution Press, 2011).

56. Dexter Roberts, "What to Know about China's National People's Congress," *Bloomberg Businessweek*, March 4, 2014, http://www.bloomberg.com/bw/articles/2014-03-04/what-to-know-about-chinas-national-peoples-congress.

57. There is now a parallel system of direct elections in urban neighborhoods for "residents' committees," but it is less studied and is generally seen as less consequential. See "China from the Inside: The Role of Elections in Representing the Chinese People and Advancing Democracy," PBS, July 31, 2015, http://www.pbs.org/kqed/chinainside/power/democracy.html. I will focus here on the village elections.

58. Schubert and Ahlers, *Participation and Empowerment at the Grassroots*, 15.

59. Tianjian Shi, "Village Committee Elections in China: Institutionalist Tactics for Democracy," *World Politics* 51 (1999): 385–412.

60. The first legislation on village elections, the 1987 Organic Law, was provisional, and left much discretion to provincial and local officials as to whether, when, and how to implement it. Schubert and Ahlers, *Participation and Empowerment at the Grassroots*, 15–19.

61. Ibid., 19–22.

62. Ibid., 143.

63. Ibid., 159.

64. Ibid., 145–146.

65. High turnover was one reason given for workers' lack of focus and engagement in the Ohms Electronics election. "Workers' Voices: Learning the Hard Way."

66. Schubert and Ahlers, *Participation and Empowerment at the Grassroots*, 145–146.

67. One observer estimated that "conflict over [rural] Chinese land accounted for 65 percent of the 187,000 mass conflicts in China in 2010." Elizabeth C. Economy, "A Land Grab Epidemic: China's Wonderful World of Wukans," *Asia Unbound* blog), Council on Foreign Relations, February 7, 2012, http://blogs.cfr.org/asia/2012/02/07/a-land-grab-epidemic-chinas-wonderful-world-of-wukans/.

68. One might also assume that this reasoning does not apply at all to unelected

company managers, but that may be less self-evident in China than it is to workers in the United States, as we will see in the next chapter.

69. Schubert and Ahlers, *Participation and Empowerment at the Grassroots,* 27 (citing Lianjiang Li, "Elections and Popular Resistance in Rural China," *China Information* 16 [2001]: 91).

70. Ibid.,163–166.

71. Ibid., 164.

72. Ibid.

73. Zhang, *Constitution of China,* 9, 28–30. Zhang traces the origins of "distrust of the political capacity of the common people" to the Confucian commitment to "social distinctions and a hierarchical structure in which the parents were to dominate over the children, husbands over wives, the nobles over the common and the superiors over the inferiors, in order to enforce rules of propriety." Ibid., 28. See also Daniel A. Bell, *The China Model: Political Meritocracy and the Limits of Democracy* (Princeton, NJ: Princeton University Press, 2015).

74. Pew finds in 2013 that 85 percent of Chinese respondents were satisfied with the country's direction, and 67 percent described their personal economic situation as "good." Pew Research Global Attitudes Project, Pew Research Center, last accessed May 9, 2016, http://www.pewglobal.org/database /indicator/3/country/45/. Kennedy finds that "[a]ll surveys examining public opinion toward the CPC conducted since the early 1990s show that over 70 percent of respondents support the central government and the party"; he and others caution, however, that survey results may reflect "citizen fear in reporting their actual feelings toward the regime," as well as "media exposure to party propaganda" and "cultural predisposition to authoritarian control." John James Kennedy, "Maintaining Popular Support for the Chinese Communist Party: The Influence of Education and the State-Controlled Media," *Political Studies* 57 (2009): 517, 520, http://onlinelibrary.wiley.com/doi/10.1111 /j.1467-9248.2008.00740.x/pdf.

75. Schubert and Ahlers, *Participation and Empowerment at the Grassroots,* 161.

76. That was once the conventional wisdom. Samuel P. Huntington, *Political Order in Changing Societies* (New Haven, CT: Yale University Press, 1968), 5; Karl W. Deusch, "Social Mobilization and Political Development," *American Political Science Review* 55 (1961): 498–499. More recent scholarship has challenged that view. See, e.g., Wayne A. Cornelius, *Politics and the Migrant Poor in Mexico City* (Stanford, CA: Stanford University Press, 1975): 77–78; and Lester Milbrath, "Political Participation," in *The Handbook of Political Behavior,* ed. Samuel L. Long (New York: Plenum Press, 1981): 197, 225–226. Milbrath concludes that "there is either a lack of, or a somewhat negative, association between urban living and political activity, especially voting."

77. Jennifer Pan and Yiqing Xu, "China's Ideological Spectrum" (research paper no. 2015-6, Department of Political Science, MIT, Cambridge, MA, November 17, 2015), http://papers.ssrn.com/sol3/papers.cfm?abstract_id=2593377. The study finds that most of the urban-rural divide is driven by other factors: "individuals with higher income and education and regions with higher levels

of economic development, education, trade openness, and urbanization are more likely to have preferences for political liberalization and market allocation."

78. On the continuing marginalization of migrant workers and the role of the *hukou* system, see C. Cindy Fan, *China on the Move: Migration, the State, and the Household* (London: Routledge, 2008), 5; and Daniel Fu Keung Wong, Chang Ying Li, and He Xue Song, "Rural Migrant Workers in China: Living a Marginalized Life," *International Journal of Society and Welfare* (2006): 34–37.

79. Samuel Issacharoff, *Fragile Democracies: Contested Power in the Era of Constitutional Courts* (New York: Cambridge University Press, 2015).

## 8. Will Workers Have a Voice in the "Socialist Market Economy"?

1. The Chinese term *(zhigong daibiao dahui)* has several translations. "Staff and Workers' Representative Congress," though unwieldy, captures the inclusion of all employees of an enterprise, including workers, technicians, management, and party cadres.

2. Wen Kuei Ma, "Industrial Management in China—How China's Socialist State-Owned Industrial Enterprises Are Managed," *Peking Review* 9 (1965), https://www.marxists.org/subject/china/peking-review/1965/PR1965-09k.htm.

3. "State-owned enterprises practice democratic management through congresses of workers and staff and in other ways in accordance with the law." Xianfa [Constitution of the People's Republic of China], article 16.

4. The SWRCs were established, first on an interim basis in 1981, then on a permanent basis in 1986, by the Quanmin Suoyouzhi Gongye Qiye Zhigong Daibiao Dahui Tiaoli [Regulations on State-Owned Industrial Enterprise Worker Representatives Congress] (effective October 1, 1986) (hereinafter 1986 Regulation on SWRCs), http://www.34law.com/lawfg/law/6/1189/law_250917172417.shtml.

5. Speech on August 18, 1980, to an enlarged meeting of the Political Bureau of the Central Committee of the CP, as discussed and endorsed by the Political Bureau on August 31, 1980, from *Selected Works of Deng Xiaoping, Modern Day Contributions to Marxist-Leninist Theory*, https://dengxiaopingworks.wordpress.com/2013/02/25/on-the-reform-of-the-system-of-party-and-state-leadership/ (hereinafter Deng Speech 1980).

6. Deng Speech 1980, note 5.

7. I thank Mingwei Liu for suggesting this point.

8. Keping Yu, "Toward an Incremental Democracy and Governance: Chinese Theories and Assessment Criteria," *New Political Science* 24 (2002):181, 184–185, http://www.tandfonline.com/doi/pdf/10.1080/07393140220145207.

9. Meei-shia Chen and Anita Chan, "Occupational Health and Safety in China: The Case of State-Managed Enterprises," *International Journal of Health Services* 40 (2010): 43, 47.

10. 1986 Regulation on SWRCs, articles 10, 12.

11. 1986 Regulation on SWRCs, article 11.

12. Joel Andreas, "Losing Membership Rights: The Impact of Eliminating Permanent Job Tenure on Power Relations in Chinese Factories" (paper presented at American Sociological Association Annual Meeting, New York, NY, August 11, 2013), 8.

13. Ibid.; Andrew G. Walder, "Factory and Manager in an Era of Reform," *China Quarterly* 118 (1989): 242, 247.

14. Quoted in Andreas, "Losing Membership Rights," 8.

15. Law of the People's Republic of China on Industrial Enterprises Owned by the Whole People (promulgated by the Nat'l People's Cong., April 13, 1988, effective August 1, 1988), articles 44, 52 (Lawinfochina) (China). Factory directors could also be chosen and removed by a "competent department of the government," though in that case after seeking the opinion of the SWRC.

16. Chen and Chan, "Occupational Health and Safety in China."

17. 1986 Regulation on SWRCs, article 4; Meei-Shia Chen and Anita Chan, "Employee and Union Inputs into Occupational Health and Safety Measures in Chinese Factories," *Social Science and Medicine* 58 (2004): 1231, 1242–1243.

18. Sean Cooney, Sarah Biddulph, and Ying Zhu, *Law and Fair Work in China* (New York: Routledge, 2013), 39.

19. Malcolm Warner, "The Origins of Chinese Industrial Relations," in *Changing Workplace Relations in the Chinese Economy*, ed. Malcolm Warner (London: Palgrave Macmillan, 2000), 27–28. See also Jackie Sheehan, *Chinese Workers: A New History* (London: Routledge, 1998), 201.

20. One 1990s study by the ACFTU found that, of the nearly three hundred thousand enterprises with SWRCs, most were able to undertake "democratic appraisal" of managerial cadres. Ng Sek Hong and Malcolm Warner, *China's Trade Unions and Management* (London: Palgrave Macmillan, 1998), 88.

21. Andreas, "Losing Membership Rights," 6.

22. Ibid., 10–11.

23. Ibid., 9.

24. Ibid., 9–10

25. Ibid., 11–12; Walder, "Factory and Manager in an Era of Reform," 252–253. Walder observes that managers also had leverage over workers given their control over a wide range of discretionary benefits and punishments (e.g., housing, education). Andrew Walder, "Organized Dependency and Cultures of Authority in Chinese Industry," *Journal of Asian Studies* 43 (1983): 51, 56–64.

26. See Andreas, "Losing Membership Rights," 8; Cooney, Biddulph, and Zhu, *Law and Fair Work*, 68–69.

27. See Zhonghua Renmin Gongheguo Gongsi Fa [Company Law of the People's Republic of China] (promulgated by Fifth session of Standing Committee of Eighth National People's Congress, December 29, 1993, effective July 1, 1994) (hereinafter Company Law), article 38 (shareholders shall supervise managers and their appointment and dismissal), article 55 (workers' opinions *should* be solicited on matters tied to their interests, and members of the trade union or

SWRC *should* be invited to attend relevant meetings as *non-voting delegates*), article 63 (SOE's board of directors *should* have a democratically elected SWRC member) (Lawinfochina) (China) (emphasis added); and Ronald C. Brown, *Understanding Labor and Employment Law in China* (Cambridge: Cambridge University Press, 2009), 46.

28. Quoted in Andreas, "Losing Membership Rights," 20.
29. Quoted in ibid.
30. Quoted in ibid.
31. See Bill Taylor, Kai Chang, and Qi Li, *Industrial Relations in China* (Cheltenham, UK: Edward Elgar, 2003): 142–143.
32. Andreas, "Losing Membership Rights," 19. See also Shaobo Wang, "A Case Study on the Workers' Rights Protection Mechanism during the Reform of a State-Owned Company," *Conflict and Cooperation: The International Symposium of Collective Labor Dispute Resolution and Regulation* 532 (2011).
33. Andreas, "Losing Membership Rights," 19.
34. Jonathan Unger and Anita Chan, "The Internal Politics of an Urban Chinese Work Community: A Case Study of Employee Influence on Decision-Making at a State-Owned Factory," *China Journal* 52 (2004):1-24, 10 (citing *China News Digest*). Similarly in Tianjin, 660 SOE managers were fired and 1,550 were demoted or transferred after losing an SWRC vote of confidence. Ibid., 10, 10n22 (citing *Workers Daily*, April 10, 1998).
35. Chen and Chan, "Occupational Health and Safety"; Chen and Chan, "Employee and Union Inputs."
36. Unger and Chan, "Internal Politics of an Urban Chinese Work Community."
37. Official government statistics showed over seven hundred thousand SWRCs in the nonstate sector as of 2007. Zengyi Xie, "Zhidaihui de Dingwei yu Gongneng Chongsu" [Reshaping the position and function of Staff and Worker Representative Congresses], *Faxue Yanjiu* [Chinese Journal of Law] 3 (2013): 110, 112 (hereinafter "Reshaping the Position and Function"). But the non-state sector includes former SOEs, joint (state-foreign) enterprises, and collectively-owned enterprises in the townships and villages. Representatives of foreign businesses operating in China report that SWRCs had little presence in their world until recently.
38. The Labor Law of 1994, which governs both non-state and state enterprises, provides that new workplace rules and other matters relating to employment "shall be submitted to the [SWRCs] *or all the employees* for discussion and adoption." Labor Law of People's Republic of China (promulgated by the Standing Committee of National People's Congress, July 5, 1994, effective January 1, 1994), article 33 (China) (emphasis added). The ambiguity was crucial.
39. A 1997 ACFTU survey found that 46 percent of private manufacturing companies that had trade unions also had SWRCs. Xiaoyang Zhu and Anita Chan, "Staff and Workers' Representative Congress: An Institutionalized Channel for Expression of Employees' Interests?," *Chinese Sociology and Anthropology* 37 (2005): 6, 13–14. But only a small fraction of such companies had unions.

40. Yinguo Sun, "Meinian Jia Xin 8% Woerma Zhidaihui Shuohua Guanyong" [Wal-Mart SWRC's advocacy proves useful in obtaining annual 8% salary increase], *Sun Yinguo Lingshou Cehua* [Sun Yinguo's retail strategy], September 9, 2011, http://blog.sina.com.cn/s/blog_4d15deof0100anah.html.

41. See Labor Contract Law of the People's Republic of China (promulgated by the Standing Committee of National People's Congress, June 29, 2007, effective January 1, 2008) (hereinafter Labor Contract Law), articles 4, 51; article 33 (LawInfoChina) (China) (emphasis added) .

42. According to conversations with lawyers for U.S. firms doing business in China.

43. Au Loong Yu, "From 'Master' to 'Menial': State-Owned Enterprise Workers in Contemporary China," *Working USA* 14 (2011): 453.

44. As reported to author by Seth Gurgel.

45. Tongqing Feng, "An Overview of the Workers' Congress System in China," in *Industrial Democracy in China,* ed. Rudolf Traub-Merz and Kinglun Ngok (Beijing: China Social Science Press, 2012), 197–199, http://library.fes.de/pdf -files/bueros/china/09128/09128-english%20version.pdf.

46. Ibid., 203.

47. Ibid., 205.

48. Ibid.

49. Xie, "Reshaping the Position and Function," 118. CASS is a "think tank" for China's State Council, its top policy-making body. That does not confer an official stamp of approval on writings by CASS professors, but it may suggest central policy officials' interest in and toleration of the views expressed.

50. Ibid., 115–118.

51. Ibid. On the productivity benefits of "participatory management" through SWRCs, see Minqi Li, "Workers' Participation in Management and Firm Performance: Evidence from Large and Medium-Sized Chinese Industrial Enterprises," *Review of Radical Political Economy* 36 (2004): 358-380.

52. Xie, "Reshaping the Position and Function," 118–119.

53. As of October 31, 2013, twenty-nine of thirty-four provinces and "provincial level" jurisdictions had regulations on "democratic management" or SWRCs. Jian Qiao, "Exploring the New Policy of Harmonious Labor Relations," *Conflict and Cooperation: The International Symposium of Collective Labor Dispute Resolution and Regulation* (2011): 438.

54. "Bu Jing Zhigong Taolun Gongsi Guizhang jiu shi Kongwen" [Company regulations not discussed by employees found meaningless], *Chutian Dushi Bao* [Chutian City News], November 28, 2009, http://ctdsb.cnhubei.com/html /ctdsb/20091128/ctdsb915310.html.

55. Shanghai Zhigong Daibiao Dahui Tiaoli [Shanghai Regulations on SWRCs] (promulgated by the Standing Committee Shanghai People's Congress, December 23, 2010), articles 2–3 (March 15, 2012, 1:21 p.m.), http://www .shzgh.org/renda/node5902/node5908/node6573/u1a1707790.html; Zhejiangsheng Qiye Minzhu Guanli Tiaoli [Zhejiang Regulations on the Democratic Management of Enterprises] (promulgated by the Standing Committee of the Zhejiang National People's Congress, March 30, 2010),

http://www.zjhrss.gov.cn/art/2010/3/30/art_156_1261.html. See also Yue Jia, "Zhejiang Suoyou Qiye Dou Yao Jianli Zhigong Daibiao Dahui Zhidu" [All Zhejiang enterprises must establish an SWRC], Zhongguo Gonghui Xinwen [China Trade Union News], September 29, 2010, http://acftu.people.com.cn /GB/67578/12849072.html.

56. ACFTU Research Department, "2012 Nian Gonghui Zuzhi he Gonghui Gongzuo Fazhan Zhuangkuang Tongji Gongbao" [2012 union organization and work development statistics] (2013), 9, http://stats.acftu.org/upload /files/1370483520528.pdf.

57. Provisions on the Democratic Management of Enterprises (promulgated by the ACFTU, February 13, 2012, effective February 13, 2012) (hereinafter ACFTU Provisions), article 3 (Lawinfochina) (China). ("Enterprises shall . . . establish a democratic management system with the employees' congress as the basic form.")

58. "Laws" in China are enacted by the National People's Congress; binding national regulations emanate from the State Council and top-level ministries. Neither the ACFTU nor other "co-sponsors" of the provisions are among those bodies.

59. ACFTU Provisions, article 13.

60. Ibid.

61. Ibid., article 9. The number of representatives must generally equal at least 5 percent of the enterprise's employees and no less than thirty individuals, and must include an "appropriate" number of female representatives. Ibid., article 8.

62. Ibid., article 24. Procedures may differ for large enterprises.

63. E-mail from management attorney to author (June 9, 2012) (on file with author).

64. "A Brief History of a Workers' Rights Group in China," *China Labour Bulletin,* September 11, 2009, *http://www.clb.org.hk/content/brief-history -workers%E2%80%99-rights-group-china.*

65. Feng, "Overview of the Workers' Congress System," 206.

66. Stephen Philion, "Workers' Democracy vs. Privatization in China," *Socialism and Democracy* 21 (2007): 37.

67. Manfred Elfstrom and Sarosh Kuruvilla, "The Changing Nature of Labor Unrest in China," *Industrial and Labor Relations Review* 67 (2014): 453, 471–473.

68. "Shanghai Maidanglao Shipin Youxian Gongsi Qianding zai Zhongguo Diyifen Jiti Hetong" [McDonald's Shanghai branches sign company's first collective contract in China], Shanghai Municipal Federation of Trade Unions, May 23, 2013, http://www.shzgh.org/renda/node5902/node5906/node6563 /u1ai574966.html.

69. Wei Gu, "Kendeji zai Zhongguo Shou Qian Jiti Hetong Zhigong Pingjun Gongzi Nian Zeng 5%" [Kentucky Fried Chicken signs first collective contract in China, workers' average annual income to rise 5%], *Xin Hua Net,* June 6, 2010, http://news.xinhuanet.com/legal/2010-06/18/c_12233334.htm.

70. Anita Chan, "Wal-Mart Workers in China" (paper presented to the International

Labor Rights Forum and National Labor College, September 29, 2008), http://www.laborrights.org/sites/default/files/publications-and-resources/Wal-Mart%20Workers%20in%20China.pdf.

71. Although the articles on McDonald's and KFC above suggest that they do help workers, Professor Chan's account of Wal-Mart's SWRC is much less sanguine. Chan, "Wal-Mart Workers." CASS Professor Xiuyin Shi found that SWRCs in foreign-invested enterprises were more successful at raising workers' wages and working conditions than SWRCs at domestic workplaces. Xiuyin Shi, "The Transformation of the Enterprise Power Structure," *Conflict and Cooperation: The International Symposium of Collective Labor Dispute Resolution and Regulation* (2011): 473.

72. Interview with Chinese industrial relations scholar, August 14, 2013 (on file with author).

73. Foshan Honda Worker Representative Committee letter, last updated June 4, 2010, https://sites.google.com/a/socialistbulletin.com/socialist-bulletin/international/foshanhondaworkersrepresentativecommitteeletter. It is ambiguous whether it was an SWRC or an unofficial employee assembly to which these workers refer, but knowledgeable observers say that it was the latter. Interview with Chinese industrial relations scholar, August 14, 2013 (on file with author).

74. Steven Greenhouse, "VW and Its Workers Explore a Union at a Tennessee Plant," *New York Times,* September 6, 2013.

75. See Steven Greenhouse, "Volkswagen Vote Is Defeat for Labor in South," *New York Times,* February 14, 2014. The UAW could petition for and win a new election, and revive the original plan for a WC. Alternatively, VW workers could still form a "labor organization" in Chattanooga, unaffiliated with the UAW, which could then agree with VW to establish a WC. Bernie Woodall and Amanda Becker, "After Rejecting UAW, VW Workers May Still Get Works Council," Reuters, February 16, 2014, http://www.reuters.com/article/2014/02/16/us-autos-vw-council-analysis-idUSBREA1F0VV20140 216. But such unaffiliated unions are rare and thought to be vulnerable to unlawful management domination. Alternatively, VW could reconfigure the WC so that workers exercise delegated managerial power rather than "dealing with" the employer through its auspices. Crown, Cork & Seal Co., 334 NLRB 699 (2001), discussed in Benjamin Sachs, "A New Way Forward for VW-Tennessee," On Labor: Workers, Unions, and Politics, May 20, 2014, http://onlabor.org/2014/05/20/a-new-way-forward-for-vw-tennessee/.

76. National Labor Relations Act, 29 U.S.C.A. § 152(5) and § 158(a)(2).

77. The definitions of "interfere," "dominate," and "support," prohibited by § 8(a)(2) of the NLRA, 29 U.S.C. § 158(a)(2) (2006), are also very broad, and are not limited to employer conduct that aims to squelch independent unionism. Electromation, 309 U.S. n.24 (citing NLRB v. Newport New Shipbuilding Co., 308 U.S. 241 (1939)).

78. See John Godard and Carola Frege, "Union Decline, Alternative Forms of Representation, and the Exercise of Authority Relations in U.S. Workplaces," *Industrial and Labor Relations Review* 66 (2013): 142-168.

79. See Richard Freeman and Joel Rogers, *What Do Workers Want?* 2nd ed. (Ithaca, NY: ILR Press, 2006), 84. See Chapter 3, note 48.

80. Joel Rogers and Wolfgang Streek, "The Study of Works Councils: Concepts and Problems," in *Works Councils: Consultation, Representation, and Cooperation in Industrial Relations,* ed. Joel Rogers and Wolfgang Streek (Chicago: University of Chicago Press, 1995), 11–16.

81. Ibid., 6.

82. Ibid., 17; Wolfgang Streek, "Works Councils in Western Europe: From Consultation to Participation," in Rogers and Streek, *Works Councils,* 313–314.

83. Carola M. Frege, "A Critical Assessment of the Theoretical and Empirical Research on German Works Councils," *British Journal of Industrial Relations* 40 (2002): 221, 222.

84. Martin Behrens, "Germany," in *Comparative Employment Relations in the Global Political Economy,* ed. Carola Frege and John Kelley (London: Routledge, 2013), 206–208, 212–215, 217–218; Walther Müller-Jentsch, "Reassessing Co-determination," in *The Changing Contours of German Industrial Relations,* ed. Hansjörg Weitbrecht and Walther Müller-Jentsch (Munich: Rainer Hampp Verlag, 2003), 39, 44–46.

85. See Walther Müller-Jentsch, "Germany: From Collective Voice to Co-management," in Rogers and Streek, *Works Councils,* 58–60.

86. Ibid., 61–62; Streek, "Works Councils in Western Europe," 314.

87. Müller-Jentsch, "Germany: From Collective Voice to Co-management," 61.

88. Ibid., 63.

89. Müller-Jentsch, "Reassessing Co-determination," 49–51.

90. Ibid., 44.

91. One German scholar of WCs in 1981 identified seven distinct "ideal types" of WCs, ranging from those that are ignored, those that operate as part of management, those that operate as "cooperative counterpower" on behalf of workers, and those that are combative on behalf of workers. Frege, "Critical Assessment of the Theoretical and Empirical Research," (discussing H. Kotthoff, *Betriebsräte und betriebliche Herrschaft: eine Typologie von Partizipationsmustern im Industriebetrieb* [Frankfurt: Campus, 1981]); and H. Kotthoff, *Betriebsräte und Bürgerstatus: Wandel und Kontinuität betrieblicher Codetermination* [Munich: Rainer Hampp Verlag, 1994]).

92. That is clear if one compares Andreas's account of the SWRCs' declining role in the SOEs and former SOEs in the "corporate era," Andreas, "Losing Membership Rights," with a leading scholarly account of the German WCs, Müller-Jentsch, "Germany: From Collective Voice to Co-management," 55. A review of the literature on German WCs underscores the consensus that, notwithstanding their variations, most WCs have a significant presence and role of some kind in workplace governance. Frege, "Critical Assessment of the Theoretical and Empirical Research."

93. Cynthia L. Estlund, "Wrongful Discharge Protections in an At-Will World," *Texas Law Review* 74 (1996): 1655–1692.

94. See "OECD Indicators of Employment Protection," Organisation for

Economic Co-operation and Development, 2013, http://www.oecd.org /employment/emp/oecdindicatorsofemploymentprotection.htm.

95. Walder, "Organized Dependency," 56.

96. Unions support WCs by providing them with expertise, guidance, and advice, and by calling official and unofficial strikes—a power WCs are denied. Streek, "Works Councils in Western Europe," 339, 343, 345.

97. Kenneth G. Lieberthal and Michel Oksenberg, *Policy Making in China: Leaders, Structures, and Processes* (Princeton, NJ: Princeton University Press, 1988); Andrew C. Mertha, " 'Fragmented Authoritarianism 2.0': Political Pluralization in the Chinese Policy Process," *China Quarterly* 200 (2009): 995.

98. See John Braithwaite, *Regulatory Capitalism: How It Works, Ideas for Making It Work Better* (Cheltenham, UK: Edward Elgar, 2008); Cynthia L. Estlund, *Regoverning the Workplace: From Self-Regulation to Co-regulation* (New Haven, CT: Yale University Press, 2010); and Christine Parker, *The Open Corporation: Effective Self-Regulation and Democracy* (Cambridge: Cambridge University Press, 2002).

99. Kuei, "Industrial Management in China."

100. "A Tightening Grip: Rising Chinese Wages Will Only Strengthen Asia's Hold on Manufacturing," *Economist*, March 14, 2015.

101. As German employers are said to have done. Müller-Jentsch, "Reassessing Co-determination," 53.

# 9. Conclusion

1. That is reflected in the descriptions of strikes in the *China Labour Bulletin*'s Strike Map. "Strike Map," *China Labour Bulletin*, accessed January 16, 2016, http://maps.clb.org.hk/strikes/en.

2. Jennifer Medina, "Higher Wages, Great! But How to Enforce?," *New York Times*, July 25, 2015.

3. "Empty Judgments: The Wage Collection Crisis in New York," SWEAT! Securing Wages Earned Against Theft, 2015, http://www.sweatny.org/report/.

4. Alan Hyde, "A Theory of Labor Legislation," *Buffalo Law Review* 38 (1990): 384, 432.

5. On the "union threat effect," studies find that "nonunion wages are higher in highly unionized industries, localities, and firms." Bruce Western and Jake Rosenfeld, "Unions, Norms, and the Rise in U.S. Wage Inequality," *American Society Review* 76 (August 2011): 517. Moreover, Henry S. Farber finds reduction in nonunion wages in a state that enacted a right-to-work law and in industries that were deregulated in ways that weakened the ability to unionize. Henry S. Farber, "Nonunion Wage Rates and the Threat of Union-ization," *Industrial and Labor Relations Review* 58 (April 2005): 335-52.

6. Western and Rosenfeld, "Unions, Norms, and the Rise," 513. In 2007, then chair of the Federal Reserve Ben Bernanke estimated that the decline of unions accounted for 10 to 20 percent of the increase in inequality. See Ben S. Bernanke, "The Level and Distribution of Economic Well-Being" (speech

given to the Greater Omaha Chamber of Commerce, Omaha, Nebraska, February 6, 2007), http://www.federalreserve.gov/newsevents/speech/bernanke 20070206a.htm.

7. Alan B. Krueger, "Inequality, Too Much of a Good Thing" (CEPS working paper no. 87, August 2002): 9, http://core.ac.uk/download/pdf/6885375.pdf (citing Robert H. Frank and Phillip J. Cook, *The Winner Take All Society: Why the Few at the Top Get So Much More Than the Rest of Us* [New York: Penguin Books, 1996]).

8. Jerome A. Cohen, "Chinese Mediation on the Eve of Modernization," *California Law Review* 54 (August 1966): 201-1226.

9. The Equal Employment Opportunity Commission (EEOC), where most discrimination claims must be filed as a prerequisite to litigation, has invested heavily in mediation of those claims; and there are many court mediation programs as well, including some devoted to employment (mostly discrimination) claims. "Mediation/ADR," United States District Court, Southern District of New York, last accessed August 2, 2015, http://www.nysd.uscourts.gov/mediation .php. ("Since 2011, counseled employment discrimination [non-FLSA] cases . . . are automatically referred to mediation when the answer is filed.").

10. For leading critiques, see Laura Nader, "Disputing without the Force of Law," *Yale Law Journal* 88 (1979): 1007–1008; Harry Edwards, "Alternative Dispute Resolution: Panacea or Anathema?," *Harvard Law Review* 99 (1986): 671–672, 675–682.

11. That includes even procedures that lower courts had found to be "unconscionable" (see AT&T Mobility v. Concepcion, 563 U.S. 333 (2011)), or a means of frustrating the "effective vindication" of federal statutory rights (see Am. Express Co. v. Italian Colors Rest., 133 S.Ct. 2304 (2013)).

12. See Zev Eigen and Samuel Estreicher, "The Forum for Adjudication of Employment Disputes," in *Research Handbook on the Economics of Labor and Employment Law,* ed. Michael L. Wachter and Cynthia L. Estlund (Cheltenham, UK: Edward Elgar, 2012), 409-426; Samuel Estreicher, "Saturns for Rickshaws: The Stakes in the Debate over Predispute Employment Arbitration Agreements," *Ohio State Journal of Dispute Resolution* 16 (2000–2001): 559-570; and David Sherwyn et al., "In Defense of Mandatory Arbitration of Employment Disputes: Saving the Baby, Tossing Out the Bath Water, and Constructing a New Sink in the Process," *University of Pennsylvania Employment and Labor Journal* 1 (1999–2000): 73-150.

13. Recent data, imperfect though it is, tends to support the critics: even apart from lower recoveries and somewhat lower success rates in arbitration versus litigation, too few employee claims are being arbitrated at all to believe that arbitration has increased access to adjudication for claims not worth litigating. Alexander J. S. Colvin and Kelly Pike, "Saturns and Rickshaws Revisited: What Kind of Employment Arbitration System Has Developed?," *Ohio State Journal on Dispute Resolution* 29 (2014): 59-83.

14. Carl F. Minzner, "China's Turn Against Law," *American Journal of Comparative Law* 59 (2011): 935-984.

15. "It is not wise to kill the chicken to get the egg" (quoting the American

Chamber of Commerce). Mary E. Gallagher and Baohua Dong, "Legislating Harmony: Labour Law Reform in Contemporary China," in *From Iron Rice Bowl to Informalization: Markets, Workers, and the State in a Changing China,* ed. Sarosh Kuruvilla, Ching Kwan Lee, and Mary E. Gallagher (Ithaca, NY: ILR Press, 2011), 36–60.

16. David Weil, *The Fissured Workplace: Why Work Became So Bad for So Many and What Can Be Done to Improve It* (Cambridge, MA: Harvard University Press, 2014).

17. See discussion in Chapter 8.

18. Cynthia L. Estlund, "The Ossification of American Labor Law," *Columbia Law Review* 102 (October 2002): 1527-1612.

19. Bruce E. Kaufman, "Company Unions: Sham Organizations or Victims of the New Deal?," *Industrial Relations Research Association Series: Proceedings of the Forty-Ninth Annual Meeting* (Madison, WI: Industrial Relations Research Association, 1997), 166, http://50.87.169.168/OJS/ojs-2.4.4-1/index.php /LERAMR/article/download/1479/1464#page=178.

20. "The apparent lack of a more aggressive state-sector reform or privatization program has distressed many economists." Arthur R. Kroeber, "Xi Jinping's Ambitious Agenda for Economic Reform in China," Brookings Institution, November 17, 2013, http://www.brookings.edu/research/opinions/2013/11/17 -xi-jinping-economic-agenda-kroeber.

21. According to one report, "the broader network of state-owned enterprises in the service sector, like telecommunications, banking, health care and electricity distribution, is likely to remain 'virtually unchanged' for the next few years." Keith Bradsher, "China's Grip on Economy Will Test New Leaders," *New York Times,* November 9, 2012. As things stand, "SOEs account for about 96% of China's telecom industry, 92% of power and 74% of autos." John Bussey, "Tackling the Many Dangers of China's State Capitalism," *Wall Street Journal,* September 27, 2012.

22. For recent accounts of China's "state capitalism," see Ian Bremmer, *The End of the Free Market: Who Wins the War Between States and Corporations?* (New York: Portfolio, 2010); James McGregor, *No Ancient Wisdom, No Followers: The Challenges of Chinese Authoritarian Capitalism* (Westport, CT: Prospecta Press, 2012); and Usha C. V. Haley and George T. Haley, *Subsidies to Chinese Industry: State Capitalism, Business Strategy, and Trade Policy* (Oxford: Oxford University Press, 2013).

23. As many have recognized, China's path from liberalization of markets to popular discontent and the rise of regulation and social protection exemplifies Karl Polanyi's "double-movement." Karl Polanyi, *The Great Transformation: The Political and Economic Origins of Our Time* (Boston: Beacon Press, 1944); Shaoguang Wang, "Double Movement in China," *Economic and Political Weekly* 43 (2009): 51–59, http://www.jstor.org/stable/40278334.

24. Gallagher and Dong, "Legislating Harmony: Labour Law Reform in Contemporary China," 39.

25. Sean Cooney, Sarah Biddulph, and Ying Zhu, *Law and Fair Work in China* (New York: Routledge, 2013); Virginia E. Harper Ho and Qiaoyan Huang,

"The Recursivity of Reform: China's Amended Labor Contract Law," *Fordham International Law Journal* 37 (2014): 973-1034.

26. Curtis Milhaupt and Wentong Zheng, "Beyond Ownership: State Capitalism and the Chinese Firm," *Georgetown Law Journal* 103 (2015): 665-717.

27. See discussion in Chapter 3 on new civil society registration rules.

28. This organizing process was prefaced by the official opening of the Communist Party in 2002 to include business owners and managers, and their recruitment into the party. See Richard McGregor, *The Party: The Secret World of China's Communist Rulers* (London: Penguin Books, 2010), 208; and Cheng Li, "The Chinese Communist Party: Recruiting and Controlling the New Elites," *Journal of Current Chinese Affairs* (2009): 20.

29. Qianfan Zhang, *The Constitution of China: A Contextual Analysis* (Portland, OR: Hart, 2012).

30. See discussion in Chapter 6.

31. It is possible that the issue of strikes and collective unrest was aired during the second day of the conference, closed to outside observers. But other sources have reinforced the impression that labor unrest is a secondary concern for major firms operating in China.

32. U.S. population data for ages 15–64 came from "National Population Estimates by Age, Sex, and Race," U.S. Census Bureau, Population Division, https://www.census.gov/popest/data/national/asrh/pre-1980/PE-11.html. U.S. striker data (reflecting U.S. workers participating in strikes involving six workers or more lasting at least one full shift) are from Florence Peterson, *Strikes in the United States, 1880–1936* (Washington, DC: U.S. Government Printing Office, 1938) (through 1936), and thereafter from Monthly Labor Reports. Chinese population data for population aged 15–64 comes from "World Development Indicators," World Bank, http://databank.worldbank.org/data/reports.aspx?source=world-development-indicators. Total population data is multiplied by the proportion in the 15–64 age range; the proportion for 2015 is estimated based on the prior growth rate. Chinese striker data is compiled from "Strike Map," *China Labour Bulletin*, http://strikemap.clb.org.hk/strikes/en#. Method of estimation is described below.

33. The CLB's Strike Map understate the number of incidents because it includes only incidents for which there is a reasonable reliable published report. On the other hand, the Strike Map reports a much larger category of collective labor protest incidents than actual "strikes" or concerted work stoppages; it appears to include what the government would have denominated labor-related "mass incidents," not all of which involved work stoppages. See China Labour Bulletin, *An Introduction to China Labour Bulletin's Strike Map*, http://www.clb.org.hk/content/introduction-china-labour-bulletin%E2%80%99s-strike-map. An advanced search option purports to allow one to identify only "strikes," or "sit-ins" (which are almost certainly strikes); but it does not capture all incidents that are described as having those features.

34. The *China Labour Bulletin* (CLB) maintains the best data known to be available, though it is likely to reflect underreporting. A generous method of estimation was followed in part to correct for that underreporting difference. CLB

data on participants for most strikes is given in ranges (1–100, 100–1,000, 1,000–10,000, and over 10,000). The great majority of strikes are in the smallest two categories, for which our estimates are based on the top of each range (100 and 1,000). For larger strikes, estimates reflect a generous reading of any numerical information that is included in a specific incident report (e.g., if a report says "more than 1,000," an estimate of 2,000 is used; if a report says "more than 10,000," an estimate of 12,000 is used). If no such information is given, then for strikes in the 1,000–10,000 range, an estimate of 5,000 is used; and for the very small number of strikes in the "over 10,000" category, an estimate of 15,000 is used. The category of strikes for which no numerical range is given is less than 8 percent on average; given the great predominance of strikes with under 100 participants and the likelihood that reports of larger strikes would include more information, an estimate of 100 strikers is used. Once estimated strike by strike, estimated numbers of participants are summed for each year. For each country, the estimated number of strikers is divided by Population between the Ages of 15 and 64 (a proxy for labor participation). No adjustment is made for percentage of the working-age population in the labor force, which is higher in China in the relevant years (on average, 77 percent; "World Development Indicators") than in the United States in the 1930s (about 56 percent; U.S. Census, Labor, "Labor Force" [Series D 1-682], chapter D, D 1-10, http://www2.census.gov/prod2/statcomp/documents/ CT1970p1-05.pdf). An estimate of strikers as a percentage of the *labor force* (versus population) ages 15–64 would show higher percentages in both countries, but would magnify the difference between China and the United States (so that failure to make that adjustment cuts against the claim in text).

35. For an argument that they cannot, and that this will undermine China's ability to emerge from its current state of unrest, see Eli Friedman, *Insurgency Trap: Labor Politics in Postsocialist China* (Ithaca, NY: Cornell University Press, 2014).

36. Jianrong Yu, *Maintaining a baseline of social stability*, Speech before the Beijing Lawyers Association," 2009, translated by *China Digital Times*, http:// chinadigitaltimes.net/2010/03/yu-jianrong-%E4%BA%8E%E5%BB%BA %E5%B5%98-maintaining-a-baseline-of-social-stability-part-6/.

37. Merle Goldman, *Sowing the Seeds of Democracy in China: Political Reform in the Deng Xiaoping Era* (Cambridge, MA: Harvard University Press, 1994).

38. Kenneth Lieberthal and Michel Oksenberg, *Policy Making in China: Leaders, Structures, and Processes* (Princeton, NJ: Princeton University Press, 1988); Kenneth G. Lieberthal, "Introduction: The 'Fragmented Authoritarianism' Model and Its Limitations," in *Bureaucracy, Politics, and Decision Making in Post-Mao China*, ed. David M. Lampton and Kenneth Lieberthal (Berkeley: University of California Press, 1992), 1–30; Andrew Mertha, "Fragmented Authoritarianism 2.0": Political Pluralization in the Chinese Policy Process," *China Quarterly* 200 (2009): 1995-1012.

39. Jessica Teets, " 'Let Many Civil Societies Bloom': The Rise of Consultative Authoritarianism," *China Quarterly,* 2013; Baogang He and Mark E. Warren, "Authoritarian Deliberation: The Deliberative Turn in Chinese Political

Development," *Perspectives on Politics* 9 (June 2011): 273; Robert P. Weller, "Responsive Authoritarianism and Blind-Eye Governance," in Nina Bandelj and Dorothy Solinger (eds), China, in *Socialism Vanquished, Socialism Challenged: Eastern Europe and China, 1989–2009* (Oxford: Oxford University Press, 2012.

40. Andrew Nathan, "China's Changing of the Guard: Authoritarian Resilience," *Journal of Democracy* 14 (2003): 6-17; Anna L. Ahlers and Gunter Schubert, " 'Adaptive Authoritarianism' in Contemporary China: Identifying Zones of Legitimacy Building," in: Zhenglai Deng and Sujian Guo (eds), *Reviving Legitimacy: Lessons for and from China* (Lanham: Lexington Books, 2011), 61-81.

41. Minxin Pei, "The Twilight of Communist Rule in China," *American Interest,* November 12, 2015, http://www.the-american-interest.com/2015/11/12/the -twilight-of-communist-party-rule-in-china/.

42. Ibid.

43. See, for example, Weiwei Zhang, "The Five Reasons China Works," *Huffington Post,* February 26, 2014, http://www.huffingtonpost.com/zhang-weiwei/the -five-reasons-china-works_b_4859899.html; Weiwei Zhang, *The China Wave: Rise of a Civilizational State* (Hackensack, NJ: World Century, 2012); and Martin Jacques, *When China Rules the World: The End of the Western World and the Birth of a New Global Order* (London: Penguin, 2012).

44. Arthur R. Kroeber, "Here Is Xi's China, Get Used to It," *ChinaFile,* December 11, 2014, http://www.chinafile.com/reporting-opinion/viewpoint/here-xis-china -get-used-it.

45. "China Overview: Context, Strategy, Results," World Bank, last updated September 18, 2015, http://www.worldbank.org/en/country/china/overview.

46. Of course, the world has provided other disillusioning examples of democracy gone awry (especially in the absence of a robust civil society and legal system). Samuel Issacharoff, *Fragile Democracies: Contested Power in the Era of Constitutional Courts* (New York: Cambridge University Press, 2015).

47. For a description and the translated text of the communique, see "Document 9: A ChinaFile Translation," *ChinaFile,* November 8, 2013, https://www .chinafile.com/document-9-chinafile-translation.

48. See Weiwei Zhang, "Five Reasons."

49. For a critical discussion, see Cheng Li, "Intra-Party Democracy in China: Should We Take It Seriously?," *China Leadership Monitor* 30 (Fall 2009), http://www.brookings.edu/research/papers/2009/11/fall-china-democracy-li.

50. Andrew Wedeman, "Xi Jinping's Tiger Hunt and the Politics of Corruption," *China Currents* 13, no. 2 (October 15, 2014), http://www.chinacenter .net/2014/china_currents/13-2/xi-jinpings-tiger-hunt-and-the-politics-of -corruption/).

51. For a sampling of views on these questions from Chinese intellectuals, see European Council on Foreign Relations, *China 3.0,* ed. Mark Leonard (European Council on Foreign Relations, November 2012); Mark Leonard, *What Does China Think?* (New York: Public Affairs, 2008); Yu, *Democracy Is a Good Thing*; and Weiwei Zhang, *China Wave*.

52. Keping Yu, *Democracy Is a Good Thing; Essays on Politics, Society, and Culture in Contemporary China* (Washington, DC: Brookings Institution, 2009).

53. Keping Yu, "Crossing the river by feeling the stones: Democracy's advance in China," *The Conversation*, April 14, 2016, https://theconversation.com /crossing-the-river-by-feeling-the-stones-democracys-advance-in-china-57557.

54. Ibid.

55. Ibid.

56. Ibid.

57. Ibid.

58. Yu's "Crossing the River" essay was published in the West; but Yu has advocated electoral competition in Chinese publications. See, e.g., Keping Yu, "Ruhe Shixian You Xu Minzhu" ["How to Achieve Orderly Democracy"], *Xin Jing Bao* [*Beijing News*], July 13, 2013, http://epaper.bjnews.com.cn /html/2013-07/13/content_448347.htm?div=-1...

59. For a moving and enlightening introduction to some of the remarkable "strivers" of China, see Evan Osnos, *The Age of Ambition: Chasing Fortune, Truth, and Faith in the New China* (New York: Farrar, Straus and Giroux, 2014).

# Index